M000189414

BERL: THE BIOGRAPHY OF
A SOCIALIST ZIONIST

JEWISH THEOLOGICAL SEMINARY OF AMERICA LIBRARY

BERL: THE BIOGRAPHY OF A SOCIALIST ZIONIST

BERL KATZNELSON 1887–1944

ANITA SHAPIRA

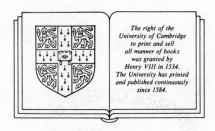

The right of the
University of Cambridge
to print and sell
all manner of books
was granted by
Henry VIII in 1534.
The University has printed
and published continuously
since 1584.

Cambridge University Press

Cambridge

London   New York   New Rochelle

Melbourne   Sydney

Published by the Press Syndicate of the University of Cambridge
The Pitt Building, Trumpington Street, Cambridge CB2 1RP
32 East 57th Street, New York, NY 10022, USA
296 Beaconsfield Parade, Middle Park, Melbourne 3206, Australia

Originally published in Hebrew as *Berl Katznelson: a biography*
by Am Oved Publishers Ltd, Tel Aviv 1980
and © Am Oved Publishers Ltd
First published in English by Cambridge University Press 1984 as an abridged edition.
English translation © Cambridge University Press 1984

Translated by Haya Galai

Printed in Great Britain at the University Press, Cambridge

Library of Congress catalogue card number: 84–7008

British Library Cataloguing in Publication Data
Shapira, Anita
Berl: the biography of a Socialist Zionist.
1. Katznelson, Berl 2. Zionists–Biography
I. Title
956.94′001′0924 DS151.K3
ISBN O 521 25618 6

DS
151
K3
S503
1984
c.2

THEOLOGICAL SEMINARY OF
LIBRARY
JEWISH ⋆ AMERICA

CONTENTS

Plates between pages 182 and 183

ACKNOWLEDGEMENTS

The publication of this book, a translated and abridged version of my Hebrew book *Berl*, was made possible through the efforts of a number of people.

I owe a special debt of gratitude to Mrs Haya Galai, the translator, and Mrs Chaya Amir, the English editor, with whom I worked in close association for over a year. They succeeded in preserving the spirit of the original version, while rendering the book into fluent English. I would like to thank Mrs Louise Braverman for her technical assistance and all the people in C.U.P. who helped me.

Some technical remarks. Most of the source material used for the book was in Hebrew. Readers with a knowledge of Hebrew would do well to use the Hebrew edition for references. In the English version I have given references only when direct quotations were used. However, a list of archival sources can be found here in the bibliographical note. Spelling of Hebrew names has been in accordance with the practice of the individuals in question. In transliterating the Hebrew we have adhered to the practice of lower-casing the definite article.

PROLOGUE

On a sweltering morning in mid-August 1944, the streets around the complex of national institutions in Jerusalem filled with a dense crowd. In the lobby of the Jewish National Fund building lay the coffin of Berl Katznelson, wrapped in a blue-and-white flag with a crimson ribbon across it. The most prominent figures in the Yishuv – heads of institutions, university professors, writers and intellectuals, party workers and movement leaders – thronged around it. Outside thousands of people milled in the streets, waiting to pay their last respects to the deceased. David Ben Gurion, Eliezer Kaplan, David Remez and Yitzhak Gruenbaum were the pallbearers. The procession wound its way slowly through King George Street and Ben Yehuda Street. No eulogies were delivered. The ceremony was simple and unostentatious, in accordance with the request of the deceased. He had hated flowers confined in bouquets. He had also hated flags and ribbons at funerals, Christian customs borrowed by the Jews. And, as in his lifetime so in his death, his will prevailed. Hushed and silent, without the relief and the consolation which people find in mourning customs, the thousands joined the long funeral cortege, which began to make its way towards Tel Aviv.

The first Hebrew city ceased its labors. It seemed that all its inhabitants were out in the streets. The funeral procession wound its way endlessly, as tens of thousands stood in silence along the route. The balconies and rooftops were black with people. The sun, which meanwhile reached its meridian, beat down on their heads, and the heat was unbearably oppressive. But the crowds continued to flock. In an eerie silence, with mournful expressions, the people of Tel Aviv awaited the man 'whom you adored even if you had no wish to. You were in awe of him as a man is in awe of his conscience.'[1] As never in his lifetime, everyone now united around his image. Members of his own party, Mapai, and of the opposition, all came, sharing the sense of great loss.

The convoy of cars crept forward slowly. It halted for a moment in front of the Histadrut offices on Allenby Street, and the great crowd fell still. And then, making its way laboriously through the sea of mourners, estimated at one hundred thousand, the convoy continued on its journey to the Great Synagogue. Here the cantor recited the prayer for the dead, 'God, full of compassion' and the mourners intoned Kaddish. And the cars moved on towards Arlozoroff House, party headquarters. Here the scene was repeated: at a given signal the crowd stood at attention in silence. Then they were asked to disperse to enable the convoy to proceed. But it was hard for them to take leave of the man to whom they had come to pay their last respects, and for a long time, in the noonday heat, they clustered in the streets in quiet, pained grief.

He had selected his place of burial while still a young man. On the shores of Lake Kinneret, in the little cemetery by the mound overlooking the lake, lay the grave of the woman with whom he had shared the pain, the joy and the torment of youthful love. Though twenty-five years had gone by since her death, her fascination and the lure of Kinneret still drew him. He wanted to complete the circle and to end his personal and public life in Palestine in the place where he had begun it. Few of the thousands who accompanied him knew the secret of Kinneret, or had experienced the captivating romanticism of the Second Aliyah days, and those who knew carefully guarded their knowledge. Only the poet delicately alluded to it:

> 'He is mine' softly whispered Kinneret
> 'And to me he returns in a dream
> Though his words bore great deeds and great echoes
> He is mute when he comes to my shore
> It is I who return him full circle
> With a stone and his name simply etched
> Yes, he's mine' softly whispered Kinneret
> 'And has been since those days long ago.'
> Nathan Alterman

There were workers who wondered why a man who was a public figure with every fiber of his being would choose, at death, to distance himself from his public? But again his will prevailed, and his private wishes were observed.

A long line of cars, two kilometers long, crept along the road from Tel Aviv to Hadera, from there through Wadi Ara towards Afula, crossing the Jezreel Valley and the Beisan Valley on its way to Kinneret.

It appeared that the whole of Labor Palestine stood guard as he passed. Outside each settlement, large or small, there awaited him comrades who had shared his path for thirty-five years, their hair graying and their faces seamed by life and by toil. There were others, young people who had heard him as teacher, educator or adversary, and small children lining the roadside. This was the sole public funeral to remain etched on their memories. In the fields all work ceased. Here a solitary farmer could be seen watering crops. But as the cortege drove by, work ceased and the figures stood at attention till it had passed. At every settlement, cars joined the convoy – at first, only representatives of the settlements, but as it came nearer to Kinneret, more and more local people joined it, men and women of the communal settlements, to whom Berl was now returning.

It was afternoon, and the heat grew heavier and more oppressive. Yet nobody budged from the roadside until the convoy had passed. It stopped at each settlement, amidst the same deep silence, and the atmosphere of communion with an irreparable loss.

At six o'clock the procession reached Kinneret. Some seven thousand people gathered in the modest little cemetery, overlooking the lake. It was there, at her request, that the poetess Rachel had been buried, amidst the anonymous heroes of the Second Aliyah. Now she was followed by the man whose image symbolized this Aliyah, come to dwell with them under the shade of the trees on the mounds. An elderly woman, Aliza Shidlovsky, said a few brief words of farewell. It was not the great leaders of the Yishuv, who bore his coffin, who eulogized him, but she, a member of Kinneret, who had known him at the beginning. David Bader, another Second Aliyah veteran, recited Kaddish, traditionally recited by the son. But Berl had died childless. Again there was a hush as each of the mourners communed alone with the man who had left them. As the sun set, the ceremony ended.

In the years which have elapsed since then, many of the best and the brightest have gone the way of all flesh; but that profound grief and sense of irreparable loss has never been repeated. Years later a writer, who was then a young man,[2] said: it was the last funeral where people truly grieved.

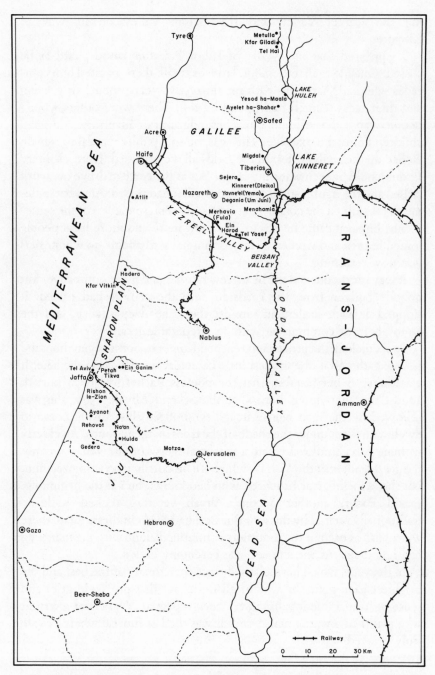

Map of Palestine showing the principal places mentioned in the text.

THE ROAD TO ZION,
1887–1909

Berl Katznelson, the son of Moshe Katznelson and Teivel-Reizel Katznelson, née Nemetz, was born on 25 January 1887 in Bobruisk, White Russia.

The region of his birth, once Polish territory, was conquered in the late eighteenth century by the Russians, and Bobruisk, till then a sparsely populated village, was elevated to the status of district capital in the province of Minsk. The town fanned out from a fortress, built (as part of the Russian network of fortifications against Napoleon) at the confluence of the Bobruisk and Berezina rivers, and was bordered by them on two sides. Before the age of the railway, the waterway was Bobruisk's natural means of transportation. Timber from the surrounding forests – the town's main source of livelihood – was floated down the Berezina, and vessels sailing to northern and southern Russia visited the port. Later Bobruisk became the junction of the railway lines to Minsk and Hommel.

Yet despite the town's importance as district capital with a population of forty thousand, Bobruisk looked like an overgrown village. It was totally devoid of charm, and the only buildings in the entire town which were pleasing to the eye were the two Polish churches. Its streets were unpaved, and during the autumn rains and the spring thaw the town was one vast quagmire, so much so that 'Bobruisk mud' became a byword. Bobruisk was typical of the small towns of the Jewish Pale of Settlement (those areas of Tsarist Russia where Jews were permitted to reside) in general appearance: they all seemed to have been strewn rather than planned.

More than half of the inhabitants of Bobruisk were Jews. Before the enforcement of the decrees of Alexander III, which deprived the Jews of the right to reside in villages (1882), the town was the hub of a Jewish rural area. Like many other small Jewish towns, Bobruisk was a self-contained world. If one can speak of a Jewish condition, it was here, in the towns and cities where the Jewish masses crowded together, eking out a living, that it evolved. The non-Jews played an important part in this world, as the authorities, as customers or even, at times, as rioters, but theirs was always a marginal role. Jewish life was conducted within the confines of a closely-knit society and system of values, determined by the Jewish law or in opposition to it. In the years of Berl's childhood and adolescence, Bobruisk, like other Jewish towns, was opening up to outside influences, but the changes were not yet strong enough to undermine the fundamental nature of the Jewish experience, which remained indelibly imprinted upon the sons and daughters of the town throughout their lives, however far they roamed.

In Bobruisk there was a saying that if one threw a stone, one could be sure of hitting a Katznelson. But there were numerous kinds of Katznelsons and Berl's family belonged to an impoverished and humble branch of the clan. His father Moshe had, as a young man, traveled in pursuit of an education as far as Vilna, which was renowned for its *yeshivas*. There he had made a match with Zelda Rachel, daughter of Shmuel Strashun of the well-known and respected Strashun family. They were married in the summer of 1879 in Cracow, where her parents lived, and took up residence there. The young couple enjoyed seven years of happiness, during which a son, Hayim, was born to them, and then Zelda Rachel died. According to family legend (as transmitted by Moshe's second wife to her children), he was inconsolable, and a number of years passed before he yielded to the urgings of his father to remarry. However, the legend is at odd with the facts. Barely four months after his loss, Moshe returned to Bobruisk and took a second wife, Teivel Reizel, the daughter of Yaakov Nemetz.

Berl's mother came from a middle-class merchant family. A headstrong young woman, of marriageable age, she had already rejected a number of suitors. When Moshe Katznelson was introduced to her as a prospective bridegroom she approved of him, finding his melancholy air intriguing. He told her that he was a widower and, in order to test her, said that he had two children. Teivel was not deterred and undertook to be a mother to them, to the chagrin of her father. Yaakov Nemetz was far from delighted at the idea of a match between his young, dowered daughter and a widower burdened with children. But as the level-headed and obstinate Teivel had made up her mind, nothing could sway her; and her father finally capitulated. The couple were married in spring 1886, and the young Katznelsons moved into the large

Nemetz household. Teivel invested her dowry in her father's ironware shop and worked there every day.

It was in the Nemetz house that their first child, Berl, was born less than a year later. Other children followed at intervals of eighteen months to two years: Israel, Isser, Stishia, Benyamin (who died at the age of one) and Hanna, the youngest, born in December 1897.

Moshe Katznelson lived in his father-in-law's house for more than ten years while he built up his own business. A timber merchant, he traveled in southern Russia in the Yekaterinoslav area, and came home only twice a year, for the festivals. Once his affairs prospered, Moshe bought a large house, and the now affluent family, with six children, finally left the shelter of the Nemetz household.

Teivel, who was considered rather intelligent and knew how to read and write, was neither educated nor particularly attracted to study. Her husband, in contrast, was a scholar and booklover, who had amassed a large library of religious works. In the attic lay volume upon volume of modern Hebrew periodicals, a secular supplement to the bookcases downstairs. Moshe Katznelson was steeped in traditional Jewish learning and the Torah, Talmud and *poskim* (rabbinical studies of halakhic questions) – were the mainstays of his spiritual world. At the same time, however, he did not suffer from a religious narrow-mindedness, possibly because his constant travels had brought him into contact with the spirit of the times and with Russian culture. In any event, works of Russian literature found their way into the household and Berl was later to describe how talmudic works, Pushkin and the novels of the Hebrew writer, Mendele Mocher Sefarim, lay heaped together in his father's study.

The encounter between traditional Jewish values and the new trends was also reflected in Moshe's attitude towards his brother-in-law, Leib Prohorovski, an early Jewish socialist. Moshe and his renegade brother-in-law were linked by ties of deep affection, and stormy debates on socialist issues were carried on whenever Moshe was at home. An air of excitement and intellectual ferment filled the house: the parlor was crammed with visitors, the water in the samovar was constantly on the boil, and the shopkeepers, merchants, and teachers of the town would sit around the table, discussing issues pertaining to Russian society and to the narrower world of Jewish affairs. Palestine and Zionism were also debated.

Berl was the favorite child of his parents, particularly of his father.

He was a handsome boy, with black curls and intelligent, merry eyes. Intellectually, he was head and shoulders above his siblings and wore the aura of the prodigy. Although he had an older half-brother, Hayim, Berl was treated as if he were the eldest, and Moshe and Teivel Reizel focused on him all the hopes which parents traditionally invest in their first-born.

Berl's mother did not play a significant role in his education; she was occupied in her father's shop, and the children were cared for by a nanny and a maidservant. It was his father who shaped the boy's world, and who selected the *melamed* (infant teacher) whose *heder* Berl attended. When he was at home, Moshe often visited Berl at *heder* and took an interest in his progress, while the child took great pride in his teacher's respectful attitude towards his father. But Berl's character was shaped by the books he read rather than by his formal studies. He was eight years old when his father brought him his first Hebrew book, a collection of stories about the Ten Commandments (or rather nine of them, since one was considered unsuitable for a children's book). Berl became very absorbed in his father's library, where he found Hebrew journals and the literature of the Hebrew 'Enlightenment',* as well as many other works usually considered far beyond the grasp of a child of his age.

Up to the age of ten, Berl was brought up exclusively on the Hebrew language and its literature, at home and at *heder*. When his father was satisfied that the boy had a firm grounding in Jewish culture, he arranged for him to be taught Russian. Berl attacked with gusto the great works of the Russian language, equally attracted to fiction and to philosophy.

He was a rather lonely child; since he was sickly, he was not sent to school or to a *talmud torah* after the *heder* years, but was taught by private tutors at home. He quenched his thirst for knowledge in his father's attic, where the Hebrew periodicals were stacked. He had no friends his own age, except for David Shimonovitz (later the poet, David Shimoni), who was his schoolmate in *heder* and reading companion, and with whom he maintained a lifelong friendship. This was not a natural situation for a child: Berl knew nothing of boyhood pranks, and had no friends with whom to make mischief and conspire against parental

---

* The Jewish 'Enlightenment' movement reached Russia in the late nineteenth century. Its essence was the creation of a secular Hebrew literature.

authority. His life centered on two things: the excitement of his father's homecomings, during which he would sit in a corner, eagerly following the fervid adult conversation, and reading, which opened up for him a world of experience and imagination.

A relative who observed him during those years believed that Berl suffered from an inferiority complex because he had no friends, had poor health, and lost his father at an early age. Berl himself often spoke in later years of his suffering as a child, always surrounded by adults, although his perception may have been colored by hindsight. It is probable that so precocious a child would, in any case, have found scant interest in the company of children of his own age.

When Berl was twelve years old, a shattering blow descended on the Katznelson family. His father Moshe contracted bronchial pneumonia while visiting southern Russia on business and died soon after on 1 October 1899. He had not lived to celebrate his 38th birthday.

Widows and orphans were a commonplace in the Pale of Settlement. Berl's father and grandfather had both lost their first wives after only a few years of marriage, and been left with orphan children. But the loss of a husband had more drastic implications, especially in a middle-class family, such as Berl's, where the father was the main breadwinner. The status of the family declined, and it was sometimes reduced to abject poverty. The plight of a widow burdened with children could hardly be compared with that of a widower.

This was now Teivel Katznelson's situation. She who had lived a cosseted life was now suddenly confronted with responsibility for supporting and educating five children, the eldest of whom was twelve years old, the youngest less than two. The shock was more than she could bear and she fell into a deep depression. A year went by before she rallied and was able to take up her yoke. The steely character which had laid dormant during the good years now came to the fore. Her father-in-law, forceful and prosperous Aharon Katznelson, was ready to support his grandchildren and his son's widow on condition that she move into his household and give the children up into his care. Teivel rejected the offer outright, turned her back on the prospect of a secure and comfortable life with her husband's family, and chose the stony path of self-support.

Barely two years later, the family suffered a further set-back: in 1902 a fire broke out in Bobruisk, which consumed most of the wooden houses in the town. The Katznelson home was spared, but the Nemetz house burnt down, as did the store in which Teivel's dowry was invested. Grandfather Nemetz became a pauper overnight, and he and his wife were reduced to living in a little hut in their daughter's courtyard. They were both dead within two years.

Teivel bought a small store in the market, where she sold rope, felt shoes and gloves to the peasants of the surrounding area. She maintained her independence despite heavy odds, and her shrewdness and common sense preserved her from the humiliation of poverty.

For Berl, his father's death spelled the beginning of a decade of wandering – both physical and intellectual. The shock of bereavement, intensified by the crisis of adolescence, drove him into a lengthy, tortuous quest for identity.

His father had been a 'Lover of Zion'.* His 'love of Zion' was not grounded in rational argumentation, but was the product of generations of Jewish tradition; it was imbibed with mother's milk, with biblical tales and legends heard in childhood, with the rituals and prayers of Sabbath and festivals. It was entwined with every aspect of Jewish life, from the mourning customs of the Fast of the Ninth of Av, commemorating the destruction of the Temple, to the merrymaking on festivals celebrating ancient harvest in a distant land.

Berl's first conscious awareness of the Land of Israel was connected with his book of tales of the Commandments. One of the stories was about a *zaddik* (righteous man), travelling through the desert in a caravan. He refused to continue the journey on Friday evening, lest he desecrate the Sabbath and was left alone in the desert. A lion came and guarded him all through the night and when the Sabbath ended, he rode on the lion's back until he caught up with the caravan. The story ended with the comment that the descendants of the *zaddik* were still living in Hebron. When the child read these words, he burst into tears – tears of joy that the Land of Israel really existed and tears of regret that he himself was not living there.

Other books helped to reinforce his sense of Eretz Israel as a real place. The news that the Jews had been granted a concession to build a

---

* Hibat Zion (Love of Zion) was a movement which advocated the return of Jews to Zion, and preceded political Zionism. It began in 1881, with the first wave of immigrants to Palestine, known as the First Aliyah (Going Up). The movement was not marked by practical sense, organizational ability or intellectual depth. At the same time, it deserves credit for initiating the first modern settlement of Jews in Palestine, with the aim of establishing productive, agricultural colonies there.

railway from Jaffa to Jerusalem conjured up in Berl's mind a Palestine resembling the railway station in Bobruisk from which his father always departed on his journeys to southern Russia. The boy loved the colorful station garden, an unusual sight in muddy Bobruisk, whose Jews considered gardens an unnecessary luxury. 'My ideal was to be a stationmaster in Palestine . . .' he later wrote. 'Not a policeman and not a soldier. I saw the Jewish state in the image of a railway station . . .'[1]

News of the First Aliyah pioneers also reached Bobruisk. The Hebrew periodicals in the Katznelson attic recorded in detail everything that happened in Palestine. And among the visitors to Berl's home was a young Jew who had himself actually been a laborer in Palestine for a year or two, one of the builders of the colony of Rehovot. He was a 'strange character', who insisted on farming in Russia as well, and found nothing shameful about driving a wagonload of manure through the streets of Bobruisk. And though he came from a middle-class family, he married a servant-girl. This man would talk at length with Moshe Katznelson, while little Berl sat, all ears, in his habitual corner.

There was another Bobruisk householder who provided direct news from Palestine, a man whose son-in-law had gone there in 1898 and was working as a laborer. His letters, though full of the problems and harsh conditions which prevailed, helped draw a picture of a country eminently accessible.

Zionism was still in its infancy and had made relatively small inroads into Bobruisk. The rich were interested in their business affairs and the intelligentsia in the Jewish socialist Bund or the revolutionary movement. Zionism was confined mainly to the middle class who read the Hebrew periodicals, *ha-Melitz*, *ha-Zefira* and later, *ha-Shiloah*. They would argue about the views of Pinsker* and Lilienblum†, and the virtues and shortcomings of Herzl‡ as they downed glass after glass of tea.

A glance at the biographies of most of the Second Aliyah pioneers,

---

* Yehuda Leib Pinsker, 1821–1891, leader of Hibat Zion; author of the famous pamphlet *Auto-Emancipation*.
† Moshe Leib Lilienblum, 1843–1910, writer and prominent figure in Hibat Zion.
‡ Theodore Herzl, 1860–1904, father of political Zionism and founder of the World Zionist Organization. It was he who transformed Zionism into a political movement, employing the instruments of political organization and of modern diplomacy. He was also the first to define the objective of Zionism as the establishment of a Jewish state. He remained the uncrowned king of the movement till his premature death.

and even those of the Third Aliyah* shows that they came from homes very like Berl's, imbued with an old-style, intuitive, naive and ineffectual 'Love of Zion'. Their Zionism was the product of a new age and a changed atmosphere, but without the background that their homes provided, they would probably never have become Zionists or immigrated to Palestine. For most of them, the transition from small-town middle-class Hibat Zion to pioneering Zionism occurred naturally and smoothly. One finds countless examples of this transition, in the biographies of David Ben Gurion, Kadish Luzinsky† (also from Bobruisk) and David Shimonovitz, to name only a few. For Berl, however, the transition was more difficult. 'By nature I am a believing Zionist', he later wrote. 'It was through despair and through heresy that I won it.'[2]

The home that implanted in him his instinctive Zionist feelings also brought him to the threshold of socialism. His beloved uncle, Leib Prohorovski, a veteran revolutionary and member of the Social Revolutionary Party (S.R.P.), was forced to flee to the United States to escape the wrath of the authorities. When he returned after several years of exile, he became a partner in Moshe Katznelson's business. Moshe, Leib and the young Berl often sat around the table, arguing heatedly about topical issues, the uncle trying to curb his nephew's 'chauvinistic' tendencies. Bobruisk had a strong revolutionary tradition: the Bund was popular, under the leadership of one Nakhke Yochbid, a talented and energetic young man, who set up an extensive underground, composed of young members of the intelligentsia and Jewish workers. A significant revolutionary incident even occurred in Berl's grandfather's house. Yaakov Nemetz was unaware that the tenants of a three-room apartment in the house were Bundists, and had a concealed printing press there, on which they printed several issues of the underground paper, *Arbeiter Shtimme*, as well as the manifesto of the Russian Social Democratic Party. The Tsarist secret police discovered the press, and Berl, then a child, was witness to the subsequent arrests.

He also learned about the party from a Bundist worker, who handed on to the inquisitive ten-year-old boy all the clandestine revolutionary literature he could get.

It was during these years that Berl also read Russian revolutionary literature – the works of Herzen, Belinsky, Dobrolyubov, Chernyshevsky,

* Second Aliyah 1904–1919; Third Aliyah 1919–1923.
† Later the Speaker of the Knesset, the Israeli Parliament.

Mikhailovsky and Lavrov, the giants of nineteenth-century Russian political and social thought, with whom he kept faith all his life. Despite the differences between them, the foundation of their socialism was a profound, unshakeable faith in the individual, his rights and his abilities. Their convictions were rooted in liberal humanism, in love of people rather than of mankind. Their brand of socialism made heavy demands – not on the 'people' in the abstract, but on living, breathing individuals. They regarded the exploitation and subjugation of the Russian peasantry by the nobility and later by the bourgeoisie as a historical injustice, corrupting both the exploiters and society as a whole. The exploiting classes, who had used serfdom for their own advantage, were under a moral obligation to restore to the masses that which they had taken from them. This obligation was based, not on any immutable and inevitable laws of development, but rather on the basic tenets of human and social justice. Russian youth were exhorted to undertake the education of the masses, arousing them to an awareness of their plight and a readiness to fight to change the social order.

This way of thinking was attractive to young intellectuals precisely because of the rigorous demands it made. It appealed to the best in human nature, to man's sense of justice, offering the vision of an ideal society. To the classic question posed by the young generation: 'What is to be done?' there was now an answer; sacrifice themselves and their lives – if need be – for the future of society. And they responded by engaging in propaganda work and by setting up the Vnarod (Go to the People) movement. Educated young people went out into the countryside to bring their message to the peasants. The peasants reacted by handing over the Narodnik agitators to the authorities, who despatched them to prison in Siberia, where, in many cases, they lost their sanity and their lives. But their fate did not deter others. From the 1870s onward, each decade brought its wave of martyrs, inspired by the moving example of those who had gone before and eager to face a life of deprivation and sacrifice. These young idealists gave up studies, careers, family ties and, at times, their lives – enthusiastically, ardently and even joyfully. Infinite dedication, asceticism to the point of self-negation, and sacrifice freely undertaken were the components of the revolutionary ethos of the movement. They handed it on to their successors in Narodnaya Volya (The Will of the People) who, in turn, bequeathed it to the revolutionary parties, and particularly to the S.R.P.

9

The Narodniks resembled anarchists in character. They believed in the individual and in his potential, abhorred coercion from above and all manifestations of authority, and hoped that socialist forms of life would evolve from independent peasant communities, voluntarily organized as free associations – in contrast to authoritarian socialism, in which the state imposed its authority on its members. For them, socialism was the domain of the individual, freely willed, aspiring to achieve total liberation.

When they realized that their methods had failed to awaken the masses and incite revolution and that the Tsar could wield a brutal police force, secret police methods and a biased judiciary against their idealism and dedication, they arrived at the inevitable conclusion that the sole effective weapon was individual terror. The attempted assassination by Vera Zasulich, in 1878, of the governor of St Petersburg, who had been responsible for the brutal flogging of an imprisoned revolutionary, heralded a new era in the annals of the movement. Political assassination now became the chief means of action of the revolutionaries, and their policy culminated in the assassination of Alexander II in 1881. Predictably, and as a consequence, they found themselves bogged down in a morass of controversy on means and ends, sacred and profane, revolutionary cadres versus revolutionary masses and statist socialism versus anarchism.

And while the Narodnaya Volya, and later the S.R.P., concentrated increasingly on terror, Marxism was offering an alternative answer to the question of what was to be done. It preached the inevitability of progress, and avowed that the revolution would arrive and socialism be realized by force of dialectical materialism. Iron logic, objectivism, historical inevitability: these now appealed to revolutionaries, who had discovered that idealism and self-sacrifice alone could not bring about the longed-for transformation.

Berl Katznelson was one of these drawn to the stormy and exciting world of impending revolution. At first he found no contradiction between his love of Russian revolutionary thought and his fundamentalist Zionist faith and attraction to the Hebrew language, but after two or three years he found himself 'torn between two worlds', buffeted from movement to movement, from belief to belief.

Berl was apparently about twelve when he first came in contact with circles of the Jewish intelligentsia in Bobruisk. His teacher of Hebrew studies, Y.L. Dubrov, a man of high moral principles and an outstanding educator, introduced him to an early Zionist student group in the town – whose members were, of course, much older. Berl felt at home among them. They were his first mentors in the maze of the revolutionary world, and with them he argued and began to crystalize his opinions. One of the students, Shimon Ginsburg, found employment for him in the popular Yiddish library, which had been established by Jews as a counter-weight to the Pushkin Municipal Library, which was intended to disseminate Russian culture in the town.

Berl belonged to the category of young Jews in the Pale of Settlement, known as 'externists'. They were a phenomenon unique to the generation which had abandoned Jewish tradition and set its sights on the secular education, the 'ticket' to European society through university studies. Under the reactionary Alexander III, the percentage of Jews permitted to attend secondary schools was drastically reduced, and without government matriculation certificates the road to academic studies, in Russia or abroad, was barred. Hence, many young Jews studied for the matriculation examinations on their own. Like the *matmid*, the diligent talmudic scholar of earlier days, the externist studied tirelessly. But now the knowledge he imbibed was secular, and his objective was to break out of the closed circle of Jewish life in the Pale.

The externists came from the Jewish middle classes: the rich could always send their children to private schools, and the working classes were too busy making a living. It was the same social class which had once produced religious scholars and who now adopted the same methods of memorizing and self-tutoring. Young Jewish scholars (like Berl's father) had always wandered, attending the renowned *yeshivas* of Lithuania in the north. Now the direction was reversed and the students went from the provincial towns in the Pale to the large cities of southern Russia.

But only a few of them actually achieved their goal. Hunger, desolation and disease were their constant companions, as was the threat of arrest and deportation for residing in areas barred to Jews without special permits. Nonetheless, those fortunate enough to find companions among their fellow-externists or students, gained access to a stimulating intellectual world in which endless debates on revolutionary issues and Jewish questions replaced traditional talmudic polemics. Berl was one of this fortunate group.

Jewish society was then taking sides in the controversy between

Ahad ha-Am and the adherents of Herzlian Zionism. The basic issue was the goal of Zionism. Herzl, who had appeared at the First Zionist Congress which he convened in Basel in 1897, like a stormy wind of change and great promise, saw the aim of the Zionist movement as the redemption of the Jewish people. Like Pinsker before him, he had arrived at his Zionism through a sense of injury, humiliation and alienation, engendered by his confrontation with anti-Semitism. Believing as he did that anti-Semitism was a dynamic phenomenon, he had become convinced of the need for a radical solution to the problem, lest the Jewish people perish. His goal was to establish a state where the greater part of the Jewish people could find a refuge, a shelter from the storm. There were two components to this theory: negation of the precarious state of exile, and the urgent need for an independent territory for the Jewish people. But Herzl's solution, brilliant in its simplicity, and aimed at slashing the Gordian knot of the Jewish predicament, encountered derision from Ahad ha-Am, the noted Zionist thinker and leader. Herzl inspired action among the young Jews envious of the daring exploits of Russian revolutionaries, and Ahad ha-Am poured scorn on their fiery enthusiasm. He soberly dissected the chances for Jewish settlement in Palestine, analyzing the country's absorptive capacity. His conclusion was that even if Palestine could absorb relatively large numbers, the rate of immigration would never outstrip the rate of natural increase in the Diaspora. Hence the Jewish problem could not be resolved in this way. He regarded the idea of mass Jewish immigration as a chimera that only idle dreamers could have conceived.

Had times been different, Ahad ha-Am's cautious, analytical approach, his idea of 'readying the hearts' of Diaspora Jews until they proved capable of setting up their own 'spiritual center,' might have found an echo among young Jews. But in an era of revolutionary fervor, of martyrdom and stirring sacrifice, his cool and calculated solution could not satisfy the natural desire for action. Sensitive and educated young Zionists accepted Ahad ha-Am's trenchant criticism of political Zionism, but not his alternative plan of action. In the prevailing atmosphere of imminent catastrophe (the Kishinev pogrom had taken place in 1903), theories were no longer enough. For the young, rejection of Herzl would have implied disillusionment with Zionism as a whole.

During his years as an externist in White Russia and the Ukraine, Berl was associated with circles of young Jews who were deeply affected by the pain of the people's disaster. Their mood was compounded of a sense of responsibility for the national destiny, an awareness of the obligations of educated young Jews, and a consciousness of the momentous implications of their final choice of action. These young people concurred with the Herzlian negation of the state of exile and foresaw hopelessness and total degeneration as the lot of Jews who remained in the Pale of Settlement. 'In our waking hours and in our dreams we saw the gleam of the twisting sword in the gloomy alleyways of Jewish Vilna, in the filth, in the hunger and in the drone of their struggle for a bare pittance, we breathed the air of extinction.'[3]

To rationalize their extreme pessimism, they evolved the theory of 'non-proletarization', which was later to appear, with variations, in the writings of Nachman Syrkin* and Ber Borochov.† According to one source, Berl considered himself one of the authors of this theory, and it seems feasible that he contributed to the discussions which eventually produced new ideas. The essence of the theory was the denial of the ability of the Jewish people in the Diaspora to make the transition from lumpen proletariat to true working-class status.

The young Jewish socialists concurred with Herzl's territorialism – i.e. the recognition of the need of a homeless people for a country of their own. But whereas Herzl cited logical and political arguments, they based their theories on socio-economic considerations: only in their own country could the Jews engage in productive labor and again become a normal people, with a broadly based proletariat.

As long as there was a chance that Herzl might obtain an internationally recognized charter from the Turkish Sultan who ruled Palestine, permitting wide-scale Jewish settlement, Palestine seemed the obvious choice for Jewish settlement. But Herzl met with continued failure in his efforts to persuade the Sublime Porte. At the same time, the British Colonial Secretary, Joseph Chamberlain, was offering a British colony in East Africa to the Jews as a homeland. And elsewhere, after a decade of relative calm, the Kishinev pogrom cast a sombre light on the relations between Jews and non-Jews in Russia. For Berl's circle, Kishinev was the writing on the wall, and the East Africa project seemed to offer

---

* Nachman Syrkin, 1868–1924, born in Russia, was one of the forerunners of Zionist socialism. He was opposed to the mainstream of socialist thought of his time, since he was anti-Marxist and believed in voluntarism.

† Ber Borochov, 1881–1917, born in Russia, was a central leader and ideologist of Poalei-Zion; his unique contribution lay in his application of Marxist theory to Zionism.

a glimmer of hope. Despite their historical attachment to Palestine and
its romantic appeal, it seemed pointless to continue to support that solution if it could not solve the urgent problems of Jewish survival. Hence,
in the vehement polemics between the 'Zion Zionists', headed by
Ussishkin, and the assorted territorialists, Berl and his comrades sided
with the latter. This group was to form the nucleus for the party known,
paradoxically enough, as the Zionist Socialist (S.S.R.P.) Party,
established in 1905 with a territorialist platform.

Berl, however, was somewhat ambivalent: he sympathized with the
'total rejection of the state of exile by the S.S.R.P.-niks, and their profound involvement with the Jewish masses'. At the same time, he was
put off by the idea of a break with Palestine. In a letter to his comrades, in
which he proclaimed his readiness to join in their activities, he wrote
that he still believed in Palestine, although the issue required further
clarification. Berl hoped that the party would eventually be forced to
reassess its stand on this question and conclude that the only 'territorial
entity' which the Jews really wanted was Palestine.

But it was not only on the territorialist issue that he differed with his
comrades. Another bone of contention was the question of Jewish self-
defense. The Kishinev pogrom revolutionized the response of Jewish
youth to such attacks. The turning-point was the publication of Bialik's
poem 'In the City of Slaughter', in which he lashed out at what he considered the shameful ineffectuality and impotence displayed by the
Jews. Self-defense units were set up, the first of them in Hommel, in
response to rumors of an impending pogrom. This urge to take up
arms and defend themselves attested to the change of values of the
young generation. The cohesiveness of Jewish life in the Pale of Settlement was so strong that the young Jew, while rebelling against religion
and tradition, could nonetheless identify with the Jewish people and
sense his affinity with it: no longer meek resignation and acceptance,
but a proud and courageous stand in defense of the honor and dignity of
the Jewish people.

One of the people closely associated with Berl's group was Pinhas
Dashevsky, a young man from Kiev, who had been arrested and tried
for stabbing Krushevan, the alleged instigator of the Kishinev pogrom.
Although Krushevan survived the attack, the attempt on his life drew
attention to the Government's role in encouraging pogroms, and
aroused many young Jews throughout the Pale. Later accounts of those
troubled times seem always to link the pogrom with Dashevsky's

assassination attempt: here, at long last, was a Jewish avenger, emulating the S.R.P. policy of responding to persecution with terror.

The Zionist Socialists condemned terror to a man and again Berl refused to toe the party line. In 1904, still only 17, he had witnessed a pogrom in the small town of Smiella and helped collect arms for self-defense. He became convinced that mere defensive action was not enough and 'that Jews must do what the S.R.P. do to the Russian Government – we must answer with acts of revenge'.[4] Revenge, he thought, would deter the rioters and have an equally important impact internally, helping to mold Jewish revolutionaries of iron determination, purposefulness and dedication.

The first Russian Revolution broke out on 9 January 1905. Berl was in Warsaw on that day, staying with his relative, Yitzhak Tabenkin. The latter was still a 'Zion Zionist', while Berl was a territorialist, but this fact did not prevent the two young men from engaging in revolutionary activity together. On that fateful day, Berl witnessed a mass demonstration, in the course of which people were shot dead in the streets. This was the eve of his planned departure for Zurich and the fulfilment of the dream of every self-taught externist to enter university. But what he saw shook him so profoundly that he canceled his trip in order to devote himself to work for the Revolution.

This is probably the most significant year in Berl's intellectual development prior to his departure for Palestine – but it is also the most uncharted. None of his 1905 letters are extant – although he spent the year travelling and was very active politically. He went back to Bobruisk, but apparently then returned to Warsaw, since in the spring he took part in a series of debates there between Borochov and the territorialists. Once again, his typical ambivalence surfaced: he appeared on behalf of the territorialists but, on his own evidence, presented the Palestinian viewpoint.

Berl rapidly became disillusioned with the Zionist Socialist Party, first and foremost because of its stand on terror. His own activistic viewpoint was undoubtedly influenced by the traumatic experiences he had undergone in Kishinev and Hommel, which he refused to discuss even years later. Moreover, on the evidence of his sister, Hanna, while organizing defensive action in Bobruisk, he was injured by a lash from a Cossack whip and the experience haunted him for years.

By summer 1905 he had left the S.S.R.P. and joined a new group, Vozrozhdenie (Resurrection), from which the Seimist Party later evolved.

This group believed that instead of engaging in a futile search for a territory it was necessary first to restore the creative powers of the Jewish people in the Diaspora. Only after the Jewish people had achieved cohesion, could they express their will and decide which territory they preferred. The members of Vozrozhdenie adopted a 'wait and see' policy on Palestine, but were more responsive to terror than the S.S.R.P. In September 1905 the group leaders met in Kroche in Moghilov Province to discuss their plans.

Berl attended the Kroche conference and delivered a speech in which he advised against turning the movement into a party. These were people whom he greatly esteemed and for whom he felt an enduring affection. He hoped they would confine themselves to criticism of existing conditions, and not try to establish a party with a platform of its own. His remarks sparked off a stormy debate and his views were rejected.

As a result of his association with Vozrozhdenie, Berl became involved in propaganda work among the Jewish and Russian masses, organizing workers' rallies and engaging in polemics with the Bund. He was active in southern Russia, apparently in Odessa and Yekaterinoslav. But, as for solid results, M. Silberfarb, one of the leaders, has attested that Berl did not succeed in setting up a single workers' circle, nor did he attract a single worker into the party. And, soon enough, Berl became disappointed with this group as well. He admired the depth and originality of its leaders' thinking, but he objected to their unfair criticism of other parties, such as the Bund. When he protested to one of the movement's leaders, the latter claimed that a distinction should be drawn between absolute justice and political justice. This argument 'immediately brought home to me the contradiction which existed between the pragmatics of political leadership, on the one hand, and declarations and ideas, on the other . . . and this, to some extent, spelled the end of my relations with the movement . . .'[5] Thus the adult Berl offered a simplistic explanation for the motives of his younger self, disregarding the confusions – and ideological uncertainties – of his adolescent years.

Berl's attitude with regard to the Hebrew language, as with regard to the question of Palestine, was ambivalent. On the one hand, he kept faith with Hebrew – his 1905 letter to the S.S.R.P. applying for membership, was still in that language! At the same time, he introduced himself to one and all as a convinced Yiddishist. In 1905 he spent some time eaching at the Bobruisk school run by the Society for the Dissemination of Knowledge, whose aim was to bring Russian culture to young Jews. His job was to teach Hebrew and Jewish studies to girls from poor families. On the assumption that he would not have time to teach them more than the Hebrew alphabet, and in order to counter assimilatory trends, he decided to teach them Jewish history and Yiddish literature. He later summarized his teaching experience in writing, and proposed modifications in the Hebrew language and Jewish history studies, and the inclusion of Yiddish in the curriculum.

From 1906, however, Berl's letters were written in Yiddish. The Seimist party (successor to Vozrozhdenie) wanted to breathe new life into Jewish cultural heritage – in Yiddish, as part of the renaissance of Jewish life in the Diaspora. And just as Jewish revolutionaries – from the Bund to the territorialists – had regarded Palestine as a 'dead land', so Hebrew was now considered a 'dead language'. On the basis of his teaching experience, Berl now concluded that the masses neither needed Hebrew nor had the possibility of studying it. But, as so often before, he was not fully convinced. In 1906, while in Vilna, he saw how young Jewish writers were deserting the Hebrew camp *en bloc* and turning to Yiddish. They regarded *ha-Me'orer* (The Awakener), the Hebrew journal published by the noted writer Yosef Haim Brenner in London, as a waste of Brenner's talents, squandered on a dead language. Berl was inflamed at the way in which these young writers dismissed out of hand their childhood traditions, slandering what had once been a cherished part of their heritage. He was unable to offer himself a satisfactory explanation of his own ambivalence. He himself confessed that his stand was not the outcome of 'Zionist faith, but rather a sense of injury, a stubborn unwillingness to be part of this generation, which lacks even the strength to die a dignified death'.[6]

Because he felt himself an integral part of the Jewish people, sharing responsibility for its fate, he could not completely identify with the Russian Revolution: 'Great waves engulfed us, the wine of revolution intoxicated us, we joined its ranks, were buffeted by its storms, smitten in its debacles. And with all that, we remained few among many, whose roots no storm could wrench out of the soil of Jewish being. We held on, steadfastly, to our own identity with the loyalty of sons banished from their father's house.'[7] His search for a key with which to transform the realities of Jewish life caused him to roam from group to group and it was this which gained him a reputation for fickleness. Many were the 'wise and good' who mocked the 'inconsistent and ineffectual boy',[8] and asked him in which congregation he was now praying.

In 1906 the nineteen-year-old boy concluded that Jewish existence in the Diaspora, devoid of living social content – was not tenable. Within the Jewish movements, involvement did not extend beyond empty rhetoric into true personal commitment, nor had a leader arisen who could elicit such commitment. Hence the futility of all discussion, and hence, to his mind, the reason why idealistic young Jews were flocking to non-Jewish movements. This conclusion was born out of the disillusionment and frustration that followed upon the high hopes of 1905. The revolutionary wave was subsiding. The Tsarist regime had rallied and was brutally suppressing all revolutionary activity. Reaction reigned supreme.

Like many others, Berl might have been absorbed into the world of the Russian Revolution had it not been for what he later termed 'the merit of my father, of blessed memory'.[9] At an early age he had ceased to be a practicing Jew, a step taken apparently without much soul-searching. Still, Passover was an event worthy of mention in a letter, and he avoided eating non-kosher food. He forced his brother, Israel, to study Gemarrah two hours daily, so that he would know something of traditional Judaism; and years later, when he learned that Israel, then living in the United States, was staying in the home of a man from Bobruisk suspected of association with missionaries, he wrote him a scathing letter. There is not one Russian name listed among his friends and acquaintances and no non-Jew ever entered his home.

Although his disillusionment with the realities of Jewish life was mixed with envy of Russian revolutionism, it did not produce self-denigration. Berl was inherently incapable of assimilation; his upbringing, his education, his very nature prevented it. On the other hand, the young Berl was too responsive to the prevailing trends to remain locked in his primary innocent Zionist faith. Many of his contemporaries of a similar background turned, in despair, to the pursuit of careers and, returning to their studies, became perennial externists. Berl too abandoned political activity in 1906, but he was still looking for 'the real thing' and at the end of the year, early in 1907, he decided to learn a manual trade. Later he would claim that his decision was inspired by another, secret resolve – to immigrate to Palestine, but this is questionable. At that time he learned that his brother, Israel, had decided to emigrate to the United States and wrote him a letter, criticizing his hasty decision, his abandonment of home and friends and all he held dear. But the letter contained no hint of criticism as to the choice of destination – America, rather than Palestine. And a year later, by which time another brother, Hayim, had also reached America, Berl heard that Israel had started work and rejoiced at the 'proletarization' of his brothers – 'a victory, a manifestation of the power to act, for once to sense your own powers, your own life . . .'[10] In spring 1908 Berl wrote of his failure: 'I am not lucky in my work, the buttered side is always down.'[11] And in the same letter he contemplated emigration to America. There it was common for young Jews to do manual work: what idealism had failed to achieve in the Pale, the struggle for survival had achieved in America. And still – not a mention of Palestine!

For about three years – till 1908 – he persevered at manual labor. First he worked for a tinsmith, then with a Jewish blacksmith in another town. Finally he managed to gain entrance to the renowned Jewish vocational school, Trud, in Odessa, as an apprentice turner. But 'not only did my hands fail to function properly, my brain could not grasp the work. My eyes did not see and I just did not understand what was going on about me. I simply lacked "manual sense". The craftsmen considered me a fool and an absolute good-for-nothing.'[12] This failure was traumatic for Berl. He had sought to revolutionize his own way of life, to demonstrate his own 'ability to act' after despairing of the creative force of the Jewish intelligentsia as a whole. But now he was the very epitome of the 'non-proletarization' of Russian Jews, incapable of earning a living by his own labor.

Berl's conclusion was that Russia was no longer the place for him. He was disillusioned not with manual labor as such, but with the life of a manual laborer in that country. He could, of course, have emigrated to the United States, following in the footsteps of many young Jews, including his own brothers. He did, in fact, consider the possibility. Why did he prefer Palestine? Was it 'by merit of my father, of blessed memory'? Or did he shrink from the alienness of the United States, fearing the loss of identity which afflicted immigrants? Was he shocked by the suicide, in America, of his boyhood friend, Leib Flakon? Or could Abba Ahimeir* be right in his claim that America was too 'definite' a place for Berl, who had been, from his youth, 'a man of

---

* Abba Ahimeir, a publicist and later the leader of an extreme right-wing group in Palestine, a native of Bobruisk, and Berl's protégé in his youth. See chapter 11.

haziness'?[13] There is probably some truth in all of these theories, except the last. Berl was, in fact, sincerely seeking a foothold in reality.

So, at the age of twenty or twenty-one, having abandoned all hope of a meaningful life in Russia, Berl reverted to the dreams of his early youth. At first he was secretive about his Zionist yearnings, but once he became convinced of his own steadfastness, he took two close friends and former pupils from Bobruisk into his confidence – Sarah Schmuckler and Leah Miron. They approved of his plans: 'It doesn't seem to them as fantastic as I feared.'[14] He then told his brother, Hayim: 'I want to go to Palestine. I want to do something. I want to live somewhere. Just a small spark, but I do not want it to die out. I am drawn to those stubborn people . . . who have turned their backs on everything in order to start a new life, to rid themselves of the Exile, to live by testing themselves.' Still he was not sure. 'As I write to you there is still a great chill in my heart. The spark is not easily ignited, but I will not let it be extinguished. I want to be more serious and I believe that once I have found myself some kind of work, new feelings will be kindled in me both with regard to labor and to my own abilities. Who knows?'

He was still repelled by the official Zionist movement and its leaders, 'who cling to empty words . . . who veil all our troubles with Zionist programs and phraseology'. The movement was at the time emerging from the Herzlian intoxication; but it had not produced a new policy, or a new slogan. It was an era of petty deeds, a Zionism of collection boxes. And as a result Berl did not pin great hopes on mass immigration: 'I have little faith in the possibility of redeeming the entire people (and who, indeed, now refers to the 'people'? – the prevailing indifference has seeped into my bones, just as it has afflicted all those I hate so much). I am thinking of myself, of ourselves. For the sake of our Jews I want us to have some other corner, another life, to escape the stifling atmosphere.' Thus, the motive for his immigration was not love of Palestine, but rather hatred of the Diaspora.

But, even after making his decision, Berl still doubted the prospects of success for his own 'individual revolution'. His failure at manual work still weighed heavily on him: 'I am mostly afraid of adding yet another ne'er-do-well to the thousands of *melamdim* and idlers already there', he confided to his brother. And, demonstrating once again his desire to be practical, he added: 'I would even be satisfied if I knew something about book-keeping, if I knew one European language.'[15]

At least a year passed before the decision was put into practice. Berl was due to be drafted into the Russian army, and he refused to act like the many young Jews who avoided military duty by fleeing to Palestine, particularly during the Russo-Japanese War. Moreover, had he deserted, his mother would have been forced to pay a fine of three hundred roubles. Instead, as was customary among Jews in Russia, Teivel Reizel approached one of the physicians on the draft board and offered him 25 roubles in return for declaring her son unfit for military service. However, the services of the physician were not required, since Berl was exempted in any case, on health grounds – probably because of poor teeth or his short stature. His mother wanted to keep the 25 roubles, since no bribe had been needed, but Berl insisted that she pay, to avoid spoiling the arrangement for other young Jews. Thus, by autumn 1908 Berl was free of his military obligations to the Tsarist Government.

Another obstacle was the question of money for the fare. Teivel Katznelson scraped out a meager living for herself and her daughters, and her son was reluctant to impose a further financial burden on her. He found a position at the same Yiddish library in Bobruisk where he had worked as a boy, and earned 25 roubles a month. He also compiled a catalog of Hebrew and Russian books, which was awarded a prize by the Society for the Dissemination of Knowledge. In this way, Berl accumulated the 350 roubles he needed.

Years later Berl wrote that that year was spent in constant preparation for immigration and described the delay as resulting from 'technical reasons'. But on the eve of Passover 1909 he wrote to Israel in the United States: 'I am still at the crossroads. I believe that in a few weeks I will be writing something about myself. I hope so, but until my mind is made up I do not want to write to you about it.' Shortly afterwards he contracted typhus and was ill for many months. According to Berl, his mother discovered his intention to leave for Palestine from his delirious ravings. Teivel, on the other hand, claimed that he had told her of his plans to travel before he fell ill. When she found a guidebook to Palestine on his desk, she realized what his destination was, wept and tried to dissuade him, 'because Palestine was strange to us then'. When he fell ill, she swore that if he recovered, she would never try to stop him again.[16]

Whatever the true version – when Berl recovered, he was firmly resolved on immigration to Palestine. In August or September 1909, he boarded a cargo boat on the Berezina, and sailed to Kiev *en route* to Odessa. He took the slower river route rather than the railway because it was cheaper, or, perhaps this was his way of bidding farewell to the country of his birth.

He reached Odessa in September, and on the eve of his embarkation for Palestine, wrote to his brother Hayim.

I am going for nobody's sake but my own. I can no longer live this way. And however bitter my thoughts about the Jewish people as a whole, if there is the slightest possibility that the remnant can extricate itself from the Exile for its own sake, even if only a few dozen remain, I shall be among them. One thing is abundantly clear to me – in all of us [all the Katznelsons] there dwells a spirit which will never allow us to resign ourselves to the Exile . . . and therefore I believe that if there is a possibility of saving ourselves and living by our own labor, we will do it. [17]

Two or three days later, a young couple named David and Rachel Zhuchovitsky (later Zakai*), who were standing on the deck of a ship sailing for Palestine, saw a short young Jew, with curly black hair, clambering up the ship's ladder, dragging a sack and a suitcase behind him. He apparently recognized them as fellow-Jews, because he placed his baggage beside them for safe keeping and rushed back to shore again, without stopping to introduce himself. At the very last moment, he reappeared, drenched in perspiration, 'with a watermelon under each arm'.[18] And it was thus, clutching two watermelons, that Berl Katznelson sailed into the unknown.

His departure made no impact in Russia. Many had left for Palestine before him, and most of them had continued their journey from there to the United States, or returned to Russia. Palestine was not considered the end of the road – and certainly not for a young man who had been associated in turn with most of the Jewish socialist movements. It is not surprising therefore, that when Ben Zion Dinaburg† heard from a mutual friend Eliezer Schein that Berl had left for Palestine, he questioned the seriousness of his decision. Schein replied, measuring every word carefully: 'Berl immigrated after lengthy preparations . . . and weighty consideration. It is a serious matter. Not only for him. It is important for Palestine as well.'[19]

Several months later, at a social gathering of former members of the S.S.R.P., all disappointed, embittered and aimless, Benny Fridland (one of the leaders of the movement) who had just returned from a trip abroad,

---

* David Zakai, later a leading labor journalist.
† Ben Zion Dinaburg (Dinur), a famous historian of the Jewish people, the first Israeli Education Minister.

described his meeting with the 'former prodigy of the revolution', on the roof of a cafe in Jaffa on the night of Berl's arrival in Palestine. Berl was dumbfounded at the news that Fridland was leaving the country on the following day. Fridland's impression was that the new arrival 'was very happy. I had the feeling that he had come to Palestine like a man whose ships had all been wrecked. And he had been saved by clinging to the last remaining plank, which had carried him to shore . . .'[20]

2

DISCOVERY AND SELF-REVELATION, 1909–1914

Jaffa

Berl was not one of the forerunners of the Second Aliyah. By the time he arrived in Palestine in 1909, the main wave of immigration, which had commenced in 1904 with the arrival of a group from Hommel and continued in the wake of the Russo-Japanese War and the failure of the 1905 Revolution, had subsided. By 1909 the Second Aliyah's patterns were fixed and its image well-established. The newly-emergent workers' parties – ha-Poel ha-Tzair (The Young Worker) with its nationalist ideology, and the socialist Marxist Poalei Zion (Workers of Zion) – were already at loggerheads. The ha-Shomer (Watchman) Association, which guarded and defended the Jewish settlements, had already lost several of its members in clashes with Arab attackers. The first socialist commune in Palestine, at Sejera (set up in 1908 in Galilee by Poalei Zion), had completed its trial year. Other communal experiments were well underway: the Kinneret farm had been established on the shores of Lake Galilee, and the neighboring lands of Um Juni (later the first *kvutza*, Degania) had been plowed for the first time. The Jewish workers in Galilee had already established the ha-Horesh (Plowman) Association. On the sand dunes north of Jaffa, the first houses of the Ahuzat Bayit suburb, forerunner of Tel Aviv, had been completed; and the sons and daughters of prosperous Russian Jewish families were now coming to Jaffa to attend the Hebrew Gymnasium (Herzliya). Close to Petah Tikva, the first *moshav* (workers' cooperative village), Ein Ganim, had recently been set up. Writers and poets such as Brenner, Agnon and David Shimonovitz were living in Palestine, as were future labor leaders Yitzhak Ben Zvi, Rachel Yanait, Israel Shohat, David Ben Gurion, Yosef Aharonovitch and Yitzhak Vilkansky.

The problems besetting the Second Aliyah had by now been defined: namely, strained relations with the First Aliyah middle-class colonists, who had little in common with the new immigrants; and the problem of 'Jewish labor', or, to be more precise, the predominance of Arab labor employed in the middle-class Jewish colonies in Judea, Samaria and Galilee. In 1908 the Zionist Organization had set up its Palestine Office, aimed at promoting settlement efforts. It was headed by a very 'correct' young Prussian Jew named Arthur Ruppin.

Berl was 22 when he arrived in Palestine. He was older than most of his fellow-immigrants, and neither his tortuous road to Palestine nor his feelings of being a refugee, fleeing a catastrophe, were characteristic of his Second Aliyah comrades. Most of the pioneers were impelled by a naive Zionist faith, by youthful self-assurance and a steadfast resolve to build a new Jewish society in Palestine. Berl later claimed that despair and disillusionment had characterized the pioneers before they took the final step of immigration but, in fact, this was true of very few. The majority – Ben Zvi and Ben Gurion; Sprinzak and Aharonovitch; Rachel Katznelson and Rachel Blaustein (the poetess); Eliezer Yaffe, Yosef Bussel and Yitzhak Tabenkin, among others – did not share Berl's torment and indecision.

After a twelve-day journey through the Black Sea, to Istanbul, Izmir and Beirut, Berl disembarked at Jaffa, a port town characterized by tumult and pandemonium: Arab boatmen loading the bewildered immigrants and their baggage into boats and rowing them ashore; a polyglot confusion of Arabic, Yiddish and Russian; new colors, new odors and the burning heat of an August day. His personal bewilderment was exacerbated by his meeting with those of 'dashed hopes'. Jaffa was not only a port of entry, but also a point of departure. And many were leaving at the time. As Brenner wrote: 'Sevenfold more depart than arrive . . . Palestine, regrettably, is a tourist country for our brethren as well. They come, they see . . . and they return . . .'[1] Immigration was not one of the imperatives of Zionism. It was possible to be a good Zionist and spend one's entire life in the Diaspora, as many prominent leaders of the movement demonstrated, among them Shmaryahu Levin, Nahum Sokolow, David Wolffsohn and Yehiel Tchlenow. Immigration was regarded as a kind of adventure, an eccentric gesture. As a result, the immigrants themselves did not perceive their step as revolutionary and irreversible. The links between Palestine and the Diaspora were strong, the borders were open and Jews traveled to and fro. According to Ben Gurion's estimate many years later, 90 per cent of the immigrants who arrived during the era of the Second Aliyah

(1904–1914) subsequently left the country.* Even if the figure is exaggerated – and there is no reason to think it is – the estimate itself attests to the scope of the phenomenon. People came to Palestine for a variety of reasons: the fare to Palestine was cheaper than passage to the United States; some were fleeing military service in Russia, particularly during the Russo-Japanese War; others were indeed motivated by Zionism. Similarly, they left for a variety of reasons: some out of hunger or disease, or simply a longing for the home and familiar landscape they had left behind; others, the 'intellectuals', in the face of the scant prospects and ineffectual field for action they discovered in Palestine; still others because of the harsh reality.

That immigration at the time was not considered final and irreversible is demonstrated by the biographies of the leaders of the labor movement: they visited Russia amazingly often! One went in order to gain exemption from military service, another in order to provide for his family, and a third to attend university. What drove these people to make so many 'home visits'? Homesickness, or perhaps the desire for some respite from the debilitating climate, disease, poor food, exhausting work? It was probably a combination of all these reasons.

It is not surprising, therefore, that Berl encountered several old-timers while still aboard ship in Jaffa. They had come to meet friends. Their first question was: 'Why did you come?' after which they launched into a harangue aimed at showing the newcomers the foolishness of their step. Years later Berl described the scene: 'Such malice, such glee at failure, such contempt for Palestine, such mockery of the poor innocents – in the course of my life in Palestine I do not know if I have ever witnessed anything more shocking and terrifying.'[2] Berl had known despair and could understand it in others. But when instead of heart-break, it generated malice and derision, to be heaped upon those who still believed – this he could not tolerate.

Berl did not consider himself a Zionist at the time of his immigration. But his initial response to the country was tinged with elements of mysticism: 'At the very moment I came ashore it was clear to me that this was my final destination. All that had gone before was ended for me . . . I knew there could be no other shore for me.'[3] Here, again, his reaction was not typical. His contemporaries, who had not wrestled with their

---

* During this decade it is reliably estimated that 35,000 Jews reached Palestine. Most were religious and settled in the 'Old Yishuv'. The term 'Second Aliyah' refers to the young pioneers, of whom there were no more than 15,000.

Zionism as Berl had, did not experience a change of heart when they set foot in the country. Although he continued to define himself as a non-Zionist and could offer no rational explanation for his immigration, Berl was nevertheless immediately, unshakeably, certain that he had found his anchor in life.

Unlike his comrades, Berl never returned to visit Russia, nor did he desire to study or take a holiday abroad. When he finally did go, it was as an emissary of the movement, under totally altered political conditions; and even then, S.Y. Agnon, the writer (who had himself gone abroad to study before the First World War), claimed that Berl's conduct was inappropriate. During his first ten years in Palestine, Berl did not even contemplate a journey abroad. He behaved in fact like a shipwrecked man, clutching at his lifeline and afraid to relax his hold.

Berl arrived at the end of the summer of 1909. In order to avoid the prospective emigrants and their malicious comments, he shunned Hayim Baruch's famous hotel, and moved into another, with his new-found friends, David and Rachel Zhuchovitzky. Every day he made his way to Ahuzat Bayit in a vain search for work. Jaffa reminded him too much of the Diaspora, and life there seemed to lack the content he sought. It was a town teeming with the old familiar Jewish controversies, 'and everything was suspended, swaying in the air, floating aimlessly hither and thither'.[4] Having passed the New Year idly and in a gloomy mood, he decided, despite the warnings of more experienced people, to leave for Petah Tikva – the largest of the colonies, and one not too distant.

His first impressions were ambivalent: 'Light and shadow intermingle . . . hope and despair. There are no clear dividing lines.'[5] It was a lush green village with an attractive main street. The houses were too pretentious for Berl's taste, and the air of luxury at odds with the idea of rural life. But the signs of Jewish sovereignty warmed his heart: the diligence service to Jaffa, the postage stamps printed by the colony, and the banknotes which were recognized as legal tender throughout the area by both Jews and Arabs. At the same time, he was unfavorably impressed by the arrogance of the colonists and by the fact that the Jewish laborers, who congregated in the renowned Rabinovitch hotel, were unemployed.

The day after his arrival, he went to Ein Ganim, where, for the first time, an attempt was being made to provide a constructive solution to the problem of Jewish employment. The early Second Aliyah pioneers had wanted to be agricultural laborers in the colonies, to 'conquer labor', firstly because there was no other work to be had; and secondly because they believed in the return to labor, to the natural life, and to the basic occupations vital for a normal Jewish society in Palestine. Their ambition was to create a Jewish working class. The slogan of ha-Poel ha-Tzair was 'The precondition for the realization of Zionism is the conquest of all manual occupations in Palestine by Jews.' Zionism, they believed, could not be realized unless the Jewish people built their country with their own hands, through sweat, effort and sacrifice. Only thus could the Jewish people re-establish their right to the country and become the majority there. These pioneers, who gloried in their atheism (particularly the Poalei Zion socialists), were uncomfortable with arguments basing the right of the Jewish people to their land on historical ties, on religion and the Bible. Just as the revolutionary movement in Russia claimed that the land belonged to those who cultivated it, they too believed that labor itself conferred the right of land ownership. This explains the shock felt by these young idealists in their encounter with the colonists, particularly in that most prosperous of colonies, Petah Tikva. These farmers, who had experienced years of hunger and deprivation before they arrived at relative prosperity, were reluctant to employ Jewish workers: experienced Arab laborers worked better than young men and women who had never seen a hoe before they came to Palestine; the Arabs had fewer needs and hence made fewer demands. Moreover, the Jewish workers openly practiced a secular way of life, conduct which offended the observant Petah Tikva farmers. Generally speaking, the farmers, who spoke Yiddish and Arabic, literally had no common language with the young pioneers, who insisted on speaking Hebrew (and, furthermore, with a Sephardic intonation). They differed in their way of life, their outlook and their approach to Zionism. It was a clash of two generations, or perhaps even of two cultures: young against old, secular versus religious, radical versus conservative. And the two camps rapidly entrenched themselves in their opposing positions: the farmers preferred to employ Arabs, and only a few of them took on Jewish laborers, either on principle or out of pity; the workers, for their part, who suffered hunger and destitution and saw many of their comrades leaving the country, regarded the farmers as 'traitors to the cause'.

The cardinal problem was not that of culture or employment, but whether an educated European Jewish worker was capable of doing backbreaking, grueling and monotonous labor and supporting himself and a prospective family that way. These questions were the source of the 'great despair' which gripped the Second Aliyah pioneers from 1908 onward. The first question was subjective and revolved around the individual's physical and moral stamina. The second, however, was an objective issue: could the educated Jewish worker, even if he succeeded in finding employment, live on the wages which the farmer paid? The young pioneers feared the stigma of charity, of parasitism: they were haunted by the fate of the First Aliyah immigrants who had accepted Baron Rothschild's patronage in return for a living wage, and thereby forfeited their independence and initiative. Hence, they avoided even the suggestion of patronage like the plague. They were unwilling even to accept assistance from institutions of the Zionist movement. Furthermore, they asked the same wages as the Arab laborers and were offended at the suggestion that they should earn more merely because they were Jews. The Arab's wage, however, was usually a supplementary income: he lived in his village, adjacent to the Jewish colony and owned a plot of land, which his family cultivated. The Jewish worker, in contrast, was forced to pay rent and buy food from his meager wages and had no additional source of income. Very few Jewish workers received financial support from abroad. The wages barely sufficed to keep body and soul together.

Buying books or newspapers or indulging in any other intellectual luxuries was out of the question. If he fell ill and was unable to work – and under the prevailing conditions this was more than likely – he was in danger of starving. It goes without saying that under such conditions, it was impossible to marry. In the first few years of the Second Aliyah, the problem was not acute: but as the immigrants matured and wearied of bachelorhood and solitude, the problem of supporting a family became more pressing. The establishment of Ein Ganim was the first attempt at a solution: each family was allotted a 15-dunam plot for a house and a small farm, consisting of a vegetable plot and a milch cow. The farm would be tended by the wife and children. It would supplement the family diet and at the same time enable the man of the house to continue gainful employment in the colony. Ein Ganim was a free community, where new members were selected by the veteran members alone, and where the principle of Jewish labor was strictly observed.

'The little free republic'[6] of Ein Ganim won Berl's heart at first sight.

Its spirit, gaiety, simplicity, and free atmosphere were immeasurably attractive to him, after prosperous, orthodox Petah Tikva. Here, for the first time, he met a real old-timer – a worker who had been there for six years; after his encounter with the emigrants at Jaffa and the embittered residents of the colony hotel, this was a refreshing change. The members gave him a warm welcome and found him a place to sleep in one of their rooms and, a day later – at long last – he started work.

Berl was tense and anxious, haunted by memories of his fiasco as a manual worker in Russia. He felt that he was facing the greatest test of his life – the supreme test for a Jewish intellectual from the Pale of Settlement. For him, the only meaningful life was that founded on physical labor, and for this he was, in fact, rather ill suited. Even when he discovered that he was capable of doing the work, he remained unsure of himself. He was afraid to miss a single day's work, lest he find it difficult to return. This fear was so pronounced that when the ha-Poel ha-Tzair conference was convened in Jaffa during the Festival of Sukkot, he contained himself and did not attend.

He was profoundly moved by his first, uniquely Palestinian experiences: the communal meal, deeply satisfying despite the paucity of the food and the slovenly surroundings; working amidst nature, in view of the Judean hills; bathing in the river after a day's work; and the pleasant feeling of lassitude at evening: 'One feels good. Good in the physical sense. So good that one can find no words to express it.'[7] And he retained this indelible impression in years to come: 'Could I but embrace that which was given to me? My days of apprenticeship at work, inhaling the air of this country. A rush mat spread on the earth after work. Ein Ganim . . .'[8] Life was hard for him, even if he refused to recognize the fact: his fatigue, that ostensibly pleasant lassitude, was so great, that he was reluctant to pick up a book or newspaper; to compose a letter was a supreme effort. He lacked the strength, even the desire, to walk over to the colony and browse at the local library. During the first three months of his stay he never left the *moshav*, and even on Saturdays and festivals he stayed close to home – all because of the 'pleasures' of toil. He was so happy to have passed the 'test', that his disinclination for cultural activity seemed to him a favorable sign, evidence of the change in his character rather than the natural outcome of constant weariness.

Although in the first flush of enthusiasm he idealized his lot, he did not ignore the shadows: the Jewish employer was a hard master, wielding a whip over the Arabs who constituted the great majority of the workers; the overseers – the better workers who were appointed watchdogs over their comrades – became insensitive to the humiliating nature of their work. The Jewish workers were also far from perfect. They labored industriously when the overseer was in the vicinity and idled when he was not around. Berl, the newcomer, was ashamed on their behalf, but at the same time understood their motives. As for the 'simple life' and freedom from material possessions – he realized that the outcome was 'dire poverty and neglect'. He also discovered that mutual aid and hospitality were positive features of communal life, but had their disadvantages: the door of the room he shared was always open and his comrades 'do not appear to recognize the right of the individual to privacy.'[9]

But these difficulties could not mar his new-found joy, which was intensified by his meeting with two men who were to become his close friends – the writer, Yosef Hayim Brenner, and Aharon David Gordon.

Brenner had arrived in Palestine about six months before Berl. His stories, describing the experiences of young Jews in the Pale of Settlement amidst political ferment and upheaval, had impressed Berl as highly authentic and sincere depictions of a world with which he was closely familiar. He also admired Brenner's loyalty to the Hebrew language at a time when other writers preferred Yiddish. Brenner's pain, his revulsion from the typical Jewish life of the Diaspora and his desperation echoed Berl's own sentiments. The two met at the home of David Shimonovitz in the Neve Shalom quarter of Jaffa on the day after Berl's arrival, and there was instant rapport between them. After his encounter with the mocking cynicism of the Jaffa 'intellectuals', Berl felt complete empathy with the writer: 'True profound despair – the heart aches to see it.'[10] Brenner's despondency was that of a man who had tried everything – and failed at everything. He had attempted to become a manual laborer, and he projected his own sense of ineffectuality to all Jewish workers, to the *yeshiva* students who had undertaken a task beyond their strength.

Berl too had been disillusioned by the ebbing vitality of the Jewish people, but there was a difference between them. Palestine did not cure Brenner of his despair, and his life consisted of a series of experiments which all ended in frustration. To a friend, Asher Beilin, who wanted to immigrate from London, he wrote: 'Beilin! You know I love you; you know how much I want to see you, but I must say to you categorically: Do not come! . . . I too, if it were not all the same to me, and if there were some place which attracted me – would leave here today!'[11] Berl, in contrast, even before he found work, eagerly awaited the arrival of friends. And less than a year later, he was urging his brothers to join him in Palestine. The country seemed to have cured his pessimism, and his attitude to the famous writer, who was his senior, was paternal and protective.

What was it that attracted Brenner to the young man who had just arrived and who had so far displayed neither talent for writing nor any other outstanding trait? Why did he bother to find him accommodation and work, and to hold long conversations with him through the winter of 1909 at Ein Ganim?

Years later, S. Y. Agnon described how he discussed this question with Brenner, after the two of them had visited Berl, then suffering from malaria.

After we left, I wanted to ask Brenner why he concerned himself so much with this man. I saw that Brenner was wrapped in thought and did not disturb him. Suddenly he glanced at me with his handsome blue eyes, then looked back at Berl Katznelson's room and said: 'A true Jew'. I looked at him inquiringly, in surprise. What was so remarkable about that? Brenner added in Yiddish: 'A yiddisher *mentsh*. He is a Jewish human being; do you understand what I mean, I said a Jewish human being. You probably want me to explain to you what a Jewish human being is. I won't do it. It's time that you understood for yourself.'[12]

Brenner was reputed to have called Berl 'the supreme Jewish intellectual'. And he dedicated an article to him with the words 'To B. Katznelson at Ein Ganim, with respect.'[13] It would appear that Berl's pitiless and uncompromising vision of his people, and his sense of doom, together with his burgeoning hope, were the meeting-points between the two men. Brenner summed up the feeling that they shared in his book *mi-Kan umi-Kan* (Here and There): 'The Jewish people, from the point of view of logic, has no future. But, nonetheless, one must labor. As long as the spirit remains alive, there are noble deeds and exalted moments. Long live humanitarian Jewish labor!'[14] This slogan was more appropriate to Berl than to Brenner.

The two men were alike, not only in their analysis of Jewish existence, but in their emotional and intellectual makeup. Both were what one might describe as Dostoyevskian characters: men of complex natures and stormy emotions, luxuriating – almost – in their suffering, aspiring to purity, almost saintliness, and racked by their lack of inner peace. Both Brenner and Berl had passed through the dark tunnel; Berl now saw the light at its end; Brenner was still oppressed by doubt.

The second person of consequence whom Berl met at Ein Ganim was A. D. Gordon. This middle-aged man of means had dragged his family from a small town in the Ukraine to a remote country, with a harsh and pitiless climate, a strange way of life and intolerable conditions. He lived in a ramshackle hut, and performed exhausting, ill-paid manual work. While still in Russia, Berl had been impressed by an article in *ha-Poel ha-Tzair* (the party weekly), signed with three asterisks, and had later discovered that the author's name was Gordon. After he reached Ein Ganim, Brenner took him to see Gordon. They found him sitting outdoors, in front of his hut, on a torn mat, 'barefoot, bareheaded, in patched trousers',[15] with young workers grouped around him. For the young pioneers, Gordon's hut was a substitute for their own parental homes. Though they would probably have denied vehemently that they were homesick for their parents, for the Sabbath and festivals, the pioneers were seeking balm for their loneliness. Berl found something heartwarming about the way in which eighteen- and twenty-year-olds were drawn to a man so much older and so different from them. But his perceptive eye was not deluded by Gordon's apparent cheerfulness. His joy had been eroded by four or five years of life under very trying conditions. Berl realized that Gordon was alien to these young people, even while he sang and joked with them. And even though he referred to his work tool as 'the sacred hoe' and considered manual work to be the be-all and end-all of existence, the sheer strain of making a living had left a deep mark on him. He was 'a Jew who keeps himself and his family on sixty kopeks a day and says that he lacks nothing' but 'rats gnawed at his heart'.[16]

Of the two, Gordon and Brenner, the latter undoubtedly had a greater impact on the workers, as he expressed their innermost feelings and thoughts. Gordon was an enigma to them, and he, in turn, had less understanding of them. He was a father figure for them and they admired his saintliness, but he lacked the 'cleft heart' which, as disciples of Russian literature, they so admired in Brenner.

Berl remained at Ein Ganim until the end of the rainy season. He did well as a laborer in the orange groves, and gradually gained confidence in his ability to persist in manual labor. In the course of his frequent talks with Gordon and Brenner during the long winter evenings, he began to formulate his first original thoughts concerning the Jewish worker in Palestine. He fell ill with malaria at this time, the baptism of fire of all new immigrants, and he and Brenner took turns nursing one another through bouts of fever.

After the rainy season, Berl started exploring the country. Only someone who had grown up in Tsarist Russia could appreciate the exhilarating freedom of the Ottoman Empire. The regime was, ostensibly, absolutist and dictatorial, but in practice, because of organizational disarray, total license prevailed. Physically the country was a revelation. Instead of the endless plains of White Russia and the Ukraine, there were low mountains and hills and strange landscapes, changing with amazing rapidity. Instead of giant forests of birch and oak, there was low Mediterranean vegetation. The flowers were different, the trees were different, the sun shone in a different way; the colors and light and fragrance were overwhelming. Galilee was an enchanted land: 'How can one describe in words these rocks, everlasting rocks, and the mighty waves of the sea, eternal hills, a narrow path between mountains and a bubbling spring on the slope? And the mountain air and the beauty of the valleys? And what is the meaning of "the morning spread upon the mountains . . ."?' he enthused.[17]

To his joy was added the intoxicating sensation of roaming freely, unattached to any particular place. One day he was in the Petah Tikva plantations – and a day later 'my mood induced me to leave Petah Tikva and go to Hadera'.[18] This gipsy-like quality – the unwillingness to become attached to a place, or job or even a particular person – is inherent in the history of the Second Aliyah. Berl called it 'the Bedouin spirit or the pauper's bohemianism'.[19] Some pioneers wandered in search of work, others explored the length and breath of the country. Still others moved around because certain places were hotbeds of malaria, and they could not stay there for long. There were those, like the ha-Shomer watchmen, who dreamed of expanding horizons and living on frontiers. Basically, however, this drifting from place to place seems to have been characteristic of young people who had abandoned parents and home and now found themselves in a new country free of authority and conventional restraints. Their clothes were shabby, their food meager, they had no choice but to remain single, and the whole world was their oyster.

Berl was typical in this respect. In his first year in Palestine he lived and worked in Ein Ganim, Hadera, Sejera, Um Juni and again in Ein Ganim. All journeys were conducted on foot, and a trek to Galilee, for example, could take days. Berl was in no hurry to tie himself down to any place, or group of people. He lived like a vagabond, moving at will, observing all, and enjoying every moment of the new experience: 'In general I feel free, I have cast off a whole world . . .'[20] This young man, who from the age of twelve had felt a heavy responsibility for his family, was now free as a bird. After having spent his life among his elders, he was now with his contemporaries. It was not surprising, under these circumstances, that despite various problems, his world was flooded with sunshine, and his letters to his brothers, summoning them to Palestine, were permeated with confidence and the cautious optimism of a man who had found himself: 'I am at home here.'[21]

The first stop of his tour of the country was Hadera. It was notorious for the malaria which had claimed many victims and driven both settlers and laborers from the colony. Berl now found a new type of work: felling trees in the Hadera forest. But he was not proficient in his occupation: 'I have learned to work with an axe and a saw, but I have not become a skillful woodcutter.'[22] He apparently found the work very hard and was often assigned to the relatively easy job of leading a donkey, loaded down with water-cans, from the colony to the forest.

Nonetheless, his stay in Hadera was a kind of milestone: he was accepted into the ranks of the 'Labor Legion'. This was a pioneering body set up by ha-Shomer which assigned its members to work and guard duty wherever needed. The association was based on complete communality: the wages of the members were paid into a joint fund, they lived in communal lodgings and ate in the general kitchen of the Hadera workers. The Legion had branches in Hadera, Sejera and Um Juni. Like all ha-Shomer's projects it is worthy of mention more because of its innovativeness than for its effectiveness. Its three branches consisted of some thirty members – no small number in Second Aliyah terms – but the enterprise lasted barely one year. Like all the institutions of ha-Shomer, for whom conspiracy was the spice of life (the legacy of the Russian revolutionary movement, but incongruous in the free atmosphere of Ottoman Palestine), the Legion was a clandestine organization, and its leaders had far-reaching powers. But there was a difference between the Hadera commune and its counterpart at Sejera. The Sejera commune was akin in spirit and human makeup to the ha-Shomer leadership and revealed certain 'dictatorial' trends: the Hadera

group was more open and 'democratic'. At that time, the Legion branch
at Sejera found itself at loggerheads with local Jewish laborers who
were not Legion members. The organization's conspiratorial manner
may have aroused resentment, or the veteran workers, most of them
members of ha-Poel ha-Tzair, may have felt that the Legion was usurp-
ing their rights. According to one story, Berl was sent to investigate the
reason for the disputes. His stay at Sejera was brief, less than one month
in March–April 1910. During Passover (in April), the first conference
of the Legion was held at Um Juni, and Berl addressed a relatively large
audience in Palestine for the first time. His remarks were controversial:
he criticized the secretive atmosphere fostered by the Legion in Sejera
and warned against creating unnecessary tensions. It was here that Berl
learned one of his first lessons in Palestinian party politics: he was never
officially expelled from the Legion as a result of his criticism, but was
never again a part of the inner cabal.

Berl's trip to Um Juni was his first encounter with the Jordan Valley:
'From the heights of Dleika this magic corner unfolded before me.
Within it was concealed the Um Juni hut.'[23] In Petah Tikva he had
heard about the little workers' 'republic' set up there. Stories were told
about the six young men – the sole girl was not considered worthy of
equal membership – who had undertaken to cultivate the Dleika lands
on the east bank of the Jordan on a cooperative basis in return for a
share of the harvest. On the other side of the river lay the Kinneret
farm, which was to play a large part in Berl's future, but on his first visit
to the Valley it was Um Juni and the novelty of the system that captivated him: Jewish workers, without overseers and patrons, had undertaken to cultivate the lands from plowing to harvest, under contract to
the Palestine Office. The six Um Juni workers had been selected carefully on the basis of a key aimed at providing representation for each
and every association which had any contact with the Galilee workers:
ha-Horesh – the Galilee workers' association; the Legion; ha-Shomer,
Poalei Zion and ha-Poel ha-Tzair. Tremendous importance was
attributed to the daring Um Juni experiment, which remained nameless
– the word 'kvutza' had not yet been coined. The six were among the
most experienced of the Galilee workers; they were a different breed
from the workers of Judea, unaffected by the Judean 'despair'. Far away
from the closed, gloomy world of the plantation colonies, they worked
the fields and wide open spaces of Galilee. Berl described them as '. . . a
group of people who had joined together for a certain purpose. This

was the essence of Galileanism. No ideological prattle, no frivolous romanticism, no self-righteousness, no excessive softness . . . I saw a spirit of profound maturity in these people, the total opposite of everything I had ever found in Jewish youth.'[24]

Berl was taken on for the harvest season at Um Juni as a temporary laborer – not as a member of the group. His job was to load sheaves on the wagons and, after a briefing from a veteran worker, he overcame his tendency to plunge the pitchfork into the sheaf like someone jabbing a fork into meat, and learned to do the job well. He was fortunate enough to take part in the famous harvest which laid the foundation for the establishment at Um Juni of Degania, the first *kvutza*. The group ended the year with a profit while the Kinneret farm, run along the old lines, sank into debt. The success at Um Juni turned an experimental project, run by the workers themselves, into an established practice.

There is no evidence that Berl was aware of the fact that he was a minor participant in a historical moment in the annals of the Palestine labor movement. He spent about a month in Degania, and left during the harvest because he fell ill. His brief stay at Degania is not mentioned in his letters, and he apparently did not attribute any significance to it. In any event, in July 1910 Berl returned to Ein Ganim, and shortly afterwards Brenner wrote to David Shimonovitz: 'I have seen Berele and showed him your postcard. His situation is not too good. He is now at Ein Ganim, trying to work. In general, everything is the same as usual: no peace. The end of summer. Everything too much to bear.'[25] Brenner's pessimistic description is confirmed by Berl himself. To his brother, Israel, he wrote: 'As you know, it was by my own choice that I made labor the essence of my life. As to what it has given me – I have no answer as yet. I am still halfway there. If my health and my former habits do not impede me, I hope to prevail, and then perhaps I will be able to deliver a report to you.'[26]

Berl's first year in Palestine had come to an end. Together with his discovery of Palestine, the joys of the free life, and his friendship with Brenner and Gordon, he was still plagued by doubts concerning his ability to persevere as a laborer.

Berl made no impact on the Palestinian labor movement during this year. Although familiar with political parties and movements from the age of fourteen, he avoided joining either of the two existing workers' parties, ha-Poel ha-Tzair and Poalei Zion. Ha-Poel ha-Tzair was a Jewish Palestine-oriented movement, reminiscent of the populist movement in Russia in spirit. Its voluntarism and subjectivism had always appealed to Berl, but it was basically elitist, too sure of itself: it was totally devoid of 'soul-searching'; and although, from the socialist viewpoint, its activities did not differ greatly from those of its sister party, there was something in the human makeup of ha-Poel ha-Tzair which put Berl off. He was later to become very friendly with several of its members, but he never felt any affinity with the party.

He was even less inclined to Poalei Zion. They supported the Ramle Platform, a Palestinian version of Borochov's theory of class struggle, i.e., a Marxist approach to Zionism. Borochov claimed that only in Palestine could the Jewish people create a base from which to conduct the class struggle. But this would be possible only *after* the creation of a Jewish capitalist society there, which would be brought about by spontaneous migration processes. Until then, it was the duty of the workers to help in the establishment of a democratic society in Palestine and to refrain from undertaking socio-economic responsibility for developing the country. Even in Russia, seesawing between parties, Berl had not liked Borochov's theories, and in Palestine he liked them even less: they seemed remote from the realities of life and the main problems of the workers. Moreover, Poalei Zion was still wrestling with the language question, while Berl had declared his allegiance to Hebrew on arrival in Palestine and condemned himself to silence until he could speak the language fluently. After a year in Palestine Berl requested his brother, Israel, to use Hebrew rather than Yiddish in their correspondence. Last, but not least, the political style of Poalei Zion did not appeal to Berl. His one attempt to approach the leaders of the movement (who were also the heads of ha-Shomer) had ended in the Legion incident, as noted above.

At this time, both ha-Poel ha-Tzair and Poalei Zion, each in its own way, believed that the Jewish workers in Palestine would eventually evolve into a wage-earning proletariat. Ha-Poel ha-Tzair believed that by appealing to the goodwill of the colonist farmers and by perseverance of the workers, Jewish labor would prevail. Poalei Zion believed that the process would occur naturally: the Jewish economy would expand through the investment of more Jewish capital, thus creating more employment for Jews. Neither as yet accepted the fact that the attempt to introduce Jewish labor into the colonies had failed. Gordon himself had not yet formulated his ideas on work as a value in itself. His idealistic view of the 'conquest of labor' as part of the general metamorphosis of the individual and society through the return to manual work was not yet commonly accepted. The concept of Jewish labor was still viewed pragmatically: in order to gain a foothold in the country and reduce Jewish dependence upon the Arabs, the Jewish farmers had to employ their fellow-Jews. The first to challenge the idea of Jewish labor in the colonies was Yosef Vitkin. He advised the workers to save money, to buy land in Galilee and to establish new settlements. His scheme, submitted to the ha-Poel ha-Tzair conference in 1908, came under vehement attack by Yosef Aharonovitch, the leader of the party, and was rejected.

At the time of Berl's arrival in Palestine, Vitkin had abandoned his attempt to influence the public, and the labor movement was in the throes of a 'great despair'. If it was impossible to be a worker in the colonies, since no Jewish worker could compete with Arabs, and if those Jews who did find work in colonies were unable to support themselves and their families, what was left to them? The life of the colonist was considered morally contemptible and degrading, and the tenant farmers on the J.C.A. lands in Galilee were proof of this. Many of them had been loyal workers who, only a few years after they became colonists, were themselves tempted into exploiting cheap Arab labor. The Judean colonists, since settling on the land twenty-five years previously, had lost all traces of the idealism which had brought them to the country. As a result, many of the workers abandoned the idea of settling on the land. Furthermore, agricultural settlement entailed the purchase of land and capital investment, at least until the first harvest. No worker was able to shoulder such a financial burden, and outside support could be construed only as patronage or charity.

Berl later claimed that in his first conversation with Gordon, on the rush mat at Ein Ganim, he had propounded his own ideas about the course to be pursued by Palestinian workers: first, since the 'conquest of labor' had failed, it was essential to find a new form of agricultural labor settlement where the members worked for themselves without recourse to hired help; secondly, the Jewish National Fund should undertake land purchase to this end. Gordon, so Berl related, rejoiced at the conversation: at last a young man had arrived, who was not only immune to the fashionable mood of gloom, but was even elaborating new hopeful schemes. There is no contemporary evidence to substantiate the conversation. It is clear, however, that very shortly after he arrived, Berl propounded some theories concerning ways of helping the workers to survive. He had been particularly struck by the workers' tremendous self-neglect, most of them being loners in an alien environment, dogged by 'solitude and orphanage'.[27] Imprisoned in their own misery, they suffered, fell sick and were broken for lack of human warmth and intimacy. They lost all interest in the physical and intellectual amenities of life, not the least through their own negligence.

Attempts were made to set up a workers' kitchen, where young workers could obtain cheap and nourishing food, and enjoy the companionship of others. But these institutions failed because of the inexperience of those who ran them. In winter 1910, Berl arranged for Brenner to lecture to the workers of Petah Tikva on the books of Mendele Mocher Sefarim. Very soon afterwards, a workers' club was set up, with the aim of providing a place where they could relax, drink tea, read the newspapers and converse in a congenial atmosphere, and sometimes, even, attend a stimulating lecture. The club was maintained by the meager funds which the workers collected among themselves. For Berl the place was a ray of light, more important than numerous debates on topical problems. 'The gift for living' – a phrase he was often to repeat – had to be reflected in the daily conduct of life in an atmosphere of simplicity and self-respect. Only thus, would the workers be able to put down roots in Palestine, and create a meaningful human habitat.

Withal, it appears that during that first year, Berl had not yet found himself. He was in no hurry to find a corner of his own or to attach himself to other people. Several months after his arrival, Leah Miron arrived from Bobruisk. She was a year younger than Berl, and had known him since she was sixteen when, together with her best friend, Sara Schmuckler, she attended a debating group on Jewish and socialist problems which Berl had organized. Leah came from a prosperous family, while Sara's family was poor. Out of a desire to prepare themselves 'to face life', the former had studied dressmaking and the latter went to Kiev to study nursing. The ties between this trio were very close: it was Sara who accompanied Berl's younger sister, Hanna, to school on the first day, and when she left for Kiev, she maintained a regular correspondence with Berl and Leah, whose friendship soon blossomed into love. Leah was seventeen when her father returned from synagogue one day and found Berl in their home for the first time. He drove him out, with the aid of a broom, pursued him down the street, and forbade his daughter ever to meet that dangerous young man again. He maintained a strict supervision over his daughter, continuing to open and read her letters even when she was close to twenty. Sara, meanwhile, carried on an emotionally intense correspondence with Leah, Berl and other friends in Bobruisk, and particularly with Batya and Eliezer Schein, Berl's good friends. It was to Leah and Sara that Berl first revealed his intention to go to Palestine.

In his first letters to Leah and Sara he wrote of his experiences in the new country. The letters reflected friendship, warmth and affection – but no passion. This may have been because several people, in addition to both girls, would be reading them, or he may have suffered from the typical Second Aliyah aversion to a public display of emotion. Any relationship between the sexes was then a deeply serious, even ponderous matter, in the spirit of the great Russian novels, not to be discussed openly and certainly never to be referred to lightly.

There are no signs, after Leah's arrival, that they decided to enter into a permanent relationship. His letters do not even reveal any particular joy at her coming. However, while Berl was at Sejera, Leah was there as well. When he returned to Ein Ganim, she remained in Galilee to seek work. It seems clear that during this first year, Berl displayed the same propensity for the gipsy life, for slovenliness and solitude, that he condemned in others.

Kinneret, 1911

In autumn 1910, Berl went up to Galilee for the second time. It was a region which the Second Aliyah pioneers considered enchanted, where everything was somehow more vivid and alive than in Judea. The agriculture was 'real' – field crops rather than plantations (which were regarded as commercialized agriculture). There the individual worker cultivated an expanse of land with his own hands: open spaces, a plow, horses, sowing, harvesting, primary acts of nature! The workers in Galilee were also regarded as more 'authentic' than their counterparts in Judea. Here each worker was billeted at the home of a farmer; he ate and slept with the family and suffered deprivation, hunger, and sickness together with his employer. In Galilee the farmer was as poor as his workers, and relations, therefore, were more intimate: in Judea large groups of workers labored under an overseer, and the individual was absolved of responsibility for the quality of his work. Whereas the Judean worker developed the mentality of the hired laborer, regarding his employer as a 'boss' who could be cheated with impunity, the

Galilean worker considered himself a half-partner in the success and failures of the farmer.

Berl wanted to share in this experience. He dreamed of working for a whole year on one of the farms, and of himself becoming a real farmer. At this stage in his life the need to acquire expertise in agricultural work was of cardinal importance. Thus every success delighted him, and every setback cast him down. After working successfully for a time at the colony of Kinneret, not far from the Kinneret farm, as one of a team of farm laborers, he moved to the colony of Menahamia, which greatly appealed to him, and became the sole employee of one of the farmers there. But he failed miserably and was dismissed after only three days. Berl found it difficult to reveal his feelings to other men, and hence turned, in his distress, to Leah, to whom he confessed his pain and his fears.

Shortly afterwards, he started work at the Kinneret farm, which was the first farm established on Jewish National Fund land in 1908 by the Palestine Office. It was located at Dleika, on both shores of the Jordan, not far from the lake. Moshe Berman, an agronomist, was appointed manager of the farm. At the same time, another group undertook to cultivate the lands of Fula on behalf of ha-Shomer. Others went to work at Um Juni, and a group of four leased part of the Kinneret lands in order to grow vegetables. These, and other endeavors such as the Sejera collective, the Legion and a plan for settlement at Merhavia, attested to the innovative mood then prevailing in Galilee. It was a hothouse for settlement experiments, which had several aims in common.

First, there was the desire of the workers to eliminate the managerial system and become their own masters. The Galilee laborers were seeking 'wholly creative' work, as Ben Zion Israeli put it, and this could only be achieved through independence. The desire for self-expression through work was typical of the best and the brightest of the Second Aliyah pioneers.

Secondly, there was the attempt to create some form of collective life. The patterns of cooperation had not yet been determined; it was not clear whether the objective was a commune or a production cooperative. The associations were usually established on the basis of personal friendship (like the group comprising the backbone of the future settlement of Kinneret – Ben Zion Chernomorsky (Israeli), Meir Rotberg and Noah Naftulsky). A few were founded on political affiliations, such as the ha-Shomer groups. In any event, cooperative life was in the air in Galilee. It was enhanced by the romantic theories brought from Russia and inspired by the ancient peasant communes – *obshchina* and *artel* – and intensified by the egalitarian aspirations, the hatred of officialdom and the longing of lonely young immigrants for companionship and warmth.

Thirdly, these young people were seeking a form of settlement which would preserve the dignity and aspirations of the settler, prevent the erosion of his idealism and respond to the needs of the Zionist movement in Palestine for wide-scale Jewish settlement.

All this ferment was concentrated in a relatively small geographical area. The journey from Kinneret to Migdal took three hours by wagon; from Kinneret to Um Juni, thirty minutes; and to far-off Merhavia, four hours at the most. Contact was continuous, news was conveyed rapidly and the workers were well aware of what was going on around them.

Berl came to Kinneret at a time of decline. The experienced workers had left, and there remained only a group of dispirited people who accepted Berman's authority. But conditions were so bad that even the most apathetic among them could not hold out for long.

In summer they slept outdoors in the courtyard, but when winter came, they were forced to crowd into one room in an old Arab house with a leaking roof and broken windows through which the wind howled; the floor was covered with water and mud; a few mattresses lay on the ground, since there were not enough beds to go round. Berman regarded this as a natural situation. Arthur Ruppin reported: 'When I asked Berman, the manager at Kinneret, where the lavatory was, he spread his arms with a regal gesture, as if to say: "The whole world is yours!" He was flatly opposed to putting up such "urban" installations in rural settlements.'[28] Among the mud and dirt in the miserable bare room, the sick and the healthy lay side by side. Many had fallen sick, since the large adjacent swamp was a source of malaria. The appalling living conditions, together with unsanitary food and the exhausting physical labor, promoted disease. There was no nurse at the farm, and medical supplies were confined to a tin box of quinine powder, which stood on the dining table, and which the workers sprinkled over their food.

When conditions became totally unbearable, the workers organized a half-day strike and presented four demands to Berman: to repair their

43

living quarters, and alleviate the crowded conditions by adding dormitories; to allot a separate room as sick quarters; to add more beds,
mattresses and some tables and chairs into the rooms, so as to enable
them to write letters; and, finally, to pay the wages of a medical orderly.
Berman promised to accede to all these demands, but did not keep his
word. A month later an incident occurred which created a furore: one
of the veteran workers at the farm fell ill with yellow fever. He was
taken to the Mission Hospital in Tiberias, and died several days later.
When word reached the workers, they asked permission to attend his
funeral. Since it was a rainy day, work had been suspended in any case,
so Berman allowed them to harness up a wagon and drive to Tiberias.
There was not enough room in the wagon for all those who wanted to
go, and the mourners harnessed up a second wagon, without asking the
manager's permission. Berman was furious and, in his typically brutal
fashion, forbade them to take the second wagon. The angry workers
abandoned both wagons, and made their way to Tiberias on foot, arriving after the funeral had ended – 'mud under their shoes and pain in
their hearts.'[29] Humiliated, tired, wet and depressed, they returned to
Kinneret. That same evening, the eve of Sabbath, they proclaimed a
strike, refusing to work until Berman left the farm. They were willing
to go on working in order to complete the sowing of the winter crops –
but only under a new supervisor. When Berman refused, all work
ceased, except the feeding of the animals. The strike lasted two weeks
(from 11 February 1911); then Ruppin arrived and, after two days of
negotiations, concluded that Berman's accusations against the workers
were groundless, while their complaints against him were justified. His
verdict was that the leaders of the strike should leave Kinneret, and that
Berman should be dismissed and a new manager installed.

Decades later, when Berl was one of the leaders of the Palestinian
labor movement, he would refer to the Kinneret strike as the symbolic
emergence of organized labor, and the predication of its relations with
the Zionist movement on its recognition of the power and dignity of the
workers. He further contended that the strike had broken the back of
the old managerial system, but this claim is not confirmed by the
facts.

The Kinneret strike was the first public event in which Berl played a
leading role. He undertook responsibility for influencing the actions of
other people. He left no written record of those days at Kinneret and
hence it is difficult to assess the exact scope of his role. But it was

apparently he who formulated the demands which the workers submitted to Berman, although a veteran worker was selected to inform Berman of the decision. At that time none of the Kinneret workers were well known in Galilee. It may be assumed that Berl was the sole figure among the despondent group at Kinneret capable of leading a strike for an extended period and, above all, of conducting negotiations with Ruppin.

Again, there is only fragmentary evidence on the meeting between Ruppin and Berl. There must have been a piquant element in the encounter between the well-dressed Prussian Jew, who spoke only German, and the tousled-headed, bearded revolutionary, in his black patched shirt, who could only try, in Yiddish, to communicate with the young director of the Palestine Office. The two sat on a log in the Kinneret courtyard and negotiated, with the help of Yitzhak Vilkansky, who apparently served as interpreter.

The strike did not end the managerial system. Some two weeks later an agronomist by the name of Golda arrived to take over management of the farm. Ruppin did not, at this stage, accept the argument of the workers that the manager's wage and living expenses constituted a superfluous economic burden on the farm, and generated tension, because of the blatant difference in standard of living between manager and workers living in close proximity. A year after the strike *ha-Ahdut*, the Poalei Zion weekly, published an article praising the achievements of Golda, under whose management the farm had developed satisfactorily.

But although the system endured, the strike was of great importance for the workers. It demonstrated their strength and convinced them that their natural partner was the Zionist Organization. A private employer would have dismissed the workers and thus ended the affair. Not so the Palestine Office: Ruppin and the workers now had a common denominator. Ruppin's readiness to accept individuals with values, way of life and cultural background differing drastically from his own, and his willingness to try to seek new paths of action, constituted the basis for cooperation. The talks at Kinneret revealed to Berl and his comrades the nature of their partner, and henceforth they were bound by ties of mutual trust.

None of the contemporary documents on the strike mention Berl's activity. This in itself is not surprising, since it was not then customary to single out individuals for mention – typical Second Aliyah reticence.

Moreover, Ruppin, in describing the affair many years later, when he and Berl were close friends, makes only vague reference to him. It may be that, in retrospect, Berl attributed exaggerated significance to the affair and to his own role in it, possibly because it marked the beginning of his public activity in Palestine.

The Kinneret strike was one of a series of events which highlighted the need of the Palestinian workers for new organizational frameworks. Ha-Poel ha-Tzair and Poalei Zion continued to regard the idea of workers' settlements as untenable. Thus, they could not constitute appropriate frameworks for dealing with workers' problems. The Kinneret strike emphasized the fact that there was no authoritative body able to represent and assist the workers in their hour of need. From this point of view the strike provided the impetus for the convening of the Galilee workers' conference at Um Juni in spring 1911. Berl attended this gathering as one of the Kinneret representatives.

This was the first non-party conference of workers, and it was no accident that it was held in Galilee. The party apparatus was weaker in Galilee than in Judea, as the central party offices were located in Jaffa and Jerusalem. In addition, the problems which preoccupied the Galilee workers differed from those with which party leaders were concerned. Hence there was room for the establishment of new associations.

It was only natural for Berl to join such an association and find his place there. From the very first he had seen work as a path to self-regeneration, an anchor against the storm, rather than a method of creating a proletariat. The new experiments in Galilee and the Kinneret strike strengthened these tendencies in him. Shortly after the strike he wrote to his brother Israel: 'I want to work, but I don't want to be a proletarian. I do not see this in any way as an injunction. To love work, to sense yourself as a human being, to be free of the yoke of landlords and officials – in order to achieve this you need to be independent, which is what the Palestinian worker wants. The roads leading towards this objective are still entirely new . . .' He lists the various experiments in settlement and adds: 'In good time these will enable each and every one of us to find his right place.'[30]

Moreover, at twenty-four, Berl was disenchanted with party life. He abhorred the empty rhetoric which characterized all parties, particularly those in Palestine, whose ideological inflexibility detached them from everyday life. Berl never felt any commitment to ideologies which he considered to be outmoded. Over the years he was to demonstrate a certain impatience towards those who were slow to perceive that the time for change was nigh. Now he simply avoided them.

In the Second Aliyah era, political parties were almost 'family' concerns. The members, and in particular the leaders, had joined together during the first decade of the century. They were few in number and knew one another well. The leadership cliques resembled exclusive clubs, whose members shared a similar style of speech and action, a common political jargon, and the same political position. Berl, like other latecomers, could not gain admission to these clubs. He therefore chose to join a new organization, which made the settlement of the workers the main item on its agenda.

Seventeen delegates attended the Um Juni conference, each of them representing eight electors. In other words, there were some 150 workers in Galilee at the time, no small figure in terms of the Second Aliyah. There were no preconceived ideas as to the form of organization or mode of action. Even the agenda of the conference was decided on at the last moment, as was the identity of the two speakers. According to one source they were Eliezer Shohat and Berl Katznelson. After protracted negotiations, a seven-member committee was elected: two from Merhavia, two from Kinneret, one from Um Juni, one from Yema and one from Migdal. Two of them, Mania and Israel Shohat, were members of Poalei Zion, and represented ha-Shomer as well; three were ha-Poel ha-Tzair supporters (Eliezer Shohat, Hanna Meizel and Zvi Yehuda), and two (Israel Betzer and Berl) were *unaffiliated*.

Berl soon became a central figure in the Galilee committee: the two ha-Shomer representatives were not very active and Eliezer Shohat and Israel Betzer, members of the Merhavia group, were arrested in summer 1911 by the Turkish authorities. There remained Zvi Yehuda and Berl. The former left on a visit to his parents in Russia so that most of the work was inevitably done by Berl.

His activities were not particularly extensive but they indicate that his main concern was to bring new workers to Galilee.

But Berl was not content, despite his activity. His main problem – to find suitable work – had not been solved. His blundering attempts at being a waggoner or at plowing and his inability to understand technical matters, however simple, were a constant source of humor at Kinneret. To this day his contemporaries tell stories of his lack of what he himself called 'manual sense'. He was 'all thumbs'[31] – he who so much wanted to be a man of mettle! Other future leaders found solutions to this problem: they simply abandoned manual labor. Some turned to teaching, others to political activity, political journalism or clerical jobs. This was not the answer for Berl. As far as he was concerned, physical labor remained the sum and substance of existence, and hence he could not avoid unhappiness and humiliation.

There was something immature about him, although he was twenty-four. Together with profundity of thought, acuity of vision as to the fate awaiting the Jewish people in the Diaspora, and singular comprehension of the historic significance of what was occurring in Palestine, he displayed a marked tendency to evade responsibility. His long, intimate relationship with Leah continued unchanged but he showed no desire to make their relationship permanent. Leah spent most of the year at Migdal, within walking distance of Kinneret, and they must have met often. He gloried in the simplicity of his clothes, and took care to wear only patched garments; when he was finally obliged to buy a new pair of trousers, he made sure that they soon looked shabby. His appearance was a reflection of his rebellion, his desire to reject convention, to refrain from accepting responsibility or commitment. Years later Berl described the Kinneret group thus: 'Everything within us cried out, stormed, erupted. The message we bore in our hearts did not adopt festive attire. It appeared in rags, torn and tattered. Our voices, our demeanor, were not marked by harmony. We rejected fine garments, good manners, whole worlds – and not always discriminately.'[32]

The same attitude was evident in other matters: 'We were, in fact, Bohemians. When we chose to, we worked; when we did not so choose, we remained idle. Anyone who suffered from a mood, could get up one fine morning, walk away and leave it all behind him.'[33] And this was what Berl did. His wanderlust had not yet been assuaged, and when in August 1911 it was combined with a desire to find new work, his involvement in public affairs in Galilee did not deter him from packing his few belongings and returning to Judea.

The year he spent at Kinneret had not brought him new friends; he was apparently rather lonely there. The Kinneret workers were simple people, without intellectual pretensions, and Berl had little in common with them. They derided his failures at work, and although they respected him enough to elect him their representative, they did not consider him in any way unique.

This view was not shared by others who visited Galilee that year. Two visitors to Kinneret that summer – Agnon, the writer, and Zalman Rubashov (later Shazar) both spoke of Berl as a *zaddik* (saintly figure), able to reveal to them new truths, a new dimension of reality and a fresh view of the future, all in the course of an evening stroll along the enchanted moonlit shore of the lake. The subject was always the same: the importance of the ostensibly insignificant deeds being carried out in Palestine. The smallest, most modest act of pioneering in Palestine, he claimed, outweighed all the great acts of the Diaspora. Immigration to Palestine and work there took precedence over all other acts. And when Shazar waxed poetic over mass demonstrations against the Tsar in Russia, Berl retorted that one wagon of hay brought into the Kinneret farmyard was of greater value to the Jewish people than all the mass demonstrations together. Agnon summed up his conversation with Berl as follows: 'And if our small deeds here in Palestine are more important to me than several vital matters of the world, I have Berl Katznelson to thank; he taught me to see what I had not seen before and to understand what I had not understood.'[34]

Ben Shemen and Ein Ganin, 1911–13

Berl returned to Judea, in autumn 1911, because he had discovered that planting and gardening was the work for which he was best suited. In order to acquire experience, he chose to work in the Herzl Forest plant nursery near Lydda, known as Ben Shemen.

His move to Judea heralded his involvement in public life and his image as a man of independent views. This was bound up with two new concepts in Yishuv life: the workers' unions and the Non-Affiliated Groups of agricultural workers who found adequate political expression in the unions.

The ha-Poel ha-Tzair and the Poalei Zion acknowledged the emergence of the Non-Affiliated Groups with a mixture of skepticism and disparagement. There was an element of patronage in their approach colored by the natural hostility of the old guard to the young Turks. On this point, as on no other issue, the leaders of the two parties found themselves in accord.

The workers' unions in Galilee and Judea began by engaging in activity unattended to by the parties. The first question they tackled was that of settlement. Although the parties were against it, the workers, by their very actions, were establishing new labor settlements and needed a body able to represent them in their negotiations with the settlement authorities, irrespective of party affiliation. From the outset, these unions could not be like trade unions elsewhere, because they dealt, first and foremost, with settlement matters, rather than with the traditional concerns of the wage-earner. Paradoxically enough, as long as the workers remained daily laborers, there was no need for such an organization. It was precisely when they cut themselves off from the 'proletarian' tradition that they felt the need for a union of their own. The endless debate conducted during the Second Aliyah as to whether the country would be built by 'idealistic' workers or 'natural' workers was never settled. But there can be no doubt that among the agricultural laborers idealistic elements prevailed. For most of them, the decision to work on the land was an individual revolution, and most of them felt that the issues which preoccupied the parties were no longer of major concern to them.

The parties which had evolved during the early days of the Second Aliyah reflected the mentality, temperament and loyalties of the young immigrants and the shared experiences of their first pioneering years. It was no coincidence that many of the active members of the Agricultural Union were people who had arrived in Palestine after 1909 – with the second wave of the Second Aliyah (the most prominent among them David Remez, Yitzhak Tabenkin and Berl), by which time the parties were well-established, with fixed hierarchies. Tabenkin, for example, joined Poalei Zion – which had been his party in the Diaspora. At its Third Conference, the party elected him as its representative to the Central Committee of Judean Workers, specifically to the Agricultural Union. It rapidly became evident, however, that he did not concur with the party's proclaimed objectives, and he soon left.

Berl was chosen to represent the workers of Lydda (Ben Shemen) at the Second Conference of Judean Workers in Petah Tikva in December 1911. This conference illuminated spheres of action which were to remain close to Berl's heart throughout his life. Its most important resolution related to the establishment of a workers' sick fund. In light of the conditions of neglect and of poverty which characterized the Second Aliyah, this decision marked a historical turning-point. At Berl's suggestion, it was decided that the fund be financed from the savings of its members. Thus, the poverty-stricken workers' association undertook the tasks of the non-existent family and of the Yishuv, not yet mature enough to shoulder its own responsibilities.

Berl also proposed that the Union undertake two kinds of workers' education: first, the dissemination of the Hebrew language to expedite immigrant workers' participation in public life. The teaching of Hebrew, he thought, could forestall the process of separation between the intelligentsia and the workers, a prospect which he viewed with concern. He often spoke of the need for the mutual enrichment and the integration of the two strata. This proposal did not win support at the conference. Secondly, Berl advocated agricultural education. He had inferred from his own experiences that the lack of vocational skills and the absence of professional literature on agricultural problems contributed to the failures and the heartbreaks of the agricultural workers. Agricultural education would also facilitate the workers' transition from the status of daily laborer to that of autonomous worker. On this specific point, Berl succeeded in persuading the conference, and it was decided to set up a mobile agricultural library. It later became the butt of numerous jokes and cartoons.

The conference underlined the suspicions of the two parties concerning their new rival, the Agricultural Union. Berl's proposals that cultural activity be carried out by the Union were interpreted as an intrusion into the domain of the parties. Their two representatives, Zrubavel and Aharonovitch, tried to confine the upstart Union to the vocational sphere, and the struggle which ensued on this issue was to continue for a decade.

Berl was elected to the cultural committee and the information committee, the equivalent of a labor exchange.

1912 was not a year of wide-scale activity for the Judean Workers' Union. In fact one man, Meir Rotberg, carried out all the routine duties, and the remaining committee members were in varying degrees inactive. Berl too was not particularly active in the Union during this year. He did, however, play a lively role in the controversy over Kapai, the Palestinian Labor Fund founded by Poalei Zion. The first article he published in Palestine was on this issue, in *ha-Poel ha-Tzair*, concerning the labor exchange which Kapai opened, and which the Union denounced as a party institution. Berl's protest did not prove effective – but it did succeed in annoying Poalei Zion. As a result, they rallied against him at the elections to the Third Conference of Judean Workers at Ben

51

Shemen in December 1912, and prevented his election. But although he was not a delegate, Berl was invited to deliver the opening address of the conference on workers' smallholder villages (*moshavim*). He was also elected a member of the Bureau, the Union's executive institution.

The conference was stormy, and the Union was attacked by both parties; nonetheless, it constituted a turning-point for the labor movement in Palestine.

In his address, Berl expounded the theory of the worker as settler. This concept had begun to take on flesh in Galilee, and now it was being elaborated into the ideology of a movement. Berl advocated workers' settlements, not as appendages to large colonies, but as autonomous smallholder villages, where the workers and their families could support themselves by cultivating their own farms. He envisaged a code of binding principles upon which the new settlements would be based. As against the practice of the colonists which, by fostering Arab labor, had been the source of the Yishuv's social and national deterioration, he proposed that Jewish labor be compulsory in the new *moshavim*. In order to eradicate the debasing patronage system, all candidates for settlement were to be screened and chosen by the members of the *moshav* themselves. Moreover, to forestall the economic difficulties and resultant personal hardships characteristic of early years of settlement, Berl proposed that the members of the *moshav* be joint guarantors for payment of debts. But all this could be achieved only if the Zionist movement undertook the responsibility to settle the workers and allocate land to them. In order to prevent speculation, the land should be allocated on perpetual lease rather than on any principle of ownership.

There were two new elements involved in this approach: permanent settlement of the workers, and a central role for the Zionist Organization in molding the image of the Palestinian Jewish worker.

The Agricultural Union took a giant step forward at this conference by assuming responsibility for settlement. The ease with which the party representatives conceded this task to the Union suggests that they were as yet unaware of the importance of the issue. One must remember that the parties were largely urban in character whereas the Agricultural Union encompassed both the hired farm laborers and the settlers in *kvutzot* and *moshavim*. As far as Berl was concerned, it was the Jewish farm worker who would constitute the nucleus of the newly-emergent Palestinian society.

Three people were elected to the 'Bureau' of the Union: Tabenkin from Poalei Zion, Berl Katznelson from the Non-Affiliated Group, and Meir Rotberg of ha-Poel ha-Tzair. Later Berl was to claim that both these men should actually have been counted as Non-Affiliated, and with good reason. There was a constant flow of people from the parties to the Unions until a solid core of active members gradually emerged. Berl defined the Non-Affiliated as 'a very small group of very good friends'.[35] He considered the profound comradeship forged through activity within the Agricultural Union as no less important than the shared public responsibilities.

It was in this year that Berl became fully involved in practical work on behalf of the Union. Mounted on a donkey or trudging on foot after a day's work, first at Ben Shemen and later at Ein Ganim, he toured the colonies, *kvutzot* and *moshavim*, smoothing out differences and settling disputes among members of the various parties. He conducted negotiations with the Palestine Office on the settlement of workers' groups, among them those engaged in 'conquering' places of work,* and was quick to defend the Unions' monopoly in settlement matters when it seemed to him that ha-Shomer was trying to intrude into this area. The same year, Berl also formulated the basic tenets of the Sick Fund and that institution, which had been founded formally in 1911, now took on life. His new public status can be measured by the fact that he began to conduct negotiations with such front-rank Zionist leaders as Ussishkin and Sokolow who met with him during their visits to Palestine, as well as by his election to the Jewish magistrates' court in Jaffa. He gained confidence and learned to phrase his ideas more clearly and concisely. By 1913–1914 both the Agricultural Union and Berl appear to have achieved maturity.

In December 1913, the Fourth Conference of the Judean Workers' Union was held at Rishon le-Zion. It represented 460 workers and aroused considerable attention. Berl made an impressive speech. He now proclaimed openly and unequivocally what he had only implied in 1912: 'The creation of a working community . . . is now the "main highway" for the Jewish worker in Palestine.'[36] The time for hesitant statements and qualifications had passed: '*It must be recognized that the settlement of the workers is the alpha and omega of the settlement of the country, that it is the sole method for national settlement.*'[37] It was up to the Zionist move-

---

* Trying to persuade Jewish landowners to employ Jews instead of Arabs in manual jobs.

ment to adopt a settlement system which would assure the Jewish workers of the possibility of settling as independent men and women, provide them with a livelihood and help them build a just society.

Berl regarded the farmers in the new agricultural settlements – who were striving to introduce modern farming methods – as the archetype of the new Jewish worker: 'Any one who has seen the few working settlements already in existence . . . will understand that these are historic training grounds, that a people is being educated here.'[38]

The improbable theory of only four years before had now become the ideological basis of a movement. It was still small – consisting of not more than one thousand men and women working on the land – but its self-awareness, sense of mission, and innovative spirit lent it weight above and beyond its numerical strength. Its patterns had not yet been determined – but the direction was clear. And Berl was its spokesman.

Berl's dominant position within the Judean Workers' Union was established at this conference: it was he who made the annual report on the activities of the 'Bureau', and he who responded to critics; he made the central programmatic speech and the conference resolutions reflected his statements and views. The disputes between ha-Poel ha-Tzair and Poalei Zion had abated somewhat and this added to the congenial atmosphere at the conference. Berl was the mediator between the parties: in order to maintain harmonious relations, he was ready to permit each party to elect its own representative to the 'Bureau' instead of holding a general ballot. Thus the new Bureau was elected unanimously – and the balance between Poalei Zion, ha-Poel ha-Tzair and the Non-Affiliated Group was preserved.

The Judean Union had become a force to be reckoned with within the movement and outside it – in the Palestine Office and the Odessa Committee, the representative of the 'Lovers of Zion' Associations – and as it grew in importance, Berl's stature increased, and he became the central figure in its leadership.

At the end of 1914 Berl was 27. A straight road seemed to stretch ahead of him: his work as a planter at Ben Shemen suited his character and his skills; his standing among the Judean agricultural workers was increasingly firm; he was engaged in effective activity, aimed at formulating a way of life and creating adequate living conditions for Jewish workers; he had also established deep friendships with some of the people who worked with him.

Yet, at the same time he was apparently still troubled by a lack of inner peace. Had it not been for the fact that his brother, Israel, and sister-in-law, Batya, arrived in summer 1912 from the United States, he would have left Judea and returned to Galilee. 'The nomadic spirit has enveloped me in its wings again . . .' he wrote.[39] He was still torn between the yearning for companionship, and the desire to be alone. At Ben Shemen he chose to live in a small, dank cellar in order to have a room to himself. And though he rejoiced at the arrival in Palestine of beloved friends and relatives, and was happy with work in the Union, he complained bitterly: 'How good it is to be alone. If I could only truly be alone.'[40] He believed in frankness, in the true baring of souls between friends – but was unable to bare his own. His letters were restrained, concealing rather than revealing his feelings.

His relationship with Leah continued without perceptible change. Their youthful years had passed, and their friendship had endured for a decade. Leah lived in Galilee, at Sejera and Kinneret, but she was often stricken with fever and found it hard to adjust to the strenuous work and the hostile climate of the Jordan Valley. From time to time, particularly during festivals, Berl would go up to Galilee to visit her: they sometimes spent time together – but never actually lived together. The 27-year-old Berl seemed still to be fleeing commitment. Perhaps he was unsure of his love, yet the ties betwen them were deep and warm and he had no desire to break off relations with her.

In autumn 1912, after numerous delays, Sara Schmuckler, Berl's and Leah's mutual friend, immigrated to Palestine. She had graduated with distinction from a nursing school in Kiev and had worked as a nurse in a rural area in White Russia for two years. Short, blonde, of delicate appearance and demeanor, despite her somewhat stocky figure, Sara was good-natured, always ready to listen and to sympathize with the woes of others – all qualities lacking in Leah's strong nature. Sara arrived after an unhappy love affair, apparently with a non-Jewish doctor. Sensitive and vulnerable, she was in the same despairing mood that had characterized Berl when he arrived. She knew little Hebrew, which further hampered her integration within the small group of Second Aliyah pioneers. It was hard for her to read a newspaper or to take part in the political discussions which interested her greatly. For a time she worked at the hospital at Zikhron Yaakov run by Dr Hillel Yaffe, who, after her death, was to eulogize her movingly, praising her humanitarianism, modesty and dedication to work. But while she was working with him, she felt herself rejected, and thought him hostile to her. Her feelings were undoubtedly subjective, and reflected her excessive sensitivity, tendency to self-punishment and yearning for affection.

Berl, Leah and Sara were bound by ties of profound friendship. The two young women loved one another dearly and Berl felt close to both. But, notwithstanding, in the first eighteen months after Sara's arrival, they did not find a way of living in the same place and contented themselves with brief meetings. This was due to some extent to the conditions then prevailing and the problem of finding suitable employment: but, at the same time, other pioneers did succeed in living family lives and setting up various types of communes. There is no escaping the conclusion, therefore, that their common privation derived from Berl's conscious or unconscious desire to preserve his liberty and his privacy, a desire of which both women, particularly Leah, were well aware.

At the same time, how he yearned for a child! The bachelor society of the Second Aliyah regarded children as sacred. Inexperienced and long parted from mothers, grandmothers and other elderly relatives, who could have helped them raise children, these young people regarded the few offspring born to them and their comrades as a kind of miracle. They inundated them with the warmth and affection with which they were so stinting in their dealings with one another. Gloomy Berl, who was so restrained in his letters to his beloved Leah, opened up completely and even jested when writing to David Zakai's little son: 'Little Yaakov, Shalom from Bewel. Well? Thpeak to me. Bewel is listening. Hello to you, hello to your nose, hello to your eyes, hello to your bewwy-button.'[41] But his love of children was not enough to persuade him to change his life.

In the public sphere his personality had matured, but in his private life he remained a boy, refusing to mature, or perhaps incapable of it. This trait also affected his public life: he was unable to persevere. Just as the mood had taken him four years before, to abandon his activities in Galilee and move to Judea, so now, still a free spirit, he abandoned his activity in the Judean Workers' Union, and in late 1914, after the outbreak of war, suddenly returned to Kinneret.

3

KINNERET, KINNERET

Kinneret, December 1914–July 1917

Berl returned to Galilee shortly after the outbreak of the First World War. The war had closed the Mediterranean to commercial shipping, thus creating difficulties in marketing wine abroad. As a result, the Judean vineyards went to seed, and workers moved from Judea to Galilee, where there were still prospects of work.

The Kinneret to which Berl returned in winter 1914 was not the place he had left in 1911. The Palestine Office had closed down the farm on the eve of war, because of the constant losses it incurred; the site was given into the charge of a well-known and experienced group of workers, led by Ben Zion Israeli. They were joined by Yitzhak and Eva Tabenkin, A. D. Gordon, and now Berl. They lived in the Kinneret enclosure, surrounded by a stone wall and an iron gate which protected them against bands of marauding Bedouin. Nearby was the girls' agricultural training farm, run by Hanna Meisel. Across the Jordan lay Degania, which was on the road to solvency. 'Down below' by the lakeside lived a group of destitute laborers for whom Eliezer Yaffe had arranged work draining the swamps, thus enabling them to support themselves and avoid the stigma of charity. The project was financed by funds sent by American Jewry during the war years to provide temporary financial relief for Palestinian Jews. Nearby, on the shore, lived a number of Yemenite families. They suffered greatly from malaria and other diseases; whole families perished, the infants being the first to succumb. To the north lay the colony of Kinneret, where there were a number of hired laborers, some with wives and children. And above Kinneret, on the hill shadowing the farm, lay the Poriya settlement, where Shlomo Levkovitch* worked.

---

* Shlomo Levkovitch (Lavi): one of the prominent figures of the Second Aliyah. Progenitor of the idea of the 'Large Kvutza', which closely resembled Fourie's concept of the Phalange (although Levkovitch apparently never heard of the French Utopist). His ideas served as a basis for the 'Kibbutz' of the Third Aliyah.

57

Shortly after Berl's return to Kinneret, the group was augmented by five young women, four of them from Bobruisk – Leah Miron, Sara Schmuckler, Batya Schein and Rachel Katznelson; the fifth, Batya Brenner, sister of the writer, had joined them in Palestine. They came in order to carry out the household tasks, and to work, together with Berl, in the vegetable garden. Berl's sister, Hanna, was already living and working at Kinneret, and some time later Leah's sister, Bluma Miron (later Slutzkin), also arrived.

There are many famous names in the annals of Palestinian Jewish settlement: Petah Tikva and the Bilu colony of Gedera, because they were the first of their kind; Hadera, because of the fortitude of its settlers in the face of the dreaded malaria; Tel Hai, because of the heroism of its defenders; and Degania, because it blazed new trails in collective settlement. But Kinneret's distinction lay in its magic. Ostensibly, it was a commune of transients; all the members – with two or three exceptions – left after the war. No dramatic new agricultural techniques were conceived there, nor did it ever become a profitable endeavor. Nonetheless, Kinneret left an indelible impression on all the people who ever lived there. Berl moved onward and upward after he left the farm, but he regarded himself as a member of Kinneret to his dying day. So did the poetess, Rachel, whose poems are permeated with longing for Kinneret.

The spell was cast, first and foremost, by the landscape. The communal farm of Kinneret lay south of Tiberias on the shore of the Sea of Galilee (in Hebrew, Lake Kinneret). Amid the arid vistas of Palestine, the bounteous waters of the lake seemed a natural miracle. It lay below sea-level, in the basin of the Syro-African Rift Valley. The grandeur of the barren hills reflected in the gray-blue lake, and the brooding quiet of the hemmed-in valley set it apart. Ben Zion Israeli described how people fell in love with the unique beauty of the place: 'Often, at night, one would come across some young man lying alone and listening to the murmur of life in this corner of the world, and to the tremor of his own heart in response.'[1] There was something seductive in its beauty. Berl called Kinneret 'the enchantress-bride, who led her bridegrooms to doom' and he, too, was caught in the snare. 'Perhaps we are not worthy of her, our destined bride (*die besherteh*)'.[2] Despite the lake, it was a bleak, almost lunar landscape; the mountains were bare and offered no shade in the blazing, pitiless heat of summer days. Neither sunrise nor sunset were visible in the enclosed vale, detached from the outside world. In summer the air was motionless, without a breeze. Yet at night, when the moon was reflected in the still waters of the lake, and there was a great stillness all around, there was magic in this tranquility. But during the long summer workday, in the furnace-like heat, with no trace of shade for relief, the valley revealed its treacherous enchantment. The immigrants from Russia, who had found it so hard to adjust to the heat of Palestine in general, suffered indescribably in the sultry Jordan Valley. They were the first Europeans who had ever dared live in this merciless clime. Various 'experts' even claimed that children could never be reared there. And, as if the heat were not enough, the settlers were afflicted with malaria as well. A great swamp adjoined the lake, and the combination of debilitating heat, exhausting work and malaria was often fatal. Kinneret was notorious for its high rate of sickness. And the natural conditions were rendered more acute by the living conditions: the housing had improved immeasurably since the days of Berman but the rooms were still overcrowded; the kitchen was makeshift and far from sanitary: water had to be drawn in buckets from the lake, and bread was baked daily in a primitive oven. In the absence of any other fuel, dry twigs were used for the cooking fires, and the meager portions of food were often scorched. The cooks were frequently reduced to tears when the comrades arranged the plates of tasteless food in a 'train' on the table, and pushed them demonstratively back to the kitchen with a deafening clatter. The boundless dedication of these young women to their thankless chores could not compensate for their lack of cooking experience, a skill they had not acquired at home. And they most certainly had no idea of how to cater for large numbers of people, a task requiring organizational talent, suitable equipment and proper ingredients – all of which were lacking.

For a worker plagued by the vicious circle of disease there was no way out, unless he chose to abandon the 'cruel enchantress' to recuperate in a healthier climate – at Sejera, Metulla or even Jaffa. They all burned with fever: Leah and Sara, Hanna Katznelson, Eva and Yitzhak Tabenkin and others. In a photograph from that period, Berl looks like an anchorite: sunken eyes, prominent cheekbones and a black beard adorning a thin face.

The atmosphere of Kinneret may have been bewitching, but it was oppressive as well. The cemetery on the rise sloping down to the lake was filled with the graves of many young men and women who had died by their own hand, because of lack of work, unrequited love or sheer despair. People demanded too much of themselves and others, and the constant tension between their own expectations and their self-judgment created misery which was intensified by the claustrophobic atmosphere. The Happy Valley became a hell on earth. Aliza Shidlovsky described it as follows:

What was there in the atmosphere of our lives in those days which caused this tension and aroused the need for constant self-assessment? . . . People feared weakness, and fear engendered cruelty, deliberate cruelty. People were cruel towards themselves and towards others. Nobody regarded the loneliness of a friend as a cause for concern, nor were depression and desperation recognized as signs that something was crying out for attention. And if, for a moment, the link binding some solitary soul to our family of lonely souls was severed, . . . his strength failed him . . .

And perhaps there were some who had envisaged life and work in Palestine in some other way, who dreamed of a life rich in heroic deeds and poetry, and lacked the imagination to find poetry in the full task of sheeptending among the barren hills, or heroism in the act of following the plow through the long, blazing Jordan Valley days . . .[3]

The landscape was peopled by a singular group of individuals in those war years: A. D. Gordon, Yitzhak Tabenkin, Berl Katznelson, Noah Naftulsky, Ben Zion Israeli, Meir Rotberg, Shlomo Levkovitch, Aharon Sher, Eliezer Yaffe, Rachel Katznelson, Batya Schein and Batya Brenner, Leah Miron, Sara Schmuckler and others. Each deserves a chapter to himself in the annals of the labor movement, and in particular in the history of innovative labor settlement in Palestine. They were solitary individuals, given to bouts of deep depression which affected the entire group. Extreme individualists, they were rebels in search of a new way of life: egalitarianism, the return to nature, social community, self-fulfillment in agricultural work. And beyond these aspirations each maintained his own outlook, each had his own personal devils. Kinneret had no fixed idea of what life in a commune should be and did not insist on examining the adaptability of each and every prospective member. In this openness, it differed from neighboring Degania which was marked by a degree of permanence and stability. The group at Degania was more closely-knit, although they too underwent various crises in their search for the proper road to cooperative life. Kinneret, in contrast, was lacking in peace, constantly striving for change and seeking new horizons:

Degania was a home, but Kinneret was a wide-open place, a focus of variegated life-styles, of ideas and experiments. The absence of any urge to create a home was the source of Kinneret's strength and the source of its weakness as well, since it encouraged mobility and impermanency in the lives of individuals and society.[4]

But profound companionship was born there, ineffable emotional intimacy and camaraderie which left their enduring stamp on all those who lived there.

'There was a sense of being one family, and although we did not speak of this, we felt that we were closer than brothers. There was a feeling of tenderness and affection for one's comrades, but it was clothed in the armor of denial and derision of "sentimentalism" '.[5] For Berl, these were the people with whom he was to feel the greatest affinity all his life. Many of those who lived in Kinneret at that time later became leaders of the Yishuv – Tabenkin, Berl, Yaffe; and most found themselves at some time or another in confrontation with Berl. But the grace of Kinneret, its joys and sorrows, colored their lives. Some basic rapport always existed between them: not one of them became a party politician in the conventional sense. Their leadership was drawn from the agricultural settlements, from the pioneering elements of the Zionist socialist movement. As we shall see, this was to be a source of both weakness and strength.

Berl was in his element among these people. Not even the most astute historian can accurately establish what determined the character of this group – the nature of the people involved, the 'chemistry' between them, or what Berl terms 'the Kinneret enigma'. Life in the Kinneret enclosure was marked by sharp contrasts: the enclosed valley and the open courtyard; the members were highly individualistic, but were nonetheless eager to abandon all self-interest and to live within and for a community. They were, like the great Russian thinkers, in love with self-denial. The poetess Rachel wrote: 'We dreaded comfort. We yearned for sacrifice, for torture, for the prisoner's bonds, with which to sanctify and exalt the Name of the Homeland.'[6] There was an air of 'emotional intensity'[7] at Kinneret, a desire to undertake great missions, 'unawareness of the barrier between our lives and the needs of society'.[8]

At Kinneret, Berl found both peace and bittersweet pain. After years of restless searching and frustration, he had found the work which suited his character and his needs, namely vegetable farming. This was a new branch of Jewish farming in Palestine. The vegetable plot, like the cowshed, became one of the distinguishing features of labor settlement, of 'authentic' agriculture – in contrast to the monoculture of the colonies. The latter had no choice but to purchase their dairy and vegetable supplies from Arab villages, while the *kvutzot* hoped to become self-sufficient in this respect. This was also seen as suitable work for the women, who resented being confined to service tasks.

Because of their lack of experience in farming in general, and farming in Palestine in particular, their approach to work was highly experimental . For every success there were two setbacks, caused by natural catastrophes – floods, frost or heat waves – or by human failings, such as illness, mechanical breakdowns or theft .The soil was not always suited to vegetable growing, and certain strains were not adaptable to Jordan Valley conditions. Primitive attempts to spray against pests met with only occasional success. Nobody knew exactly when to plow, sow and harvest or when and how much to fertilize. The seeds were often of inferior quality. Berl kept a logbook, in which he painstakingly summarized his years of work scientifically.

The sum conclusion was failure – with an occasional bright moment. Nevertheless, Berl derived great satisfaction from the very act of tracing the growth of a plant, tenderly nurturing saplings, seeking original solutions to recurrent agricultural problems. He was later to recall it wistfully: 'My attitude towards the cultivation of vegetables was a great deal more spiritual than my approach to editing work.'[9] He was not a born farmer, but an intellectual trying to adapt to manual labor, and gardening suited his personality more than any other farm chore. He brought to it an intelligent and straightforward approach, a responsiveness to innovation, and painstaking attention to detail. This work was very different from the monotonous and backbreaking work he had done before. Now he was taking part in acts of creation. For the first time in his life, he was content with a day of physical labor and had no desire to seek wider horizons.

This may help to explain why he was not particularly active in public affairs during the war years. Kinneret was the center of the labor movement in Galilee, and such conferences as took place were held there. In summer 1915, a conference of women workers at Kinneret proclaimed the establishment of the women workers' movement. No men were permitted to attend, apart from Gordon, Bussel, Eliezer Yaffe and Ben Zion Israeli. Berl, who was very close to the young women, sharing their work and sympathizing with their hopes of achieving equality in the new society, is not listed among the participants. This may be because of his eschewal of public activity. This assumption is borne out by Rachel Katznelson's report from the Galilee Workers' Conference, held at Kinneret in October of the same year. It was the first conference that she had attended since arriving in Palestine, and an unforgettable experience for her: 'The conference was a trial, a crucible. I had never dreamed of such heights. We judged one another, sometimes harshly. I felt myself borne on waves which carried me aloft and cast me down.'[10] Berl apparently attended the conference, but although the subject under discussion was cultural issues, a subject close to his heart, the central figure at the conference was Tabenkin, and not Berl. Tabenkin, Rachel Katznelson and Berl were elected to the 'Cultural Committee'; but the focal point of Berl's life was now the vegetable plot, in sharp contrast to his Judean period.

Still, Berl found time for cultural work. He established an agricultural library at Kinneret despite the difficult conditions. His comrades there never forgot his delightful Hebrew lessons, which commenced at ten in the evening, for the sake of the women who worked in the kitchen: Leah Miron and Sara Schmuckler were not yet fluent in Hebrew. He would take a certain Hebrew root and teach all its meanings and declensions. These lessons were also attended by the swamp workers, who found respite in them from the dreariness of their daily existence.

The most typically 'Kinneret' project of all was ha-Mashbir. The idea was conceived by Meir Rotberg in the spring of 1916, when there was a shortage of staple foodstuffs. The Ottoman authorities were confiscating grain crops, and there was growing fear of famine among the population. Shortly before the grain harvest, Rotberg proposed the organized purchase of the crops of all the labor settlements by a labor institution – ha-Mashbir. The theory was that when the grain in Judea ran out, and prices rose steeply as a result of speculation and hoarding, ha-Mashbir would sell the grain to the workers at cost price. Rotberg proposed this idea to Berl, who adopted it enthusiastically and gave it its name ha-Mashbir (The Provider), recalling the biblical Joseph. Many workers at the time believed that the name derived from the similar-sounding Hebrew word for crisis, *mashber*, a word then in vogue and familiar even to those with very little knowledge of Hebrew.

The scheme could only work if the settlements agreed to sell their crops at the beginning of the season at a low price, even though they would forfeit considerable profits. Kinneret adopted the idea wholeheartedly and the members agreed immediately to sell to ha-

Mashbir at relatively low prices. Not so Degania. Lengthy debates raged on the question of whether to sell the crop to ha-Mashbir or at considerable profit on the open market. Shmuel Dayan* of Degania expressed the *kvutza*'s viewpoint: 'The danger is that if the farm failed economically, the noble idea of the commune would also be obliterated. Degania could not accept this.'[11] This was essentially a debate between the stable homestead of Degania and the unstructured openness of Kinneret. The desire for permanence and security of people who owned little was at odds with the voluntary impoverishment of those who had even less. For the first time the interests of the *kvutza* and the interests of society were in conflict. Kinneret's eagerness to take up public tasks and social responsibility, and Degania's bourgeois caution presaged future developments in the labor movement. A delegation was sent from Kinneret, consisting of Berl, Meir Rotberg, Ben Zion Israeli, Shlomo Levkovitch, and headed by Gordon, to persuade the Degania settlers to sell their wheat crop to ha-Mashbir; after long nights of stormy, acrimonious debate, Degania finally agreed to place the general good ahead of its own interests.

The concept of ha-Mashbir played a considerable part in the post-war consolidation of the labor movement. It was the first country-wide institution of the movement. The sense of mutual responsibility, as well as the organizational ability it generated, pointed to the inherent unity of the movement and the marginality of its partisan conflicts. The siege atmosphere of the war years provided the elite of the movement at Kinneret with the respite they needed for contemplation, and enabled them to view the future of the movement in a detached fashion.

It was the close contact between practical people like Meir Rotberg and the Kinneret intellectuals which engendered an ideological approach to the comprehensive role of the Agricultural Union with regard to the workers in Palestine. The Friday evening discussions which Berl organized were devoted to the problems and failures of the world labor movement in the wake of the war, and a search for new theoretical formulations commensurate with the lifestyle emerging at Kinneret and places like it. Considerable intellectual daring was required to criticize forms of socialism sanctioned by traditional socialist thinkers. During these long evenings, Berl and his comrades

---

* One of the leaders of ha-Poel ha-Tzair, later among the founders of the first *moshav* Nahalal; father of Moshe Dayan, who was born in Degania in 1916.

forged their fundamental *Weltanschauung*. This group of comrades from Kinneret were later to remain loyal to Berl through thick and thin, when the Ahdut ha-Avoda Party was founded in 1919.

Berl appeared to have found stability at Kinneret and when he decided to return to public activity in the Galilee Workers Union, he was welcomed with open arms. Nonetheless, by summer 1917, he was again restless, and this mood augured his departure from Kinneret. He complained of the 'hubbub at Kinneret' which left him no time for relaxation. The contrary pull of public activity, against his desperate need for privacy, raised its head again.

Even now, at the age of thirty, he may have found it hard to confine himself to one place and one occupation. But this is not enough to explain his departure from Kinneret, since he undertook the organiz-ation of the 'vegetable growers' in Jerusalem, in many ways a continu-ation of his work at Kinneret. His move to Jerusalem was not motivated by the desire for a new type of work, or a different company, or an aversion to public work. There was only one implication: he wanted to flee Kinneret. And the reason lay in his private life.

As we have noted, Kinneret was enveloped in a romantic aura. In several cases it was deliberately selected as the site for suicide. Love affairs flourished there – some happy and some doomed. But, in typical Second Aliyah fashion, a veil of reticence has been drawn over all of them. The anguished love affair between Berl, Leah Miron and Sara Schmuckler was among the most notable among the young people of Kinneret. For fifteen years a delicate balance had been maintained by this strange triangle; suddenly the balance was disrupted. Berl fell in love with Sara. Neither of the young women was particularly pretty: Leah was distinguished by her dedication, strong will and sober outlook on life; but Sara possessed qualities of compassion and kindness, which endeared her to all who knew her. She had the emotional makeup of the heroine of a Russian novel, veering in her moods between ecstatic enthusiasm and profound desperation, and it is not difficult to under-stand why Berl fell in love with her. Since his affair with Leah had plod-ded on for years in a tranquil and routine fashion, his infatuation with Sara came like a draught of intoxicating liquor.

From their letters it appears that their love blossomed during their stay at Kinneret. They tried to ignore and suppress their feelings. Berl believed in loyalty to one's first love, and suffered from deep guilt feel-ings where Leah was concerned. Sara, for her part, was afraid of experiencing another unhappy love affair, particularly since it involved betrayal of Leah, her dearest friend. But, in the close intimacy and lack of privacy of communal life, the lovers could not escape one another. Leah accepted the situation more calmly than the other two. Or perhaps this is only an impression, because she was not given to writing and never recorded her feelings. Some sources suggest that her attitude towards Sara and Berl had maternal overtones, a desire to take the new couple under her wing. She would vacate her room in order to enable them to be alone together. Sara, after lengthy vacillation and refusal to believe in the sincerity of Berl's emotion, finally admitted her love – and abandoned herself to it with all the fibers of her romantic being. Berl, on the other hand, was beside himself. Sometimes it seemed as if the trio from Kinneret was trying to act out a Russian novel: they behaved with great 'nobility', trying to act like 'adults', 'understanding' and 'explaining' emotional situations, which were beyond their control, shunning such base emotions as jealousy. Berl and Sara spent hours 'explaining' to Leah that their love was 'decreed' from above and that they were unable to control it. Leah, for her part, showed 'understanding' and gave them her blessing, like a mature human being, who knew of such situations from literature and regarded them as her model. Berl was not content with this reaction. Suffering and emotional upheaval are spice to 'great' love affairs and Berl apparently was enjoying his misery. He was incapable of irrevocably breaking off relations with Leah. He seems to have feared that she might be driven to suicide, although it is hard to believe that so stable a person as Leah would have contemplated so dramatic a step. And thus, with two young women passionately in love with him, Berl continued to torment himself and them. It should be recalled that they were not adolescents but adults in their early thirties. The whole affair was no secret to the other Kinneret pioneers and apparently did not enhance Berl's reputation. At first, he hoped that Leah would make a clear break, but she showed no such inclination. Sara called Berl 'an incomplete person'. Clearly, it was Berl's hesitation which caused both young women protracted suffering.

Thus, even in the intensely romantic yet puritanical atmosphere of Kinneret the Berl–Leah–Sara affair was considered unusual, though no public criticism was ever voiced, and for half a century the story was hardly known.

After several attempts at living together and subsequent partings,

Sara and Berl decided on a self-imposed exile from Kinneret and a separation. They hoped to demonstrate to Leah, through their dignified and ennobling suffering, that their love was meant to be.[12]

Sara became the village nurse at Yesod ha-Maala in the far north and Berl went to Jerusalem. At one point, unable to contain himself, he asked her to join him – but they withstood temptation, and very soon the conquest of Jerusalem by the British and the siege of Galilee, which remained in Turkish hands, rendered their voluntary parting a forced separation.

Shortly after Berl moved to Jerusalem, sober Leah wrote to her friend Sara in a somewhat stilted Hebrew: 'Who needs it, this nonsense? Certainly not me. But I hope it will have an end at last, and then things will be better, at least better than now . . .'[13]

The Jerusalem vegetable growers

Berl arrived in Jerusalem in August 1917 and remained there, intermittently, until he joined the Jewish Battalions in July 1918. During those ten months the south of the country was conquered by the British, a Palestinian Jewish volunteers' battalion was established, Berl wrote his article 'To the he-Halutz Movement', made one of his greatest speeches, 'Facing the Days Ahead', met Chaim Weizmann and edited and wrote an article for a volume called *ba-Avoda* (At Work). It was, historically speaking, a time of great upheaval; and though Berl was very prolific during those stormy ten months, his life in Jerusalem was, in fact, marked by an almost unnatural quiet. The typhoon raged all around, smashing everything in its path, and at the eye of the storm was a quiet spot, the Jerusalem group in 1918.

It was hard to determine exactly why Berl chose Jerusalem of all places. There are no indications that he was drawn by its charm or its history. It would appear that because it was a town with a considerable Jewish population and, therefore, a potential market, it was a good place to set up his group of vegetable growers.

He leased plots of land from Arab landowners, near 'the tomb of the kings', and found accommodation for the group in an old, deserted Arab house. There were several young women in the group – among them, Rachel Katznelson and Hanna, Berl's beloved younger sister. Berl was a cross between the leader of the group, its father figure and guardian angel of the girls. He enjoyed the company of women and seemed to be more at ease working with them than with men, who usually outdid him. The group cleaned the house, readied it for occupation and prepared the plots for sowing before the first rains. It was October 1917 and General Allenby's troops were at the gates of the city. The shooting went on day and night, and the thunder of cannons disturbed their pastoral peace. Preoccupied as he was with finding good seeds and assuring the success of his produce, Berl was obliged to exercise caution to avoid being apprehended by the Turkish army on a charge of evading military service, especially since his papers were not in order. This is clear from a worried letter from Sara, who had no illusions as to her lover's resourcefulness: 'Don't forget that if they catch you, you're not a *berieh* [old hand] at escaping and things like that.'[14]

After some two weeks of feverish activity, the old building began to look like home: 'Everything is whitewashed, clean and pleasant, and there is even a lamp burning on the table.'[15] There was an aura of peace in this corner of Jerusalem which impressed Berl. His long and candid letters to Sara reveal an inner contentment, a satisfaction with his creative work and a new tranquility.

The house was owned by an Arab, and Arab families lived nearby. The group had no plow of its own and was at the mercy of an Arab plowman who appeared fitfully and worked well or carelessly, as the spirit moved him. For the first time since his arrival in Palestine, Berl was living on non-Jewish land, in an almost totally Arab environment. The sense of alienation, which had troubled him in Russia, now returned to haunt him in Jerusalem, of all places. As far as he was concerned, Palestine was a Jewish place, where he should have been free from dependence on Gentiles. He did not like non-Jews. Long before, when Sara was preparing for her immigration, he had sent her a list of suggestions, and advised her, *inter alia*, to purchase a boat ticket which did not include meals, since 'one should not, in my opinion, eat with Gentiles. And, generally speaking, it is best to stay as far away from them as possible.'[16] A sense of 'alienness, bereavement, sorrow and lack of security, the security we enjoy in all the places where we work'[17] afflicted him in the rented house in Jerusalem, 'as if it were not Palestine'. And it was no coincidence that boyhood memories were revived: 'Moonlight and fears, as in Kiev, long ago'.[18] The Arab neighbors stole seeds and it was necessary to stand watch from sowing to harvest. One clear and cold winter's day, the Arab plowman abandoned his work halfway through. What exactly occurred between him and Berl is unknown; what is certain is that a scuffle broke out between them, and it may be assumed that the Arab gained the upper hand. Berl burst into the house without a word and offered no explanation. But Rachel Katznelson was struck by his appearance: 'Injury and fury and the fervor of rebellion against age-old helplessness were in his countenance.'[19] Years later he had still not forgotten 'the day of Ibrahim' as he called the incident. The disparity between the will and the power to act which plagued Brenner's protagonists, troubled Berl as well: he longed for a Jewish genius, a strong and courageous Jew, independent and free of reliance on non-Jews. And now he found himself again in the grip of those same fears and complexes which had characterized the traditional relations between Jews and Gentiles.

This situation intensified his nationalist feelings as well as the hopes he pinned on the British occupation of Palestine. Although he was then busy, in addition to his exacting farming work, in drawing up plans to expand the supply of fresh vegetables to Jerusalem and conducting negotiations with Sir Ronald Storrs, Governor of Jerusalem, for the cultivation of abandoned plots near the city, Berl began to pay brief visits to Judea, the coastal plain. He became increasingly involved in the activities now beginning there again after years of stagnation. At the same time, he developed a new attachment to Jerusalem. After six months in the Holy City, Berl visited the Temple Mount for the first time on the first day of Passover. On the seventh day of the festival he repeated the visit: 'A walk around the city wall and a visit to the Wailing Wall; the Temple Mount makes the heart beat faster and overflow.'[20] It was nine years since he had arrived in Palestine, and this was his first visit to the place so sacred to the Jews.

The Jerusalem group gradually declined. When Berl left to join the Jewish Battalion, he did not dream that he was abandoning an entire way of life. He never returned to communal life, nor did he ever again work as a farmer.

4

FACING THE DAYS AHEAD,
1918–1919

All national movements are based in some measure on irrationalism, even anti-rationalism. This was certainly true of the Zionist movement, which lacked even the ordinary territorial foundation for the expression of its national aspirations. The theories of the fathers of Zionism reveal numerous pathetic endeavors to provide logical explanations for the inexplicable, as do those of the Second Aliyah pioneers, as well. Ostensibly, they advocate a positivist, rational, clearly-defined, often even somewhat deterministic *Weltanschauung*. But beneath the surface lurked an alien fire, fed by totally different visions. Occasionally, in times of crisis, this inner world was exposed, casting a new, fascinating light on the psychological makeup of these people. With Berl Katznelson, in 1918–1919, the struggle between rationality and deeply-buried instincts and desires – the 'life-force' – is particularly striking.

Berl, it will be recalled, had come to Palestine to escape the 'spiritual life' in Russia, which was marked by lofty rhetoric and unrealistic hopes. He was searching for 'real life', for tangible realities, to no small extent under the influence of the great Russian thinkers. But he was also swayed by the theories of 'vitalism' which he learned from Micha Yosef Berdichevsky. Berdichevsky was the voice of the irrational in Zionist thought, the antithesis of Ahad ha-Am, who represented the influence of European rationalism. Through Berdichevsky, young East European Jews absorbed anti-rationalist trends. Their thinking rejected the rule of reason and was directed at the primeval world of the senses, in the spirit of *fin de siècle* Central European *Lebensphilosophie* in the writings of Nietzsche, Schopenhauer and others.

It was no accident that Berl and Brenner were drawn to one another. They both identified with subterranean currents of the national spirit which they saw as the true source of the people's vitality. Inhibited by life in the Diaspora, this vitality was now reviving in the new Palestine.

They were both engaged in a search for the down-to-earth and cor-
poreal, as opposed to the complex logical and ideational structures of
the young intelligentsia in the Pale of Settlement. The way of life adopted
by Berl and his comrades had anarchistic origins – vagabondage, non-
conformism, rebellion against bourgeois morality. It sought a direct and
simple approach to human relations and to nature, perfection and a
'meaningful' life. There were points of psychological contact between
the nihilistic saints and amoral revolutionaries in Dostoyevsky and the
irrational views of Nietzsche, and these found expression in the stories
and articles of Brenner and Berdichevsky.

Those who take up the burden of sorrow, lace up their boots and take the wanderer's
staff in hand will create an entirely new political-economic-folk community; it is
those on the move who will build and consolidate a nation, landless as yet, and not
those who remain outside that longed-for land, even if they speak of it at councils, and
believe they can attain it by councils and words . . .[1]

This proclamation of pioneering Zionism was not written by Berl: its
author was his mentor, Berdichevsky.

In the first article he wrote in Palestine, 'mi-Bifnim' (From Within),
Berl employed Berdichevsky's terms throughout:

The legacy of our forefathers, the suffering of generations and the ravages of history
are gradually giving way though in the teeth of considerable opposition – to the *new
forces rebelling against them. A change of values* is approaching . . . a change in matter and
in spirit. In place of the murky atmosphere of ghetto life – a life of labor on the soil: in
place of the spiritual life of the ancient and modern ghetto – a *dignified human being*. We
have a long road to travel to the defiant man of the soil, but we are on the right
path.[2]

During the Second Aliyah, belief in the life-force of the people was
nurtured in secret, for fear that it would be mocked as a pipe dream. But
now that the Balfour Declaration had been granted and the British
Army had occupied the country, the atmosphere was conducive to soaring hopes and messianic beliefs. What had been regarded as a fantastic
dream in Herzl's day – the attainment of a charter under international
sponsorship for the establishment of a Jewish national entity in Palestine
– had been achieved by Chaim Weizmann. At this hour, rationality
yielded place to the voices of instinct.

Berl, living in Jerusalem with his vegetable growers, was well aware
of the changes taking place. Through the haze of war, rumor reached
him that a new immigration movement, he-Halutz (The Pioneer), was

being organized, and he addressed a letter to its members, though there was no guarantee that it would reach its destination. In it, he referred to he-Halutz as 'a movement of *will* and *action*', rather than of the 'social scholasticism' of the existing parties and movements. The pioneering movement, the manifestation of the *will* of the people through selected individuals, was 'the loyal emissary of history, the emissary of national providence'[3] he wrote. Using 'vitalist' terminology, and Berdichevskian theory, he bestowed on he-Halutz the title of history's elect, who by force of *will* took upon themselves the creation of a new life and a new people.

There is a strange contradiction in Berl's letter between its tone of ardent 'vitalist' enthusiasm and high-flown rhetoric and its crystal-clear pragmatic import. Berl advises he-Halutz first not to bind itself to political parties or dogmas, but to preserve the movement's unity and allow its ideological content to grow out of the Palestinian reality. Secondly, he emphasizes the need to prepare for life in Palestine by training in manual work and learning Hebrew, two deficiencies which had hampered him and his comrades every step of their way. His 'vitalism' in no way obscured his sense of reality.

The same duality is evident in a speech he delivered several months later, in March 1918, at the Seventh Conference of the Judean Workers' Union in Rehovot. The British had occupied the south of the country and Jerusalem three months previously. Galilee was still occupied by the Turks and Judea was cut off from the Diaspora and from the leadership of the Zionist movement. The conference was convened in an atmosphere of unrest and uncertainty, the outgrowth of numerous factors: the change of regime in which most had been passive onlookers; the tribulations of the war years – famine, disease, forced labor, persecution, disintegration of the Yishuv leadership; and concern for their relatives in Eastern Europe. The delegates yearned for a reassuring word, an inspiring message. Berl, in close rapport with this audience, neither preached nor exhorted. He preferred rather to conduct a dialog with them. It was, after all, a unique moment, a pause for contemplation on the threshold of a new era, for people who had been forged in the crucible of the Second Aliyah and the war years. Berl titled his speech 'Facing the Days Ahead'. He could have called it 'Facing the Newcomers' for this cohesive group was about to absorb groups larger than itself, and all the problems relating to this eventuality colored the deliberations.

The motto of his speech was a quotation from Ferdinand Lasalle who, exhorting the working class to recognize that they were the class of the future, paraphrased the words of Jesus to Peter: 'Upon this rock I will build my Temple.' Like Lasalle, Berl tried to inspire this small, exhausted and apprehensive group of people with a sense of mission. Berl believed that he and his comrades were the chosen few, Berdichevsky's – and Jewish history's – elect. Lasalle attributed the historical mission to a class which constituted the majority of the people; Berl spoke of the 'active minority, bearing the future within them'.[4] He referred not to the Jewish working class as a whole, but to the Palestinian workers alone, this 'new force' which must now 'track out a path for the people'. There are overtones of the 'avant-garde' theory of the Bolsheviks, just then coming to power in Russia. While there may be no indications of direct influence, the elitist theory was common to both messianic socialism and to Nietzscheanism.

Berl then digressed and spoke reverently of Herzl's genius and prophetic vision, adding: 'How sorely we need this faith in human life, a living, pure and binding faith, whose power and force can add so much to our future lives.'[5] This is faith without religion, messianism without a god. Berl was enamored of traditional Jewish eschatological concepts: redemption, suffering, visions, messengers of good tidings, the Return to Zion, Divine revelation are all expressions which recur in his speeches. But this redemption was to be secular.

Berl went on to analyze the essence of the national movement. He reverted to the basic question of how to transform the aspirations of individuals into a mass movement, and believed that the answer lay in infusing the national movement with social content. The movement must reflect and respond to the needs of the pioneers who sought both national and social redemption. A Zionism which did not satisfy both these aspirations, would find itself deprived of these people, who were in fact the mainstay of the movement. Though Berl never actually used the word 'socialism' it was an integral part of pioneering Zionist belief and he admonished the bourgeois leadership of the movement to reconcile themselves to this fact.

Berl did not derive his two central assumptions, the preeminence of a socialist conception of Zionism and the historical 'mission' of the workers, from Marxist thought. His analysis rested on both logic and his instinctive feelings, and oscillated more to the latter – his keen sense of the social psychology of both labor and bourgeois elements in the

Zionist camp. He envisaged, not a class war in which the workers would eventually prevail, but rather voluntary withdrawal from power by the Zionist bourgeoisie, who would concede their place to the pioneer-workers. The objective he describes – 'liberating and liberated labor' – recalls the great socialist utopias or the anarchistic societies, organized from below by autonomous workers' cells. He held that the 'leap forward' from capitalism to the society of the future would occur through a peaceful evolutionary process, by virtue of the national vision which sanctioned the revolution.

His apparently rational conceptual structure was essentially irrational. But Berl's audience were not seeking an immaculate consistent philosophy. They were not troubled by the strange amalgam of nationalist impulses and social pathos, creative spontaneity and social messianism. The 'survivors' of the Second Aliyah required that someone give meaning and dimension to their suffering and sacrifice, and voice to the latent emotions.

Like Berl, they were torn between a propensity for the noble and arcane and the desire for practical action. And hence Berl, after echoing their profoundest emotions, turned to more mundane matters, and listed a number of demands which he proposed should be submitted to the Zionist leaders, then about to visit Palestine to draw up plans for development of the country in the wake of the Balfour Declaration. Berl foresaw an alliance between the workers and the Zionist leadership. The former would contribute energy and initiative, the latter would lease land to them. All the unoccupied land in Palestine would be handed over to the Jewish people or, in other words, nationalized, so as to prevent any form of settlement other than 'labor settlement'.[6] In addition, national credit would be extended to 'labor settlement'. Berl envisaged the establishment of an institution whose aim would be the promotion of settlement, even if this involved financial losses. This institution would be controlled not by the 'property owner' but by 'a society of workers who are mutual guarantors'.[7] In the same spirit, he went on to enumerate the vital conditions for the absorption of a massive immigration which would be transformed into a 'labor community'. On the face of it, there was no connection between the two sections of Berl's address: the first half consisted of ideology and fragments of philosophical theories, and the second of a working program. But, in fact, the former provided the legitimization for the latter. The Jewish worker's mission and sense of vocation empowered him to demand national lands and national funds – as well as autonomous control of settlement. In its own interest, the nation must create the possibility of settling and consolidating the workers.

It should be noted that the future which Berl conjured up in his speech was based entirely on an agricultural society. The Palestinian workers to whose needs Berl was responding were those in the labor settlements.

The Seventh Conference of the Judean Workers Union was aimed at the establishment of a single labor federation, which would deal with all the 'economic, spiritual and civil' matters of interest to the labor public as well as with all settlement affairs. There are no indications that this federation was to extend beyond the confines of the agricultural sector into the urban sphere. One could argue that this was because there were no Jewish urban workers in Palestine at the time. But the real reason lay, not in the presence or absence of non-agricultural workers, but in the field of vision of the beholder.

Berl's awareness of the need for unity of the workers evolved before he realized the necessary scope of this unity. It therefore seems only fair to state that, in 1918, he had not yet formulated his theory of the 'all-inclusiveness' of the Palestinian labor movement, and confined himself to the agricultural workers alone; and further that his basic conception of the unity of the labor movement crystallized during the war and matured towards its close.

Volunteering for the Jewish Battalions

The British occupation of Palestine aroused great hopes among Jews, and evoked mixed feelings in the Yishuv. The British were welcomed as the saviors of Palestinian Jewry from Turkish oppression, which had become particularly severe in the past few years. But the young generation felt a certain shame at the fact that Australian and British soldiers were spilling their blood for the country while the Jews watched from the sidelines. Word came from Egypt that units of Jewish volunteers had been set up within the framework of the British Army – the 38th Battalion of the Royal Fusiliers for Jews from Great Britain, and the 39th for Jewish volunteers from the United States. There were reports of plans by Jabotinsky, a prominent Zionist leader and one of the architects of the Battalions, to establish a Jewish Legion, of the Palestinian Jews. From Russia came vague rumors of revolution, and they enhanced the hopes that a new world order was imminent. The Jews had taken part in the war, fighting on both sides, but this had affected neither the outcome of the war nor their own future, since they had fought under alien flags and for the national aspirations of others. It was now believed that fighting for one's country bestowed the right to self-determination. There would be a general reckoning and recompense for suffering, an idea which was reinforced when the demands of various new nations were supported in Wilson's 'Fourteen Points'. The need to win Palestine by fighting for it seemed particularly urgent now that there was another claimant to the country just emerging as a force on the stage of history – namely, the Arabs. The Balfour Declaration of November 1917, which constituted British recognition of the national rights of the Jewish people to Palestine was a strong bargaining card. At the same time, the claims which the Jews planned to submit to the forthcoming Peace Conference were blatantly weak: the Jewish people could not represent itself as one of the combatant nations, despite its sufferings during the war and its contribution to victory. Hence the importance of the Jewish units within the Allied forces. Another significant consideration was the chance to provide military training for young Jews, who would serve one day as the nucleus of the future Jewish army. In practical and immediate terms, those who volunteered for service in the Jewish Battalions hoped to take part in the battle for Palestine – only the southern area of which had so far been occupied by the British – and to bring the message of liberation to the Jews of besieged Galilee. What clearer illustration of the revolutionary change in the status of the Jewish people could there be than the spirit of the Palestinian volunteers, eager to liberate their own country!

From the very outset, the idea of volunteering for service in the Jewish Battalions of the British Army aroused tremendous response. There was a general thirst for some dramatic action after the years of barren misery. The first volunteers were the young middle-class graduates of the Herzliya Gymnasium in the new town of Tel Aviv, led by Eliyahu Golomb and Dov Hos.* They were idealists in the best Narodnik tradition. (Golomb was involved in the labor movement and had spent some time working at Degania and Kinneret.) They had

---

* Golomb subsequently became the founder and head of the Hagana. Hos was a labor leader, known for his lobbying contacts with the British Labor Party. They and their friend, Moshe Shertok (Sharett, later Israel's Foreign Minister and Premier) were related by marriage and known as 'the brothers-in-law'.

already demonstrated their organizational skill in setting up a union of Herzliya graduates, aimed at serving national interests. The second group which responded to the call was Poalei Zion, whose spokeswoman was Rachel Yanait. During the period of the Second Aliyah, Poalei Zion had already displayed its political resourcefulness in such matters as the establishment of ha-Shomer, and the despatch of Ben Zvi and Ben Gurion to Constantinople to study law in order to prepare themselves for political activity in Ottoman Palestine. The slogan adopted by the Battalions, 'In blood and fire Judea fell, in blood and fire it will rise again', had also been the slogan of ha-Shomer. The driving need to rely on oneself rather than on others, which had motivated the Hommel self-defense activities in Tsarist Russia and had been reflected in ha-Shomer and the other defense organizations in Palestine, was evident in the volunteering spirit.

The ha-Poel ha-Tzair Party, on the other hand, objected vehemently to the volunteering scheme. They regarded such open and unequivocal support of the British cause as adventurism. Formally speaking, the Zionist Organization, whose executive office was operating out of neutral Copenhagen, had not given its blessing to the volunteering movement. Trumpeldor and Jabotinsky had set up the Zion Mule Corps and the 38th Battalion of the Royal Fusiliers in the teeth of that body's opposition. Furthermore, Galilee was still under Turkish rule and there was good reason to fear acts of barbaric revenge against the Jewish community once the Turks learned of the 'treachery' of the Jews of the south of the country. The memory of how the Nili group of young people from the old colonies had collaborated with the British in intelligence operations and endangered the entire Yishuv was still fresh. Moreover, ha-Poel ha-Tzair tended towards pacifism, and were repelled by the idea of winning a country through bloodshed. Palestine, they believed, should be won through labor. Finally, the creative energies of a movement could not be directed at two objectives simultaneously: if they were focused on war, they would be diverted from work. Enlistment, in their eyes, was the result of a militaristic psychosis, of false messianism. They continued to insist on the path of self-fulfillment through work, without impetuous action. Redemption of the country was a lengthy process, and could not be achieved in one fell swoop.

The mobilization was organized by young people. The 'gymnasists' were about ten years younger than the Second Aliyah pioneers, and had no public standing. The Poalei Zion leaders, Yitzhak Ben Zvi, David Ben Gurion, Israel Shohat and Alexander Hashin, were all out of the country. Though Rachel Yanait's efforts in the volunteering movement were sanctioned from afar by her future husband, Ben Zvi, she was not a leader of Palestinian workers, and was certainly not well known to the Yishuv in general. Thus, lacking a recognized, respected leadership, the volunteers were considered a cross between reckless adventurers and the saviors of the nation.

Berl, all this time, was absorbed in his work in Jerusalem. In February, 1918, he went to Jaffa, *inter alia* in order to inquire into the Battalions issue with Golomb and other leaders of the volunteering movement, and they were convinced of his support. As far as the volunteers were concerned, the recruitment of Berl and Shmuel Yavne'eli – leaders of the Agricultural Union and the Non-Affiliated Group – constituted a breakthrough. From the status of a fly-by-night scheme it became a widely based public movement. But Berl's support appears to have been somewhat halfhearted: he avoided active participation and deplored the controversy which was creating a rift within the small community of workers. If Golomb and his comrades had hoped that Berl would give the signal to the Non-Affiliated Group to join the Battalion, they were disappointed. Berl did not attend the first meeting of the volunteers at Jaffa in March, nor did he come to a subsequent meeting with Jabotinsky. Despite the urging of his friends, he did not overcome his indecision. It is not surprising, therefore, that he was accused of opportunism, of trying to satisfy both sides, of 'posturing diplomacy and a false heart'.[8] These charges impelled Berl to confide in his friend and fellow-member of the Non-Affiliated Group, Mordechai Kushnir, who was in utter disagreement with him on the question of the Battalions. Berl was basically a pacifist. Although he had once abandoned his Seimist comrades in Russia because of their reluctance to employ terrorist measures in retaliation for pogroms and had worshiped Pinhas Dashevsky, the Avenger, as the personification of the new Jew, he condemned the war. He distinguished between acts of terror in revenge for outrages against the Jewish people, and total war, which did not differentiate between the innocent and the guilty, and in which human dignity and life were lost in a great, purposeless blood-bath. When the First World War broke out, and all hopes of international solidarity of the workers against the war were swept away by a

universal outpouring of patriotic enthusiasm, Berl was bitterly disillusioned. He longed to be in Europe in order 'to sanctify the name of
Man by refusing to fight, even at the cost of my life'. A false rumor at
the beginning of the War, that Karl Liebknecht had been killed because
of his anti-war stand, aroused his enthusiasm: 'I trembled with joy.' So
strong was his aversion to war that, at the outset, he refused to pin any
hopes on it: 'If they were to ask me if I want this war in order to gain
Palestine as a result – I would not be capable of this evil, even for the
hope of our future.'⁹ But, paradoxically, the very spirit which made him
a pacifist led him to the Battalions. He could not remain indifferent to
the messianic ardor which inspired the volunteering movement. As a
disciple of Dostoyevsky and of Berdichevsky he perceived 'the human
within the inhuman, the noble within the degraded, and the evil within
good as well.' However suspect its origins, this movement might, in its
own way, bring about the 'supreme awakening, which elevates the
individual and the community'. As a disciple of Narodnaya Volya, he
believed in the 'deed' which generates great revolutionary ardor. In
fact, all his reasoning was a kind of rationalization of his profound
emotional need to share the sense of common destiny, the 'joy of sacrifice', which possessed the volunteers. Moreover, Berl believed in the
mysterious ways of fate:

And I still hold the view that there is a history in this world, whose decrees and com-
mands and paths are unknown to us, and it murmurs to me that this is the road that history has chosen to test the strength and the enthusiasm of the people. Would it be
honest of me to deride this enthusiasm? No, no such man am I!¹⁰

Berl did not subscribe to the myth that the country could be won
through blood, nor did the vision of a Jewish army attract him greatly.
He regarded it as one of the manifestations of the national renaissance
movement – no less, but no more. As far as he was concerned, it was
merely a means, incidental to the exhilaration it evoked, incidental to
the new public spirit it would foster.

The political parties took a clear position *vis-à-vis* volunteering; the
Agricultural Union did not. This fact rendered Berl even more eager to
find the golden mean between the two positions. He tried to encourage
an atmosphere of conciliation, and did in fact succeed, before the Battalion
left for training, in restoring the unity and trust which had been undermined in the course of the acrimonious debate. The pamphlet *ba-Avoda*

(At Work), an early editing effort of Berl's, is imbued with the mood of spiritual conflict and intense emotion which characterized the volunteers who shared Berl's views.

A soldier in the 40th Battalion of the Royal Fusiliers

Berl and the other volunteers enlisted in July 1918 and were sent to the Halamyia training camp in Egypt. This period was to change his entire life and leave an indelible stamp on his personality. It was a year of soaring hopes and of bitter despair, of peaks in his public life and abysses in his private relationships. He was thirty-one years old when he first donned a British uniform, but he still lacked the keen sense of decisiveness which usually comes with maturity. Six months later he wrote to his brother, Hayim, in the United States: 'I am as I was. Thirty-two years old and feeling at times as if I were still a boy, although I have many gray hairs . . .'[11]

The first weeks of military service were pleasant: Berl's fears of failure to adjust to military life, which had been among the factors which deterred him from supporting the volunteering movement, proved exaggerated. He was certainly far from being a model soldier: short and scrawny, his head and his beard shaven in deference to military regulations, he looked strange and out-of-place in uniform. Golomb and Ben Gurion were also short men, but somehow the uniforms looked more natural on them. On Berl it looked like a costume. Never an outstanding soldier, he acquired military skills, like all other mechanical skills, with only partial success and with great effort. But the problem of successful adjustment apparently ceased to trouble him soon after he joined his unit: there was no repetition of the misery which accompanied his efforts to adapt to manual labor. He considered that he had tasks to fulfill in the Battalion other than mere soldiering duties: and these, as we shall see, were the center of his world. As a result, he was spared humiliation despite his ineptness and his characteristic lack of physical resourcefulness.

The first days of service were marked by exhilaration because of the sense that redemption was close. But this joy soon turned sour in the pedestrian routine of military life. Life in a training camp did not appeal either to Berl or his comrades. It is unlikely that the British army ever took in volunteers more enthusiastic and more foreign to the nature and demands of army life. It was only with great reluctance that the military authorities agreed to accept these strange and enthusiastic ragamuffins, and they were fully determined to transform them, so far as possible, into rank-and-file soldiers without special privileges. British reserve had a damping effect on the impassioned volunteers, and a clash between the two was inevitable.

Jabotinsky had warned the volunteers on the eve of their enlistment about the boredom and routine of army life, and these proved even worse than the Palestinians had dreamed. Army discipline, uncompromising and often mindless – particularly for recruits who were fond of asking questions and probing – aroused resentment. The humiliating floggings for violations of regulations were unacceptable to the Second Aliyah rebels. Life in the unit was enervating and tedious and did not satisfy the expectations of such volunteers as Berl and Shmuel Yavne'eli. Squabbles soon followed: Berl and his comrades insisted on stressing the Jewish character of the Battalion. They held extempore Hebrew lessons for overseas volunteers and insisted that orders be given in Hebrew. The British officers, both Jews and Gentiles, found it hard to accede to this demand for obvious reasons, and a storm erupted. Berl and Yavne'eli, conditioned as they were by their political experience in civilian life, and apparently unable or unwilling to 'compromise' their struggle for the Hebrew language, contemplated nothing less than a strike! It is not difficult to imagine how this would have been greeted by the British officers, who greatly feared 'Bolshies'. Only after fierce arguments, did the 'rebels' agree to retreat and submit a memorandum to Weizmann to be conveyed to Balfour.

But the Battalions, which were envisaged as a unique historical event, were reduced to a fleeting episode, when the British captured Galilee without their participation. Rumor had it that the British High Command deliberately vetoed the participation of Jews fighting under a Zionist flag in the battle for Galilee, so as to forestall the possibility that they would submit political demands after the event. This may have been only a rumor, fed by the characteristic suspicious attitude of Eastern European Jews towards Gentiles, but it may also have had some basis in the hostility of the military administration towards Zionism and Zionists. In any event the volunteers were bitterly disappointed. What was the point of suffering army life, with its strenuous training and pointless discipline, without the recompense of the great, uplifting deed? The Battalions never recovered from this blow. From now on army life was nothing but dull routine, interspersed here and there with operational activity. The center of activity now shifted outside the Battalion, which was now a burden rather than an achievement: it was hard to bear, but to abolish it would mean to bestow an easy victory on the enemies of the National Home. And thus the Battalion dragged on for another year, in a spirit of disillusionment and indifference.

Berl shared in the general frustration and confusion, and his optimism dwindled. The wonderful fellows from the Battalions no longer seemed so wonderful to him. He lived 'with a vague, deeply confused feeling: we are superfluous'.[12] His hair became streaked with gray in the space of a few days. His misery was compounded by physical disability: he fell sick, and for several weeks failed to recover, which led him to comment: 'For all the pleasure the King gets out of me – he could do without me.'[13]

But, despite his depression and weakness, he still found the strength to take on an awesome task – an attempt to unify the labor movement.

Unification: Ahdut ha-Avoda

Among the reasons Berl had cited in favor of enlisting was the need to unite the labor movement. In a frank letter to Mordechai Kushnir, he wrote: 'I regard my enlistment as a continuation of my work for the unification of the workers. Various hopes urge me on as I go . . .'[14] Before six months had passed, Ahdut ha-Avoda (Unity of Labor), the socialist Zionist association, had been established. What could be more natural than to attribute its ultimate realisation to Berl? It was he who had seen unification as the natural outcome of the organic development of the movement, the corollary of internal trends and of the 'true' will of the workers in Palestine. 'It was not created out of a void. It came to us from the depths of real life, and grew out of constant action.'[15] Even before the unification became a fact, Berl was referring to it as an almost inevitable, historical phenomenon of the Palestinian labor movement, a legacy of the Second Aliyah agricultural unions, which had inspired the entire movement and compelled it to accept its historic mission. Those who attacked it – he claimed – were aiming at the movement's heart. The entire movement accepted this view to the point where the word 'unity' (*ihud*) became sacrosanct and 'split' (*pilug*) derogatory. The Palestinian labor movement, he theorized, was progressing towards the complete and total unification of the working class in Palestine. To digress from this aim was an error which bordered on betrayal of the cause.

Without dwelling at this early stage on the question of whether Berl was correct in his conception, it should be noted that the kind of unity he envisaged never materialized.

A cautious examination of the sources casts doubt on Berl's claim that the unification of the labor movement proceeded, unabated, from the Second Aliyah period onward. Belief in the valid assumption that the workers in Palestine shared common interests could not alone prevent dissent. It did lead to the adaptation to Palestinian conditions of political theories originating in the Diaspora, such as the Poalei-Zion-style Borochovism, but this did not suffice to bring about the disbanding of existing political frameworks and the creation of new ones; in the final analysis, when the countless arguments and ideological exhortations are set aside, therein lay the revolutionary significance of the establishment of Ahdut ha-Avoda. No labor movement anywhere was immune to schism, common interests and class solidarity notwithstanding.

What, then, actually occurred in 1919 which crystalized vague aspirations for cooperation into a driving political force, which was destined to reshape the image of the movement, determine the patterns of its development and affect its history and that of the entire Palestinian Jewish community for at least two decades?

In September 1918, the Palestinian Battalion met with the other Jewish Battalions. Several days later, when the excitement at this historic encounter had abated somewhat, Berl began to conduct discussions with the 'Americans'. Berl probably tried to interest them in the aims of the Agricultural Union, which were constantly being obstructed and checked by the parties. But there is no record that the establishment of a new political entity was discussed. *Ba-Avoda* (At Work), the journal of the Agricultural Union, which appeared at the end of October, written in a florid style, reflected the mood of the group of comrades from Kinneret rather than the program of a political body. In November, several days after *ba-Avoda* reached the Battalion, Ben Zvi and Ben Gurion decided, as a countermove, to produce a party journal for the Poalei Zion members within the Battalions and elsewhere. Their activity in the following weeks was conducted strictly on party lines: there are no indications as yet of any desire for unification.

In January, Berl came back from leave in Palestine, and his return marked the beginning of relentless negotiations which culminated two months later in March, in the establishment of Ahdut ha-Avoda. Two persons were undoubtedly responsible for the launching and success of these negotiations, Berl and David Ben Gurion. During the period of the Second Aliyah, Ben Gurion and Berl had not been active in the same circles. Ben Gurion belonged to Poalei Zion, which was anathema to Berl, and when Berl became active in public life, Ben Gurion was in Istanbul, studying law. Psychologically, they differed greatly: Ben Gurion was a man of decision, he had adjusted to life in Palestine with alacrity and he saw his way clearly and forcefully. Their approach to socialism was also different: Ben Gurion was a follower of Borochov, and continued to use Marxist ways of thinking. Berl, who never accepted Borochov's theories, was loyal to the individualistic subjectivism of the First Russian Revolution and to Berdichevsky's philosophy of the Will. On one occasion they had walked together all the way to Jaffa (apparently from Petah Tikva) and did not even manage to find a subject of conversation. But in the army tents at Tel el Kabir in Egypt, they developed an abiding rapport: to call it political is to minimize its depth. If one were required to enumerate the achievements of the Battalion, Berl and Ben Gurion's discovery of one another should surely head the list. According to various reports, Ben Gurion read Berl's article 'Facing the Days Ahead' in *ba-Avoda*, and concluded that his objectives were identical with those of Berl, and sought a way of making contact with him. For the task of mediator he chose Shmuel Yavne'eli*, his friend from Galilee days, who was also friendly with Berl and a supporter of the Non-Affiliated Group. Yavne'eli was fired by the idea of unification. According to Ben Gurion: 'Berl was not like Yavne'eli – capable of enthusiasm; he would always ponder matters and try to see both sides of the question. He said, unenthusiastically: "All right, let's go and see the ha-Poel ha-Tzair people." '[16] It transpires from Ben Gurion's description that the initiative was his, and that Berl joined in skeptically and hesitantly. This description is substantiated by a letter which Ben Zvi wrote on the day of Berl's return from Palestine:

The latest news: Berl Katznelson returned from Palestine and we had a private (unofficial) consultation with him with the participation of several of our comrades, and

---

* Well known political journalist and labor movement leader. Sent during the Second Aliyah to Yemen to recruit Jewish workers, aroused messianic fervor which led to the immigration of groups of Yemenite Jews to Palestine.

people from ha-Shomer and ha-Poel ha-Tzair. David [Ben Gurion] proposed the amalgamation of all the workers of Palestine – Berl expressed his agreement, and so did Yavne'eli . . .[17]

Berl gave vent to his feelings on the matter in a letter to Sara. 'Since the day of my return to Egypt I have vowed to dedicate myself to a final effort for unification. I do not know if I will succeed. But I wish for it desperately, as the last hope and attempt.'[18]

Ben Gurion's proposal for 'unification' was totally different from anything Berl had intended. Berl dreamed of rallying the workers around the Agricultural Union, which he believed personified the creative, pioneering Palestinian elements of the labor movement. There is no evidence that Berl's vision of the unification of the labor movement in this period extended beyond the framework of pioneering and agricultural endeavor in Palestine. He demanded a wide sphere of action for the Union – but did not touch on the parties' right to exist. And herein lies Ben Gurion's main contribution to the unification: it was he who advocated the abolition of the parties and the establishment of a joint organization for socio-economic and political action.

This proposal derived from his desire to abolish Poalei Zion. And, in fact, the most important change on the political map of Palestine as a result of the establishment of Ahdut ha-Avoda – the new unity – was the disappearance of Poalei Zion. It was Ben Gurion who persuaded his fellow party-members, some senior to him and more renowned, to agree to an act of political suicide. His stand should be understood in the context of the situation then prevailing in his party, both in Palestine and abroad. Ben Gurion had returned to Palestine after a fierce debate among Poalei Zion members in the United States. He differed with American Poalei Zion on the question of the 'primacy' of Palestine and its implications. Poalei Zion in America were then under pressure as a result of the controversy with anti-Zionist leftist elements. The more they were accused of non-proletarian tendencies, the more they tried to emphasize their working-class credentials by distancing themselves from their commitment to Palestine. There were two main issues at stake: the question of a national language and the question of the relations between the movement in Palestine and in the Diaspora. The ardor with which the Yiddishists defended the supremacy of that language was matched only by their hostility towards Hebrew. On the face of it, there was no contradiction between the two languages, and they could co-exist. Among Berl and his comrades, love of their mother

tongue was not affected by their preference for Hebrew: Yiddish literature, stories and anecdotes were part of their everyday lives. But the
Yiddishists placed the two languages in confrontation. A *Kulturkampf*
erupted between the national-populists, who considered Yiddish to be
the language of the masses, aspired to Jewish autonomy in the Diaspora
and believed that, ultimately, the solution to the Jewish question would
be found in their countries of residence, and the national-Zionists. The
struggle against Hebrew was, in fact, a battle against Jewish Palestine, if
not in theory then in effect. Poalei Zion adopted an ambivalent stance
on this question: anxious to emphasize their socialist outlook, they tended
to agree that Yiddish should be the language of the Jewish masses, but,
as Zionists, they could not reject Hebrew. Hence, as a compromise,
they denounced the campaign against Yiddish which they claimed was
being conducted in Palestine. Ben Gurion, from the beginning of his
life in Palestine, was a dedicated 'Hebraist'. During his stay in the
United States, he waged a fierce battle on behalf of Hebrew – without
marked success. His comrades in the American party continued to conduct polemics with the Bundists in that country, to stress their own populist character and to play down their Zionist leanings. Zionism became
an appendage to their socialism, liable to be discarded at the first indications of a brewing storm. And these were, in fact, stormy times: the
Russian Revolution, which raised hopes that a solution to the Jewish
problem might be at hand with the construction of a socialist society,
struck the socialist Jewish world like a lightning bolt. Potential reserves
for Zionist pioneering became intoxicated by the Revolution and abandoned the 'parochial' Zionist milieu. As a result, Ben Gurion lost faith
in the force of the movement in the Diaspora. The question of the
primacy of Palestine was now transformed into the question of the
primacy of Zionism over socialism. Ben Gurion knew where he stood;
his movement was still vacillating.

Back at home, in Palestine, Ben Gurion became concerned by the
state of his party. Most of its veteran leaders had abandoned it; no
young leadership, nurtured in the Palestinian, socialist Zionist spirit,
had emerged to replace it. The party core was focused around ha-
Shomer, where Ben Gurion was not particularly popular. This core,
which was something in the nature of a military order, could not serve
as the substitute for a party.

The controversy over the Hebrew language threatened to cleave the
Palestinian party as well; among the Battalion veterans who reached

Palestine there were a large number who were profoundly attached to Yiddish, and were irritated by the zeal for Hebrew, a language they did not know. It was clear to Ben Gurion that his old party was incapable of taking up the challenge of building the country at this difficult time. Coming from the outside, he could see the entire picture lucidly: the old Poalei Zion was disintegrating. The new immigrants had not arrived. The time was ripe for dismantling old frameworks and establishing new ones. In 'Facing the Days Ahead', Ben Gurion recognized a partner worthy of him: a man who was a Palestinian through and through, raring for action.

The same conditions which encouraged the political 'suicide' of Poalei Zion were responsible for the fact that ha-Poel ha-Tzair did not join in the unification. The ha-Poel ha-Tzair leaders had remained in Palestine throughout the war, and were not particularly affected by it; their prestige remained unimpaired. Their zeal for Palestine and for the Hebrew language was only reinforced by the Yiddishist onslaught, and their hostility towards dogmatic socialism was intensified by reports of events in Russia. Moreover, rumors reached Palestine from Russia that 60,000 members of Tzeirei Zion,* affiliated to ha-Poel ha-Tzair, were about to immigrate to Palestine. There was no reason for the party to disband and renounce its distinctive character by entering into some dubious venture of all Palestinian workers. Furthermore, it was loath to join a body which accepted the theory of class struggle and was ear-marked to become part of the World Alliance of Poalei Zion, an international federation of Poalei Zion in Europe, the U.S. and Palestine.

Ha-Poel ha-Tzair, like Poalei Zion, was a socially cohesive organization, fostered by fifteen years of joint effort. They were moderate people, not given to the excessive enthusiasms which characterized the Battalion volunteers, and made them ready to jettison their differences and forswear old loyalties.

Ben Gurion was not satisfied with the mere establishment of a new framework; he also postulated a program for it: (a) recognition of the class struggle, (b) organizational ties with Jewish workers throughout the world or with the Poalei Zion Alliance; and (c) membership in the Socialist International. Ben Gurion was aware that his fellow party-

---

* A populist Zionist party, close in character to ha-Poel ha-Tzair which expanded greatly in the period between the deposal of the Tsar and the setting up of the Bolshevik dictatorship.

members would not settle for less, and even on the basis of this platform he found it difficult to convince them to join in the unification, as it implied renouncing Borochovism.

Berl was remote from dogmatic socialism. He wanted to establish as widely-based a socio-political body as possible, and to this end he needed a platform which would give expression to the varied, even conflicting, trends among the workers. Ben Gurion's formula was too unequivocal and inflexible. And it was here that Berl stepped in and infused a historical event with ideological scaffolding – inadvertently, perhaps.

Ahdut ha-Avoda was planned to combine the roles of party and trade union. It was supposed to be an association, composed of autonomous trade unions, rather than a party whose members were expected to keep faith with a certain credo. In this formulation there was undoubtedly a touch of syndicalism, and a dash of Kropotkin. But, there are no indications that Berl acted with prior intent to create this type of all-embracing body. It seems to have grown out of the desire to construct a social-political-trade-union organization, on the widest possible basis. It could not be founded on clearly defined political convictions, since the slightest rift would jar its stability. Berl chose to emphasize the common way of life of the Palestinian workers and the fact that under prevailing conditions, all were equal, without division into exploiters and exploited. He stressed the brotherhood of laboring people rather than dogma. Its form of organization was borrowed from the Agricultural Union; its scope was the outcome of Ben Gurion's proposal that all parties be eliminated. The main tasks of the new association would be in areas in which the Union had operated or aspired to act: settlement, developing the country, acting as a labor exchange, helping new immigrants. Berl and his colleagues believed that the socio-economic and cultural objectives were more important than the political aspects. This view of matters was characteristic of the immediate post-war period, when the political role of the Zionist Organization (as well as the tasks of the parties) appeared to have diminished in significance. The implementation of the Balfour Declaration after the British occupation was considered to spell the end of the political era of Zionism and to usher in the epoch of development of the country.

Of Ben Gurion's three demands, two were incorporated into Ahdut ha-Avoda's program: participation in the World Alliance of Poalei Zion and participation in the Socialist International. The principle of the class struggle was not.

The platform was socialist insofar as its orientation was towards the workers and its vision was of a self-organizing non-class society. It bore little resemblance to any of the accepted socialist theories. There was an essential difference between the syndicalists, for example, and the founders of Ahdut ha-Avoda: the former did not undertake the task of developing a country and hence could preserve the integrity of their theory, which opposed central authority. It also condemned them to barren inactivity. The founders of Ahdut ha-Avoda set themselves the objective of developing Palestine, and its political structure was based on a curious blend of centralization and decentralization: the cells were envisaged as trade unions, but the central body of the association was to be elected at a general conference of all the workers. This method of election was aimed at bestowing supreme authority on the central body and freeing it of dependence on the particularist constitutive bodies. The central body was to represent the *volonté générale* – as against the *volonté de tous* which would find expression in the sectoral unions. Ahdut ha-Avoda accepted the primacy of Palestine over the Diaspora and recognition of Hebrew as the official language. It sought the unification of the Jewish labor movement in the Diaspora with the aim of establishing a large-scale pioneering movement. It considered its essential aim the setting up of a body capable of action, which would direct all the creative energies of the movement into constructive channels.

The establishment of Ahdut ha-Avoda marks the introduction of the labor movement as a central force in the Jewish community in Palestine. Ahdut ha-Avoda determined the patterns of action and methods of organization for the future and, most important of all, gave the movement a leadership. On the face of it, the Agricultural Union appeared to have accepted the basic tenets of Poalei Zion as regards the Socialist-International and the World Alliance. But one should differentiate between appearance and reality: when Ahdut ha-Avoda came into being the Non-Affiliated Group constituted the majority within it, and this was more than a question of numbers. In effect, no veteran leader of Poalei Zion played a central part in Ahdut ha-Avoda, apart from Ben Gurion. The distinct impression is that Ben Gurion entered into an alliance with a new leadership group, which evolved into the historic leadership of the labor movement: Berl, Tabenkin, Remez, Yavne'eli – all leaders of the Agricultural Union. Eliyahu Golomb, who had become friendly with Berl in the Battalions, would soon join them as a junior partner. Hence, even if ostensibly Ahdut ha-Avoda adopted certain Poalei Zion positions, Poalei Zion, with the help of Ben Gurion, disappeared in effect from the political horizon. Yitzhak Ben Zvi was not greatly enamored of his comrade's conduct, but he was not strong enough to undermine the mighty partnership created between Berl and Ben Gurion.

The relations between Berl and Ben Gurion were different from Berl's previous patterns of relationships, based as they had been on intimacy, close political and intellectual affinity, a shared cultural background and experiences. These were replaced by dialog on the public-political plane, mutual understanding and appreciation: each considered the other a personality of the first rank. Together they were capable of impelling forward the Jewish settlement endeavor in Palestine.

At the same time, Berl's relations with A. D. Gordon – one of his closest personal friends – deteriorated. Gordon, who had lived with Berl in a tiny room at Kinneret throughout the war years; who, together with him and with Tabenkin, Israeli, Mordechai Kushnir and Noah Naftulsky, had dreamed of the unification of the labor movement, and opposed all manifestations of party politics – now objected bitterly to the establishment of Ahdut ha-Avoda. He interpreted its platform as a surrender to Poalei Zion and their repugnant socialist dogmas and internationalist theories. After Ahdut ha-Avoda came into being, Gordon, the non-party man, joined ha-Poel ha-Tzair and became its treasured symbol. Berl took the rift to heart, and tried to placate Gordon, but he never regretted his step.

The establishment of Ahdut ha-Avoda was one of the high points of Berl's life. He dominated the inauguration conference on 24 February 1919, in Petah Tikva, delivered the keynote address, formulated the resolutions, and supervised the election of its central body. Berl was now one of the chief leaders, if not *the* leader, of the most important body of the Palestinian labor movement. One of the characteristics of the Second Aliyah leadership was their conviction that they held the key to the construction of a utopia which conferred upon them the right, even the obligation, to lead others. Berl's haste in setting up Ahdut ha-Avoda derived, *inter alia*, from his desire to guide the expected new immigrants along the path of the unified labor movement under its united leadership, and to ensure that only one choice was open to them.

The Petah Tikva conference resolved Berl of the Second Aliyah into Berl the leader. He was well aware of the changes taking place in his life, and when the unification was imminent he began to plan his future life with Sara. Of all the places for which he had felt affection since his arrival in Palestine, he chose to live with her in urban Jaffa, the center of Ahdut ha-Avoda's activity. He continued to agonize over the trials of public life, but knew himself well enough to realize that his predilection for public activity was stronger than his desire for seclusion. He may have been influenced by Ben Gurion, who always tried to be at the center of events. At all events, he regarded the unification as a vote of confidence in him as a public leader. When Agnon met him in the early 1920s, for the first time since their pre-war conversations at Kinneret, the writer gained the impression that Berl 'is a man who has measured his own strength and knows that he is capable of action, but his modesty prevents his greatness from showing.'[19] From now on, he appeared outwardly as a leader, confident in his powers and in the course his life was taking.

After a separation of more than a year, Berl and Sara met again for the first time when he spent his leave in Palestine after the liberation of Galilee, in November 1918. Sara, who had spent the year dreaming of their life together when he returned, found a different Berl. Her Berl had preserved loving friendships, going back fifteen years to his youth in Bobruisk – friendships with Batya and Eliezer Schein, Leah and Sara herself. The new Berl greatly admired Zalman Rubashov and was impressed with the intellectual powers of Rachel Katznelson to the point of infidelity to Sara. The inability of Leah and Sara to write articles or deliver speeches suddenly appeared to him as a failing. At their long-awaited reunion he poured cold water on Sara's enthusiasm: 'What shall we do together?', he asked: 'I want the whole world, you want only love', and he launched into an analysis of the plight of modern woman, unable to content herself with housework, but also unable to make progress in any activity outside the home. He continued to swear that she was 'the ruler of my destiny' but hesitated to marry. In a letter she wrote him, permeated with jealousy and heartbreak, she quoted Evgeny Onegin's words to Tatiana:

> If I were one of those who rather
> Enjoy staid domesticity
> If as a husband and a father
> The kindly fates had fancied me.
> Where should I seek a dearer treasure?
> If for a moment I found pleasure
> In cosy scenes of fireside life,

You, you alone would be my wife.
I must confess, though loth to hurt you,
I was not born for happiness . . .
I am unworthy of your virtue;
I'd bring you nothing but distress.
My conscience speaks – pray let me finish;
My love, first warm, would soon diminish,
Killed by familiarity;
Our marriage would mean misery.

(*Poems, Prose and Plays of Alexander Pushkin*,
Modern Library, New York 1943, p. 186)

His affair with Rachel Katznelson and his sophisticated remarks about their relationship aroused in Sara profound doubts as to the sincerity of his feelings. She was obsessed by the idea that he was growing away from her, that she had become a burden to him, like Leah before her. Any delay in the post was agonizing for her. While Berl was immersed in feverish activity in connection with the unification, she remained – tormented by doubt and fear – at the remote and isolated village of Yesod ha-Maala. In the months which elapsed between his return to Tel el Kabir from his first leave in Palestine (December 1918) and the establishment of Ahdut ha-Avoda (end of February 1919) the two did not often meet. Berl was still in the army and political activity took up all his spare time. Despite his endeavors to appease her and allay her suspicions, she did not hasten to accept his suggestion that she find accommodation and employment near Jaffa. On one occasion, when he visited Galilee on behalf of the unification, she sat quietly in a corner during a workers' meeting, impressing all who saw her by her delicacy and the soft timbre of her voice. She joined the delegation from Kinneret to the Petah Tikva meeting and saw Berl at his finest hour, the crowned leader of the movement, borne aloft by his followers. Three weeks after the conference she wrote to him: 'You know, I am still under the impact of the meeting . . . you three [apparently Berl, Tabenkin and Ben Gurion] were like a living drama, with all the finest and most tragic and noble things, but this time it was not on stage, it was in real life.' But she also experienced difficult moments during the conference: 'Our spiritual relations have cost me a great deal.'[20] In his relations with her, Berl remained 'an incomplete man', as she herself had defined him.

At Passover 1919, Berl visited Yesod ha-Maala. The family of the local teacher, Petahia Levtov, had gone on a visit to Judea and left their house to Sara and Berl. They celebrated Passover alone: Leah refused to join them, on the pretext that it was the busy season at Kinneret. At Yesod ha-Maala Berl found the peace he needed, and it was there that he transcribed the speech he had delivered at the Ahdut ha-Avoda conference. It appears that during those Passover days they experienced a fullness of emotion and tranquility that they had lacked till then. According to one version, they decided to marry a month later. This sounds unlikely, since neither ever displayed a desire to give religious sanction to the ties between them. They may have decided that Sara would move to Judea, where Berl wanted them to set up home together. But this too seems unlikely, since at about that time Berl wrote to his brother Hayim, in the United States, a long and detailed letter, in which he sent him regards from all his Bobruisk friends, including Leah, Sara, Batya Schein and Tabenkin, and concluded: 'Not one of us has reached harbor'[21] without mentioning any ties to Sara.

Shortly after Berl's return from Yesod ha-Maala to his army unit, Petahia Levtov summoned him to Safed; Sara had fallen desperately ill with yellow fever, and had been taken to the Safed Hospital. When her condition deteriorated, she asked that Berl be called. On the same day, while *en route* to work in the Kinneret fields, Leah was filled with foreboding and an urgent compulsion to see Sara. She left her work and hastened to Upper Galilee. On the way, she learned that the nurse from Yesod ha-Maala had been taken to hospital at Safed. When she reached the hospital, she found Sara in a critical condition. Berl arrived the following day, Monday, by which time Sara was in a coma. Early on Tuesday morning she died, aged thirty.

In her lifetime, Berl's attitude towards her had undergone fluctuations; he had caused her great misery by his relations with Leah and, later, by his infidelity, the instability of his emotions, his denial of her instinct to consummate love in family life. After her death, however, Sara became the focus of his emotional life. His contemporaries were amazed that during her funeral at Kinneret, this usually reticent man wept bitterly and flung himself into the open grave. In her lifetime, he seemed unaware of her importance in his life, although for fifteen years, she was always in the background, his link to youth, to his home at Bobruisk. Her death supplied him with the constant pretext for torturing himself. His collapse at the graveside resulted from his pangs of conscience. He blamed himself for her death: he had not known how to make her happy.

The distinction between Berl as a private individual and as a public figure became even sharper after Sara's death. When the seven days of mourning were over, he returned to camp, profoundly depressed and impatient. He buried himself in work, particularly in editing, concealing his sorrow behind a wall of public activity, which none of his friends could breach. An open display of feelings was considered unseemly, and Berl faithfully observed this code of behavior.

The only person to whom he opened his heart was Leah Miron. After Sara's death, the 'threefold link', as Leah called it, was renewed.

From the beginning, Leah had been the most mature of the three. She displayed a fierce urge to protect the two people she loved, who were intellectually her superiors but lacked her emotional stability and physical sturdiness. Her renewed relationship with Berl, after Sara's death, emanated from her love for Berl and for Sara. As far as Leah was concerned, the guilt feelings and regrets which obsessed Berl for years after Sara's death, were justified. She never tried to comfort him by alleviating them. Rather the contrary: about a year after Sara's death, Leah could still write to him: 'For the thousand and first time the question surfaces: why couldn't you make Sara happy in her lifetime?'[22] Berl's infidelity was apparently the central theme in the painful talks between them. In his misery Berl reacted by displaying loyalty to her memory: months after her death, he wrote to Leah: 'And those were the days when in all I did and wherever I turned, I was with her. (Remote from betrayal. The miracle, which we hoped for all our lives, came to be . . .)'[23] He had also written: 'What is most important now for my life is that you recuperate and grow strong.'[24] And, a week later, in a note, he said: 'Today, the thirteenth Tuesday [i.e. the thirteenth week after her death] . . . I may come tomorrow. Where? It is as if I were ripped away from all my worlds. Is it possible that I may come and find a room for me, for you, far away from the city?'[25]

What should a woman feel when her lover writes to her: 'If I could only believe that one more meeting, one more look were possible . . . I spend my life amidst alien people, in matters which are superfluous . . . all the rest, my evenings, my nights, my mornings, for one person' – referring to the other woman, and in the same breath he adds: 'And with you, with the solitude of your days and nights, I live.'[26]

Before Berl left on his first mission to Europe (autumn 1919), the two of them apparently lived together in a room near Jaffa; but once Berl sailed, Leah returned to Kinneret. Berl could not let her go. She was his sole hope of setting up a family and home of his own. It was out of the question for him to establish a relationship with any other woman. Upon his return to Palestine, he asked her to return to him, to Jaffa: 'And by the time you come, I will find us some corner. Let us not be parted.' In his usual fashion, he appealed to her maternal instincts: he stressed his misery, his fatigue, his helplessness, and, in particular, his loneliness. When she was slow to reply, he hastened to despatch another letter, to tell her that he had found them a home near the workers' commune, organized by Ben Zion Israeli, south of Jaffa. This *kvutza* attempted to solve the problem of *kvutza* members who, because of their public obligations, were cut off from their own *kvutzot*, but wanted to continue to maintain a communal way of life. And again Berl emphasized his helplessness: he would not move there until she came . . . 'I lack the strength to arrange things . . . when you come, we will summon up strength.'[27] Leah could not resist his pleadings and joined him at the Jaffa *kvutza*. But she was not happy there. The relations between them took on a typical bourgeois pattern: she was allotted the role of the housewife providing her man with a comfortable and peaceful home. Moreover, she did not feel that Berl's heart was with her. Only a few months later, Berl, who had promised that he would not undertake any more journeys abroad, left again (summer 1920). Leah took the opportunity of his absence to try to break away; she returned to Kinneret, her refuge. When Berl learned of this, he sent her the nearest thing to a love letter he had ever written her:

You are in Kinneret. So I have heard. I will soon be back – and where shall I seek you? We have built up our pathetic little nest twig by twig, and now it has been abandoned. Shall I return and find it gone? Must we start again? If you only knew, Leahnka, how my heart trembles, like a leaf in the wind, wherever I go.

But even in this letter, intended to melt a woman's heart, Berl could not resist mentioning Sara: perhaps, perversely enough, he did so in an attempt to ensure Leah's fidelity to him and to her dead friend: 'Leahnka, you are there. You sit by the stone which covers my beloved. Tell her, tell her that I am keeping faith . . .' And then he appealed again to her emotions: 'Leahnka, why aren't you with me? At this time when my heart yearns for you, for your aid, when it is clear, and not only in thought, what we are and who we are, when the meager spark of life is

ignited.'[28] But Leah was not convinced of the sincerity of his sentiments. Nobody knew as well as she how profoundly he had despaired
after Sara's death, or to what extent 'you consumed all your emotional
energy in order to hold fast'.[29] 'There can be no life for me without
total spiritual content', she wrote to him. Not for her the routine family
life which was not based on deep emotion. 'To continue this life would
degrade me in my own eyes and clip my wings.' Leah loved him, as she
always had, but possessed sufficient inner strength to tear herself away
from him:

There are days when I feel exhaustion – I would have given my fate into the hands of
chance and into your hands. And then a human spirit inspires me, and, even now, at
my age, after 17–18 years, I am ready for anything. And if our hearts do not beat in
unison [sentence in Russian], as S [Sara] wrote to you, then we too are finished. This
is apparently our destiny. As for you, don't pity me. I am not yet lost. To bow my head
and live . . . like all 'decent' people . . . that I have not yet learned.[30]

Berl apparently succeeded in persuading her of the sincerity of his
love, or perhaps she was incapable of leaving him, despite her doubts.
Several times she tried to return to Kinneret, and from time to time,
when Berl embarked on his various missions – and between 1919 and
1921 he was abroad three times – she would pack her few belongings
and try to return to the way of life she had known before Berl became a
public personality. When she gave up hope of being able to remain at
Kinneret, which was then undergoing a severe crisis, since most of the
Second Aliyah group had left, she tried to settle at Ein Harod, a new
kibbutz, founded in 1921. She tried zealously to maintain her independence and to avoid being overshadowed by her life's companion. As a
true revolutionary, she shrank from giving official sanction to her
relationship with Berl: they never married. They did not even contemplate a secular ceremony, as did their friends, Rachel Yanait and Yitzhak
Ben Zvi. Because of Leah's irresolution, it was a protracted process
rather than a decisive step which rendered their ties permanent. Only
two years after Sara's death did Berl dare to give their relationship some
official stamp: when he was required to take out a membership card in
the Histadrut (Labor Union) for Leah, he filled in a form and wrote
that she was married to Berl Katznelson. As a result she was registered as
Leah Miron-Katznelson, and he apologized to her: 'Please do not be
angry with me because of the way they wrote the name. I wrote only
one word (the well known word to which we are not accustomed) and

they, on the basis of this, sent me a card with this name.'[31] Berl was about thirty-five and Leah thirty-four when they accepted the fact that they were destined to live together permanently. Their youthful love had long since faded and had been replaced by true intimacy: a self-revealing frankness on his part, a profound and sober understanding on hers, a bond of mutual dependence, which could never be severed. Berl could not live without her – and recognized the fact. But could he content himself with this in the long run as a substitute for love?

5

REVOLUTIONARY TIMES,
1919–1921

The Balfour Declaration and the British occupation of Palestine turned Zionism into a recognized national movement with legitimate and tenable aspirations. For the visionary Second Aliyah pioneers, the Balfour Declaration was considered a declaration of intent to establish Jewish rule in Palestine after a brief interim period or, at the least, to prepare the ground politically for immigration and wide-scale Jewish construction which would, within a few years, lead to the creation of a Jewish majority in Palestine. With 'politics' out of the way their main task appeared to be the building up of the land. This view was shared by such 'men of the world' as the leaders of the American Zionist movement, headed by Judge Brandeis. Among Eastern European Zionists, the Declaration was widely perceived as a step towards the immediate establishment of a Jewish state, and they came to the first post-war Zionist conference armed with lists of prospective ministers of the future state.

Disillusionment with the British authorities was soon to follow. Up to July 1920, the country was ruled by a military administration whose anti-Zionism was – according to some – overlaid with anti-Semitism. The British officers, trained in the pan-Arab Cairo school of thought, regarded the Balfour Declaration as a historical error perpetrated by politicians in Whitehall, ignorant of Middle Eastern conditions. They hoped to save the day by sabotaging government policy. The legal situation provided General Allenby and his colleagues with an anti-Zionist lever: under guise of preserving the status quo, as required of an occupying power, they managed to restrict the Zionists, while encouraging nationalist tendencies among the Palestinian Arabs. Their aim was to bolster the standing of Feisel, son of Sherif Hussein of Mecca, whom Lawrence of Arabia had chosen as future ruler of the Arabs of Syria and Palestine. This policy was reflected in numerous ways from refusal to recognize Hebrew as one of the official languages of Palestine to non-publication of the Balfour Declaration in the Middle East. Quite a few misunderstandings resulted from the differences in mentality between the British conquerors and the Jewish Yishuv, who had pinned great hopes on the British Army and were eager to extend a warm welcome to them. The British regarded these strange 'natives' with suspicion and distaste mingled with contempt. They had never met their like in the British Empire. They were people ambitious for immediate self-rule, over-fond of giving advice, and wont to make excessive and tiresome demands.

In Upper Galilee, which was a kind of no man's land between French-occupied territory in Syria and British-occupied Palestine, irregular Arab forces conducted raids in winter 1920 against the settlements of Metulla, Tel Hai, Kfar Giladi and Ayelet ha-Shahar. These culminated in a clash at Tel Hai on 2 February 1920 in which Trumpeldor (one of the founders of the Jewish Battalions and the leader of he-Halutz) and his fellow-defenders were killed. The Tel Hai affair did not undermine the Yishuv's confidence in the British. Rather the contrary: the courageous stand of the settlers in the North was perceived as justifying the extension of British occupation to Eastern Upper Galilee, including the sources of the Jordan. But only a month later, attitudes changed.

During the Moslem Feast of Nebi Mussa, in April 1920, an Arab mob attacked Jews in Jerusalem. The military authorities did not distinguish between attackers and victims; Jews who defended their families were arrested together with murderers and rapists. Zeev Jabotinsky was incarcerated in Acre fortress for organizing Jewish defense in Jerusalem, and his British judges refused to take into consideration the mitigating circumstances and his past record in the British Army as organizer of the Jewish Battalions.

Berl was not surprised by the conduct of the military administration: the Jews of the Pale of Settlement had always expected the worst of 'the authorities'. He considered the Arab attack a pogrom, the biased trials against the Jews and the suspension of immigration as encouragement for the rioters. Berl did not know of Allenby's plan to place Palestine under Feisel's rule, nor had he analyzed the aims of British Middle Eastern strategy. His reaction was born out of his instinctive hostility towards the stranger, the Gentile, the ruler – whether Russian, English or Arab. These emotions were as much second nature to Berl and his friends as their Yiddish speech, as the pages of Talmud they had learned by heart in childhood. In describing the funeral of the riot victims in Jerusalem (which Jews were banned from attending), Berl could not help adding: 'Only a Jew-baiting Russian Orthodox family stood on the balcony looking on.'[1] The military administration evoked associations with Amalek and Hadrian, the traditional enemies of the Jewish people. But whereas his perception of the situation issued from centuries of Jewish suffering, his response to it was the upshot of the rebelliousness of the generation of the First Revolution. Their disillusionment with the British led Berl and his comrades to rely once again on their own resources, as they had done in the Second Aliyah period. This attitude found expression in the establishment of the Hagana defense organization by Ahdut ha-Avoda.

In the wake of the San Remo Conference, the military administration was replaced by civilian government, and Herbert Samuel, a Jew and a Zionist, was appointed first High Commissioner of Judea. The Jews rejoiced: Samuel was compared to Nehemiah, Governor of Judea on behalf of the Persians, who revived Jewish settlement in Palestine in the Second Temple era. Berl did not share the general euphoria, and adopted a policy of 'wait and see'.

On 1 May 1921, riots broke out in Jaffa, sparked by a clash between Arabs and Jewish May Day demonstrators in the Neve-Shalom quarter. This time the attacks were broader in scope, and dozens of people were killed in the Jaffa Immigrant Center, in the streets and in the suburbs between Jaffa and Tel Aviv. On the following day, Brenner and several of his friends, who lived in an isolated house on the outskirts of Jaffa, were murdered. Berl was mortified and guilt-ridden at the death of the writer and he blamed himself for not having done enough to save him.

However, his sense of personal bereavement did not prevent him from conducting a reckoning with Samuel. On 3 May, the High Commissioner delivered a conciliatory speech aimed at allaying Arab apprehensions and ensuring the peace and quiet so vital for the expansion of the National Home. He further proclaimed the temporary suspension of immigration until the problem could be examined.

Berl and his colleagues were incensed by Samuel's policy. He had expected nothing of the British, and could not, therefore, claim to be disappointed with them. But he passed harsh and incisive judgment on Samuel, the Jew, for what he considered his cowardly failure to exact a toll for Jewish lives. He totally disregarded the complexity of the political situation, which had impelled Samuel, a sophisticated politician, well-versed in the intricacies of British policy, to act as he did. As far as Berl was concerned, Samuel was a renegade, an archetypal obsequious Jew.

At this time, he attributed scant importance to the sphere of political relations between the Yishuv and the Mandate Government. His priority was the organization of the Palestinian labor movement. Yet, instead of engaging in this work, as he would have wished, he traveled abroad a great deal during this period, gaining close acquaintance with Jewish communities overseas.

At the end of September 1919, Berl was sent on his first mission as a representative of Ahdut-ha-Avoda, with his two fellow party-members, Ephraim Bloch-Blumenfeld and Yisrael Shohat. They attended a conference of Poalei Zion in Stockholm and a session of the Zionist Actions Committee in London. The Zionist movement he discovered in London seemed to him powerless, uninspired and oblivious to its real challenges. The Jewish world was disintegrating: Russian Jewry had been severed from the rest of the Jewish people, its institutions were in disarray, and its society doomed to atomization. In Eastern and Central Europe, crisis had followed crisis – war, revolution, economic slump – and Jewish institutions had become enfeebled. At this momentous hour, the Zionist leadership had proved itself incapable of recruiting outstanding personalities into their ranks, and most certainly had not succeeded in enlisting the masses. 'Its leaders,' Berl commented, 'are old politicians',[2] detached from the young generation and unable to satisfy their thirst for action. Berl was now thirty-two, and he felt slighted by the attitude of the veterans: 'Neither logic nor justice can help. And by the time we too become old, we will be just like them – we have no hope of making things clear.'[3] This was almost certainly hyperbole. The leaders of the Zionist movement, though older than Berl, were far from being old men. The movement may not have been inundated with outstanding intellectual talents, but its leaders did include such impressive figures as Shmaryahu Levin, Menahem Ussishkin, Arthur Ruppin and, of course, Chaim Weizmann. Berl's complaints reflected the frustrations of a young man, very sure of himself, who has encountered people with a differing viewpoint and suffered defeat at the hands of the majority.

Nine months later, in July 1920, the first annual Zionist conference since the war was held in London and it assumed the form of a small-scale Zionist Congress. It was attended by the veteran Actions Committee members, and by representatives of national associations, many of them young people, responsive to new ideas and ready to accept revolutionary influences. Ahdut ha-Avoda sent an impressive delegation consisting of Tabenkin, Ben Gurion and Berl, and they were joined by young Poalei Zion delegates from England. The conference aroused strong emotions in Berl, a combination of affront, anger and the helpless resentment of a man stranded on the margins of historical events. His descriptions of the conference were biting. In a letter to his comrades in Palestine he described the convention hall and the splendid platform and added:

If there had been nothing but the audience down below and this sight above them – how wonderful it would have been. But for our edification the platform is full of gentlemen in stiff collars whose whole appearance has the charm of political mummies a century old. Each of them sits there in regal splendor trying to maintain a frozen expression on his face.[4]

There was indeed an element of absurdity in the elegance of the Congresses, the formal dress and elaborate etiquette (introduced originally by Herzl, and now but the last vestiges of his impressive leadership). But Berl's heavy sarcasm was undoubtedly misplaced. It resulted from the fact that he found himself in a new and disconcerting atmosphere. The leaders of the movement treated him with the patronizing and gently mocking affection which adults bestow on a precocious child, as yet untouched by life. This must have been trying for him, as he considered himself worthy of Zionist leadership.

Here, as at the Zionist Actions Committee session in summer 1919, Berl became increasingly depressed as the deliberations proceeded. Weizmann delivered a highly critical address on the conduct of the Yishuv, its demands and complaints, and the unbecoming reception it gave to the Zionist Commission sent to Palestine to represent the Zionist Organization.* Ben Gurion responded with a violent attack on the Commission and on the policies of the Actions Committee towards the Jewish community in Palestine: its neglect of the Jewish Battalions

---

* The Yishuv was organized in a legal body known as Knesset Israel, to which every Jew was affiliated unless he opted out (as did representatives of Agudat Israel, the anti-Zionist religious party). The members of Knesset Israel elected a parliamentary body known as Asefat ha-Nivharim (Elected Assembly) from which a Vaad Leumi (National Committee) was elected, in which all the parties in the Assembly were proportionally represented.

then facing demobilization and its failure to aid Jabotinsky and the other Jews imprisoned as a result of their participation in Jewish defense against the rioters. Weizmann counter-attacked: an experienced speaker of considerable rhetorical powers, and the Balfour Declaration to his credit, he easily vanquished Ben Gurion – adopting the same chiding, paternal manner which so infuriated Berl. His somewhat lighthearted attitude towards the ponderous seriousness of the Palestinian labor delegates was deeply offensive to them: they felt that the Zionist movement must accept their plans, criticism and standpoint if it hoped to become a popular movement. For Weizmann and his colleagues they were the representatives of yet another of the many bodies constituting the Zionist movement.

The main subject of dispute between the Palestinians and the great majority of the Zionist Organization was the question of the role of private capital and national capital in developing the country. The labor delegation submitted a draft resolution, according to which 'the purchase of land in Palestine is to be concentrated solely in the hands of the Jewish National Fund, as the eternal possession of the Jewish people'.[5] The implication was that the purchase of land in Palestine by private Jewish capital should be banned. Moreover, they proposed that the funds of the Zionist Organization should not be used to extend credit to privately-owned farms; it was to be used solely for purchase of national lands and for the consolidation of farms established thereon. These demands derived from the view that private capital would seek the most profitable investment rather than one which served the national interest. It would therefore contribute to the employment of Arab labor – cheaper and more efficient than Jewish, and work to the detriment of Jewish workers. They demanded that the Zionist movement direct its resources to settlement based on nationalized land. In other words, they wanted the socialist ideal realized through the instruments of the Zionist Organization.

The London Conference rejected the proposals of the representatives of labor Palestine, and indeed the Zionist Organization could scarcely have banned land purchase by Jews in Palestine. This would have aroused a furore among potential Jewish settlers, to say nothing of how the British would have reacted to such a socialist demand. But Berl and his comrades regarded this as a humiliating defeat and a demonstration of distressing shortsightedness on the part of the Zionist Organization.

This was the first of numerous attempts to force the Organization to accept the national and socialist outlook of the workers with regard to the role of national capital in the settlement and development of Palestine, and its failure caused Berl to level bitter criticism against the parliamentary system of the Zionist Organization. He was not really familiar with the system, and did not like what he saw of it in action in London. He lacked the patience to play the 'democratic game', and felt that democracy frustrated the weak and non-influential – like himself. 'We are not worthy of our task', he wrote to Leah, and this was a bitter pill indeed for the up-and-coming leader of the Palestinian labor movement.[6]

His critical view of the 'formal' democracy of the conference corresponded to his disparaging view of the delegates who, in his view, represented the interests of their constituents rather than those of Palestine. The problems of Palestine were a closed book to them and they were naturally wary of resolutions submitted by unknown young people, suspected of Bolshevik tendencies. They preferred to rely on the judgment of their revered leadership. The frustrated Berl attributed this conduct to personal ambitions and to the undue influence of Weizmann. When the labor delegates realized that the Zionist Organization would not accept their viewpoint, they moderated their demands and proposed instead that Jewish National Fund land and financial aid be guaranteed for labor settlement. And, in fact, the Zionist Organization did accept as a basic tenet the obligation of financing the settlement of impecunious workers. Ruppin reflected this approach by proposing the establishment of a workers' bank, to finance various workers' groups and cooperatives, its primary funds to be drawn from the budget of the Zionist Organization.

The labor movement was almost totally dependent on the Zionist Organization, yet Berl nevertheless fought zealously against the dangers of political patronage and succeeded. The Zionist Organization was to finance the bank, but representatives of labor were to manage the bank and decide on the allocation of funds.

The weakness of the labor movement at the London conference mirrored the weakness of the Yishuv in general within the Zionist organization, then in its prime. Just as the Yishuv had rebelled against the authority of the Zionist commission, preferring to conduct its own affairs, so Berl and his comrades rebelled, insisting upon and gaining autonomy for their movement and authority over their constituents. No other body in the Yishuv could match this success.

Many of Berl's comrades in the Poalei Zion Alliance contemplated leaving the Zionist Organization. Not Berl. In spite of all his criticism, he had no doubts that the place of the labor movement was within the Zionist movement, both on principle – in order to preserve national unity, and for practical reasons: settlement work could not be carried out in Palestine without the Zionist Organization. Berl's fury was that of an opposition aspiring to power, not to breaking up the game. He hoped that the Zionist Organization would change when a young and daring generation of leaders took over. But for this to happen, a widespread, influential labor movement had to emerge in Palestine and in the Diaspora. Regrettably, the Zionist labor movement in the Diaspora was in a most precarious position at the time, on the verge of collapse.

The event which had the most forcible impact on the labor movement at the time was the Bolshevik Revolution. The challenge of building a new, just and egalitarian society, and molding better and more humane individuals, kindled the enthusiasm of millions. It swept aside national allegiances all over the world and within the Jewish people as well. Jews followed events in Soviet Russia with bated breath. the great majority of them, recent emigrants from Russia, were still inextricably linked to the country which had so cruelly treated them. The revolution offered salvation from oppression to Jews in Russia, giving them equal rights, and they responded to it with the eagerness of the outsider suddenly welcomed in. The pleasures of belonging, of feeling at one with the great Russian nation, of taking part in the construction of a new world, overcame the restraints imposed by tradition, and long, bitter experience. The Jewish parties in Russia renounced their national bonds. The Zionist socialist parties, like Poalei Zion, were the first to respond, at first, out of a desire to belong and later, for fear of reprisal for holding aloof. Abroad, where coercion was not a factor, similar processes operated. Distance obscured the ruin of Jewish communities, the destruction of Jewish life, the impoverishment of the Jewish masses. From afar, these appeared as unavoidable evils on the road to the creation of a new society, in which the Jews would find their rightful place.

In Palestine as well, the Bolshevik Revolution had a profound impact. Fears for the safety of friends and family mingled with soaring hopes. Horrific reports came through of pogroms and of the ravages of the Civil War, but there was also stirring news of the new order. A delegation from the Poalei Zion Alliance, which visited Palestine in 1920, brought something of the flavor of the Revolution with it. One of its members even voiced the hope that the Red Army would come from Caucasia, and import the Revolution to Palestine. There was great enthusiasm in labor circles. Criticism, when it was voiced, was directed mainly against the Jewish socialist parties, and above all, against Poalei Zion, which had hastened to jump on the bandwagon, dissociating itself from its Jewish ties.

Berl witnessed events in Russia with mixed feelings. On the one hand, he saw in the vanquishing of a despotic regime, the democratization of society, the great land reforms, the elevation of the status of women and children, the granting of equal rights to national minorities, and revolutionary simplicity, the culmination of his youthful dreams. On the other hand, he was not blind to the violent and bloody nature of the triumphant revolution. The images of Herzen – the socialist inspired by moral truth, humanitarianism and recognition of man's value, and Nichayev, the nihilist – destroying a world in order to rebuild, believing in the good born out of an evil impervious to human suffering – these two men symbolized for Berl the basic duality of the Revolution. During the Civil War, Berl published anonymously in *Kuntres* (Pamphlet), the Ahdut ha-Avoda weekly, his reflections on Russia, the Revolution and Russian literature:

'If the world's happiness is to be achieved at the expense of an infant's tear – then I wash my hands of happiness and of the world, and I return my bond to my Creator' – thus speaks Russia through Ivan Karamazov.

What, therefore, is the path you are pursuing, near and distant Russia, steeped in blood?

'If I ever attain the highest level of human progress and happiness, I shall demand of historical Providence a reckoning for every lost soul, and if no answer is forthcoming, then I shall cast myself from the highest storey and smash my skull' – thus Vissarion Belinsky. Which road, therefore, are you treading, tortured and weary, sacred and crazed Russia?

And who can understand you? Childishly pure as Raskolnikov or darkly profane as Smerdiakov? Distant-near homeland, alien yet dear.[7]

The moral yardsticks by which Berl measured the Revolution emanated from his fundamental belief that the aim of socialism was the liberation of man. A revolution which brought in its wake the devaluation and degradation of humanity was incapable of nurturing a new individual who would build a socialist society. Evil – namely terror –

could not be the means for achieving good – i.e. socialism. Berl was never tempted by Bolshevism even when his close associates in Ahdut ha-Avoda, Ben Gurion, and even more so Tabenkin, were captivated by its resoluteness, drive and sweeping action. Berl conceded the achievements of Bolshevism, but did not consider that they justified the loss of humanity. He could not subscribe to the Russian proverb: 'When one chops down trees – splinters fly.'

His negative assessment of Bolshevism was also colored by Zionist considerations. He was perhaps unique in his early comprehension of the significance of the great enthusiasm for international communism which touched large sections of the Jewish intelligentsia, and particularly the young generation: every young talented Jew who chose to dedicate his life to communism was a loss to the Zionist movement. The same idealism, self-sacrifice and readiness to take up a burden for the common good, 'the joy of sacrifice', as Berl called it, which characterized the best of Jewish youth, could lead them either to communism or to pioneering Zionism. Hence, the element of jealousy and competition in his attitude towards the 'world of the future'.

The arena for the struggle between socialist Zionism and communism at that time was the Jewish labor movement. When Ahdut ha-Avoda was established, it was assumed that, as the heir of the Palestinian Poalei Zion, it would join the World Alliance of Poalei Zion. The decision was made largely out of a desire to appease the Poalei Zion leaders who had joined Ahdut ha-Avoda, such as Ben Zvi, Blumenfeld and Shohat. Berl, Tabenkin and their comrades did not pin great hopes on the Jewish parties in the Diaspora. In 1919 it appeared that young Jews were beginning to organize immigration to Palestine outside the existing parties – in he-Halutz in Russia and in similar organizations elsewhere in Eastern Europe. The Alliance was not considered vitally important. But, at the same time, it was the largest socialist Zionist association and its apparatus, its financial resources and its propaganda organs could be used to advantage for the development of Palestine.

In summer 1919, the first post-war gathering of representatives of the Alliance was convened in Stockholm. It was a prolonged series of discussions, lasting three whole months, with delegates from various countries coming and going all the time. Berl came with Blumenfeld and Yisrael Shohat, who were former members of Poalei Zion, and although they did not concur with the theories of their partners to the

Alliance, they were very much at home in its political jargon and way of thinking. Berl had never held Borochovist ideas, and the rhetoric and philosophizing of the leftist bloc left him cold. Ahdut ha-Avoda was accepted into the Alliance after a debate, although its non-Marxist prognosis was held suspect by the Polish members of the Alliance. Moreover, the representatives of Ahdut ha-Avoda were enthusiastic Hebraists, an isolated few among the great mass of Yiddish speakers at Stockholm. They were charged with debasing Yiddish in Palestine and forced, so as to keep the peace, to abandon their extremist position on this question, and reconcile themselves to the preferred status of Yiddish in the movement abroad.

Berl felt like an outsider at Stockholm. He resembled the suitor for the hand of a favorite daughter, whose credentials are scrupulously examined by the bride's family. But the crux of his differences with his comrades was his particular view of Jewish reality. A disciple of the Second Aliyah, he saw all of life through the prism of Palestine. He judged every question, every new phenomenon, by one yardstick: was it advantageous or detrimental to the development of the Jewish community in Palestine? In the eyes of the others, Berl and his like were self-centered people, intent on creating a separatist tribe in Palestine, independent of the Diaspora. They were impervious to Berl's charm and he was alienated from them.

Berl concluded, as a result of his encounter with the higher echelon of Poalei Zion, that the Alliance, despite its weaknesses, was capable of rallying all as yet unorganized Jewish workers to the cause of Palestine – on condition, *inter alia*, that it absorb into its ranks the non-dogmatic pioneering socialist elements within Tzeirei Zion. The latter had become a mass movement in Eastern Europe, and sections of it had displayed a leaning towards Ahdut ha-Avoda. This association could serve as a counterweight to the leftist leanings of several Poalei Zion parties, particularly that of Poland. His despair at the existing Zionist and Jewish labor establishments whose leadership was frittering away its days in intellectual squabbles, was offset by the masses of young people who were eager to act, and were serious about Palestine. These seventeen- and eighteen-year-olds, who were joining he-Halutz, Tzeirei Zion and other pioneering movements, were for Berl the great hope of Zionism.

The Stockholm conference was the prologue to the great drama which was played out in Vienna a year later, during the Fifth Annual Conference of the Poalei Zion World Alliance. In Stockholm, the exuberant encounter between delegates from Eastern Europe, the West and Palestine had, for a time, masked the crisis which Poalei Zion had undergone in the wake of the revolution. But the year which elapsed between the two gatherings saw an intensification of internal conflict. The Third International, the Comintern, was established and split the socialist parties in Europe into communist and socialist bodies. The latter maintained their allegiance to the Second International.

The burning issue at the Vienna Conference was the attitude of the delegates to the Third International. The representatives of Russian Poalei Zion (who had already split into three separate parties, differing slightly with each other with regard to communism) sported red flowers in their buttonholes, signifying that they represented the cradle of the revolution. They and particularly the representative of the Jewish Communist Party – Alexander Hashin, a former leader of Palestinian Poalei Zion – demanded unqualified acquiescence to the Comintern's conditions for acceptance: dissociation from the Zionist Organization, and total commitment to the Revolution as the sole answer to the Jewish problem. All the Eastern European delegates supported this stand. Kaplansky,* on the other hand, proposed that Poalei Zion join the Third International on condition that the International accept the unique nature of every movement for national liberation, i.e., the right to self-determination of the world Jewish proletariat, and its right to create a Jewish socialist society in Palestine. This proposal won the support of Ahdut ha-Avoda's delegates, and the representatives of the United States and of Great Britain.

The Ahdut ha-Avoda delegation was of outstanding caliber – Ben Gurion, Tabenkin, Ben-Zvi and Berl. But the 'Russians', reinforced by the 'Viennese', set the tone of the conference. The focus of attention was the question of how to win the sympathy of Soviet Russia. Ben Gurion, Ben-Zvi and Tabenkin, all former members of Poalei Zion, were listened to attentively.

Berl remained an outsider. He, who had worked indefatigably for the unification of the Palestinian workers, set his sights on a split. Not having been in at the birth of the Alliance, he felt no sentiment towards it: as a bystander, he found it easy to perceive the acuteness of the con-

---

* A leader of Poalei Zion in Vienna, an outstanding intellectual, and among the first Ahdut ha-Avoda representatives on the Zionist Executive. In Palestine he advocated viewpoints somewhat to the left of the central policy of Ahdut ha-Avoda.

flicts. Those for whom the world revolution was 'the greatest issue of all',[8] assessed every act of omission or commission in Palestine according to one sole criterion – whether it was good or bad for the revolution. For Berl and his comrades, the central question remained: to what end were the creative energies of the movement to be harnessed – to the world revolution or to the development of Palestine? The debate was, essentially, a highly practical one.

The split at the Vienna conference illustrates Berl's attitude towards questions of unity and division: unity was a positive force, when it linked similar elements and prevented the squandering of effort on imaginary conflicts. But organizational unity, which merely plastered over fundamental differences – as at Vienna – was negative, and Berl preferred a split. The schism at Vienna transformed Ahdut ha-Avoda into the leading force within the Poalei Zion Alliance. It now became the nucleus for a new Alliance, of smaller scope but of greater cohesiveness and capacity for action.

The movement in the Diaspora was intended to serve as the reservoir for the Palestinian movement, a source of manpower and of funds. But the veteran Poalei Zion members were growing old, while the young flocked to Tzeirei Zion. Berl felt that if Ahdut ha-Avoda did not find the way to a union between Tzeirei Zion and Poalei Zion, it would forfeit the young generation, the pioneers. This would have immediate implications for the situation in Palestine. Tzeirei Zion provided the major source of immigrants to Palestine, and if they moved away from Ahdut ha-Avoda, the latter would lose touch with the emergent labor movement in Palestine and would lose its ascendancy over ha-Poel ha-Tzair, which was also battling for the hearts of Tzeirei Zion.

The grandiose Zionist schemes devised after the Balfour Declaration had produced scant results: in the four years since the British took Palestine, almost nothing had been done to develop the country. Berl and his friends had placed great hopes in the availability of national capital – but it never materialized, nor were lands purchased on a large scale. The only striking achievement was the purchase of the Jezreel Valley lands from the Arab Sursuk family. No initiative for settlement was taken until after the 1921 Zionist Congress at Karlsbad, when Shlomo Levkovitch's scheme for the establishment of a 'large *kvutza*' in the Jezreel Valley was approved. Apart from this move – which came relatively late, two years after the Third Aliyah began – national capital played little part in Palestinian development. Both veteran workers and newcomers were directly affected by this stalemate. The Zionist Organization astounded prospective immigrants by advising them not to come – partially for this reason. It also explains the failure to absorb American veterans of the Jewish Battalions who wanted to settle on the land in Palestine, and who, for lack of opportunity, returned to the United States or to Britain.

Rescue for the Third Aliyah pioneers came from an unexpected quarter – the Mandate Government, which undertook a wide-scale roadbuilding project in the north. In these 'labor universities', the Labor Brigade, the Jezreel Valley group and even ha-Shomer ha-Tzair (The Young Watchman), the main components of the Third Aliyah, were consolidated. The daily wage of the roadbuilders was small, but it enabled them to keep body and soul together until the settlement schemes materialized. The work was carried out on a contractual basis by the political parties: one road was built by Ahdut ha-Avoda, another by ha-Poel ha-Tzair and another by the Mizrahi, the Religious Zionist Party. The work provided welcome respite but this was scarcely the grand development project which had been envisioned.

The dire economic situation adversely affected not only individuals but the political parties as well. Ahdut ha-Avoda could hardly afford to employ a single functionary no matter how meager the wages. The publication of *Kuntres*, the party weekly, and *ha-Adama* (The Soil), the literary journal edited by Brenner, required considerable financial outlay. Such minor matters as the despatch of party lecturers to the roadworkers' camps or to immigrant hostels entailed payment of fares, even if speakers' fees were dispensed with. It was too costly to send telegrams abroad. The Agricultural Center, which concerned itself with settlement matters, suffered from a lack of active workers, ha-Mashbir accumulated heavy deficits, and members of the party executive found it necessary to spend most of their time seeking ways to support themselves. If Ahdut ha-Avoda was to survive, money had to be found. Consequently, Berl decided that the acquisition of funds from Poalei Zion sources was an urgent task. He appealed to the movement in the English-speaking countries, where he felt that there were good prospects. This was one of the main reasons why Ben Gurion was sent on a mission to Poalei Zion in London. Before he had had time to settle down there, Berl wrote to him: 'You must find the hidden keys there in London – or else, we will perish in our poverty.'[9] But very little came of it.

When Berl returned from his second trip to Europe, he was shocked at what he found in Palestine. Whole families were on the verge of starvation; Brenner was looking for gainful employment as a manual laborer; and while the teachers employed by the Cultural Committee were still at their tasks, they had not received any payment for months on end. Yitzhak Tabenkin, the only member of the Party Executive who had not left Jaffa in search of some kind of work, was unable to achieve anything. The only ray of light was the profit which accrued from the roadwork and enabled Berl to subsidize the journals and other party institutions.

The fact that the roadbuilding project saved Ahdut ha-Avoda from destitution points to the fundamental change which had taken place in Palestine during Berl's attendance at the London and Vienna conferences in the summer of 1920. The Third Aliyah had become the decisive factor in the labor movement, if not in quality – so Berl apparently thought to the end of his days – then at least numerically. The young pioneers from Tzeirei Zion, he-Halutz and the Z.S. (Zionist Socialist Party in Russia), had rapidly become the majority of workers in Palestine. In the Diaspora the various pioneering groups had a history of political mergers and splits. By this time Tzeirei Zion was only loosely affiliated with the Palestine ha-Poel ha-Tzair and he-Halutz was declaratively non-partisan. In effect, upon their arrival in Palestine, the new immigrants encountered two political camps, two contracting offices, two labor exchanges, each vying for their sympathies. Ha-Poel ha-Tzair had stolen a march on Ahdut ha-Avoda in organizing immigration and thus won considerable influence among the new arrivals, both for bringing them to Palestine and for finding them employment upon arrival. On the other hand, these young people came at the peak of the revolutionary wave in Central Europe and in Russia, and their socialist Zionist views harmonized more with those of Ahdut ha-Avoda than with the non-socialist ha-Poel ha-Tzair.

At this time there was a campaign underway to establish an all-embracing trade union, launched at the initiative of Joseph Trumpeldor, the leader of the non-partisan he-Halutz. It was aimed at rectifying the disgraceful situation whereby each newcomer was met at the port by representatives of both labor parties, each seeking to recruit him the moment he set foot on Palestinian soil. Berl, despite his past efforts at unifying the labor movement, was not enthusiastic about Trumpeldor's scheme, nor was he taken with the mood prevailing among the roadworkers. The union they planned would encompass all the Palestinian Jewish workers, but without the anarcho-syndicalist philosophy which was germane to Ahdut ha-Avoda.

It was to be a strictly trade-union body. Politics and culture would be left to the parties, which, while not being abolished, would relegate some of their tasks to the new union. Berl objected to this conception, fearing that the large, amorphous new body would lack ideological content.

In November 1920, Berl toured the roadworkers' camps and centers of new immigrants. It was the first encounter of the Third Aliyah pioneers with the man who had come to personify the Second Aliyah. They had grown up in a world of chaos, war and revolution, at a time when the Jewish community and the Jewish family were disintegrating. Many of them had been cut off from Jewish tradition at too early an age to have been permanently influenced by it. Some of them had absorbed the spirit of the Bolshevik revolution, others had been drawn to the theories of Freud or of Buber. Berl's heroes were alien to them, his ideas different. Some found his style of speech and lengthy discourse reminiscent of the *bet midrash* (school of religious studies) – and no compliment was intended thereby. Nonetheless, with his indefatigability and his customary rapid-fire delivery, he was apparently reasonably persuasive. Within a month the new immigrants had agreed to include a considerable part of Ahdut ha-Avoda's platform in theirs. They recognized, for instance, the need for activity abroad and for the establishment of an organization in the Diaspora which would support labor Palestine. But, accustomed as they were to the separation of political and trade-union activities, they refused to accept Ahdut ha-Avoda's monistic approach. Although many of these young pioneers joined Ahdut ha-Avoda immediately after the establishment of the Histadrut, they were adamant in their refusal to accept Berl's basic viewpoint.

He was obliged, therefore, to concede to them. When the decisive moment arrived at the Conference in Haifa, in December 1920, and the General Federation of Jewish Workers in Palestine (the Histadrut) was established, he withdrew his demand for total unity, and accepted the verdict of the majority. The labor movement urgently needed a representative body of legal standing, able to appear as a party to agreements with the Zionist Organization (on the workers' bank, for example), and with the Mandate Government (namely roadbuilding projects). Berl, well aware of the problem, could not remain aloof, merely because the new body did not meet all his expectations. Moreover, he was convinced that the affinity of the Third Aliyah immigrants to Ahdut ha-Avoda would contribute ultimately to the internal unity of the Histadrut and the scope and sphere of its activities would expand naturally. History vindicated Berl in this respect.

The leadership of Ahdut ha-Avoda at the time was composed of people of unusual organizational and intellectual talents, singularly dedicated, energetic and imaginative. They were men and women of strong, sometimes overpowering, personalities, and their ability to work as a team derived to a large extent from their interdependence, their profound sense of camaraderie and the sense of urgency which drove them on: they believed that they, and they alone, carried the burden of Jewish redemption on their shoulders, in the face of a hostile or indifferent Gentile world and a deteriorating Jewish world. There were three recognized leaders in the group, Berl, Ben Gurion and Tabenkin, but Berl was the *primus inter pares*. When he returned from his second trip to Europe, the Ahdut ha-Avoda Executive convened in order to discuss his future work. The discussion was summed up by Eliyahu Golomb, who said: 'Because we are not satisfied with much of what we have done, we think that everything can be remedied by Berl, by bringing him into all the projects . . .',[10] Ultimately, Berl chose those areas which appealed to him most – and his colleagues hastened to accept his choice. After the founding convention of the Histadrut, at which Shmuel Yavne'eli made the most impressive speech, it was still Berl who attracted the most attention, who evoked the most affection, who aroused the highest hopes. He was a man of whom great things were expected and who could never disappoint his admirers. Berl conducted the party's correspondence with the Poalei Zion Alliance, with Ben Gurion, who was then in London, and with *Die Zeit*, the American Poalei Zion paper. He was in charge of the movement's other foreign contacts, and in addition, had absolute control over the party's propaganda organ, *Kuntres*.

Berl's status within the party was determined to no small extent by the attitudes of Tabenkin and Ben Gurion: they had absolute confidence in him which, combined with profound admiration, bordered on self-effacement.

It was apparently Berl's common sense (a quality which Tabenkin attributed to him) which appealed so strongly to his fellow-leaders. His analysis of the situation, both in Palestine and abroad, and his understanding of the spirit of the pioneering movement, proved, in most cases, correct. His rare eloquence lent particular weight to his opinions and proposals. But his pragmatism, his simple ability to get things done, was his hallmark: he extracted funds from the settlement institutions of the Zionist Organization, found Jewish donors in London and Vienna willing to finance the party's projects, and mobilized the Jewish labor movement in the United States to raise funds for the purchase of machinery and tools and their despatch to Palestine. He was not above canvassing for subscribers to *Kuntres*, or bargaining with Poalei Zion leaders in the United States for payment for cables, or reminding a potential donor that he had not yet made good his pledge.

Berl responded to the indulgent affection and esteem of his fellow-leaders. He accepted it as self-evident, and did not exploit it to dominate his colleagues. The trust was mutual. Moreover, it seemed that his ability to act was based to no small extent on his sense of being loved, and being depended upon.

But there were two areas of difficulty. Within the movement, the Third Aliyah did not accept Berl's authority unquestioningly. The Labor Brigade and ha-Shomer ha-Tzair were cohesive groups with their own leadership, and for them Berl remained an outsider, representative of the 'old' leadership of the Second Aliyah. While this did not affect Berl's immediate status within the movement, since at the time these groups were not crucial, it did portend trouble for the future.

Of greater significance was Berl's own ambivalent view of his position. With his colleagues and in public, he radiated self-confidence, immersed as he was in activity in Palestine and abroad. But to Leah, he confided his trepidation at the immensity of his tasks. The old inner strife still plagued him and he longed to return to agricultural work and to the peace and satisfaction it granted. Public activity really was the focus of his life, and success in this sphere brought him happiness. But he remained apprehensive of any group of people with which he did not share complete rapport. Furthermore, the memories of Brenner and Sara Schmuckler haunted him, and for years he could not, or would not, seek release from them.

This inner dissatisfaction was not a pose, as is sometimes the case with successful politicians, who 'long for' respite but cannot let go. Continually tormented with doubts, he wrote to Leah: 'Woe to the

115

labor movement whose leaders we are.' Berl was mourning Berdichevsky, who had been a spiritual father to him and to Brenner. Of Berdichevsky he said: ' "Leader" – how pointless is this word when used with regard to him. In our times, when leaders are neither saints, nor teachers nor poets, but any tyro politician who knows how to win the heart of a party or to win himself a group of disciples.'[11]

Berl's malaise did not stem from a sense of inferiority where his colleagues were concerned. He did not hesitate to undertake those tasks which he and the movement considered vital at the time. His doubts, as expressed in his letters to Leah, derived from the gap between will and ability, the old affliction which Brenner had described. Berl judged himself according to the absolute criteria which he himself had established, and found himself wanting: he was neither a saint, nor a Rabbi nor a poet: he lacked the divine spark. Mere political leadership did not satisfy him; charismatic leadership appeared beyond his capacities. He considered himself, finally, unworthy of being a leader. But, as the years went by, he came to accept his weaknesses, if only out of comparison with his rivals.

6

MISSION TO THE UNITED STATES,
1921–1922

The most crucial question facing the Zionist movement as a whole and the Histadrut in particular, after its founding at the end of 1920, was the economic development of Palestine. The Keren ha-Yesod fund-raising campaign of the Zionist Organization had set itself a target of £25,000,000 sterling, a sum which could have generated much-needed economic activity. Unfortunately, the results of the campaign were meager. Much more abundant than funds, were plans, some of them large-scale and serious, others merely hare-brained schemes. For Berl and his comrades, it was often difficult to tell which was which.

To Berl's credit, and to Ben Gurion's, is the fact that they were both strongly taken by Pinhas Rutenberg's plan for the construction of a hydro-electric power system for the country. Moshe Shertok, for example, doubted Rutenberg's credibility and derided the idea.

Rutenberg, an irrigation engineer by training, had in his youth been a fervent S.R.P. revolutionary activist and had taken part in the plan to execute the *agent-provocateur*-priest, Gapon. No doubt, Rutenberg's stormy past and fiery temperament enhanced Berl's enthusiasm for the power project and when Rutenberg insisted that Berl go to the United States to help raise money and support, Berl readily accepted. As usual the trip abroad was exploited for additional purposes: Poalei Zion conferences, the Zionist Congress at Karlsbad, fund-raising for the Hagana (Jewish defense units), among others.

Berl left Palestine in June 1921, but reached the United States only in November, having spent time in Europe on the conferences. During this time, Rutenberg succeeded in obtaining a concession for his scheme from the British, making Berl's efforts on his behalf less than crucial. Berl's trip took another focus. It will be recalled that the Zionist Organization had agreed to support the establishment of a workers' bank, but it had made its support conditional on the provision of matching funds from the workers themselves. This now became Berl's task.

117

Berl arrived in the United States as a member of a Histadrut delegation: Yosef Baratz represented ha-Poel ha-Tzair and Manya Shohat and Berl represented Ahdut ha-Avoda. This was the first deputation sent on behalf of organized labor in Palestine, rather than on behalf of a particular party. But it was not the first time that the workers of Palestine had appealed to their comrades in the United States. For the Jewish world, decimated and impoverished by the First World War and its aftermath, American Jewry was both the cornucopia and the new center of gravity of the Jewish people.

The trouble was that American Jewry was not yet ready to accept responsibility for the fate of the Jewish people, and even less so for the development of Palestine. The old American-Jewish establishment of German origin was ready for philanthropy as was the Joint Distribution Committee in Russia and other Eastern European countries. But they had little sympathy for Jewish national aspirations, considering them a threat to their full integration in American society.

The Jewish immigrants from Eastern Europe, and particularly those who had arrived in the first two decades of the century, were different. They worked hard for a living and their main drive was for economic security and subsequent integration in American society. For the present, however, they lived within a closed immigrant society. They had brought with them from the Pale of Settlement a spontaneous sense of national solidarity which was sustained by the life they shared in the ghettoes of the East Coast. The leadership which came from labor and trade union circles, and from the Jewish socialist parties, subsequently fostered popular Yiddish culture. There were numerous newspapers, publishing houses and a flourishing theater. The *Forverts*, edited by Abe Cahan, had half a million readers, and there were other dailies, such as *Der Tog*, *Der Morgen Journal*, and an important monthly, *Die Zukunft*. A Poalei Zion paper, *Die Zeit*, appeared between 1921 and 1922.

American Jewry had a national consciousness, but it was not Zionist in orientation. The minority who were actively interested in politics gravitated to the ideas of the Bund: socialism, the improvement of the lot of the masses and the fostering of national awareness, – but not Zionism and Palestine. The Zionists were regarded as reactionaries, tied to religious tradition and to the middle classes and suspected of persecuting the Yiddish language in Palestine.

Berl arrived in the United States in November 1921 aboard the *Kremania*, with much publicity and fanfare. He had hoped that his comrades in the American branch of the Poalei Zion Alliance would organize an impressive tour for him. But the party had no outstanding leaders, only a mediocre party organ, and an ineffective apparatus. It was further divided between left and right, sworn Yiddishists and those who hardly cared. Some of the prominent members were indifferent, even hostile, to the Palestinians. Berl's support came from a relatively narrow circle of intellectuals and trade union leaders who were affiliated neither with the Bund nor with the *Forverts* circle, nor identified formally with Poalei Zion. Nonetheless, the first few days of his stay seemed promising. Trade union leaders proved willing to help; the *Morgen Journal* publicized the delegation and its objectives, using warm words of praise for Berl, and Manya Shohat arranged a meeting between Berl and Dr J. L. Magnes, leader of the New York Jewish Community and one of the founders of the American Joint Distribution Committee. Magnes, scion of an old American-Jewish family, was very influential in labor circles because of his pacifist stand during the war, and his moral integrity. Magnes not only welcomed the delegation, he involved himself wholeheartedly in activity on its behalf. At a meeting in their honor, he introduced them in Hebrew, thus demonstrating his support for that language in the face of the onslaughts of the Yiddishists. It was Magnes who breached the wall of the *Forverts* for them by inviting them to his home to meet Abe Cahan. Berl described the conversation as follows: 'Manya talked a lot. Baratz talked about Degania, and I – about the Histadrut.'[1] Cahan took the traditional stand of the Bundists: if this had been a delegation of English workers, he said, he could have helped, but Hebrew and Zionism were involved, and hence, the matter was objectionable. He later softened and said: 'I differentiate between "ism" and "ist". The idea is strange and utopistic, but we bow to every idealist.'[2] He agreed to publish a letter from Magnes presenting the delegation to the readers of what was the most important and widely-read Jewish paper in the United States. The letter appeared on 28 November 1921. Magnes was careful to avoid any mention of Zionism and Zionists. He stressed rather the fact that since the gates of the United States were closed to the needy Jewish masses, one should help the Jewish workers' organizations in Palestine provide employment for those intending to go to there. One consequence of this letter was an endless round of meetings with trade union leaders, labor activists, the Joint and the People's Relief Committee, etc. Another was the assault from all sides on precisely those questions which Magnes had refrained from mentioning. Chaim Zhitlowsky, a Yiddishist with Poalei Zion affiliations, attacked Magnes and claimed that Palestine without Yiddish was not a Jewish country. *Die Zeit* published a series of articles by Abraham Revusky, a Poalei Zion leftist, describing the persecution of Yiddishists by the workers of Palestine. The veteran Bundist leader, Vladimir Medem, who was enraged by the publication of Magnes's letter in the Bundist *Forverts*, persuaded Cahan to adopt an uncompromisingly negative stand on the delegation and to exert heavy pressure on the trade union leaders associated with *Forverts* to break off contact with the delegation and boycott the planned joint committee for the establishment of a labor bank. Some of the delegation's supporters hastened to beat a retreat; others, like Max Pine, one of the first to help Berl, now hesitated, afraid that the Jewish trade union movement might split on this issue. A few, like Abraham Liessin, stood firm and prepared for a fight. Magnes did not exert counter-pressure, and although he continued to help the delegation, it was not enough to overcome the vigorous onslaught of the *Forverts* circles.

After the initial success with Jewish labor, the attack shattered all prospects of consolidating a wide public front in support of the labor bank. Eventually, Berl succeeded in establishing a 'Committee of American workers on behalf of a workmen's Bank in Palestine', chaired by Joseph Schlossberg: Magnes was treasurer; and Hayim Ehrenreich, secretary. Ehrenreich, a Poalei Zion functionary who had been entrusted with the task of organizing the campaign, displayed considerable ineptness. On 20 December, six weeks after Berl's arrival, readers of the Yiddish press learned of the establishment of the Committee in a manifesto, addressed to 'the Jewish workers of America'. They were urged to lend a hand, 'like true proletarians',[3] to their fellow-workers in Palestine, to alleviate the Jewish plight and to realize 'the great ideals of the international labor movement . . .' Again, the word Zionism is nowhere to be found.

The fund-raising campaign was inaugurated at an American-style 'concert' at the Manhattan Opera House. The cantor, Yossele Rosenblatt, several popular singers, and even a cellist, were prominently featured on the program. The bottom line noted that Dr Magnes and others would speak. The number of 'others' was not specified so as not to scare off the audience. Berl and his comrades were not even mentioned in the invitation. Familiar with the inefficiency of the organizers, they were pleasantly surprised to discover that the hall was jam-packed. The audience, while restless, did nonetheless buy some 1,500 shares of the 'Workmen's Bank' that evening, and Berl's heart lightened.

Originally, Berl had hoped to collect a quarter of a million dollars for the bank, but Poalei Zion insisted that he lower his sights to 100,000 dollars, and even this modest sum proved elusive. The American Jewish public was sated with campaigns: a parallel fund-raising operation by the Keren ha-Yesod, more efficiently organized, had succeeded in raising only one million dollars. Circles outside the labor movement were not willing to help, and even the Joint Committee refused. Bernard Flexner, one of the Joint Committee directors, objected to the idea of a separate workers' bank, and preferred to extend direct assistance to Jewish workers in Palestine. The campaign to raise tools and agricultural machinery for Palestine, an imaginative scheme supposed to lead to the modernizing of Palestinian farming and industry, never got off the ground. Rumors that certain funds had been diverted to rescue *Die Zeit*, then struggling for survival, undermined public confidence in fund-raising campaigns on behalf of Palestine.

Berl did not manage to gain access to the very rich American Jews; his activity was confined to labor and ex-labor activists. The Jewish masses were, in the main, preoccupied with eking out a living; some were opposed to Zionism, most indifferent. A single delegation, however effective and talented, could not hope to arouse them to active commitment to Palestine.

The delegation dispersed in mid-January, to tour the continent and sell bank shares. Berl went northeast to comb the great industrial cities – Chicago, Detroit, and the smaller towns *en route*. In Chicago, a conference of representatives of workers' institutions and trade unions, branches of the Arbeiter Ring, (Jewish Unions), the National Arbeiter Verband, etc., convened in Berl's honor, provided him with some gratification. He spoke freely, without the nervousness which usually afflicted him at mass meetings, and for the first time since his arrival in America felt that he had created rapport with his audience. Most of the time, however, he felt alienated from his public and haunted by fear that his mission would fail. On previous missions success or failure had been measured by relative criteria, since only political propaganda was involved, and its impact could not be assessed at once. Now there was only one criterion: the number of shares sold. He knew that 'the eyes of

121

the workers of Palestine are fixed not on the bread which I am casting on the waters, but on the bread which will be sown in Palestine as a result of this journey.'[4]

Apart from trains, hotels and meeting halls, Berl saw almost nothing of America. He paid scant attention to the landscape. Niagara Falls was mentioned only in the context of a meeting supposed to take place there with Baratz. New York left no impression on him. Europe's cultural heritage had impressed him, but now he was indifferent, even hostile, to his surroundings. When he was taken to the theater to see *Anna Christie*, he commented that he had not expected to find such profundity on Broadway. His hosts took him to see the Ford plant at Detroit – but even the wonders of modern technology did not move him.

During the eight months he spent in America, the sole Gentile he mentioned in his diary was a woman, whose home he reached because of some confusion. His lack of fluency in English undoubtedly restricted his contacts. But there was something more involved: the Palestine labor movement, like the entire Zionist movement, still saw America as a source of money – but not of political importance. When he visited England, Berl went out of his way to meet with leaders of the labor party; in the United States he did not make the slightest attempt to contact leaders of the American labor movement.

Nor did he feel at ease among the Jews of America. At public meetings he was 'sold' to the audience in true American style, at the end of a long evening. He was not a great orator. Small in stature, alone on a large platform, he did not cut an impressive figure. His appeal lay in his logic, his powers of persuasion, the ring of truth in his words, but these fell flat in a large, cold auditorium at midnight.

In the small, remote towns, however, Berl met with a warm response and with unanticipated success. There, at small gatherings, his warmth, humanity and deep conviction, combined with his ability to express himself superbly in Yiddish, strongly impressed those who came into close contact with him. His strength lay in direct contact and when this was made possible, he was in his element.

Beyond the public significance of the tour, his visit to the United States was the closest Berl had yet come to visiting the world of his early years.

There was much in common between Palestine and America for emigrants from the Pale of Settlement. Both were supposed to provide an answer to the problems of Jewish existence in Eastern Europe. Both forced the individual to take his fate in his two hands, to abandon a homeland, family and familiar landscape, and to set out for the unknown. The qualities demanded of the Jewish immigrant to the United States, were relatively similar to those demanded of the pioneer who chose Palestine: readiness to work hard, to struggle for a living; the ability to fit into new frameworks and to adjust to a different way of life. There was both open and covert competition between Palestine and America for the soul of the Jewish immigrant. At the same time that Berl, and a few others from his town, left for Palestine, many of his childhood friends and fellow party-members were abandoning Bobruisk for the United States, among them his eldest brother, Hayim. Berl awaited his meeting with them with curiosity and dread, and it proved, indeed, both pathetic and tragic.

Hayim met Berl at the dock when he arrived and took him to spend two weeks at his home. This brother, the closest to Berl of any of his siblings, a revolutionary and a party man, had become a small shop-keeper, spending his days behind a counter. Personal tragedies had aged him before his time. He had withdrawn into his shell, and there was nothing in his world except his business. All the ex-Bobruiskites were anxious to see their 'Berele' and they greeted him with open arms. 'Our Bobruiskites', he wrote to Leah, 'were not born for America. They have not become rich, have not become settled citizens.'[5] They were lost souls, wandering in search of a life of purity which they could never find in American society.

Berl was both distressed and encouraged by his encounter with his friends from Bobruisk: distressed because of the waste of human lives which could have been different if these people had found the courage to take the giant step to Palestine; encouraged because he discovered 'that in every country there are many who cannot acclimatize and for whom this is not the right place';[6] for a Second Aliyah pioneer, who had witnessed the frustrating phenomenon of emigration, there was a measure of comfort in this thought.

Berl was obliged to remain in New York for long months to ensure that the funds donated for the bank would reach Palestine and not fill some gap in the local Poalei Zion budget. Once the 17,000 dollars had finally been despatched to Palestine, Berl permitted himself to leave the United States.

There was a great disparity between his hopes of raising a quarter of a million dollars and the actual sum raised. However, contacts were established between the Histadrut and the *Geverkshaften* – the American Jewish trade unions; seeds were sown even in *Forverts* circles, and would bear fruit in Cahan's subsequent visits to Palestine; and the friendships which ensued with Liessin, David Pinsky, Schlossberg and others would prove of vital importance in the second half of the 1920s. Then a Histadrut fund-raising campaign, headed by David Remez, would reap what Berl had sown. In 1926–1928, a period of dire economic deprivation, the funds which flowed into Palestine from the American Jewish labor movement were crucial for maintaining Histadrut projects – among them *Davar*, the daily newspaper and ha-Mashbir, the supply cooperative – and for constructing workers' housing and supporting various cultural institutions.

The workmen's bank – Bank ha-Poalim – was one of the greatest success stories of the labor movement in Palestine. Unlike other economic creations of the movement, such as ha-Mashbir and Solel Bonneh (a large building concern), it never suffered economic or financial disaster. It was a reliable source of credit for all the Histadrut's activities, from workers' housing and settlement projects in town and village, to industry, agriculture, and even cultural areas. In order to bring Berl's mission full circle, one of the first actions of the new bank was to adopt a resolution approving its participation in the organization of P. Rutenberg's hydroelectric project in Palestine and the appointment of Shlomo Kaplansky as its accredited representative in London.

7

THE THIRD ALIYAH CRISIS,
1923–1925

In August 1922 Berl finally succeeded in extricating himself from America and set sail for Europe. His sister, Hanna, was undergoing medical treatment in Vienna and Leah, practical and devoted as ever, had accompanied her to Europe. Now, after more than a year of separation, Berl was reunited with his loved ones. The mood of gloom which had permeated his letters to Leah lifted, and his love of life surfaced again.

Meanwhile his comrades in the party had sent him a delegate's ticket to the annual Zionist Conference held in August 1922 at Karlsbad. The gathering was not inspiring, according to Berl's account. Similarly uninspiring were the deliberations at the Poalei Zion Alliance office in Vienna, which, as usual, revolved around the question of amalgamation with Tzeirei Zion, and relations with the left wing of Poalei Zion. The discussions were inconclusive, and the only thing decided upon was that the Poalei Zion conference would be convened a year later to discuss the whole range of questions.

Berl apparently returned home at the end of November 1922 after an absence of about a year and a half. He arrived in Palestine at the height of the Third Aliyah crisis, that is, the winter of 1922/3. He toured the country extensively and found 'much that is great and new, but also, a great deal of unparalleled distress and pressure'.[1] He went up to Galilee to visit 'the traces of my life's memories'[2] and *en route* found the new settlements of Beit Alfa, and Benyamina. But he also found 'a heavy cloud on each countenance, and long lines of people weary of the land awaiting exit permits'.[3] Tel Aviv was utterly transformed. 'I walk down the street, meet workers, enter offices, and nobody knows me',[4] he wrote, rather nonplussed. Still, he immediately found himself 'in the boiling cauldron of public life', occupied 'in mending matters',[5] without a moment for himself, without the time to organize his life with Leah or find them a home. Most of his friends now had children: Ben

Gurion, Tabenkin and Remez, not to speak of such long-married friends as David Zakai; he alone was childless. Leah had gone to help her sister, Bluma, and her brother-in-law, Slutzkin, to set up a convalescent home in the Jerusalem hills which Berl envisaged as a memorial to Sara Schmuckler. Leah was also active in setting up a training farm for women workers in the Borochov Quarter – to the resentment of Berl, who complained that their meetings were snatched and hasty, and little resembled regular family life. It was only six months after his return to Palestine that he found time to rent a room. His longing for a child became intensified. He wrote of his sister-in-law's family: '. . . like all good people in Palestine, they have a lovely little girl,'[6] and the implication was: 'Only I have none.' But he took pleasure in his nephews and nieces, whom he used to spoil unabashedly. Family affairs continued to trouble him: his brother Isser, was unemployed; Hanna was still in Austria, where she underwent a thyroid operation. His mother, Teivel, arrived at the end of December 1922, and Berl was pleasantly surprised by her rapid adjustment to life in Palestine, her tolerant and relaxed attitude to the conditions, to the food and to the strange Hebrew language. Her arrival, however, was an additional burden upon him since he was obliged to support her.

Immediately after his return, a number of important conferences were convened. They had been postponed again and again – first, because of Berl's absence and then because he and Ben Gurion were attending the Karlsbad Conference. Within Ahdut ha-Avoda the demand was being voiced that the party be disbanded in the wake of the establishment of the Histadrut, which had assumed the tasks of development, and in December 1922 the Third Ahdut ha-Avoda conference was held to debate the party's continued existence. Berl came down in favor of continuation. He saw the party as an avant-garde within the Histadrut which, while placing itself at the Histadrut's service, would nonetheless direct it in the spirit of the original Ahdut ha-Avoda.

Two months later, the Second Conference of the Histadrut took place in Jaffa, at the peak of the economic crisis. It was an impressive event, and among the renowned guests were Albert Einstein, J. L. Magnes, and Ahad ha-Am. The conference hall was crammed, and the profound rapport between the public and its representatives and everyone's intense interest in the proceedings greatly impressed the visitors from abroad.

This conference determined the image and organization of the Histadrut for the future. Hevrat ha-Ovdim (the Workers' Company) was set up with two subsidiaries: the Labor Settlement Company (Hevrat Hityashvut ha-Ovdim), the main instrument for labor settlement, and the Joint Company for Public Works and Building. The conference also formulated the Histadrut constitution which spelled out such matters as the relations between the individual member and the Histadrut, rights and obligations, etc. A wage scale was established for all Histadrut enterprises, based not on vocational skills but on the size of the wage-earner's family, and it now remained only to implement it. The participation of the Histadrut in the Trade Union International at Amsterdam was approved, thus sanctioning the Histadrut's affiliation to the international labor movement but without the political implications entailed in affiliation to the Socialist International.

Berl was gratified by the achievements of the Conference: 'Its resolutions would have sufficed for ten conferences of Gentiles',[7] he wrote to Eliyahu Golomb, who was then in Vienna. But he was not pleased with the ceremonial aspects of the occasion, and expressed his feelings succinctly in his diary: 'Pagan customs. Both the parliamentary debate and the applause.'[8] He was infuriated by the excessive attention paid to the members of the small Communist Party. They were headed by Daniel (Zeev Averbuch), a brilliant polemicist, who turned the debate with the left into the central issue of the deliberations, and was supported by Revusky and Zeev Abramovitch, future Left Poalei Zion Party leaders. Berl deplored the applause accorded to the representatives of the extreme left and the form of the debate which, in democratic European style, permitted adversaries to express their views, however controversial. He did not state explicitly what form of debate he would have preferred but he would have been happier if the extreme left had been excluded altogether. The press, particularly the overseas correspondents, was more taken with Daniel's sparkling witticisms than with the sober, down-to-earth remarks of Ben Gurion, Tabenkin and Berl, and gave them wider coverage. It may have been Berl's sense of frustration and his impatience at this pointless debate which led him to propose the expulsion of the Communists from the Histadrut. He declared that both freedom of opinion and discipline of action should reign together within the Histadrut, which meant, ostensibly, that no one should be expelled because of his opinions. But he went on to state that 'certain people' were slandering the Histadrut as a chauvinistic body, thus creating hostility and discord between Jewish and Arab workers. The Histadrut could not tolerate this; freedom of opinion or of debate was acceptable as long as it remained within the bounds of the socialist-constructionist consensus.

The conference resolutions were formulated by the Ahdut ha-Avoda leaders, headed by Berl, who was the traditional drafter of resolutions.

Berl reassumed the editorship of *Kuntres* and also became a member of the directing board of ha-Mashbir. Meir Rotberg, progenitor of ha-Mashbir, had submitted his resignation, apparently because his colleagues were neglecting their duties, and Berl hastened to lend him a hand. The wide scope of its activities made ha-Mashbir one of the most important factors in the Palestinian economy, and as it acquired more and more capital it became one of the central pillars of the labor economy. In these matters, Berl proved himself a born 'capitalist'. He continued to devote himself to the affairs of Bank ha-Poalim and was considered by many to be the central figure in that institution. But these were not his only preoccupations. Whereas Ben Gurion was totally absorbed in running the Histadrut, Berl remained at the helm of Ahdut ha-Avoda and served as its mentor, father confessor and castigator. He travelled all over the country, held 'comradely discussions' on Friday evenings in remote settlements, a great part of them devoted to a collective self-criticism. The subjects of discussion were depressing: hunger, unemployment, suicide, the ineffectuality of the Histadrut – and people were eager to talk and to listen. At the First of May celebrations in 1923, Berl delivered the central address at the Eden Theater, then Tel Aviv's largest hall. His May Day speech became an institution. It was said that people walked on tiptoe in Berl's home as 1 May approached: Berl was preparing his speech! He never wrote it out, but jotted down headings, important points, catchphrases. When Beit ha-Am (a kind of town hall) was built, with its large auditorium, thousands would wait for hours just to hear Berl speak. The quasi-mystical contact between Berl and his audience made up for his drawbacks as orator. He spoke rapidly, stopping from time to time to sip water. His speech was low-keyed, neither stirring nor exciting his listeners, and one can only ask: how did he succeed in captivating his audience, without a microphone, in a crowded, hot and uncomfortable hall? In a letter to her brother, Moshe Shertok, Rivka Hos described Berl: 'His soul is attuned to every sound and every pain.'[9] Many felt that way about him. And Berl wrote: 'The knowledge that it is possible – even if only by words – to alleviate some stress, to add some interest, at a time when people, for some reason, expect something of you, and pin unjustified hopes on your words – this imposes an obligation on me, and I submit.'[10]

Unlike Ben Gurion, who was completely at home in his activity on behalf of the Histadrut and reveled in feverish activity, Berl was dragged into public life reluctantly. While his friends worshiped him and felt that he was indispensable, he took a detached view of his life, as a bystander, ironically observing his own loss of image and the obliteration of his own personality within the collective persona of the movement. Whereas Ben Gurion did not differentiate between private and public life, Berl regarded them as two separate worlds. The engulfing of his private world and his immersion in public life pained him; the time had passed when he could flee public activity and hide in his own corner. He surrendered to his *alter ego*, that of the leader, possibly because he could not live without this total commitment, which at the same time repelled him; or because, since Sara's death, he had never again experienced passionate love or torment, and found recompense for his emptiness of spirit in complete dedication to movement affairs. Over the years his identification with the movement was to grow stronger. Only his sarcastic bent and his talent for self-torment remained with him.

The crisis which had been fomenting with the Third Aliyah culminated in the split at Kibbutz Ein Harod. The 1921 Zionist Congress at Karlsbad had adopted the plan of Shlomo Levkovitch (Lavi) for the establishment of a large *kvutza* on the Jezreel Valley lands, recently purchased by the Jewish National Fund. The Second Aliyah *kvutzot* had consisted of several dozen people each, the assumption being that a *kvutza* must be based on spiritual affinity between members. The large *kvutza* (later known as a kibbutz), was planned to have hundreds and even thousands of members, with an extensive economic and social makeup. It was believed that in so large a body, it would be easy for individual new immigrants to find their place. When the opportunity presented itself, the young Third Aliyah pioneers of the Trumpeldor Labor Brigade undertook to implement the plan and settled in the Jezreel Valley near the Spring of Harod. Two kibbutzim were soon established – Ein Harod and Tel Yosef. Several Second Aliyah veterans, including Tabenkin and Shlomo Levkovitch, joined the younger pioneers and became members. This move freed Tabenkin of the burden of seeking a livelihood, and enabled him to devote more time to public activity.

The amalgam of young people and veterans was not a success. There were disputes between the Brigade leaders, headed by Menahem Elkind, and the older workers, led by Levkovitch, who was backed by Tabenkin. The financial hardships which the kibbutz encountered (like all other workers' groups at the time) aggravated the situation and, as might have been expected among people living in close proximity, life soon became intolerable.

Levkovitch appealed to the Histadrut's Agricultural Center, charging the leaders of the Brigade with appropriating funds intended for Ein Harod, to cover the deficits of other Brigade units. The Center, which consisted of Second Aliyah veterans, despatched committees of inquiry and attempts were made to settle the dispute. Elkind was ready for a compromise, provided that the principle of economic communality, guaranteeing an equal allocation to each member for sustenance, be maintained. The argument evolved into a debate between two opposing concepts. Levkovitch maintained that the large *kvutza* was an autonomous unit, settled in a particular area and expanding in accordance with its economic possibilities. Thus Ein Harod was to be its own focus of development. Elkind, on the other hand, conceived of a country-wide commune of kibbutzim (*kibbutz artzi*), centrally supervised and subject to the authority of the Brigade Center. Ein Harod was considered to be one of many such units. Ostensibly, it was a theoretical discussion over organizational differences of conception. In fact, it was a struggle between the Second Aliyah and the Third for domination.

Ben Gurion and Remez, the Histadrut leaders, responded to Levkovitch's appeal for 'outside' interference and backed Tabenkin in his struggle against the majority in the Brigade. The latter interpreted this as a form of coercion exercised by the old guard against the younger generation. The leaders of the Brigade were defending their right to create independent patterns, to be different, to refuse to accept the authority of the 'founding fathers'.

When Berl returned home in November 1922, as noted above, the dispute was at its height, and the differences were irreconcilable. He visited Ein Harod on several occasions, but did not appear to have impressed the young Brigade leaders. They were a closely-knit group and impervious to outside influences. Even those who lived among them – like Tabenkin – found it difficult to sway them. The split, which took place in 1923, was unavoidable. Berl later related that he had offered to mediate and been turned down. There could be no greater insult as far as he was concerned. Many years later, when he examined the affair in retrospect, he accused himself and his comrades of failing to understand and properly absorb the younger people, but this was hindsight. At the time, he was unable to take a detached view of matters. He reacted with anger and incomprehension at their refusal to accept the authority of the Histadrut leaders. They, after all, had created the Palestinian labor movement through the establishment of Ahdut ha-Avoda and of the Histadrut, and would not sanction any sidetracking. The allegiance of the Brigade members to their own leaders' point of view violated Berl's concept of an all-inclusive, disciplined labor movement.

The split in the Brigade occurred simultaneously with the failure to unify Tzeirei Zion and Poalei Zion in the Diaspora. From both affairs Berl concluded that the Ahdut ha-Avoda leadership had to prevent the creation of a grass-roots leadership among the pioneering youth, in Palestine and abroad. If the party wanted to shape the young generation in its own image, it had to become decisively active in organizing and educating them – in accordance with its conception of party centralism.

Years later the excessive centralism practiced by the party was to be laid at the door of Ben Gurion, the Histadrut Secretary. Berl was considered a pluralist and hence, a decentralist. And, indeed, within the framework of the comprehensive party he established, Berl regarded pluralism as the sole way of guaranteeing the movement's scope. Furthermore, it suited his emotional makeup; he was not dogmatic, despised rigid formulae and monolithic philosophies. But this in no way implies that he wanted the movement to organize itself spontaneously from below. It was his ambition to mold it into the patterns he advocated. Pluralism was acceptable, as long as the authority and the directives of the leadership were accepted. The days of the creative anarchy of the Second Aliyah had passed.

In spring 1923, Berl resumed work on *Kuntres*, which had suspended publication during his stay in the United States. The first new issue appeared on 23 March 1923, and in it Berl tried to convey the acuteness of the crisis, summoning the leaders of the Zionist Organization and well-to-do Jews in the Yishuv to aid the unemployed worker. Publishing a weekly edition of the *Kuntres* was a constant struggle and Berl worked almost single-handed. He never had time to write real articles; his notes were written at the very last moment, while the presses were waiting.

In July 1923 he was elected by the Ahdut ha-Avoda Council as a delegate to several conferences about to be held in Europe: the Sixth Conference of the Poalei Zion Alliance in Berlin; the 13th Zionist Congress at Karlsbad, and finally, the newly-conceived Conference on Labor Palestine.

It was evident that the Poalei Zion conference would be as stormy as its predecessor, and this in fact was the case. Ahdut ha-Avoda was attacked by all the national parties of Europe, from Vienna to Poland. The American party rallied to its defense, as did a scattering of delegates from other parties. Deliberations lasted for six days and nights, and left Berl totally exhausted. He described it as a 'nightmare' and the relations between Ahdut ha-Avoda and Poalei Zion as follows: 'A couple who cannot refrain from making one another's lives a misery, and only when the cup of bitterness and insult overflows, do they weary and agree to concessions and reconciliation.'[11]

At the heart of the debate were the language question and the issue of unity with Tzeirei Zion – and they were interdependent. Poalei Zion, which opposed the unification, used the tactic of preventing it through submitting inflexible resolutions on the Hebrew language which would deter Tzeirei Zion. The resolution finally adopted was aimed at balancing the viewpoints of the Yiddishists and the Hebraists, favoring the latter.

But the most bitter moments of the conference were during the discussion of the merger with Tzeirei Zion. The debate raged through the night and resulted only in the establishment of a committee of three – David Remez, Berl Locker and Shlomo Kaplansky – who were to continue discussions and hopefully arrive at some acceptable decision. Berl's previous reluctance to play a leading role in Poalei Zion (dating from his first encounters with the Alliance) disappeared, and he presented the case of the Palestinian delegation confidently, displaying a talent for negotiation and for compromise. An analysis of the conference resolutions shows that on most issues the Palestinians' stand prevailed. But Berl was sapped by the protracted negotiations, the tension, the squabbles and the mutual exchange of insults.

It was only weeks later, and after the success of the Conference on Labor Palestine, in which seven Diaspora associations had rallied to the

Histadrut cause, and agreed to work jointly for Palestine, that Berl took a positive view of the overall achievements of that summer's exertions.

Between the Poalei Zion conference and the Conference on Labor Palestine, the 13th Zionist Congress was convened; it made the least impression on Berl of the three gatherings: 'There was an audience and an air of expectation in the hall, as if Kol Nidrei [the solemn Day of Atonement prayer] were about to take place. The spectacle itself may have been important, but the stage and the players were totally unworthy.'[12] It was at this congress that Berl adopted a pattern of conduct he was to follow at all subsequent congresses: 'I try to keep away from any mandate or political position', he wrote to his sister. 'The relations between the factions are repugnant to me, and I cannot deal with them.'[13] His gloomy mood resulted from the refusal of Poalei Zion to appear at the congress in one bloc with Tzeirei Zion. In years to come the arguments would change and the issues vary but one fact remained unchanged: Berl never became a member of the Zionist Executive.

The above-mentioned three-man committee set up to promote the merger of Poalei Zion and Tzeirei Zion failed owing to the fact that Locker and Kaplansky refused to accept the Lithuanian Tzeirei Zion into the alliance: it was Hebraist and ran Hebrew schools, and in the year which elapsed after the Berlin Conference, Ahdut ha-Avoda, occupied as it was with everyday affairs, gave less prominence to the question of the merger. But Berl was in 'great moral distress' about it: he feared that Tzeirei Zion would be drawn into petty party squabbles and lose its great pioneering impetus. This time he decided to conduct the struggle on his own ground. The fourth conference of Ahdut ha-Avoda was hosted by Ein Harod on 12–19 May 1924. Its members were a responsive audience to the speeches of its favorite leaders, including, of course, Berl. The conference opened ceremoniously with the singing of the International – to the gratification of the three guests from abroad who attended, all members of the Poalei Zion Alliance Bureau: Kaplansky, Locker and Rubashov. The choice of the conference venue had not alerted them to what lay ahead. The gentle, inoffensive Rubashov was enchanted by the beauties of the Jezreel Valley and the country as a whole, and planned to settle in Palestine. It was clear from the outset that he would adopt a stance of compromise, and try to tie the loose ends together. Berl opened the conference with warm remarks about the role of Ahdut ha-Avoda and enumeration of the issues on the conference agenda. And, having lulled his audience, he threw down his challenge to 'our good friends, who have been standing guard for so many years in the Diaspora' who 'on this occasion are here with us'. Although he welcomed them warmly, he immediately demanded 'Palestinian hegemony' in the Poalei Zion movement.[14] It may be assumed that his audience greeted these remarks enthusiastically. As usual, he was expressing their feelings. They had no doubt that they were the focal point of the Zionist movement and the Jewish people. The audience was less sympathetic towards Kaplansky and Locker. The representatives of the labor settlements and agricultural workers, who constituted the majority of the delegates, were mostly former sup-porters of the Non-Affiliated Group. They had little enthusiasm for the old Borochovist slogans, or for the Poalei Zion Alliance, for that matter.

The storm erupted in the wake of Kaplansky's political proposals, a detailed plan the crux of which was the establishment of a quasi-parliament in Palestine. The lower house would be composed of pro-portional representatives of the population – this implying, of course, an Arab majority – while the upper chamber would consist of equal numbers of Jews and Arabs. This was intended as a counter-proposal to the High Commissioner's proposal of a legislative council, and it was hoped to present it to the new Labor Government in Britain as a posi-tive contribution to solution of the constitutional problem in Palestine. The great majority of Ahdut ha-Avoda rejected these proposals, for a variety of reasons. Berl was the sole delegate who did not confine him-self merely to rejecting them: he subjected them and their two advo-cates, Kaplansky and Locker, to ridicule. He quoted the remark of Syrkin that Jewish socialists, in their debates with the S.D. (Social Democrats), had moved to the left and 'adapted the theory to the dis-putation'. He described Kaplansky's proposal as the outcome of the uncomfortable situation of 'our comrades who often come into contact with the outside world and must explain our case there', i.e., as a propa-ganda device, aimed at enhancing their standing in the eyes of socialists in London. Having demolished the ostensibly democratic aspects of the proposal, he declared that the Kaplansky proposal should be shelved. He further depicted the notable guests as strangers, interfering in mat-ters they did not understand. Following this, a debate ensued on the amalgamation of Poalei Zion and Tzeirei Zion.

134

The discussion was opened in a minor key by Zalman Rubashov, whose views were summed up in one significant sentence: 'There are those who hope that through the merger, this force [i.e. the labor movement] will be reinforced and will be able to fulfill its tasks more effectively, and there are some who fear that through this unification the power to remain a workers' movement will be forfeited'.[15] Berl now took the floor and diverted the discussion to the question of Ahdut ha-Avoda's place in the Alliance. He started by saying that 'the presence here with us of our comrades from abroad makes it possible and even essential to expose our wounds, to show things as they are, mercilessly and frankly'.[16] And he kept his promise. He accused the Alliance of failing to work on behalf of the Palestinian labor movement, of making overtures to the left, within the Alliance and subsequently on its periphery, as in the case of the party in Eastern Galicia (which returned to the Alliance after the 1921 split, and was subsequently accorded 'special treatment' lest it secede again). For the sake of this party – claimed Berl – the unification with Tzeirei Zion had been thwarted, and conditions subsequently posed which were unacceptable to Tzeirei Zion. The culmination – according to Berl – had been their refusal to enter into an alliance with Tzeirei Zion in Lithuania, because of the latter's Hebraist zeal. Berl demanded two things of the Alliance representatives: first, the 'purging of the Alliance', i.e., a new split and the expulsion of Eastern Galicia. 'And we do not want men of peace to come and propose organizational compromises';[17] secondly, freedom of action in Hebrew cultural activity in the Diaspora. He concluded with the hint of a threat: 'The Alliance must not forget that its strength lies in Ahdut ha-Avoda, and not elsewhere.'[18] Locker responded to Berl's attack. His emotion-laden remarks concerning the profound psychological difficulties of the Poalei Zion in Vienna, and the great sacrifices they had made, made little impression on his audience. They were indifferent to the emotional problems of Poalei Zion, and shared Berl's view that a movement which had not succeeded in sending pioneers to Palestine was not worth its salt.

Ben Gurion paraphrased Berl's ideas in his less eloquent closing remarks. Some of the former Poalei Zion members, not to mention the guests, had apparently been offended by Berl's causticness, and must have commented that it stemmed from his alienation from Poalei Zion, since Ben Gurion found it necessary to say: 'Berl's remarks were moderate – because he has been in Poalei Zion only five years. If I had made those remarks – they would have been much harsher, since I have been in Poalei Zion for twenty years, and I really know its faults.'[19]

The conference called for unification with Tzeirei Zion 'without curtailing their freedom of Hebrew educational activity in the Diaspora'. The unification was to take place as soon as possible; if not, Ahdut ha-Avoda reserved freedom of action for itself and the right to maintain contact with Tzeirei Zion and other socialist Zionist groups. Berl's veiled threat, reinterpreted by Ben Gurion, that Ahdut ha-Avoda would secede from the Alliance, now received official sanction. The Poalei Zion Alliance could hinder Berl and his comrades in Berlin but not at Ein Harod. Here the old Berl–Ben Gurion alliance, dating from the establishment of Ahdut ha-Avoda, prevailed.

In 1925 the two alliances finally amalgamated and the question was removed from the agenda.

8

On the afternoon of 1 June 1925, a group of workers assembled near the ha-Poel ha-Tzair printing press in Mazeh Street in Tel Aviv and stood there as if awaiting word of a birth. And, indeed, about an hour later than expected, the first Hebrew daily of the Palestinian Jewish labor movement, *Davar*, came into the world.

The establishment of *Davar* was natural enough in the development of a movement, which had been distinguished since its inception by journalistic talent and the inner need to record itself in writing. More than any other sector of Palestinian society, the labor movement was responsive to the written word, to education, to dialog – an attitude which attests to the non-proletarian origin of its members. Its faith in the power of words was an integral part of its belief that society could be changed by educating mankind, and raising their social consciousness. The written word was considered as the most effective weapon in the contest with both right- and left-wing elements in the Zionist movement for the soul of the workers. When Ahdut ha-Avoda was established, Berl immediately began to publish the weekly *Kuntres*, the party organ. At the same time, Berl and his comrades undertook to produce a literary monthly, *ha-Adama* (The Soil), edited by Brenner, the man they regarded as embodying the noble spirit of the Second Aliyah.

Berl's predilection for editing and publishing was first manifested in *ba-Avoda*. Berl's personal taste – a fondness for a simple but original style – were reflected both in the anthology *ba-Avoda* and later in *Kuntres*. *Ha-Adama* waned after Brenner's death and *Kuntres* was read by party supporters alone and closed to rivals by definition. Berl was far from satisfied with this situation. He wanted a paper which would reach and influence every worker's household.

The idea of publishing a Histadrut paper as against a party paper had been mooted since that body was established. While Berl was in the

137

United States, a Histadrut bulletin, *Pinkas* (Notebook) began to appear. *Pinkas* reported scrupulously and in great detail all of the activities and achievements of the Histadrut and its various institutions, from the milk yield of kibbutz cows to the debt–credit ledger of the Bank ha-Poalim. While it was certainly highly informative, it was also dry as dust and it is no wonder that even sworn party loyalists took to reading, openly or in secret, the much livelier 'right-wing' daily of Itamar Ben-Avi, *Doar ha-Yom* (Daily Mail).

From the time he returned from the United States, Berl was intent on producing a Histadrut daily. He apparently persuaded Ben Gurion, then Secretary of the Histadrut, of its importance and then succeeded in persuading the Second Histadrut Conference to adopt a resolution to that end. Many members of the Histadrut Executive doubted the economic viability of Berl's brainchild. This was at the height of the Third Aliyah crisis: the momentum of immigration and settlement had been checked, the immigrant groups were destitute and labor unions were undergoing financial problems. At this precise time (autumn 1923), Berl claimed at the Executive that a Histadrut daily was of crucial socialist and Zionist importance, and he argued that the sale of 1,500 copies daily would cover the costs. A two-man committee was set up, consisting of a highly respected representative of ha-Poel ha-Tzair, Yosef Aharonovitch, and Michael Assaf of Ahdut ha-Avoda, a member of the Cultural Committee, to examine the question in depth and convey its conclusions to the Histadrut Council.

At the Tenth Histadrut Council session, in spring 1924, a decision was made to elect Comrade Berl Katznelson editor of the projected Histadrut paper. The editorial board was to consist of Berl and one representative each of ha-Poel ha-Tzair and Ahdut ha-Avoda. The latter did not constitute a problem – Berl was to be allowed to make his own choice. But when ha-Poel ha-Tzair proposed Yitzhak Lufban, editor of *ha-Poel ha-Tzair*, as its representative, a scandal broke out. Berl announced categorically that under no circumstances would he work with Lufban. Ha-Poel ha-Tzair was incensed and 'diplomatic negotiations' ensued between the two parties. The incident ended in agreement that the editorial board would consist of a chief editor – Berl – and four other members – two from each party. Ha-Poel ha-Tzair was to be represented by Chaim Arlosoroff and Aharonovitch, both of them acceptable to Berl. But Lufban had his revenge: he published an article in *ha-Poel ha-Tzair* accusing Ahdut ha-Avoda of exploiting the Histadrut platform to slander his party. He substantiated his charges by citing remarks alleged to have been made by Ben Gurion and Berl at public meetings that same week. Now Berl was incensed.

The allegation that he had exploited the Histadrut for party purposes deeply offended him. He still regarded himself as the representative of the whole labor movement and to be identified as a party man contradicted his self-image. He hastened to write to *ha-Poel ha-Tzair*: 'I would like to state that the remarks attributed to me by Y. Lufban in his article in Issue No. 12 of *ha-Poel ha-Tzair* are a total fabrication.'[1] The editors of *ha-Poel ha-Tzair* printed the letter, but used their prerogative to add an 'editorial comment' refuting Berl's denial. The intention was undoubtedly to add fuel to the flames of the controversy, since by the time the letter and comment appeared, it was common knowledge that the affronted Berl had taken a step he was to repeat often under similar circumstances: he sent the Histadrut Executive a letter of resignation as editor of the paper. He argued that Lufban's article attested to ha-Poel ha-Tzair's lack of confidence in him. It was all Berl, *par excellence*: the personal note in his letter, the injured tone, his insistence on tokens of personal confidence in him personally as the precondition for public activity. He was one of the few people in the movement, perhaps the only one, who was regarded by his comrades, with what may be termed love. There were, of course, those who hated him, like Lufban, an emotion heartily reciprocated by Berl. But most of his comrades saw in any attempt by political rivals to injure him a cardinal sin. The need to mollify Berl was also taken for granted: it was considered intolerable for him to resign or to feel slighted. There was something feminine in his conduct, which caused people to court him, to try to placate him. The tough Ben Gurion, who never aroused such warm sentiments in his comrades, who created the impression that he needed nobody, hastened to Berl's defense, or perhaps to ensure Berl's return to public life. In any event, in the wake of Berl's resignation, Ben Gurion included Lufban's charges on the agenda of the Histadrut Executive. Thanks to the Ahdut ha-Avoda majority, augmented by Hugo Bergman of ha-Poel ha-Tzair (Berl's personal friend), the Executive decided to summon Lufban before a Histadrut tribunal on a charge of slander.

Before the scandal, Berl had been content with the status of 'first among equals' on the editorial board: but things were very different now. The question of his resignation was raised at the Eleventh Histadrut Council, in January 1925. By the end of the Council session in January

1925, the idea of a collective editorial board had been shelved. Berl was appointed sole editor, and he was answerable, not to the Histadrut Executive but to the Histadrut Conference alone. The editor was now a figure apart, elected on a personal basis by the Histadrut Conference which was convened infrequently, and hence dependent neither on his fellow party-members nor on the Histadrut Executive.

Years later it was claimed that Berl, from the outset, strove to attain the status of managing editor and abolish the editorial board; but this is not confirmed by contemporary sources. If ha-Poel ha-Tzair had agreed to one of the earlier proposals pertaining to their representation on the board, Berl would have been obliged to acquiesce. One may well ask whether such an editorial board could have worked effectively in the long run. Still, it is clear that Lufban's attack worked in Berl's favor. It afforded him the opportunity of presenting himself as a martyr, and forcing his colleagues' hand. When he finally agreed to become editor, he voiced his doubts: 'If you harness me firmly to this project – perhaps I will lack the strength to refuse you, but I have no faith that under these circumstances the endeavor will succeed.'[2] Such reluctant acquiescence on the part of anyone except Berl would have been regarded as hypocrisy. But in Berl's case, his remarks were accepted at face value. Even his rivals in ha-Poel ha-Tzair refrained from attacking him personally, arguing only over issues.

With the Histadrut Council behind him, Berl began making energetic preparations to produce the paper.

At this time, the Yishuv read two papers: *Doar ha-Yom* mentioned above, and Moshe Gluecksohn's moderate General Zionist *ha-Aretz* (The Land). The former was a literally 'yellow' paper, both in color and in content. *Ha-Aretz* was solid, attractive in its layout – and boring. Both were constantly on the verge of bankruptcy, and the news that a third paper was about to appear, and undoubtedly rob them of readers, was not good news. According to one story, Gluecksohn offered to allocate to Berl half of the pages of his own paper, to edit as he chose, if he would only abandon the idea of producing a labor newspaper. Berl naturally turned him down.

He did not spare himself and took care of both the important and the minor details of publication. As soon as the 11th Histadrut Council ended, Berl asked Dov Hos, then in Holland, to purchase the necessary machinery. For a month he wrote to him frequently, urging him to deal with the matter, but soon came to the conclusion that it would be wiser to use one of the existing printshops. The likely candidates were the Ahdut press which printed *Kuntres*, and the Tversky Press, which printed *ha-Poel ha-Tzair*. Ahdut apparently could not meet the stringent requirements of a daily paper, and it was, paradoxically enough, the *ha-Poel ha-Tzair* press which was selected. In mid-March 1925, a contract was signed between the press and the directorship of the still nameless newspaper.

In March, after long debates, it was named *Davar*. Berl had consulted a number of eminent people about the name, among whom were those who favored *Am Oved* (A Working People). Others thought that the unpretentious name *Pinkas* (Notebook) was suitable for a workers' paper. The issue was decided by H. N. Bialik, the national poet, who chose *Davar*, a Hebrew word which means speech, or the word, but also deed, vision or prophecy. The polysemy was irresistible.

The paper was established without working capital. The assumption was that the great majority of the paper's readers would be subscribers and would pay their subscriptions in advance. Thus, even before the paper appeared, a subscription campaign was launched among the workers. Berl proudly informed Mordechai Lipson, a Jewish writer from New York, that in some factories and unions more than half of the workers had taken out subscriptions. It may be assumed that the pressure exerted by the *Davar* managers contributed to the high proportion of subscribers. In any event, one month after the paper commenced publication, Berl boasted of having 3,200 subscribers, and 4,500 copies were printed – equal to the combined circulation of *ha-Aretz* and *Doar ha-Yom*.

In addition to these prosaic concerns, Berl was preoccupied with such questions as who would contribute to *Davar*, and, more importantly, who would constitute the staff. In 1924, a young physician of Russian origin, named Moshe Beilinson, who had lived and studied in Italy, and knew Russian, German and Italian fluently, arrived in Palestine and attempted to become a laborer in the colonies. Failing this, he began to work for *Kuntres*, to which he had sent letters from Rome. He brought to the paper something of the flavor of the European and particularly Central European press. His articles were as yet written in Russian and translated into Hebrew. Also included on the editorial staff was Zalman Rubashov, a skilled Hebrew stylist, who was well-versed in Hebrew literature, and in general, a man of broad knowledge. He was, as well, familiar with the Jewish labor movement and an experienced editor. Berl also recruited his old friend, David Zakai, who had written a column for *Kuntres*, and now contributed short articles to *Davar*. The fifth member was Moshe Shertok, a brilliant young man and graduate of the Herzliya Gymnasium. Shertok had studied in London in the early 1920s at the London School of Economics, together with many future leaders of national movements which sought liberation from the British Empire. Berl, who was acquainted with Shertok's articles for *Kuntres*, written under the pen-name of *Ben Kedem* (Son of the East), had urged Shertok in summer 1924 to return to Palestine in order to join the editorial staff. He was the only member of the staff who knew English and could translate news from the English-speaking world.

While he was assembling the permanent staff of the paper, Berl also contacted a number of free-lance journalists, reporters and writers, among them some who had published in veteran Hebrew journals, such as *ha-Shiloah*, *ha-Olam* and even *ha-Poel ha-Tzair*, in its early Second Aliyah days. One of them was Rabbi Benjamin, a veteran political journalist; another was Ya'akov Rabinovitch. One of his greatest achievements was to persuade S. Y. Agnon to become a regular contributor. He also recruited lesser-known writers: David Hofstein, a Jewish writer who had immigrated from Russia and was trying to settle down (he later failed and returned to Russia); Yehuda Burla, a promising young Palestinian writer; Uri Zvi Greenberg, a Hebrew poet (Greenberg had begun writing in Yiddish and was drawing dangerously close to the world of the revolution when he was restored to Hebrew and to Palestine); Zalman Yitzhak Anokhi, a writer who started out in Yiddish and switched to Hebrew; Hugo Bergman from Prague, beloved of Berl, whose cultural world was entirely different from that of the others. Although he was not overly fond of Shlomo Kaplansky, Berk also asked him to contribute to the paper, as he did veteran contributors to *ha-Poel ha-Tzair*, Yosef Aharonovitch and Azar (Alexander Siskind Rabinovitz).

When the first issue appeared on 1 June 1925, it was no mean achievement – a daily of Palestinian Jewish workers. Its name appeared on the masthead in elegant curved Hebrew letters, and is unchanged to this day. Few knew that the attractive graphic design was the work of Lily Zadek, the niece of Edouard Bernstein. She had become interested in Zionism and immigrated to Palestine in the early 1920s and developed a profound friendship with the *Davar* staff, particularly with Zalman Rubashov and Berl. The first edition was ceremoniously set in six columns, but on the next day it changed over to five columns, a form it preserved for many years. It contained four pages, including advertisements on the back page. The first page, edited by Moshe Shertok, featured an editorial by Berl, as well as 'cables' from all over the world. The 'cables' were news items, outdated in the outside world, but still 'hot news' in Palestine. The sole news agency operating in the Middle East in the mid-1920s was Reuters of Cairo, which sent *Davar* bulletins by train, printed by hectograph on long, yellow sheets. Unfortunately, it took them three days to arrive! European newspapers took much longer. The *Frankfurter Zeitung*, one of Beilinson's main sources of information for his articles on world affairs, reached *Davar* only ten days after its appearance. It was only in the early 1930s that news agencies such as S.T.A., I.T.A. and United Press opened offices in Palestine and *Davar*'s world coverage was able to match – in immediacy – its coverage of the local scene.

In that first issue, Berl wrote a long editorial addressed 'To our Readers', setting out his credo with regard to the newspaper. The literature, and particularly the journalism, of Hebrew labor, he wrote, were inextricably linked to the emotional, social and moral needs of the Jewish worker. Berl believed fiercely in the intellectual ability and understanding of the Palestinian Jewish worker, and it was this conviction which, he added, made sensationalism and blazoned headlines unnecessary. *Davar*'s readers would be offered the best of Hebrew journalism, and learn to enjoy theoretical, even esoteric articles.

At heart, Berl was something of a teacher, intent on leaving his stamp on his disciples. At some level of consciousness he wanted to mold the labor movement in the image of his group of comrades from Kinneret. As long as the labor camp was small, it was possible to reach practically everyone through the spoken word, only occasionally would he resort to the written text, as in *ba-Avoda*. But as the labor community grew and became highly variegated in composition, Berl discovered that the spoken word was not sufficient. As a result, the newspaper became the instrument for creating a common ideological, social and cultural clime. The Histadrut, led by Ben Gurion, was creating the wherewithal of a labor society; *Davar* would fashion its *Weltanschauung*. Berl strongly believed in the power of literature as an educational tool. He was convinced that a book by Gorky engendered more socialist awareness than any treatise by Plekhanov, and a work by Agnon greater insights into the Diaspora than any historical or sociological survey. Brenner, it should be remembered, reflected the mood of an entire generation. For

Berl, the new Hebrew literature was one of the manifestations of national renewal and revolution, and he undertook the task of nurturing it in its embodiment of new values, a new life-style and a changing language.

Moreover, it should be noted that literature was practically the only form of art easily accessible to the immigrants from Eastern Europe. They had little experience of great art, sculpture or architecture, nor had they been trained to admire visual beauty, except, perhaps, the beauties of nature. Berl, himself, had been impressed by the museums of Europe and brought reproductions of paintings back to Palestine. But art was never apparently an inseparable part of his intellectual makeup, as literature was. The same was true of music. The melancholy Russian and Ukrainian songs, nostalgically sung by the pioneers, were the sole music (apart from cantoral chants) which was familiar to them. Thus, Berl dedicated himself to fostering the literary section of *Davar* and rapidly transformed it into a literary supplement (edited first by him, and later by Zakai, then by Dov Stock (Sadan). This predilection certainly was part of Berl's Russian heritage, the influence of his formative years. In no other nation did literature play so decisive a role in influencing moods and fashioning political and social norms as among the Russian people in the second half of the nineteenth century and the beginning of the twentieth.

It is questionable, however, whether *Davar* really gave voice to the moods prevailing among Palestinian workers. The paper was supposed to be a partisan *political* organ, a weapon of the workers – and not only a means for their education. While its outlook should reflect the general policy of the Histadrut, which Berl believed to be the voice of the movement's inner truth, he maintained that the paper should provide the opportunity for airing the different viewpoints: 'free expression for *all* the trends in the Histadrut'.[3] It should be open to political criticism from the opponents of the general policies within the movement and public and social criticism from the various Histadrut institutions.

Before long it transpired that the principle of free criticism could not stand the test of the onslaught from all sides, especially from labor institutions. The local 'leaders' of labor councils did not always welcome the idea of free expression, particularly when they themselves were the target. They tended to feel slighted by what *Davar* did or did not write about them and their achievements.

This did not mean that Berl was prepared, indiscriminately, to publish everything. When a group of disgruntled workers physically assaulted Berl Repetur (a labor leader known for his integrity) on the pretext that he had shown favoritism in selecting workers for the better-paid jobs at the Naharayim power station, Berl refused to print an article justifying the attack. Criticism of the conduct of public emissaries was acceptable – if proper proof was provided; the use of violence was never sanctioned.

The relations between *Davar* and the minority parties in the Histadrut constitute a chapter in itself. In the 1920s the main minority groups were ha-Shomer ha-Tzair and the Labor Brigade. Ha-Poel ha-Tzair had its own reputable paper, and its members rarely wrote for *Davar*. Abba Ahimeir claimed years later that Berl did not allow ha-Poel ha-Tzair access to his paper, but perusal of back issues shows that this was not true. Luckily for Berl, the P.C.P. (Palestine Communist Party), on the one hand, and the Revisionists, on the other, never put the editor of *Davar* to the test: they didn't bother to submit articles to the paper. Thus Berl could continue to claim that *Davar* printed everything it was sent, and that if any member of the Histadrut felt that the paper did not reflect his views, he was free to write and *Davar* would print his comments. When the fifth anniversary of the Labor Brigade went by without any mention in the paper, a member of the Brigade protested to the editor. Since every Friday evening workers' meeting was reported in detail in *Davar*, its silence on the anniversary seems somewhat strange. Berl replied in an open letter 'To Those who Remain Silent'. In it he attacked the views of those who divided society into simple people who kept silent, and writers, whose task was to write. There was no room in Palestine, Berl wrote, for professional writers who described life; literature should emanate from those actively engaged in the life of labor. This viewpoint (vehemently attacked by the young poet, Abraham Shlonsky, who thought it dilettantist) was exploited by Berl, who used it to justify the fact that he allotted scant space in the paper to trends he considered deviationist. But, of course, when Berl was interested in a particular issue, he did not wait till some anonymous reader wrote to the paper about it, but commissioned a professional writer. The complaints of the Brigade members, and later of ha-Shomer ha-Tzair, that *Davar* discriminated against them, were not entirely groundless.

Berl was ambivalent on the question of freedom of the press. He believed that anyone who wrote an article worthy of publication was treated fairly; but in fact his evaluation of articles was affected by his entire frame of reference at the time. When Beilinson wrote an article for *Kuntres* in the wake of the de Haan murder*, denouncing political assassination of Jews by Jews, Berl shelved the article – or at least toned it down – although he was thereby offending Beilinson, his friend. It is not clear whether Berl justified the deed itself, but he undoubtedly thought that controversy on the matter in a labor newspaper was to be deplored: the perpetrators were members of the movement, and hence caution had to be exercised. Some years later, this policy of turning a blind eye to members of the movement guilty of violence was to come home to roost: when Berl wanted to denounce such acts during the struggle against the Revisionists, he found himself in a minority within the party.

Beilinson defined the *Davar* policy in the early 1930s as follows: 'We are loyal political "maximalist" Zionists. We are moderate "reformist" socialists. I, in particular, am very close in the German S.D. This is the policy which we observe and which it is incumbent upon us to maintain.'[4]

It was Berl rather than Beilinson who determined *Davar*'s policies, although the latter wrote most of the editorials. There was a measure of self-deprecation in Beilinson's attitude to Berl: this intellectual, from an assimilated background, who had absorbed Russian, Italian and German culture but had arrived at Hebrew relatively late and with great difficulty, regarded Berl as the fundamental, authentic Jew. The achievements and qualities of the Second Aliyah leadership profoundly impressed all those nurtured on the Russian socialist philosophies of the turn of the century. Beilinson, in addition, revered Berl as a human being. He accepted Berl's views to such an extent that they appeared to be identical with his own. But it is enough to read Beilinson's letters to Berl in order to see that this was not the case. Prior to the 1929 disturbances, Beilinson showed some sympathy for the Arab position and an open-mindedness on the issue of the scope of Jewish labor. But after 1929 he became Berl's instrument in the struggle against Brit Shalom, the association which worked for Jewish–Arab *rapprochement* at the price of Jewish concessions (see chapter 10). He accepted as self-evident the

---

* Jacob Israel de Haan, a Dutch Jew, came to Palestine as a Zionist, went over to Agudat Israel and was 'foreign minister' of the extreme orthodox anti-Zionist circles. He was suspected of collaborating with Arabs in anti-Zionist activity and was murdered by an extremist group in the Hagana in 1924.

fact that *Davar* had a clearly-defined ideology, and that its staff was required to toe the line. Like Berl, he justified the coercion entailed in maintaining editorial policy. Moreover, he did not perceive it as coercion but rather as the manifestation of the general will of the labor movement.

From the early 1930s, the paper began to hold meetings with its readers – '*Davar* Evenings' – in order to ascertain reader-response, and considerable praise was lavished on the paper on these occasions. It was indeed the best of the Palestinian newspapers in the 1920s and 1930s. At the same time, certain differences were revealed between the editors and the readers, although not on all issues and with varying degrees of disagreement.

With regard to British policy in Palestine, *Davar* took an uncompromisingly negative position. Berl's basic mistrust of the foreign rulers, which was shared by Beilinson, colored every report of British deeds and intentions. (See chapter 10 for a fuller discussion of this subject.) This policy was highly popular with the public at large, though less so with Berl's own labor colleagues. Chaim Arlosoroff, head of the Jewish Agency's Political Department, and Ben Gurion after him, viewed *Davar*'s intransigence in the matter, and the anti-British hostility it generated, as extreme, often impeding the conduct of any constructive dialog between the Yishuv's representatives and the High Commissioner.

With regard to the Arab problem, *Davar* also enjoyed broad public support for its position. While usually moderate and never inflammatory, it did little to advocate *rapprochement*. The Palestinian Arab national movement was consistently described as the outgrowth of incitement, lacking authenticity. Articles were frequently peppered with terms such as 'pogroms', 'effendi', and 'gangs', disregarding the national aspects of the Jewish-Arab dispute.

There were two issues, however, on which *Davar* was often at loggerheads with its readership: its socialist orientation and religion.

Beilinson, it will be remembered, presented the paper's socialist outlook as social-democratic and reformist. Socialist Zionism was basically a constructionist ideology, aimed at building the country and establishing the hegemony of the labor movement, in the Yishuv and in the Zionist movement as a whole, as the central social and educational force. The political implications in foreign policy were expressed in an affinity with the socialist, democratic and reformist parties in Europe and, concomitantly, in a rejection of revolution and the dictatorship of the proletariat. *Davar* fiercely denounced developments in Russia, the deposing and exile of Trotsky, the persecution of Zionism and the purges of the 1930s. Beilinson went so far as to compare communism to fascism, thus infuriating workers all over the country. There was tremendous curiosity about the events in the Land of Revolution, about Soviet achievements in Russia, but Berl and Beilinson chose to emphasize other aspects of Soviet rule – manifestations of despotism, the undermining of human dignity, the betrayal of socialism. Tabenkin claimed that *Davar* should not have printed Trotsky's version of his relations with Stalin, without affording Stalin the opportunity to reply. Berl and Beilinson were not troubled by their 'unfairness' towards Stalin. This became the source of a dispute, which surfaced whenever a meeting between readers and editors took place. Berl was accused of basing *Davar*'s attitude towards the U.S.S.R. on 'Zionist revenge' for the persecution of Zionists in Russia. To this he replied that 'our reckoning with Russia is above all a socialist reckoning'. His opposition to what was going on in the Soviet Union was based, first and foremost, on the distortion of the image of socialism there. Berl was unwilling to behave like certain English socialists who, so he claimed, 'accept socialism for Russia and reject it for England'.[5] As far as he was concerned, the criteria were moral and absolute, and on this point he never gave in to public opinion.

The subject of 'clericalism' provoked sharp criticism of *Davar*, to the extent that one might have thought – God forbid! – that *Davar* was a religious paper. In fact, this criticism was leveled at relatively minor 'sins': why Maimonides' centenary was noted and Marx's ignored; why the religious festivals were given such prominence in the children's supplement, and so on.

Another more serious issue was the complaint, voiced from time to time, particularly by people from the ha-Kibbutz ha-Meuhad (United Kibbutz) movement, that the paper tended to adopt a neutral stand in internal Yishuv matters, not identifying with labor positions nor siding with labor institutions. Some of the more extreme members of this movement accused the paper of playing down the conflicts in the Yishuv and the Zionist movement, of over-zealously preserving equilibrium: the editors of *Davar* were 'too responsible', lacking the temperament and the forcefulness of a fighting paper, going too far in criticizing certain actions of the workers. Tabenkin summed up the question concisely: 'The paper must not be more righteous than the workers.'[6] If the workers were destined to err – then their paper must err with them. Berl could not accept this view. *Davar* was usually to the right of its public on matters of socialism, trade union fights, the class struggle and the conflict with the Revisionists.

But the tension between the paper and its readers did not derive solely from ideological conflicts. There was simply a gap between Berl's idealized, intellectual, politically astute, theoretically inclined reader and the people who actually bought the paper. He dismissed a proposal to print detailed sub-headlines, summarizing the content of articles (as was customary in Russia), arguing that *his* readers were above that. Until 1934, he adamantly refused to print photographs in the paper – for the same reason. Over the years, Berl was forced to retreat and make the paper more popular in style. Headlines and sub-headlines appeared, as did photographs and a very popular column for new immigrants, in simple, voweled Hebrew. An evening edition, bordering on the sensational (in connection with the struggle against the Revisionists), also appeared. But not everyone welcomed the change. The Palestinian non-labor intelligentsia, which at first had been enthusiastic about *Davar*, protested: Ernst Simon warned Berl that the decline in the standards of the paper would lead them to abandon it. But the trend continued unchanged.

Concomitantly with the decline in the level, Berl began to distance himself from the paper. His name continued to appear on the masthead as chief editor, but his activity tapered off. He was apparently somewhat disappointed with the development. Rather than educating the Palestinian workers to accept his ideas, Berl was now obliged to adapt the paper to the needs of the public.

Disillusioned with *Davar*, Berl lost interest in editing. He was replaced by Beilinson and after the latter's death (in 1936), the post was handed on to Zalman Rubashov. Moshe Shertok had left in 1931 in order to pursue a political career, and Berl never forgave him. The camaraderie which characterized the editorial board in the early years gradually dissolved in quarrels, intrigue and self-aggrandizement. In the late thirties, he wrote to Rachel Katznelson, his beloved friend from Kinneret days: 'My relations with the *Davar* staff are like my relations with other institutions. I am weary to death of them.'[7]

On its tenth anniversary, the paper printed a cartoon by Aryeh Navon, captioned: 'The editor hastens to *Davar*.' The picture showed

Berl jumping over six different chairs on his way to *Davar*. The chairs represented the Histadrut Executive, the Jewish National Fund Directorate, the Hebrew University Board of Governors, the Nir Directorate, the Mapai Central Committee and the Youth Center. Berl never belonged exclusively to *Davar*, though it was his more than any other institution. He had abandoned the Agricultural Union, ha-Mashbir, *Kuntres* – all his own creations – when he found them too confining, and moved in other directions.Twice he tried to leave *Davar*, and changed his mind. His curiosity was boundless – where people as well as actions were concerned; but he soon grew weary, or possibly bored. Reality was always inferior to his vision, and when the two clashed, disillusion followed. For him, *Davar* was one of a series of endeavors which he had built – and which had failed him.

History apparently judged Berl's favorite child less harshly than he did. For all its failings, it was the paper which formulated Jewish public opinion in Palestine during the Mandate. One can still gauge its impact by talking to its veteran readers today, almost fifty years later, who remained loyal to it even during its later periods of decline. Their political, social and economic views on what occurred in Palestine and abroad during the Mandate bear a uniform and familiar stamp, the stamp of *Davar*. Needless to say, there were sectors of the population which read other papers and took a different view of the annals of the Yishuv. Yet, there was indeed such a concept as 'Yishuv public opinion', the opinion of the majority, and it included most of the Jewish community's teachers through whom *Davar*'s outlook on the world was bequeathed to the next generation. Few newspapers can claim to have molded two generations.

9

IN TRANSITION,
1925–1929

The 1920s were years of maturation; a prelude to the stormy 1930s. The exciting or fateful events took place at its very beginning and end. This decade was the dividing line between the great hopes generated by the Balfour Declaration and the British occupation and the bitter struggle of the 1930s between the Jews and Arabs, and between the Jews and the British. They began with the ambitious scheme to settle one million Jews in Palestine and create an immediate Jewish majority there, and ended with the emergence of a viable and politically significant Jewish community, but without the hoped-for majority status. They began with a Zionist movement grounded in the middle classes and led by notables and ended with the rise of popular, democratic elements to the key positions, thus ultimately changing the face of the Zionist leadership. The beginning of the decade witnessed the consolidation of the labor movement and the establishment of its central institutions: ten years later it had reorganized and moved into the predominant position within the Yishuv, the Zionist movement and the Jewish people.

At the beginning of the decade, Berl was thirty-three years old. By its end, he had passed from protracted youth to premature age. There was something mature and tranquil about Berl's middle years. An element of permanence emerged in his relations with his life's companion, Leah, and with his fellow party-members in Ahdut ha-Avoda. No period in his life was as strongly marked by a mood of stability and reconciliation as the 1920s.

The veteran members of Ahdut ha-Avoda would look back in later years on that period with affection and nostalgia. Ahdut ha-Avoda was then a cross between a romantic youth movement, and an organized political party, characterized by power struggles. The party counted some 3,000 members and resembled an extended family: relations between members were characterized by personal loyalty and friendship. The party continued to foster the ties established during the Second

151

Aliyah days, but also absorbed newcomers, who accepted the authority of the veterans and, to a certain extent, at least in the 1920s, conceded to them. This was true of the 'gymnasists', Eliyahu Golomb, Dov Hos, Shaul Meirov and Moshe Shertok. They were leaders in their own right, but did not enjoy the same independent status as the Second Aliyah group. The same applied to the Third Aliyah immigrants who found a place within the party, such as Berl Repetur and Golda Meyerson (Meir); they were later joined by the Fourth Aliyah, headed by the Z.S., a number of leaders of the persecuted and storm-ridden pioneering movement in Soviet Russia, among them, Israel Idelson (Bar Yehuda), Bat-Sheva Haikin and Zalman (Ziama) Aharonovitch (Aran).* They were ten to fifteen years younger than Ben Gurion, Tabenkin and Berl, and during the Ahdut ha-Avoda era, they accepted their authority as self-evident, and regarded them with affection and esteem. Towards Berl the two emotions were equally balanced; towards Ben Gurion, esteem outweighed affection. The young people could not compete with their mentors either on an intellectual level or in force of personality. The Second Aliyah leaders were individualists and rebels. Those that came after them joined an already existing movement, for better or worse. They lacked the singular drive and creative impulses which so attracted them to the Second Aliyah leaders, to the point where they were rendered powerless. The ideological foundations of Palestinian socialist Zionism had already been laid. Socialist constructionism in the style of the Second Aliyah, with its utopistic elements and pragmatic significance, offered an original solution to the problems of socialist Zionist existence in Palestine. The new immigrants accepted the entire system of ideas and concepts consolidated by the veterans, and in so doing, also accepted the authority of the creators. The intellectual daring of the Second Aliyah generation was replaced by an energetic conformism of the next generation. The Second Aliyah myth took root quite early, and the later immigrants, who were absorbed into the central stream of the labor movement in Palestine, accepted it for the time being unquestioningly.

When the first of the Third Aliyah pioneers arrived in Palestine, Berl was wearing the mantle of the founder and helmsman of Ahdut ha-Avoda. His quiet authority drew the young to him as did his simplicity of demeanor: the yellow silk shirt, buttoned at the side and tied at the

---

* Idelson (Bar Yehuda) and Aran later served in various Israeli cabinets.

waist with a rope belt; the peaked cap, perched slightly to one side and covering his curly black hair (now speckled with gray); the smile that originated from his eyes and spread down his face to his impressive moustache. He was venerated for his ability to listen and his talent to persuade and for his sincere interest in young people. And when he spoke at meetings or in public his listeners gained the impression that he was an inexhaustible source of knowledge, plumbing unsounded depths in Hebrew and Russian literature, in socialist theory, in history and in current affairs. The impression was of an encounter with a giant force to whom nothing human was alien. Berl was a peerless polemicist, and there was an element of ruthlessness in the way in which he would divest his rivals of layer after layer of pretence, distortion, incomprehension or mere superficiality to the gratification of his audience. In a party and in a country where ideology held considerable sway, a man of eloquence was greatly admired. It was precisely because the Zionist movement in general and the labor movement in particular were bogged down in petty deeds in the 1920s that debate on matters of principle were considered highly important. Moreover, at that time it was still believed that a man could be swayed and led to change his mind through fair debate. It now seems that, ultimately, people nonetheless voted according to their party line. Still as conferences and ideological disputation were of major public interest, Berl's talents were in heavy demand.

Officially speaking, Berl occupied no prominent positions, except as editor of *Davar* – which paid his salary. Ostensibly, he was only one of many, and did not hold higher office than others; but Berl's power never derived from his position.

Ben Gurion, who was not a charismatic figure at the time, based his influence within the party and within the Histadrut on his ability to get things done, to define objectives and achieve them. Berl's strength emanated, first and foremost, from his personality. During the Ahdut ha-Avoda, it was standard practice to consult Berl on various matters, even those far removed from his official tasks. His counsel was sought on questions of defense and arms purchases, acts of retaliation against Arabs who had raped Jewish girls, labor disputes with such notable employers as Rutenberg and even personal problems or disputes among kibbutz members. Every promising young man who joined the party 'had to' meet Berl, and the interview with him was usually fateful for the future of the young recruit.

The most important task entrusted to him was the preparation of lists of candidates for office. Ahdut ha-Avoda was known for its 'family atmosphere', and the family did not always observe strictly democratic procedures in these matters. All office holders were elected, but the members whose names were put forward were chosen, and it was Berl who chose them. His proposals were generally well balanced between urban and rural candidates, although he tended to prefer the latter. He tried to bring newcomers into the leadership and was anxious to open up positions to Third and Fourth Aliyah people; still most of the important jobs were reserved for Second Aliyah veterans. If he had been questioned, he would most probably have replied sincerely that he selected people on the basis of their qualifications. One could ask, however, whether he was really receptive to new people and new ideas.

Be that as it may, Berl was undoubtedly the party's one-man nominations committee. His veto could cut short a political career. Ahdut ha-Avoda was a rather unstructured party, organizationally. There were spasmodic attempts at organization when elections were imminent, but they usually petered out. Power was vested not in formal positions, but in individuals.

Still, in the 1920s, the party was evolving from the intimate leadership groups of the Kinneret days to the broadly-based heterogeneous class party to which Berl aspired, and which was to emerge in 1930 as Mapai. The intimate atmosphere of Ahdut ha-Avoda was on its way out, dispelled by processes operating from above and from below.

The agricultural workers were the backbone of the Non-Affiliated Group. But it soon became clear that they were a minority in the party. Members of the Fourth Aliyah, which commenced in 1924, chose largely to live in the towns, which now became the main centers of absorption, and urban workers became the majority of the Histadrut's membership, providing Ahdut ha-Avoda with its electoral force. The party was slow to respond to this structural change in its composition. But in the mid-1920s, and particularly after the leaders of the Z.S. group took over the organization of the party, a new type of party activist emerged – the municipal labor council representative. The growing strength of the municipal labor council leaders reflected the increasing importance of the party apparatus in the towns, which exerted control over most of the workers. It was an inevitable process, of which Berl was aware intellectually, though he did not internalize this awareness. He was and remained loyal to the Agricultural Union, its problems and aspirations, and saw in it the creative sector of the Palestinian Jewish labor movement. The problems of the urban wage-earner were of little interest to him: they resembled the problems of wage-earners anywhere else in the world, who were interested primarily in their own immediate well-being. Attempts to establish urban cooperatives were short-lived, tending to deteriorate within a short space of time into private enterprises.

The shift in importance from the agricultural settlements to the towns presaged the changes which were to come over the labor movement as a whole during the 1930s, and over Berl's position within it.

The leadership of Ahdut ha-Avoda was grounded on the triumvirate which had set up the party – Berl – Ben Gurion – Tabenkin. Cooperation between these three guaranteed harmony within the party and inner fraternity. In the years we are discussing, it seemed that this coalition was alive and well. But here, too, as in the case of the urban workers, certain phenomena signaled the beginning of developments which were to lead to the breakup of the inner harmony.

In the early days, the party had regarded the large kibbutz as the ideal form of settlement, and hence its enthusiasm for the Labor Brigade. This was enhanced to no small degree by the fact that rival ha-Poel ha-Tzair had 'adopted' Nahalal, the first *moshav*, a smallholders' farming cooperative. Those members of Ahdut ha-Avoda who leaned towards the *moshav* form of settlement were uneasy within the party. This situation is illuminated by Ben Gurion's remarks to the Nahalal settlers during a speech he delivered there. 'You are sitting on the border', he said. 'Beyond you lies capitalism.' This was the view of most of the Ahdut ha-Avoda people in the first half of the 1920s.

The party gradually abandoned its conviction that the large kibbutz could accommodate the masses. A special council in the mid-1920s devoted to *kvutza* matters revealed the disparity between the stand of the party members in general and the kibbutz members in particular. Tabenkin, the leader of the most important kibbutz movement, ha-Kibbutz ha-Meuhad, found himself isolated. His fellow-leaders, who lived in towns and were well acquainted with the urban workers, no longer deluded themselves into believing that collectivist settlement would ever encompass the entire country. There was no confrontation, and certainly no open clash on this occasion; but beneath the surface, the foundations of the Ahdut ha-Avoda triumvirate were weakening.

The influx of the largely middle-class Fourth Aliyah (1924–1928) led to disillusionment with the view that Zionism would be realized through national capital, directed to labor settlement and to pioneering immigration and that labor hegemony of the Yishuv would prevail. The frustration was particularly acute in the Labor Brigade and in Ein Harod, with its socialist-collectivist *Weltanschauung*. Numerous problems were to beset these two large groups in the years to come, ending in the disbanding of the Labor Brigade (and the emigration of some of its members, led by Elkind, to the Soviet Union). Many of those who left Ein Harod felt that instead of being the vanguard of a large movement, they were becoming a small minority within a public which was increasingly remote from them. Berl was aware of this and felt himself helpless to do anything about it. The settlement movement was practically deadlocked and was not to revive until the early 1930s. Few new settlements were established, and most of them were middle-class villages in the central Sharon Plain. The labor movement was now largely composed of wage-earners, and Berl lacked the necessary means – capital and land – to alter these processes.

The disbanding of the Labor Brigade and the disputes at Ein Harod were part and parcel of the crisis within the labor movement in the years between the end of 1926 and 1929. The young Jewish community experienced its first period of 'prosperity' followed immediately by mass unemployment, deprivation, despair and emigration. The first to suffer were the urban workers. Tel Aviv, where houses sprang up during the boom years like mushrooms after the first rain, now became the main victim of the slump. When immigration ceased, building work was halted: no new sources of employment were created, and contractors and factory owners went bankrupt. At the height of the crisis, one-third of Tel Aviv's workers were unemployed. It was obvious that without massive aid from abroad labor institutions, *Davar*, Solel Boneh, Kupat Holim, etc., would not survive. In order to save them, Dov Hos and Zalman Rubashov were sent to the United States at the end of 1926 (or in early 1927) to raise funds from the same source to which Berl had appealed in the early 1920s – the Jewish labor movement. The considerable sums raised by the delegation (the first instalment of £4,000 arrived apparently in March 1927) were of inestimable importance. They injected new life into the blocked arteries of labor institutions. The severest problem facing the Histadrut was the bankruptcy of Solel

Boneh building contractors, the largest such institution in the Histadrut – and perhaps in Palestine as a whole.

At the Third Conference of the Histadrut (1927), one of the main subjects on the agenda was the issue of corruption, exposed by the failure of Solel Boneh. Berl felt that a public airing, conducted in a restrained and unhysterical fashion, was essential. He himself was considered above reproach, and it was to him that people always complained about the corrupt practices of others. Berl and Leah lived very modestly; he took loans from *Davar* when necessary, and was granted preferential repayment terms, but there was nothing unethical or unacceptable in this conduct, according to the criteria of the time. At the same time, he often displayed leniency towards comrades who had stepped out of line. In those years, professional embezzlement was unknown. Malpractices were minor, although they were, of course, unacceptable on principle, particularly in a society which had set itself the goal of egalitarianism, simplicity and personal restraint. Berl understood the predicament of people who 'borrowed' public funds to solve their personal problems and, despite all good intentions, were unable to extricate themselves later. He launched a vehement attack on 'advance payments' and excessive salaries at the Third Conference. He also attacked the spread of bureaucracy in the Histadrut, but his criticism was qualified. He did not forget to mention that those facing the charges had been 'pioneers in the thick of battle for many years'.[1] He blamed the failure of Solel Boneh on a lack of organizational ability and on excessive confidence, deriving from the intimate nature of relations in the Histadrut. But ultimately he demanded collective responsibility for what had happened, since without mutual responsibility, anarchy and mutual recrimination would run rife in the movement.

The Solel Boneh affair was inextricably bound up with the relations of the labor movement to the World Zionist Organization. When the Third Histadrut Conference was convened, the fate of Solel Boneh was as yet undecided. The Histadrut leaders had obtained a guarantee from the Zionist Executive to help pay the debts and not allow the company to come to a shameful end. Despite and no doubt also because of the great difficulties in Palestine – the economic slump, the Solel Boneh affair and the Ein Harod dispute – Ahdut ha-Avoda made an effort to send an impressive delegation to the World Zionist Congress, which included Berl, Ben Gurion, Harzfeld and Remez. Berl hoped to persuade the Congress to resume land purchase through the Jewish

National Fund. The crisis in Palestine, however, was only a reflection of the general crisis of the Zionist movement. Fund-raising was at a new low, and the possibilities of undertaking new commitments were very restricted. In fact, the movement was unable to meet its old obligations. This dire financial predicament roused the Zionists of America to demand the establishment of a 'practical' directorate – rather than a party directorate – consisting of experts, who were able to withstand insupportable pressures. The practical implication of this demand was the setting up of an Executive without leftist and rightist wings. Weizmann supported the demand, assuming that its fulfillment would guarantee the financial support of American Zionists for the new Executive. The labor party delegates, albeit reluctantly, voted for the Executive of experts for fear that otherwise there would be no Executive at all.

Ten days later a blow fell which indicated to Berl the changes which were to follow in the wake of the election of the new Executive. On 22 September 1927, Israel Cohen (General Secretary of the Executive) informed Remez and Harzfeld that the new Executive was unable to participate in payment of Solel Boneh's debts and planned to reduce considerably its participation in the budget of the Histadrut's Cultural Committee. The previous Executive (which included labor representatives) had agreed to subsidize both budgets.

It may have been the surprise and shock evoked by this hasty and unequivocal decision on the part of the Zionist Executive which inspired Berl's subsequent uncharacteristic outburst. He poured out his wrath on the unfortunate head of a personal friend and political ally, Kurt Blumenfeld, leader of the liberal trend in German Zionism. The progressive German Zionists had supported the election of the new Executive, for reasons which did not differ greatly from those of the labor movement. Thus, Berl's attack was more an expression of his frustration than of his belief that Blumenfeld and his colleagues had willfully supported the wrong policy. The alliance of the workers with other progressive forces in Zionism, Berl wrote angrily to Blumenfeld, an alliance which he had urged on his comrades, had failed in its hour of trial. Hence, the 'Zionist victory [of the labor movement] has to be sought in other ways, with total adamancy, and through battle, however cruel'.[2] This declaration was the closest Berl ever came to formulating an ideology of the class struggle. Blumenfeld was offended by Berl's letter: 'Why such a preemptive letter, when only a few days ago we sat together, expressing totally different sentiments?' he wrote. He denied

Berl's charges and appealed to his friendship. But despite his affection for Berl, Blumenfeld was aware of his friend's lack of restraint in times of political struggle: 'I know,' he added, 'that you will do everything possible to slander our group politically, and – regrettably – personally, as well . . .'[3] And, truly enough, Berl's failure to distinguish between political criticism and personal acrimony was no secret to those of his allies with a discerning eye.

Berl drew an important lesson from the ousting of the labor movement from the Executive at the Fifteenth Congress, which brought in its wake the abrogation of promises of the previous Executive and the despatch of a committee of experts to examine the economic feasibility of the *kvutzot* and *moshavim* (its report was to shock the kibbutz movement). He concluded that the labor movement could not content itself with its traditional concern for settlement budgets and other matters of minor importance, and leave the running of the Zionist movement to the liberal center, led by Weizmann. In a lecture at Beit ha-Am in Tel Aviv, immediately after his return from Europe, Berl called for 'conquest of the Zionist movement. There is no future for Zionism unless it is conquered by the labor movement, and no other way for the worker: labor must take over the Zionist movement completely so that our spirit prevails in the economy and in cultural affairs.'[4]

The precondition for conquering the Zionist movement was to capture Zionist youth in the Diaspora. According to Berl, the labor movement could be forged into a great educational and political force, first and foremost, by healing the rift between the youth movements in the Diaspora, a situation which mirrored conditions within the movement in Palestine. (Prior to the he-Halutz conference in Danzig, in 1927, Berl expressed his apprehensions as to the effects the old rivalry between ha-Poel ha-Tzair and Ahdut ha-Avoda would have on 'the children from abroad'.)[5] The labor movement could attain hegemony within the Zionist movement only if it were united from within. In urging the unification of ha-Poel ha-Tzair and Ahdut ha-Avoda in Palestine, Berl reverted to his original idea from the time of the founding of Ahdut ha-Avoda – namely, that unity was the source of strength.

Three years before, in 1925, an attempt had been made to unite the two movements. It then became evident that the Second Aliyah leaders of both parties were capable of speaking the same language, and that it was the rank and file who were in conflict. As a result, the idea of merger was shelved for several years. The World Alliance of Poalei

159

Zion had yet to come to terms with the amalgamation with Tzeirei Zion, which had been forced upon it by Ahdut ha-Avoda, and any further merger was as yet unthinkable.

It was the crisis in relations with the Zionist Executive that apparently spurred both parties to break down the barriers between them. Berl responded eagerly to a proposal by ha-Poel ha-Tzair for unification, and took steps to ensure that the party approved, thus transforming a somewhat dormant desire for unity into an acceptable political policy. When Berl revealed his intentions to Ben Gurion, the latter rallied to his support, although only two weeks previously he had been reserved on this issue.

Tabenkin's stand was more ambiguous. When the matter was put to the vote at the Ahdut ha-Avoda council in October 1927, the merger proposal won a resounding majority, only the three ha-Kibbutz ha-Meuhad delegates – Tabenkin, Ostrovsky and Idelson – abstaining: ha-Kibbutz ha-Meuhad moved towards the amalgamation with the greatest reluctance, in dramatic contrast to the enthusiasm with which Tabenkin had, in 1919, harnessed himself to the task of setting up Ahdut ha-Avoda. Ha-Poel ha-Tzair was hostile towards the idea of the large *kibbutz artzi* (nationwide kibbutz), founded by ha-Kibbutz ha-Meuhad. Berl was aware of the tensions between ha-Kibbutz ha-Meuhad and ha-Poel ha-Tzair but hoped that the merger would obliterate them. It would also, he hoped, put an end to the separatist tendencies in the party and the Histadrut, originating in the various settlement movements (as reflected in the Labor Brigade and ha-Shomer ha-Tzair). The tragic fate of the Brigade had shown what could happen to a pioneering settlement body detached from the main current of the movement. Berl was careful to refrain from explicitly attributing any such divisive intentions to ha-Kibbutz ha-Meuhad; but his remarks implied that there was a danger in the establishment of parties based on a particular form of settlement.

It is possible – although no direct evidence exists – that Berl's urge to unite the two workers' parties was grounded in his reservations with regard to ha-Kibbutz ha-Meuhad's educational methods in he-Halutz (see chapter 12). After the 1927 Congress, Berl took part in the he-Halutz Council at Danzig and also addressed the ha-Shomer ha-Tzair conference, held at the same time. In drawing conclusions from his analysis of the failure of the Brigade, he attacked ha-Shomer ha-Tzair for its separatism which, he claimed, was leading towards the establishment of a new political party. He defined the process as follows: 'First a body is created – and then, in its name and on its behalf, a political point of view is created, and ways of domination are sought.'[6] And he added: 'To repeat to the young people, morning, noon and night: kibbutz, kibbutz, kibbutz is useless; we must not turn living endeavors into dogmas.'[7] Sometimes a certain road to realization comes to naught – frustrating those who have pinned all their hopes on it. This danger can be avoided by educating people in the general spirit of the movement, and not for a particular way of life. These remarks also implied strong, though oblique, criticism of the educational methods of ha-Kibbutz ha-Meuhad emissaries to he-Halutz. Berl feared the emergence of youth movements in the Diaspora who would be loyal to specific settlement movements in Palestine. A broad class party could win the loyalty of the various movements, he hoped, and prevent further schism. His colleagues in ha-Kibbutz ha-Meuhad regarded the establishment of the broad party he was advocating, as a means of weakening their influence both in the party and in he-Halutz.

The atmosphere attending the proposed unification of ha-Poel ha-Tzair and Ahdut ha-Avoda in no way resembled the exhilarating atmosphere of the 1919 amalgamation, in which personal and political differences were laid to rest. The negotiations dragged on through the winter of 1927–1928. In spring 1928 Berl composed Ahdut ha-Avoda's draft platform for the unification. On the evening of 25 May 1928, the car carrying Ben Gurion and Berl to a lecture at Ben Shemen overturned and their injuries, particularly Berl's, further postponed unification. At the end of September 1928, an Ahdut ha-Avoda council meeting was convened and ratified the platform proposed by Berl; it also decided that talks should be initiated with ha-Shomer ha-Tzair to bring it into the amalgamation. This clause was added on the demand of ha-Kibbutz ha-Meuhad, the party's leftist element, in order to increase the weight of the left in the united party and to complicate the amalgamation process even further. Only in May 1929, about a year and a half after Berl had launched his renewed efforts, were the platform and the organizational agreement for unification of the two parties finally agreed upon.*

---

* The platform was closer to the spirit of Ahdut ha-Avoda than to that of ha-Poel ha-Tzair, and served as convincing evidence that the latter were beginning to accept the socialist Zionist views of Berl and his comrades, including participation in the Socialist International and the unification of the two world alliances.

The Palestine Workers Party (Mapai), which was born out of this union, did not encompass the entire working class: the Marxist ha-Shomer ha-Tzair, also a *kibbutz artzi* movement, like ha-Kibbutz ha-Meuhad, did not join the party. Still, the party represented more than 80 per cent of the workers of Palestine, and was destined to leave an indelible stamp on the annals of the Yishuv and the Zionist movement.

Berl's dedication to the unity of the labor movement exceeded the bounds of contemporary political pragmatism. He believed that a party representing the entire working class could arrest the development of division and sectarianism which threatened labor movements everywhere. The united party formulated a plan of action and a common view regarding the relations between capital and society in Palestine and elsewhere; it stressed the central role of the labor movement and of workers in Zionist achievement. But one can seek in vain a philosophical preamble, usually so integral a part of the platforms of socialist parties. For the sake of scope, Berl was ready to dispense with philosophical hair-splitting. He hoped that the new party would provide a cohesive framework, inculcating political maturity in the Jewish masses, and particularly in Jewish youth.

There was a paradoxical element in Berl's yearning for unity: the establishment of Mapai expedited processes, which had commenced in the 1920s and were destined to undermine his own standing within the movement. Berl was and remained a man of the Second Aliyah, of the early labor settlement movement. Within the intimate atmosphere of Ahdut ha-Avoda, he was in his element. The establishment of Mapai created a relatively mass party, no longer based on personal acquaintances and contacts. And, as it expanded, Berl's influence within it decreased. Specific professional and sectoral focuses of power and identifications emerged, and Berl was not part of them. And thus, in retrospect, one sees in Berl's effort to create unity the factor which led to the waning of his leadership.

The 1920s were years of transition for Berl, in his personal life as well. After the torments of the early 1920s, his life with Leah took on routine patterns. In 1934 they finally moved into a 'respectable' apartment in the workers' housing estate built by the Histadrut in Mazeh Street. Their home was run with a simplicity bordering on penury; Berl contributed part of his salary to his mother's household expenses. The evidence points to his having been a model son, visiting his mother frequently and attending to her needs. Some sources claim that it was Leah who concerned herself with the practical details of caring for Teivel. There are no reports of tension between wife and mother-in-law, nor indications of excessive affection between them. Leah recognized Berl's debt to his mother, but drew the line at sharing a home with her. However, there was always some relative or other staying with the Katznelsons, eating at their expense and burdening the already scant household budget.

The apartment lacked even simple conveniences: Leah cooked for years on a primus stove, and an electric refrigerator was an unthinkable idea. Berl never owned a wristwatch. Only in the late 1930s did the household acquire a clock, the gift of his physician, Dr Kunin, to enable Berl to take medication at regular times. There was no radio in the house and for many years it was Berl's habit to stand silently under the window of his more affluent neighbor, Yosef Kitzis, Secretary of the Tel Aviv Labor Council, who owned all the latest technical wonders, to listen to the news. He never owned a car, and at a time when various party workers had cars at their disposal, he would wait patiently – sometimes after long tiring meetings – for a lift, usually from Eliyahu Golomb. His one concession to modern technology – since he often worked at home – was a telephone, Tel Aviv 34.

The problems of his brothers and sisters and their families continued to trouble him. His sister Hanna, the youngest and the best-loved by Berl, became a nurse in Jerusalem, but the others were in constant financial straits. Unlike Ben Gurion, Berl was deeply attached to all his family. Yet he refused to use his position to better their lot. His mother's sister sold bagels outside the Tel Nordau school, and in the mid-morning break, when the children crowded around her, Teivel would come to assist her.

Amidst the hubbub of a house which was always filled with visitors, Leah managed the finances and day-to-day organization. The household revolved around Berl, and Leah, (at least in the 1920s) contented herself with the role of housewife, pampering her husband, coddling him like a child and putting up with his idiosyncrasies.

The ties between Berl and Leah never came so close to love as in those years. The strongest link between them was their longing for a child. Various legends were rife in Palestine about Berl's childlessness: some people claimed that he had sworn on Sara's grave never to bring a child into the world. Others, less romantic and more malicious, claimed that he was sterile. This was probably political gossip, aimed at Berl, rather than at Leah. But all these theories were fanciful, deriving from Berl's unabashed love of children and Leah's failure to give birth. Berl easily established contact with children and young people. His love of play was so unusual, in a society of humorless and grave leaders, that it was often singled out for mention. The man who had never experienced a real childhood, who became an adult before he could taste the pleasures of childhood freedom, recreated his lost childhood in the company of children. It was difficult to distinguish between the adult and the children with whom he played. Children aroused his curiosity and he never tired of them – whereas, in the company of adults, he was often bored.

In Leah's case, the hope of becoming a mother was the focus of her life. Twice she conceived and miscarried. Her sisters had married and when they gave birth Leah was always there to help, and she did the same for old friends. Her life revolved around the illnesses, births and deaths of others. When she abandoned her attempts to work outside the home, her world shrank until it encompassed, beside her own family, only Berl. By the end of the 1920s, she and Berl were already in their forties – and the hope became fainter: time was pressing. And then, in May 1928, Berl was injured in the accident on the way to Ben Shemen.

An erroneous belief prevailed that Berl's injuries, like Ben Gurion's, were slight. An examination of medical documents reveals that he was forced to stay in bed for close to a year with the leg raised; his leg was put in plaster six times, yet the break failed to heal. In the end, he was obliged to travel to Berlin and there, after a brief stay in hospital, his condition improved beyond recognition, and he was released without crutches. He limped, however, for the rest of his life.

The year in which he was incapacitated was a lost year as regards the conception of a child. Berl returned from Berlin and plunged straight into the political turmoil which followed in the wake of the 1929 riots. Before long, at the end of 1929, he was sent by the newly united party to attend conferences in Germany, and then on a political mission to London, and was away for at least four months. At that time, Leah apparently made her last attempt to change her situation. After being examined by physicians in Jerusalem and by the specialist, Professor Asherman, she entered hospital for treatment. Her letter to Berl expressed her mood of despair: 'Once again anaesthetics and all the "pleasant" procedures.

But to remain by myself after all this – that I don't want and it is also useless . . . and although political affairs are so complicated now, you must change your arrangements to take our situation into consideration.'[8] She spent a week of solitude and suffering in hospital and when she returned home, broken and dispirited, she learned from Beilinson that Berl, at the insistence of his comrades, would remain in London for some time. This infuriated her: 'I asked Beilinson not to do this,' she wrote to Berl, 'but they apparently don't take people's private lives into consideration.'[9] She began to hint to Berl that she might join him in London – but he remained impervious to the hints. Politically speaking, his trip was a success, and he was widely acclaimed. Very cautiously he informed her that he would apparently be obliged to stay in England till the spring – against his own wishes, of course. She tried to lure him back to Palestine on the pretext that the newspaper required his presence and added, one last comment: 'And, apart from that, it is so inconvenient for us now. Perhaps you can still change the situation.'[10] But he ignored this appeal as well, either because he shrank, as was his wont, from revealing his feelings or because he had resigned himself to the fact that they were doomed to remain childless. Swamped by his numerous tasks, he found recompense in political work. Leah had no such compensation; she lacked intellectual interests, did not read books and never engaged in public work. Her world was confined to the four walls of her home. She lavished on Berl all the love and concern which she had reserved for the child who was never born, and her attitude towards him became increasingly maternal and possessive. She worried about his health, ensured that he visited his physician, that he did not forget to take his winter coat lest he catch cold, that he bought himself a new hat. And, while he flourished as a result of his triumphs abroad, the lines of bitterness around her mouth deepened.

10

FIRST POLITICAL BAPTISM,
1929–1931

The year 1929 was a turning-point in the annals of the Yishuv and the Zionist movement. The stormy summer of 1929 spelled the end of the years of placidity which had lasted since the riots of 1921 and the 1922 White Paper, and ushered in a new era, confronting the Zionist movement and the Yishuv with essentially new problems. The lethargy of the 1920s went hand in hand with a false sense of security, originating in the incorrect assumption that the Arab nationalist movement in Palestine had been weakened, or had even evaporated completely, and that the Zionist movement had unlimited time at its disposal to settle the country. Economic and financial problems were then the main preoccupation of the movement and it was around these issues that the 1929 Congress deliberations revolved. Weizmann led the fight – in the teeth of both left- and right-wing opposition – to establish the Jewish Agency, a body which would conduct economic and political activity on behalf of the National Home, in which Zionists and non-Zionist Jews would be represented. The aim was to grant rich and influential Jews a stake in building the country, even if they were non-Zionists. Their inclusion affected the democratic and representational structure of the Zionist movement, bestowing considerable influence on notables who had never stood for election.

The establishment of the Jewish Agency in Zurich in August 1929 was an impressive occasion. Even the skeptics, who were only partly persuaded of the validity of the concept, were moved by the ceremoniousness of the event and began to believe that great achievements would follow.

But on 23 August, before the delegates dispersed, bloody riots broke out in Palestine, and dashed all the hopes. The 1929 riots marked the end of the old Zionist world, and plunged the Zionist movement and the Yishuv headlong into the stormy 1930s. If there was any event in the annals of the Yishuv which can be called 'traumatic', it was the 1929 riots. Stunned and horrified, the Jews watched acts of atrocity in Hebron and Safed, at Motza and Hulda. The Hagana defense organization showed itself to be weak, in comparison with the Arabs, and the sense of helplessness was reflected in the fact that the riots were referred to as 'pogroms'.

The 1929 events rendered the Arab problem the central issue facing Zionism. The problem was not new, and had existed since Jewish settlement was first launched in Palestine. But after August 1929, the problem became acute. For some two years, it remained at the top of the agenda of the Yishuv in the press, in deliberations within and among the parties, and among groups which tried independently to tackle the problem. The most important and prominent of these groups was Brit Shalom (The Covenant of Peace), an association of Jewish intellectuals, most of them from the Hebrew University and the younger Zionist Executive officialdom, founded by immigrants from Central Europe. It was set up in the mid-1920s to promote understanding between Jews and Arabs in Palestine.

Berl's stand on the Arab problem was formulated relatively early. It is surprising how little he actually dealt with this issue. Whereas Ben Gurion constantly sought ways and means of achieving a dialog with the Arabs, Berl devoted scant attention to the problem. During the Second Aliyah, Ben Gurion and Ben Zvi had sought the common ethnic origin of the Arab *fellahin* and the Jewish worker, and they attributed to the *fellahin* Jewish lineage from the Second Temple period. In 1924, during the discussions at the Ein Harod conference of Ahdut ha-Avoda on the Arab question, Ben Gurion declared: 'The fate of the Jewish worker is linked to the fate of the Arab worker. We will rise together or sink together . . . We Jewish and Arab workers are the sons of the same country, and our paths are united for ever.'[1] During the 1920s Ahdut ha-Avoda advocated a 'Joint Union', the establishment of a Jewish–Arab workers' alliance, as a means of solving the Arab problem. This program was grounded in the socialist conviction, still prevalent in the 1920s, that the source of all national conflicts was social, and that fraternity between the workers of the two peoples could resolve them. It was the hostility of backward Arab effendis towards progressive Jewish workers, bringing social advancement to the country that impeded cooperation. If the Arab displayed hostility towards his Jewish counterpart, it was a result of incitement on the part of the class enemies of both Arab and Jewish workers. Advocacy of this view postponed the need to relate to the anti-Zionist Arab national movement; this would have been painful for socialists who believed in the brotherhood of peoples and in the right to self-determination. Today this theory appears naive and evasive, but in the 1920s, in the face of the ineptitude of the Arab national movement in Palestine, it seemed feasible. Perusal of Ben Gurion's book *We and Our Neighbours*, reveals a slow process of maturation and shows how a realistic statesman emerged from the orthodox socialist of the 1920s.

Berl, in contrast, had no illusions about the Arab problem, and did not share the endearing and simplistic optimism of the advocates of a Jewish–Arab Labor Alliance. As a socialist, he saw no point in opposing the idea – it expressed the aspirations of Jewish workers to improve the lot of the Arab worker. Throughout the 1920s he was tolerant of new ideas on the Arab problem. On 2 July 1925, Hugo Bergman published an article in *Davar* entitled 'Let Us Speak Frankly', in which he called on both labor parties to include planks in their programs on the Arab problem, proclaiming that there were two nations with equal rights in Palestine, the common homeland. Berl, as editor, not only printed the article, but wrote a letter of encouragement to the author, lauding his attempt to clarify vital questions 'courageously and with pure intentions.'[2] In the same letter, he explained his own stand on the issue. His solution was the establishment of two separate national autonomies with wide-ranging powers. He went on: 'The painful aspect, so it would seem, of any agreement with the Arabs is that we explicitly wish *to cease to be a minority* [italics in original]. And we cannot deny this desire, firstly, because this would be an untruth and secondly – it would destroy the national will operating within us.'[3] In his considered opinion, all wild-goose schemes which did not relate to the basic problem, namely the existence of a majority people and a minority people in Palestine, were not worthy of attention. As far as he was concerned, Zionism lacked significance without the consolidation of a Jewish national entity in Palestine, based on a Jewish majority. For him, the right of the Jews to develop the country was beyond question. The Arabs enjoyed rights in Palestine – but not the right to prevent the Jews from creating a new reality in Palestine. The Arabs were still the majority – that much was true – but this fact could be altered through immigration, purchase of land and settlement, and hence these three components of Zionist action should be the focus of attention. The definitive act was not the search for social and political means of arriving at agreement between

Jews and Arabs, but the alteration of the conditions in Palestine. The Jewish problem, and not the Arab problem, was the crux of the matter. His interim solution envisaged the coexistence of two autonomous national units, each entitled to its own independent and separate development in all areas, without infringing on the rights of the other. This outlook apparently originated in theories which prevailed in Eastern and Central Europe at the turn of the century where the question of the relations between majority and minority peoples, differing in nature and culture, was one of the central issues.

The separation between the two autonomies was the cornerstone of Berl's outlook, first, because he assumed that bringing Jews and Arabs together in one political body, under the prevailing conditions of Arab numerical superiority, would give them an edge in the formal democratic guise; secondly, because he believed that when two cultures differed so greatly, they could not function together within the same framework – the more backward of the two would hamper the development of the more advanced. Berl presupposed a relatively protracted period of growth which would prove advantageous to the Zionists and, at the same time, produce more democratic elements among the Arabs.

Berl never idealized the Arabs, as did many of the leaders of the labor movement. He had been acquainted with Arabs since the Second Aliyah, and was not enamored of what he saw. All the movement leaders shared a hostility towards the Arab effendis – the archetypes of everything abhorrent to them: eagerly profiteering from sale of land to Jews and yet inciting against them, *inter alia*, in the hope of increasing the value of land thereby. Yet they took a different view of the Arab *fellahin* and worker, as we have already noted. This romantic outlook lingered on in the 1920s. Yet Berl could scarcely be accused of sentimentalism in his attitude towards the Arabs. Rather, he seemed to have transferred his hostility towards the Russian peasant and the Ukrainian 'pogromchiks', to the Arab *fellahin*. Berl did not like foreigners, particularly those hostile to Jews. He refused to see any element of justification in the riots, and the fact that most of the rioters were simple people in no way mitigated his hatred. He said in 1930:

The talk here about the Arabs of Palestine, all the sentimentalism on this topic, reminds me of that period in Russia when young people and workers talked about the *muzhiks*. How they sang Shevchenko's songs, how they learned Nekrasov by heart!

169

Though they found the stink of tar on his boots intolerable, they imagined that same *muzhik* to be pure and noble, and thought that they could infuse him with those feelings of compassion and brotherhood which they refused to bestow on their fathers and mothers, or on the local shopkeepers or artisans. I have the feeling that the Arab in Palestine is beginning to fulfill the same highly romantic role as the *muzhik*.[4]

Berl went on to elaborate the similarity between the Russian *muzhik* and the Palestinian *fellahin*: the organization of the Russian or Polish workers did not prevent riots – and neither would the organization of the Arab workers. Any effort invested in this work should be tempered by a healthy degree of skepticism as to the advantages accruing from it.

Withal, Berl maintained a humanitarian attitude in the wake of the riots. *Davar* warned against ideas of revenge. Its tone was restrained, and it soon began to print 'Gleams of Light in the Darkness', descriptions of cases in which Arabs had rescued Jews from the rioters, sometimes at risk to themselves. Berl's demand that the Arabs be treated humanely derived not so much from love of Arabs as from fear of Jewish dehumanization in acts of savage revenge. One could not build a nation with a socialist, or at least humanistic outlook, and at the same time license it to spill the blood of another people.

The 1929 riots, or to be more precise, the reaction of the Jews to the events, changed Berl's attitude towards the Brit Shalom and other intellectuals who favored *rapprochement* with the Arabs. He was fond of intellectuals and spoke their language. This had been true in Russia, and was the basis of his friendship with such writers as S. Y. Agnon and Dov Stock (Sadan), and his rapport with intellectuals from different cultural backgrounds to his own – i.e. from Central Europe. Berl became very friendly with Hugo Bergman after their first meeting in Germany, despite the latter's official affiliation to ha-Poel ha-Tzair. He was later to establish a special relationship with Gershom Sholem, the renowned Kabbala scholar. Berl also admired Robert Weltsch, the political journalist. But, despite his affection and esteem for these people, he responded vehemently to what he regarded as Brit Shalom's panic-stricken reaction to current events. The Brit Shalom members, particularly the Jerusalemites, Ernst Simon, Hans Kohn and Hugo Bergman, were greatly perturbed by the riots and concluded that if dialog and agreement between Jews and Arabs was not forthcoming, there was no hope of implementing Zionism. Strongly influenced by the teachings of

Ahad ha-Am, this group did not advocate maximalist Zionism. It was ready to sanction an agreement based on concessions and changes in the terms of the Mandate, which would introduce majority rule, leaving certain issues to the jurisdiction of the High Commissioner. This reaction resulted from a blend of moral scruples, guilt feelings at Jewish collusion with the British Empire, and fear of renewed Arab nationalistic violence. But Berl was less shocked by Brit Shalom's reaction than by the confusion within the young generation of the labor movement, influenced by it. The tolerance with which Berl had formerly greeted unconventional views on the Arab question now abandoned him. Several days after the riots, voices were raised in Jerusalem in favour of negotiation, implying readiness to forgo the Balfour Declaration and mass immigration. Speaking at a semi-closed meeting, Berl referred to the Brit Shalom minimalists as 'uprooted people'. He hinted at their Central-European assimilated background, lacking roots in Jewish popular culture. His remarks exposing the differences between the Jews of Western and Eastern Europe, which were as old as the Zionist movement itself, roused a storm of protest, and his undiplomatic statement was later often used against him. *Davar* began to censor Brit Shalom's statements. The manifesto entitled 'Our Evaluation' was printed in full by *ha-Aretz* but *Davar* suppressed it, though it printed the mocking and abusive responses of the popular Arab paper, *Filastin*. An article in which Hugo Bergman defended Hans Kohn and his views was also shelved by *Davar*. Berl saw no point to quixotic gestures in times of crisis. He considered them of dubious value in a society battling for survival, for whom belief in the justice of its own cause was essential.

The defense of Zionist loyalties and Zionist maximalism were among the central themes of Berl's European tour in December 1929. His first stop was the conference of German Zionists at Jena in December. German Zionists were under the dominant influence of Robert Weltsch, who shared the beliefs of Brit Shalom and the pacifist views of Magnes, now Rector of the Hebrew University. Since Kurt Blumenfeld, who headed the Left Center Party and was also Chairman of the German Zionist Association, supported Weltsch, the latter was unassailable. At the conference, Berl encountered the very trends which he had fought in Palestine; but here he was a guest and his hosts were ranged against him. However, he was not alone nor was he the most important person present. The central figure at the Jena conference was Chaim Weizmann. Weizmann found himself in a strange situation: the Revisionist right wing applauded every forceful remark he made; while his supporters in the center and on the left adopted a qualified attitude towards him. Berl was introduced as the editor of the labor paper *Davar*. His speech was not a success, and made little impact on the audience. In private encounters with the prominent German Zionists, Oscar Cohen, Bloch, Kalisky and Schocken, he met with greater success than on the rostrum, but the atmosphere oppressed him. Berl apparently spoke a rather Yiddishified German, and his arguments, even fiercer than those of Weizmann, were anathema to the German Zionists. Berl's deficiencies as a public speaker outside Palestine were revealed again when he appeared at the Poalei Zion conference in Germany, after the Jena meeting. On his initiative, it should be noted, the conference adopted a resolution calling for complete solidarity with the Histadrut and expressing reservations on the positions of militant Revisionists and pacifist Brit Shalom; he even succeeded in rallying around him a strong and loyal group of party members. But in the general debate, he was only partially successful. After his speech, his interlocutors declared that there was a vast gap between them and the Palestinians, that they were the disciples of Romain Rolland and of Gustav Landauer, that is to say, of the pacifists, while the Palestinians were 'different'.

At the beginning of January 1930, Berl left Germany. In Berlin he had shared a gloomy room with a strange Jew in a little *pension*. In London, he stayed in the modest but warm home of the Hoş family, with whom he had been on affectionate terms since their joint stay in Vienna in the early 1920s. After the German aloofness, Berl was now bathed in affection: Dov Hoş adored him, Weizmann was affectionate and Pinhas Rutenberg coddled him like a child (hastening to replace Berl's peaked cap, which he had insisted on wearing, with a more elegant hat). The contrast with Germany was refreshing. Like Weizmann, Berl needed a congenial atmosphere in order to function properly. The warm reception in London prepared the ground for his subsequent success.

This was not his first trip to London. But it seemed to be the first occasion on which he tried his hand at something besides attendance at a Zionist conference. Berl was incapable of conducting a conversation in English without an interpreter. He had served in the Jewish Battalions under British officers, but had never learned English. Even his relatively long visit to the United States had not sufficed to make him fluent. Apparently he lacked the iron discipline which characterized Ben Gurion's decisions to learn languages, or perhaps he simply refused to speak a language in which he was less than highly articulate, a characteristic of eloquent people. He intended to confine his efforts to instructing and encouraging those engaged in political work, but his activities soon extended beyond Hebrew- and Yiddish-speaking circles.

Berl lacked official status. He was a member neither of the Zionist Executive nor of the Jewish Agency Executive. He was the Histadrut's emissary to Poalei Zion in London. But immediately upon arrival he was invited to attend meetings of the Zionist Executive on behalf of the Vaad Leumi, the representative body of Palestinian Jewry. Berl supported those members of the Executive who opposed the idea of a legislative council in Palestine, an idea then being revived in London. Three previous attempts by Herbert Samuel to establish such a council had failed in the 1920s because of Arab opposition. Now the Jews objected for fear that the council would reflect Arab numerical superiority.

The two most prominent Zionist leaders then in London were Chaim Weizmann, President of the World Zionist Organization, and Pinhas Rutenberg, Chairman of the Vaad Leumi. It was widely known that they were incapable of working together. As a matter of fact, when Berl went to London, one of his chief priorities was to try and mediate between the two, and his long relations with both leaders stood him in good stead.

The alliance between Weizmann and the labor movement was rooted in Weizmann's approach to the problems of building Palestine. A 'practical' political Zionist, he strongly supported the pioneering movement in its efforts to settle the country. But his ties with Berl apparently went beyond the affection and trust which marked his relations with other labor leaders. Berl was never one of Weizmann's coterie, like Sprinzak or even Ben Gurion at times, but he admired Weizmann and considered him the foremost Zionist of his day – a man of profound political comprehension. The element of competition, which clouded Weizmann's relations with Ben Gurion, was lacking in his relationship with Berl, who never sought the limelight, preferring to act behind the scenes. The two men had much which drew them together: both were sons of Eastern European Jewry, deeply saturated with the Yiddish folk culture of their childhood days. The suave aristocrat and noted scientist, who had entry to the corridors of world power, and the self-educated socialist with his simple ways shared not only a

common language but a deep love of their common roots. The fact that
'Chaim' confided in him, inviting him to discussions and taking counsel
with him, was flattering to Berl, although he tried to conceal his
gratification.

His relationship with Pinhas Rutenberg was of a different nature. *En
route* from Palestine to London, Berl had stopped off at Capri to visit
Maxim Gorki, the Russian writer. The encounter was disappointing.
Berl attempted to explain the Zionist enterprise to him, in light of the
1929 riots, which had been described in the Soviet press as an uprising
of the Arab masses against British imperialism and its Zionist lackeys.
Although the writer took a positive view of the Zionist endeavor, he
was careful to avoid criticizing the Russian regime and blamed its negative manifestations on the mistakes of ignorant individuals. The conversation never really got off the ground. The only breakthrough in the
conversation came when Gorki asked Berl what Piotr Moisevich –
Pinhas Rutenberg – was doing in Palestine. When Berl began to describe his achievements, Gorki interrupted him and said: 'Yes, yes,
since then, since Petersburg, I have known that he is a great man, and
will do great things.' At the time, Berl reflected: 'There was in these
remarks an element of jealousy that that man had not remained there.'[5]
Berl's own admiration of Rutenberg was coupled with his anger at the
fact that other young Jews, men of vision and talent, had preferred to
dedicate their energies to the Russian revolution, depriving the Zionist
movement of their gifts. Berl loved Rutenberg, the S.R.P. leader, a unique,
impulsive and unpredictable person, whose breadth of vision was suited
to a larger canvas than that of Palestine, but who stuck to his choice with
the loyalty of the convert. Rutenberg was endowed with some primor-
dial power, and his weaknesses were as notable as his strengths. His
strong character made it very difficult to collaborate with him, and
many preferred to avoid him altogether. But in times of crisis, he was
the person to whom people naturally turned for help. His unique
energy and his ability to influence both Jews and Gentiles who were
remote from Zionist sympathies were unquestioned. Thus, after the
1929 riots, he was appointed Chairman of the Vaad Leumi.

In London, Berl hoped to use his influence to facilitate cooperation
between Rutenberg and Weizmann: he was the confidant of both, and
they regarded him as the archetype of the wise, impartial labor leader.
But it was not easy. Rutenberg's inclination to reject the authority of the
Zionist Executive and to act independently, and Weizmann's wounded

pride, which he wore on his sleeve, threatened to destroy the precarious coalition which had been established. Although Berl abhorred the outward trappings of power, he was not averse to pulling strings behind the scenes. Berl found no small satisfaction in the fact that these two giants were exposing their somewhat infantile weaknesses to him, and that he was succeeding in prevailing upon them to do as he chose.

The trip to London brought Berl other unexpected successes. He took part in the closing session of the Conference of the British Zionist Federation, which was attended by representatives of the Jewish Agency, the Jewish National Fund and the Keren ha-Yesod. He delivered a speech in Yiddish, which, surprisingly enough, made a considerable impression on his audience. The Chairman of the Jewish Agency in Britain, d'Avigdor Goldsmith, who had only recently begun to take an interest in Palestinian affairs and in Zionism, and knew no Yiddish, described the speech as 'brilliant'; the rank-and-file delegates clustered around him; representatives of provincial towns invited him to appear. His speech was unique in that it did not deal with rarefied abstract political affairs, but with concrete plans. And from this point on, an exceptional relationship developed between Berl and the leaders of Anglo-Jewry.

Berl became the darling of Jewish high society in Britain. Receptions were held in his honor. Dinner parties were given for him with members of 'The Family': the Sachers, Marks and Sieffs. Berl used these occasions to persuade the Anglo-Jewish plutocracy to support two projects close to his heart: land purchase and the Hagana; and although the money he raised was only a drop in the ocean, it reflected the beginning of a link between Berl and The Family which was never to be severed. From now on Berl had secret funds for clandestine projects. More important, he now had the necessary contacts which, in times of need, could help him to obtain hard cash.

What was it that attracted the Anglo-Jewish aristocracy to this labor leader from Palestine? He was an incongruous figure in their elegant drawing-rooms, yet he seems to have charmed them more than any other Palestinian leader. Both men and women were fascinated by him. One can only assume that a combination of factors was at work. Berl was at his best in intimate discussions with people. His engaging conversation was free of phraseology and hyperbole, somewhat akin to British understatement. He radiated a profound conviction which sat well with his shrewdness and intelligence, and he was always practical, not theoretical or ideological. The British Jews were entirely different from their ponderous German counterparts with whom Berl had had such little success, and it was not only because the German Jews were diametrically opposed to his views. They were afraid of a too overt Jewish national commitment. The leaders of Anglo-Jewry were not. They were, in fact, awaiting a message, a call to action, and this Berl provided.

While in London, Berl further devoted a considerable amount of time to contacts with non-Jews. The first Labor Government was in power, and it was considered vitally important to establish contact with its leaders. The Poalei Zion Alliance office in London was run by Dov Hos, who had succeeded in developing good contacts with Labor Party circles, and he arranged for Berl to meet Henry Noel Brailsford, one of Labor's best political journalists. The pessimistic Brailsford told Berl that he gave the Zionist movement another 10–15 years before a parliamentary regime was established in Palestine and he doubted whether this period would suffice for the consolidation of a viable Jewish community. He also impressed Berl with his evaluation of some of the changeovers in the Colonial Office. Apparently, a certain member of the Labor Party, an uneducated miner by origin, who had emerged from the trade union movement, had been proposed for the office of Colonial Secretary. Brailsford claimed that the new candidate would be worse than Passfield and would not understand Palestinian affairs. 'What is needed is a man with a different education and wider understanding.'[6] One may assume that Berl's comrades recalled this warning when Labor came to power after the Second World War.

As Berl extended his contacts with Labor Party members, journalists and M.P.s, he felt increasingly hampered by his lack of fluency in English. His meetings with ordinary people – Jews and non-Jews – in the provincial towns, no less than his meetings with intellectuals and political people, persuaded him that there were extensive propaganda opportunities for the Zionist cause in England, if the appropriate funds and manpower were available.

His language difficulties notwithstanding, Berl swiftly grasped the advantages of the British single-member constituency electoral system for Zionist action. In Palestine, for some reason, the leaders, and Berl among them, seemed ashamed of using power politics – preferring to emphasize the more spiritual aspects of leadership. But in Britain, Berl gave his instincts free rein, with refreshing candor. A month after his arrival he conceived a method for promoting the Palestinian cause in the House of Commons, which was to become an inalienable part of Zionist work in Great Britain, and, subsequently, in the United States. Berl proposed that in those constituencies where Jews lived efforts should be made to ensure that pro-Zionists be elected, and hostile candidates defeated. 'I have seen here the careerism entailed in elections and candidacy,' he wrote to members of the Mapai Central Committee, 'and I realize that we can exploit not only the good instincts of true friendship, but also the evil instincts prevailing during elections.'[7] It is interesting to note that it was Berl, every inch a Palestinian, and remote from the affairs of the Zionist movement overseas, who dreamed up this astute political tactic.

Berl returned to Palestine at the end of March, 1930. On the 31st of the month, the Report of the Commission on the Palestine Disturbances of August 1929 (Shaw Report) was published, ushering in a new era in relations between the Zionist movement and the Mandate Government. The Report shifted focus from political questions to economic issues, and, foremost among them, the question of land, Arab tenant farmers and their dispossession by Jewish settlement. It cast doubt on the ability of the Zionist movement to settle more Jews in Palestine without dispossessing Arabs. Whereas direct blame for the riots was attributed to the Arabs, the Committee found 'mitigating circumstances' in the conduct of the Jews. The Report had a bitter taste for the Yishuv and the leaders of the Zionist movement. In the months after its publication, British Government policy became increasingly hostile towards the emergent National Home, particularly in the sphere of immigration: immigration quotas were drastically curtailed to the point of actual suspension. On 6 May 1930, Sir John Hope-Simpson was appointed by the British Government to investigate the land reserves in Palestine and assess the possibilities for Jewish settlement while guaranteeing the rights of the Arabs. He arrived in Palestine on 20 May. Concomitantly, the Macdonald Government conducted a series of discussions with an Arab delegation in London, which demanded the suspension of immigration, the reduction in the scope of sale of lands to Jews and the immediate establishment of an Arab national government in Palestine (or at least a legislative council). The nature of Hope-Simpson's questions in his discussions with representatives of the Histadrut Executive was ominous: he was particularly interested in the principle of Jewish labor and its implications, and ascertaining whether Arab workers had been ousted from the Jewish economy.

During the summer of 1930, the Zionist leadership was compelled to accept certain political compromises which resembled, to some extent, the positions of Brit Shalom. It was considered both impossible to avert the decree and essential to arrive at a *modus vivendi*, which must be preceded by an agreement with the Arabs. This view was accepted by Weizmann, Arlosoroff, Sprinzak, Ben Gurion, Ruppin, Kaplansky and others. They differed on tactics, but all of them accepted the fact that there was no escape from a peace agreement, and that it was both desirable and attainable. As Avraham Katznelson said: 'Thank God, now progressive Zionism is commencing.'[8] Berl's stand was conspicuously different: he was much more militant and inflexible than his colleagues on a whole range of issues.

This became evident during John Hope-Simpson's visit. Berl was dissatisfied with the way in which negotiations with the British representative were conducted. He claimed that the Jewish representatives were not emphasizing sufficiently the possibility of settling Transjordan, the Negev and the hilly areas, and were confining settlement schemes to the Sharon Plain, the Beisan Valley and the Huleh. He found Arlosoroff's moderate answers unsatisfactory. Those members of the Mapai Central Committee who attended the discussions ostensibly accepted Berl's views but the mood inclined to Arlosoroff's cautious approach.

Berl's militancy was evinced in several other areas. He proposed that U.S. Jewry be mobilized to help counter British Government pressures on the Zionist Executive and that the Vaad Leumi send a delegation to the U.S. to this end. The idea was not rejected outright, merely shelved 'for the time being'. When the Passfield White Paper was published (on 20 October 1930) sanctioning the anti-Zionist conclusions of the Shaw Commission and the Hope-Simpson Report without accepting any of the latter's positive recommendations, Berl advocated the convening of a special Congress to express the formal protest of the Jewish people. He was opposed by most of his colleagues, led by Ben Gurion, and nothing came of the scheme.

In September 1930, Ben Gurion organized a Congress of Labor Palestine in Berlin and despite the fact that he had brought a distinguished Mapai delegation with him, he insisted that Arlosoroff, Head of the Political Department of the Jewish Agency, and Berl, also attend. The fact that both were fully occupied at home, and awaiting the visit of the Under-Secretary for Colonial Affairs, did not change his mind. Arlosoroff remained at home, and Berl went, though unwillingly. The Congress was successful, as was Berl's appearance. He had hoped to hasten back to Palestine (among other reasons, because Leah was undergoing treatment) but he was sent on a ten-day lecture tour of the Baltic countries – his first visit there. The Passfield White Paper was published while he was abroad, and disrupted his plans to return home. Instead he went on to London.

He was tired and dejected during this visit. Whereas, a year before, he had believed in the power to influence the British Government by various propaganda and information activities, he now felt that the Shaw Commission and Hope-Simpson Reports and the White Paper had demonstrated the uselessness of such efforts. 'It is not a question of justice.'[9] Unlike his comrades, who saw this as evidence of the need for greater flexibility, Berl saw it as evidence of the need for a more bitter and resolute fight, without diplomatic legerdemain. The problem was not rooted in the hostility of a particular High Commissioner or Minister; it was rooted in the situation in Palestine, in the relative strength of Jews and Arabs, and would ultimately cause any administration of Palestine to become anti-Zionist.

In the second half of November 1930, a special Cabinet Committee was appointed to negotiate with the representatives of the Zionist Executive and the deliberations culminated in the document known as the 'Macdonald Letter'. Berl did not participate directly (since he was not a member of the Executive) but he tried to persuade Weizmann to adopt a more militant stand in the talks, without discernible success.

Alone in his room in London, despairing of his chance of doing something useful and anxious about the situation in Palestine, he wrote to Leah: 'I feel, within my heart, a burgeoning sense of bitterness against my comrades, a feeling which has always been alien and, essentially, even abhorrent, to me.'[10] The incessant clashes with his fellow-leaders, who rejected his political line, were compounded by the Whitechapel affair. In November 1930, by-elections were held in Whitechapel, a London district with a large Jewish population. On the assumption that large sections of Labor would shortly support the amendment of the White Paper, and that therefore it was worthwhile to maintain the goodwill of the Labor Party as a long-term natural ally, Hos and his colleagues appealed to the Jews of Whitechapel to vote

179

Labor rather than Liberal. The Palestinian Jewish public did not approve of these tactics and even the loyal Beilinson rebelled. Berl supported Hos, and reacted to the attack with a bitterness whose roots went deeper than the Whitechapel affair: 'What happened to us as human beings during the years of crisis, financial and economic, in the sphere of personal-economic trust,' he wrote, 'is now happening to us in the sphere of personal-political trust. Once again we are in the throes of agitation and defamation, and the more the better.'[11] As was his wont, Berl did not distinguish between personal and political relations. But Berl was still vigorous enough to turn the tables and impose his will on his comrades. He returned home in the second half of December 1930, and left his colleagues to complete the negotiations with the Cabinet Committee. From afar, he found it easier to criticize their acts of commission and omission, and preferred to conduct his reckoning with them in the arena where he was most at ease – the party council.

The third session of the Mapai Council was held on 5–8 February 1931, in Tel Aviv, several days before the official publication of the Macdonald Letter, its contents already known. Berl's speech included a vehement attack on the acceptance of the legislative council scheme, advocated by many party leaders, headed by Arlosoroff. He recommended a 'do nothing' policy as the most effective Zionist policy – as in the well known anecdote about a village Jew who promised the local landowner to teach a bear to read the prayer book within three years, explaining to his friends that during that time, either the bear would die or the landowner would die. He dismissed the idea that the council could be accepted in principle and then rendered ineffectual in practice through being hedged with restrictions. Once the idea was accepted – he said – the situation became fluid and unpredictable, and the restrictions would not be worth the paper they were written on.

But the main reason for Berl's devastating assault on the idea of the legislative council was the fact that it implied recognition of majority rule. Though Berl objected to the belligerent and provocative vocabulary of the Revisionists, he could not resign himself to an Arab state in Palestine, wherein the Jews would be a perpetual minority. The Zionist movement could only agree to a council based on national parity. His own ideal scheme was and remained separate growth of the autonomous ruling institutions of each national entity and the gradual curtailing of the powers of the Mandate Government. Although Berl claimed that the British would accept this idea, the chances were actually slim. Its importance lay, from the outset, in the fact that it offered a Jewish answer to the legislative council, without abandoning ground or altering the letter of the Mandate.

Arlosoroff rose to the defense of his scheme. He considered Berl's plan to be both utopian and destructive: utopian – because the modern state could not confine itself to the anemic tasks Berl assigned it; destructive – because the Anglo-Arab alliance in Palestine would be perpetuated thereby. The British would allow the Jews to do as they chose to the best of their ability, and would continue to regard themselves as the champions of the Arabs; since they held the reins of power, the Jews would suffer as a result. Moreover, if the Jews barricaded themselves within their autonomy, and the Arabs gained control of the Mandatory Government's institutions, they could stifle the National Home. The British – so Arlosoroff claimed – would establish the legislative council in the teeth of Jewish opposition, and the Jews would be forced to acquiesce and accept it without the restrictions which could have been demanded as a precondition.

Arlosoroff's scheme was the more sophisticated of the two, but Berl, though a novice in diplomatic procedures, made the more correct prognosis. Arlosoroff's basic assumption – that, since the establishment of the council could not be prevented, the Jewish community should face the problem head on – did not stand up to the test of reality: implementation was, in fact, postponed because of both Jewish and Arab objections. The idea resurfaced from time to time, but meanwhile, in the wake of the Nazi rise to power, the situation in Palestine and throughout the world changed; when the dormant Arab–Jewish crisis erupted again, it was accompanied, for better or worse, by a revolutionary proposal – namely, partition. Thus, Berl's 'do nothing' policy was vindicated by the historical developments of the early 1930s.

Arlosoroff represented a new type of Jewish statesman – educated, brilliant, able to converse with the British in their own language and on their own terms, relating to them on the basis of understanding and, to a large extent, even mutual trust. Berl never established rapport with the British, and his approach remained that of Eastern European suspicion and hostility towards the non-Jew, and particularly towards the 'authorities'. He attributed to the British more malicious intentions than they actually displayed, and his fight on questions of principle was adamant and desperate. The tragic paradox of the matter was that his inflexible approach was justified by subsequent events. In the future Berl was often to claim that it was necessary to fight to the bitter end, submitting – if at all – only at the last moment, and he would cite the legislative council affair as evidence.

The Mapai Council decided in favor of the parity proposal, including Berl's proposal that the autonomy evolve on a municipal basis. They rejected Arlosoroff's advocacy of the legislative council. What is remarkable in the whole affair is the fact that the people who represented the party and ran the Political Department of the Jewish Agency – Arlosoroff, and later Ben Gurion – were not able to dictate their political line to the party. The rank and file was more sympathetic to Berl's grass-roots approach to the 'authorities' than to the innovative and diplomatic approach of those officially in charge of conducting policy.

Berl's father, Abraham Moshe Katznelson.

Berl, Leah and Sara in Bobruisk.

Berl and a group of students in Bobruisk, *c.* 1906.

From left to right: Leah Miron (Katznelson), Sara Schmuckler and a friend in
Kiev, 1907.

Sara Schmuckler: Kiev, 1907.

Berl in Palestine, 1912.

Berl and a friend in the Jewish Battalions, 1918.

Berl at the Study Month at Rehovot, 1941.

Berl at the Study Month.

Berl reading, during the fateful Kfar Vitkin Conference about the British breakthrough at El-Alamein, October 1942.

The four Miron sisters (probably 1944): Leah is third from the left.

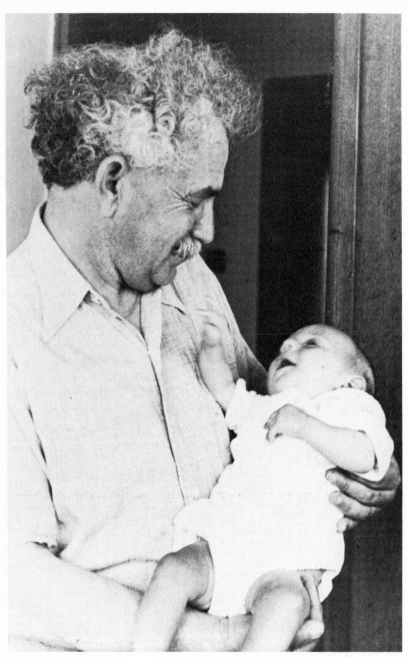

Berl, a week before his death: he holds the new-born baby of his niece.

11

THE LEADER AND HIS PARTY,
1931–1935

Once the Macdonald Letter was published, Zionist political activity abated. The Letter abrogated most of the clauses of the Passfield White Paper, and the National Home in Palestine entered on a period of renewed growth. Paradoxically enough, Weizmann's achievement paved the way for his being deposed from the Presidency of the Zionist movement. As long as negotiations with the British were imminent, Weizmann's presence was vital. But now his controversial personality, the interviews he granted to the press and his independent standpoint hampered the consolidation of the movement and the establishment of an effective coalition at the forthcoming 17th Zionist Congress, due to convene at Basle (30 June to 15 July 1931). At meetings of the Mapai Central Committee convened prior to the Congress, Berl actively supported a resolution to establish coalition, with or without Weizmann – as long as it was anti-Revisionist. This resolution reflects the change in the nature of the topics of the agenda of the movement. The 1929 riots and the subsequent two years of political struggle had diverted attention from events in the outside world: the world economic crisis which rocked the United States, and, in its wake, Germany and Austria and to varying degrees the other countries of Europe, had little impact on the Palestinian economy. The preoccupation with Palestine's affairs overshadowed the destructive processes occurring in Central and Eastern Europe: in Germany, anti-semitism was on the rise, and the Nazi Party was gaining strength; for Poland – which contained the largest Jewish community in Europe – hatred of Jews was part of the national cultural heritage. In the atmosphere of intensifying nationalism in Central and Eastern Europe, the Jews became the scapegoats of frustrated nations whose newly-found independence had not achieved its goals.

The 17th Zionist Congress marked the appearance of two parties which represented the masses – Mapai and the Revisionists – both of which reflected the growing influence of Zionism among wide sections of Jewish society. Zionism was becoming a matter of life and death: it was imperative that Palestine become a refuge for large numbers of Jews. The Zionist movement could no longer proceed at a slow and steady pace. The sense of urgency, which gave force to these two movements, also sparked off the clashes between them.

One can scarcely conceive of a movement or an individual further removed in character from Berl than Revisionism and its leader, Zeev Jabotinsky. The first encounter between Berl and Jabotinsky occurred during the heady days of the Battalions – Jabotinsky, the moving force behind the Battalions and Jewish activism, might have been expected to elicit a response from Berl. But, from the outset, there was a certain alienation: Jabotinsky's predilection for militarism and its codes, including blind discipline, did not appeal to Berl, although Jabotinsky charmed him in certain ways. There was a world of difference between the two. Jabotinsky came from an assimilated family, steeped in Russian culture. He came to Jewish culture only in adulthood and Russian remained his foremost language of communication. His Hebrew was clear and precise but singularly limited: he lacked familiarity with its biblical and talmudic sources, which were second nature to Berl. Although both were 'addicted' to literature – Jabotinsky was considered a gifted writer – there was a world of difference in their tastes. Berl loved the emotional depths of Tolstoy and Dostoyevski and considered Kafka the foremost twentieth-century writer. Jabotinsky was enamored of the structural beauty of Italian and English literature. This was reflected in their approach to public speaking. Whereas Berl was always concerned primarily with issues, Jabotinsky gave great weight to rhetoric: his speeches were theatrically calculated for effect. Berl was at his best with an audience that understood and sympathized with him. Jabotinsky could impress any audience.

Jabotinsky had been nurtured on European liberalism, which he had absorbed in the course of his studies in Italy. Despite the rebellious tendencies of his youth, he rapidly abandoned the convoluted conceptual world of Russian revolutionarism. Nor was he in sympathy with the traditional symbols of Judaism. Berl, the disciple of Russian revolutionaries and, at the same time, of Berdichevsky, combined rationalism with something beyond logic and intellect, and felt a profound affinity for traditional Jewish symbols. When Jabotinsky settled in Paris, he and his group came to be associated to some degree with the anti-revolutionary Russian emigrants. Berl, although not fond of the

Bolsheviks, felt no sympathy for White Russians, among whom were numbered many anti-semites and pogromists.

There were also fundamental differences between them in their approach to Zionism. Jabotinsky had grown up in the mixed Jewish–Gentile society of Odessa, free of the traditional restrictions imposed on Jews elsewhere in Russia. He did not display the characteristic aversion of the Jews of the Pale of Settlement to any contact with non-Jews. Jabotinsky trusted Gentiles, and particularly the British. Perhaps he was influenced by his contacts with them during the First World War, or attracted by British liberalism and democratic institutions. He believed that Great Britain would keep its promise to the League of Nations to establish a National Home for the Jewish people in Palestine. Were they to fail to do so, then British public opinion could be roused to force them to honor the commitment. Jabotinsky did not believe that the National Home could be achieved without active British help, and doubted that practical achievements, such as new settlement, economic development and the like, could eventually bring about radical change and ensure a Jewish majority in Palestine. He regarded political activity as the most urgent Zionist priority, and considered demonstrations, petitions and other gestures aimed at winning public sympathy, as the most effective means of influencing the British Government.

Berl doubted – a priori – the readiness of the British to help in the establishment of a National Home. His Zionism was based upon everyday achievements in building the country and the nation. Action was immeasurably more important to him than political maneuvering. He considered Jabotinsky's mode of action ineffectual and educationally abhorrent: self-reliance was for him the essence of the Zionist revolution.

For Jabotinsky, Zionism meant Jewish independence in a sovereign state. For Berl, it implied, first and foremost, the building of a Jewish nation, the first stage of which was the transfer of the Jewish working masses to Palestine where they would live a productive life. The successful integration in Palestine of the Jewish worker was of crucial importance, essential to the implementation of Zionism. Thus, when Berl fought for social justice and for decent living conditions for the workers, he was, in effect, struggling for the realization of Zionism. Jabotinsky, on the other hand, favored postponement of the fight for social justice and the subjugation of class interests to national needs until after the State had been established. In the conditions prevailing in

Palestine at the time, the practical implication of this stand was renunciation by the workers of any social gains – to the benefit of the employers.

The differences between these two approaches to Zionism began to surface during the 1920s, commencing with the debate on the defense of Tel Hai in 1920 (see p. 99). Jabotinsky believed that the French, who had taken over Syria, would defend the Tel Hai settlers; if they failed to do so, the settlers should withdraw. Berl and his comrades attributed cardinal importance to the consolidation of Jewish settlements all over Palestine, and adamantly opposed the idea of abandoning any spot where Jews had established a foothold. Whereas Jabotinsky advocated the organization of a Jewish 'legion' within the framework of the British Army, the labor movement leaders went ahead with setting up a small but independent underground force – the Hagana. The debate also touched on the question of the Jewish Agency: Jabotinsky regarded it as a violation of the democratic principles of the Zionist movement, while Berl and his comrades were prepared to waive principle in return for the accelerated development of the country, funded by the non-Zionists in the Agency. Another controversy revolved around the Wailing Wall. On the Fast of the Ninth of Av, 1929, Betar, the Revisionist youth movement, held a demonstration at the Wall. The British and the Arabs later claimed that this act instigated the 1929 riots. This attempt to demonstrate Jewish ownership of the site was condemned by wide circles in the Yishuv: it was considered a superfluous provocation of the Arabs.

Berl and Beilinson were among the first to compare the actions of the Betarists with the conduct of Italian fascists: when a group of young Betarists attacked and dispersed a communist demonstration, Beilinson wrote: 'This is exactly how the acts of "heroism" of the Italian fascists began.'[1] In 1928, Jabotinsky, who lived mostly in Paris, visited Palestine and delivered a speech in which he advocated the theory of 'monism': during the period of construction, all justice and morality should be subordinated to the one central national objective. In the wake of his remarks, *Davar* published a series of critical articles, the most penetrating of them by Shlomo Levkovitch. It was now clear where both camps stood.

Nonetheless, in autumn 1930, when Berl visited Lithuania and Latvia, he initiated a meeting with the Riga Betarists and they invited him to their club, where he conversed with them through the night. His impression was that these were 'wonderful young people, despite their incorrect views. Their attitude towards me, their adversary, was very civilized. I wish that our young people knew how to welcome their opponents in this fashion.'[2]

At the elections to the 17th Congress (1931), after the shock of the 1929 riots, and the Passfield White Paper, the Revisionists won 21 per cent of the vote, and the labor movement 29 per cent. The most significant result was in Poland: here the number of votes rose from 48,905 at the 16th Congress to 72,550, and among these the Revisionists gained 20,498 votes (against 4,229 at the previous Congress) and labor 22,487 (against 14,163). The Revisionists appeared to be the rising force among the Jewish masses. Jabotinsky demanded from the Congress that the 'end goal' of Zionism, namely a Jewish state, be proclaimed – this at a time when the campaign for the Macdonald Letter had only just ended, and its interpretation was still being debated. The other leaders of the Zionist movement considered it unwise to endanger existing gains for the sake of slogans which could not be realized in the immediate future. The labor delegates succeeded in defeating Jabotinsky's motion for a general debate on the 'end goal', fearing that it would generate unnecessary tensions between the Jews, the Arabs and the British. They preferred to emulate the policy of Gambetta *vis-à-vis* Alsace-Lorraine: 'Never talk about it, always think about it.' Berl compared Jabotinsky to a man walking through a forest full of bears, shouting at the top of his lungs, thereby attracting the attention of the predators. Jabotinsky tore up his delegate's card and made a dramatic exit from the assembly hall. A new Executive and President were elected. Paradoxically enough, though Weizmann was deposed because of the dissatisfaction prevailing in the movement at his moderate political line, the new Executive intended to continue his policies. The new President was Nahum Sokolow. The Executive was a coalition, and included the labour parties amalgamated in Mapai and represented by Chaim Arlosoroff and Berl Locker. The rivalry between the labor movement and the Revisionists and their battle for power in the Zionist Organization now became the central issue in internal movement relations. The struggle between the left and fascism in Europe at the time lent this rivalry a dimension of drama, desperation and urgency.

Berl's trip to the Congress gave him the unique opportunity of observing at first hand the collapse of the economic and social order in Central and Western Europe, and the impact of revolutionary trends on the public. From Basle he went on to Vienna to a socialist congress. His initially negative impression ('This congress does not bolster faith in the value of socialism today,' he wrote, 'just as the Zionist Congress does not enhance faith in contemporary Zionism')[3] was offset by his encounter with leading socialists, and with socialist Vienna, in particular. 'I have realized that the socialist movement, despite its errors and weaknesses, is nonetheless a great movement, and at this hour of plight, it may be preserving mankind from total ruin.'[4] He was impressed by a popular celebration in memory of Matteoti, the victim of Italian fascism, organized by the socialist municipality of Vienna, and saw in it 'burgeonings of socialist culture',[5] that very cultural singularity which he had sought so eagerly in the Palestinian labor movement.

With the sensitivity of a seismograph, he noted the changes in the labor movements, and among the young in particular. Despite conflicting ideologies, he found a common denominator for all of them: 'We live in a period when any movement – communism, fascism, socialism, Zionism – tries to realize its aims. Today one cannot win the hearts of the young by those theoretical and visionary means, which captivated young people when we were young. The main arguments are not in the sphere of ideals.'[6] What now attracted young people to the left was not communist ideology, but news from the Soviet Union that the Five-Year Plan was making good progress or that there was no unemployment there. The need for concrete answers to existential problems applied to the Zionist movement as well. The Jews of Poland would be drawn to whichever movement was able to provide immediate answers to the question of their survival. If the labor movement did not act decisively to renew immigration on a large scale the young people would abandon it, 'and Zionism will fall *irretrievably* [italics in original]' into the hands of the Revisionists. Haunted by a sense of urgency ('I feel it each and every day, when I awake and when I retire'), he urged his comrades in Palestine to concern themselves with obtaining immigration certificates; otherwise 'we will most certainly perish'.[7]

The twin tasks of checking the Revisionists and gaining control of the up-coming generation of Zionists were paramount for Berl in the coming four years, involving him ultimately in profound personal and political crises.

Concomitant with the Jabotinsky–labor rift in the world movement, a new brand of Revisionism was evolving in Palestine, around Uri Zvi Greenberg, Abba Ahimeir and Yehoshua Heshel Yeivin, all three 'graduates' of the labor movement. Palestinian Revisionism resembled those trends in the international labor movement which had moved from syndicalism and anarchism towards Nietzschean and elitist views, characterized by a leader cult, the use of force, and a contempt for democracy, bourgeois morality and the law. Whereas Jabotinsky emphasized the political differences between Revisionism and the labor movement, his Palestinian counterparts channeled a blatant social and economic hostility both toward the idea of the class struggle and toward the organizational strength of the Histadrut. Jabotinsky regarded himself as a devotee of liberalism and rationalism. Those who considered themselves his disciples and crowned him their leader moved towards a form of extreme populism, using methods borrowed from Italian fascism. Their paper, *Hazit ha-Am* (*The People's Front*) was unpleasantly aggressive, and its vituperations against the labor leaders were notorious. Ben Gurion, for instance, was referred to as 'Stalin'. *Jerusalem Waits*, a pseudo-historical novel, published in installments in the paper, and later as a book, was a distorted and savage caricature of the labor leaders. Berl was the villain of the story, and Greenberg the hero. The *Davar* editorial office was described in detail and though the names were changed, readers could easily identify the protagonists and enjoy the piquant political and personal scandal-mongering. Between 1931 and 1933, when *Hazit ha-Am*'s attacks on Berl reached their zenith, *Davar* chose to disregard them completely.

In October 1932 a small-scale civil war erupted in the Yishuv and lasted some two years, ignited by a strike at the Froumine factory in Jerusalem. The Jerusalem Labor Council demanded that the factory accept unionization and dismiss a female worker who was not a member of the Histadrut. Froumine refused to dismiss her and proposed arbitration, which was rejected by the workers. He then approached the Betarists and invited them to replace the striking workers. The Betarists argued, with some degree of justice, that the demand that the factory employ only organized labor was aimed at excluding them from employment, since the Histadrut had not recognized their right to establish a separate union. They could either abjure their Revisionist views, which rejected the idea of class struggle, and join the Histadrut or try to find work directly through the employers. Some chose the former path, while the more militant preferred the second. When Froumin approached the Betarists, they agreed to become scabs, claiming that the strike was political rather than economic. In the course of the strike, Jabotinsky published several articles, including his famous article: 'Yes, Break Them!', which sanctioned strike-breaking, calling upon his followers to shatter the Histadrut's monopoly of the labor market. The Froumine strike was the subject of debate in every Jewish household in Palestine, and reverberated in the Diaspora as well.

The strike ended ultimately in defeat for the Histadrut, which was forced to resign itself to the employment of Betarists by the firm. In winter 1933 another strike broke out, this time in the building trade in Petah Tikva, over the trade union's struggle for organization and decent working conditions. On the invitation of the contractors, Betarists flocked from all over the country to break the strike for the same reasons enumerated during the Froumine strike. Passions ran high, blows were exchanged, and even blood was shed.

Davar adopted an unequivocal stand on the question of strike-breaking: the Betarists were depicted as assailants, the Histadrut workers – as victims. In reports of events, the facts were screened and actually obscured. Berl was on vacation in March 1933, and Beilinson wrote to him: 'Have you seen what trouble the Petah Tikva affair has caused us? Or to be more precise: have you sensed it? Because there are some things we did not report.' He proposed that the Histadrut's Executive examine the question of the strike's and concomitant violence, adding: 'The communists would have used this strike as a model and thrown out its leaders, and they would have been right.'[8]

On 27 and 28 March 1933 the Histadrut Executive held two very lengthy debates on the implications of the strike. Ben Gurion wanted to blackball Betar workers all over the country and throw the weight of the Histadrut into the 'decisive battle' against them and the employers who supported them, come what may. Berl disagreed: a movement which had set itself the aim of building up a people and a country could not permit itself the romantic gesture of recklessly fighting a 'final battle'. Berl proposed that the labor movement take the wind out of the Betar slogans by adopting them: the Histadrut should advocate a 'national authority' in labor relations, call for collective agreement with employers, establish a 'neutral labor exchange' (i.e. forgo labor council control of employment) and negotiate a federative agreement with Betar. Berl wanted, in this way, to neutralize the valid Betar claim that they were, in effect, barred from employment except under the aegis of the employers. The singularity of the labor movement, he claimed, lay in the fact that it had succeeded in absorbing into its ranks immigrant workers of every shade and persuasion, making *ad hoc* concessions in order to further unity later on.

Everyone was shocked at Berl's proposals and their underlying analysis, although several of those present – Remez, Beilinson, Sprinzak, and to some extent Arlosoroff – tended to agree with him. His opponents included Ben Gurion, Tabenkin and Ziama Aharonovitch, Yosef Bankover and Berl Repetur (Third and Fourth Aliyah people), and apparently many others who did not actively participate in the debate. Tabenkin strongly opposed the slogan of 'national authority', the neutral labor exchange and compulsory arbitration. Were strike-breaking not contained immediately, it would spread like wildfire. He rejected Berl's contention that the Betarists were 'our own flesh and blood' and refused to consider them idealists. Even Eliyahu Golomb, Berl's old friend, dismissed his proposals as incapable of checking a movement like Betar, as did the younger leaders of the movement, from the labor councils in towns and colonies, who were in daily confrontation with Betar. They were not prepared to accept any restraints either on their right to strike or on their right to defend themselves against strike-breakers, whatever that entailed.

After a lengthy debate, in which he had been attacked vehemently, Berl took the floor: 'This time I find myself at odds with comrades with whom I have worked in harmony for many years. One comrade who heard me yesterday predicted that if I continued in this direction, I would forfeit my reputation within the labor public.'[9] Still, he was not willing to revoke his proposals. While he agreed that strike-breaking was an immoral act of violence, and that force could be met with force, he pointed out that however justified certain acts of violence, one had to weigh their usefulness. There was no point in rushing into a civil war if it could be postponed – even if one were convinced that it was inevitable. The movement had gone off the rails in its trade-union struggle: authorized violence could only lead to moral corrosion. A way had to be found to conduct a dialog with the Revisionist workers, just as it had been done before with other groups, such as ha-Shomer ha-Tzair, the founders of the Labor Brigade, and ha-Poel ha-Mizrahi, the religious workers' association.

Berl's speech wound up the discussion and, apparently, summed it up as well. The general feeling was that the Executive must tighten its supervision of the labor councils and seek an understanding with the Revisionist workers.

191

Less than one month later, on 17 April 1933, things got out of hand. A Betar convention was being held in Tel Aviv during Passover, which was to culminate on the seventh day of the Festival in a march through the streets of the city. Berl was not in Tel Aviv during the first days of Passover, and when he returned on the eve of the seventh day, he was informed that Tel Aviv Labor Council activists, headed by Ziama Aharonovitch and Dov Hos, planned to disrupt the march. He tried – unsuccessfully – to dissuade them. The thin ranks of the Betarists, wearing brown uniforms, marched through a dense crowd of workers, kibbutz members, 'Young Socialists' and youth movement members lining the streets. At first the counter-demonstrators contented themselves with booing and spitting. Then someone decided that it would be amusing to grab the cap of one of the Betarists. The anticipated clash ensued at once. A number of young marchers were injured – most of them junior Betarists at the tail end of the parade.

The day after the clash, *Davar* appeared with the headline: 'Tel Aviv insists that the filthy Hitler uniforms be removed from our midst!' This demagogic headline, composed by Zalman Rubashov, attests to the fact that Berl had absented himself from the *Davar* editorial office. After three days of seclusion, he sent a letter, announcing his resignation from the Party's Central Committee and all other positions in the movement. He wrote:

I have been deprived of the emotional capacity to regard myself as a representative of our movement . . . What others regard as an expression of mass sentiment, closing ranks against the enemy, and strengthening class unity, I see as a delusion, destroying the inner force of the working class, handing it over to the forces of chaos and darkness among the workers, and destroying the basic social fabric – without which there can be no basis for national and socialist construction work . . . I do not believe that the Devil can be exorcized by imitating his actions.[10]

The question Berl posed was: what happens to a people and to a movement when they resort to violence? The picture he drew was ugly and depressing:

Our lovely children are brought out in thousands to witness a foolish demonstration by others, to hoot them and spit at them and harass them in a convulsive frenzy, waving their fists and stealing hats. Will they be able to build a socialist economy and establish a new society, to understand the fate of our storm-tossed people, and constitute a true force when the time comes?[11]

Yosef Aharonovitch, Moshe Beilinson and Moshe Shertok openly condemned the incident, but most of Berl's colleagues – in some degree – justified the workers' conduct. They may have seen it as an outlet for the anger and frustration generated by the Betar strike-breakers, as a way of stopping Betar from gaining control of the streets, or appealing to the public as a militant alternative. Berl disagreed. As far back as the 1920s, he had been convinced that the revolutionary movement in Russia had reached a watershed when it chose to employ terror out of despair at the slow progress of constructive action. The use of terror – for Berl – was a barren attempt to force the issue and accelerate the process. One can draw a straight line from Berl's uncompromising stand against the brutality of the Bolshevik Revolution to his objections to the use of violence against Revisionism: he did not believe that good could ensue from evil. Violence, in his view, was the contemporary malaise, present in both right- and left-wing revolutionary movements. 'For some time I have been contemplating the question of evil, which is not confined to a particular sect or sects',[12] he wrote shortly afterwards. He regarded the incident as a manifestation of anarchy and of contempt for resolutions adopted previously by the party, and therefore, 'if I lack the power to prevent the movement's downfall, let me at least not be part of its aimless leadership.'[13]

The Party's Central Committee met on the same day to discuss Berl's resignation. Rumors about it had spread like wildfire all over Tel Aviv, and the workers were baffled. So was the Central Committee. Ben Gurion was in Poland at the time, and when the meeting commenced, the impression was that the opponents of violence – Sprinzak, Aharonovitch, and Beilinson, among others – would carry the day. The discussion dealt with two issues: the strategy of labor's struggle against the Revisionists, and the question of Berl's letter. The great majority of those present were loath to condemn the provocation outright, even if they did not actually condone it. The general view was that it had provided an outlet for the pent-up hostility of the workers.

As for Berl, everyone agreed that he must not be allowed to retire from public life. As Elyahu Golomb put it: at a time when the workers were confused and in need of guidance, Berl could not simply decide for himself to abandon the arena.

It was considered vital for the movement that he return to the leadership, even if only in order to stave off the vilifications of the

193

enemy. Nonetheless, after all was said and done, those forces which regarded the all-out struggle against the Revisionists as the major issue – around which the workers should be rallied – prevailed. Berl's demand for 'peace in the Yishuv' was rejected even in the shadow of his pending resignation.

Berl, in fact, could not permit himself to resign at so crucial a time. The rise to power of the Nazis in Germany had created a new situation *vis-à-vis* the Zionist movement, the possibilities open to it and the risks it faced. Thus, on 1 May 1933, only ten days after his putative resignation, he addressed a large public meeting, and exhorted against the panic which had gripped the labor movement in the face of Hitler's victory in Germany. Faced with the debacle of democracy and the rise of totalitarianism in Europe, the public tended to believe that the use of violence was the sole path to victory, and the only way of checking 'home-grown' fascists – that is, Betar. Berl attacked this view, stressing his belief in the inevitability of the victory of the workers in the Zionist movement.

But this new-found hope for moderation was shattered on Friday evening, 16 June 1933, when Chaim Arlosoroff, Director of the Jewish Agency's Political Department, was shot and killed on the Tel Aviv beach while strolling with his wife. Rumor had it that the Revisionists were responsible, and public tempers flared. Berl tried to defuse the tension and to restore calm. He published several leaflets, the best known among them entitled 'Brothers in Pain,' calling for clear-sightedness and, above all, restraint. Only a few days later the investigation narrowed down to Avraham Stavsky, a young Betarist from Poland whom Sima Arlosoroff – widow of the victim – identified as the man who had shone a torch on her husband while his accomplice shot him. The second suspect was Zvi Rosenblatt, also a Betarist. Stavsky was arrested in Ahimeir's room in Jerusalem, where he had been living. The shock was stunning. Dov Stock compared his feelings to those of the children of Israel assembled at Bethel after the incident of the concubine at Gibeah: '. . . And they lifted up their voices and wept sore; and said, O Lord God of Israel, why is this come to pass in Israel that there should be today one tribe lacking in Israel?' (Judges 21:2–3).

During and after the trial, and as the years went by, it was increasingly claimed that the charges against Stavsky, Rosenblatt and Abba Ahimeir were false and had been fabricated by the left deliberately in order to check the rise of the Revisionists in the stormy

elections campaign then underway in Poland to elect delegates to the
18th Congress. These suspicions seem highly exaggerated, though not
totally unfounded. The labor movement was highly responsive to the
idea that the Revisionists had committed the murder; but this is a far cry
from suggesting that a premeditated blood libel was involved.
Moreover, it should be emphasized that the conduct of the Revisionists
was indeed suspect, particularly that of Ahimeir and his associates in the
Brit ha-Biryonim (Alliance of Warriors), an elite group of Ahimeir's
disciples. On the eve of the murder, *Hazit ha-Am* had vilified
Arlosoroff as a traitor and vowed to get even with him. Ahimeir's
interrogation, and the examination of his papers, revealed the existence
of the shadowy world of a terrorist-inclined group. In their deliberations on the value of a revolutionary deed, they had concluded that the
quantity of blood shed was the measure: it was not hard to believe that
they were capable of acting on their convictions.

During the course of the first year after the murder, Berl was convinced of Stavsky's guilt and believed that Ahimeir's philosophy must
be uprooted from the Jewish community before it spread its poison.
Still, he endeavored to dissuade the labor public from acts of revenge
and untrammeled aggression.

It was precisely because of his fear that the labor movement might
itself resort to fascist conduct, that Berl sought constitutional ways of
preventing both character assassination and the use of terrorist
methods, and urged the expulsion from the Zionist movement of those
who employed them. It was hoped that the 18th Zionist Congress, convened in summer 1933 in Prague in the shadow of the murder, would
do this.

The atmosphere in Prague was highly charged. Rumors were rife that
the Revisionists might try to attack labor leaders, and Berl reassured
Leah when he wrote: 'From the point of view of "security", we have
arranged matters well: we are all concentrated in one hotel.'[14] On 17
August, at the opening session of the Actions Committee, Berl demanded
the appointment of a commission of inquiry to examine a file of documents in his possession which he claimed proved the existence of
terrorist groups within the Revisionist party. The Actions Committee
set up a six-man commission of inquiry and Berl handed it the file,
which contained 16 documents. (It subsequently disappeared and was
never found.)

Labor did its best to ostracize the Revisionists, preventing their election to the all-representative Praesidium of the Congress, and working to exclude them from a broad coalition Executive.

The commission of inquiry proved a traumatic experience for its members, including middle-class representatives such as Leo Motzkin (Chairman), Menahem Ussishkin and the leader of the religious party, Rabbi Meir Berlin. The two latter, at least, tended to take an understanding view of the militant political stands of the Revisionists. From the documents, they gained the impression that there was, in fact, 'a group of Zionists' in Palestine which accepted violence as a political weapon. Nonetheless, the commission determined that the documents did not prove a connection between the terrorist group and the official institutions of the Revisionists. Though Ussishkin insisted that the group be denounced at the Congress, members of the Actions Committee feared that an unequivocal condemnation might influence the outcome of the murder trial then underway in Palestine. The Actions Committee, instead, decided to recommend to the Congress the establishment of a tribunal, to investigate the evidence and draw conclusions, i.e., to procrastinate until the trial ended. The Congress accepted this recommendation, and set up a new tribunal of inquiry, headed again by Leo Motzkin.

Ten years later in a changed atmosphere Berl claimed that never for a moment was he reconciled to the idea of 'lopping off a "tribe" from Israel'.[15] Notwithstanding, from his conduct at the Congress and fragments of information and hints that have reached us it seems that there was a moment when he was willing to accept such a drastic step – under the impact of the murder and his great dread of what might ensue if terror infiltrated the Zionist movement, and Jews spilled the blood of other Jews.

At the time of the trial, Berl did not doubt that Stavsky, Rosenblatt and Ahimeir were responsible for the actual murder, although he was haunted by troubling thoughts of a broader responsibility: 'My heart is not at peace about Arlosoroff's murder. A great deal of emotional preparation was required of these people before they arrived at this state. And who can tell whether or not one of us did not expedite this process?'[16]

But, there are indications that during 1934 Berl changed his mind. He was influenced by the affair of Rivka Feigin, a young woman who claimed that she had reliable evidence of Rosenblatt's guilt. She was eventually sent abroad, on Berl's advice, when it transpired that she was an unstable person. Berl may have deduced from this that other witnesses were also unreliable. He may also have felt some degree of doubt as to the guilt of Ahimeir, whom he knew personally. Chief Rabbi Kook, who sided with the defendants, may also have influenced him. Be that as it may, the guilt of Stavsky and his colleagues was a tenet of faith for the leaders of the Histadrut and Mapai, and nobody dared openly to refute the charges. Berl was no exception. But one can deduce his doubts from his silence on the matter after his return to Palestine at the beginning of 1934 and his failure to attempt to activate the Congressional tribunal even after the trial ended.

1934 was a crucial year in the annals of the Zionist movement, the Yishuv and the labor movement. It was the year in which the Zionist Executive, under Ben Gurion's leadership, proved worthy of its task: a year of mass immigration, economic prosperity, and the commencement of the settlement of the Huleh Valley. It ended in an attempt by the former adversaries, Ben Gurion and Jabotinsky, to arrive at agreement.

For Berl, it was a year of tragic duality: to all outward appearances he wore the aura of the warrior battling against the Revisionists and their allies, but he found himself isolated from his closest comrades on a question which he regarded as the central issue of the movement, namely the use of violence.

If official positions are the yardstick by which to measure the status of a leader within his movement, then Berl remained at the helm of the labor movement. True, before and during the Prague Congress he withstood the pressures of his comrades to accept a position on the Zionist Executive (even without portfolio). He was reluctant to tie himself down to any activity which required routine work; he was, however, a member of the Zionist Actions Committee and the Jewish National Fund Directorate. Within Mapai he continued to serve in all the truly decisive institutions: when the Central Committee elected a 'political committee' to guide the movement's representatives on the Zionist Executive, it was taken for granted that Berl would be a member. He was the natural candidate for posts which called for humanitarian judgment and moral rectitude. But his status can also be measured by two other yardsticks, his comrades' attitude towards him and his image of himself. And, in these respects, 1934 marked the beginning of a process of alienation between Berl and considerable sections of the movement. What would have been inconceivable two years

197

before – that Berl's opinion would not be accepted, that he might be sidestepped and his wishes ignored – became a fact. And Berl, for his part, was beginning to be afflicted by this sense of alienation, pain and failure.

The debate, renewed in early 1934 (in the course of the Arlosoroff trial), was, to a large degree a repetition of the controversy which had raged in the wake of the Petah Tikva strike. The group of young leaders who had come to the fore in the Party were all of one opinion: the 'street' is violent, the public is a motley mob and admires the display of force. This was the lesson to be learned from the history of the S.D. in Germany. These leaders were experienced in organizational work among urban workers; they had emerged from the labor councils and ruled the party apparatus. Their attitude towards Berl was a blend of rebellion and scorn. They were willing to accept his authority on subjects in which they were not yet involved – such as political policy, but refused to do so in matters that touched on their own sphere of control. In these matters they felt that they understood more than the leader who was detached from the everyday realities of the urban workers. They had been nurtured in the spirit of the October Revolution and regarded Berl's nineteenth-century moral and educational criteria as irresolute and misleading. The pathetic defeat of the German S.D. Party, they believed, resulted from the failure to meet force with force. The heroism of the Austrian Schutzbund, on the other hand, had also failed but had at least provided the proletarian masses with a legacy of active resistance to tyranny. The members of this unofficial, lower-echelon leadership continued to treat Berl with respect – it was party practice and he could have checked their advancement within the movement – but they harbored resentment against him, which he did nothing to allay. Berl was not particularly fond of the trade union people, and their strong-arm methods, although he recognized the political usefulness of the council apparatus. As a result, he consequently reconciled himself, for example, to Abba Houshi, a typical member of this group, head of the Haifa Labor Council, despite the notorious 'bossist' machine Houshi used to pressure the workers. But he did not bother to conceal his loathing of them.

Despite the growing importance of the union leaders and the fact that they already wielded enough power to block any resolution denouncing their methods, the central power of the movement remained within the *troika* which had set up Ahdut ha-Avoda – Berl,

Ben Gurion and Tabenkin. Ben Gurion adopted a pragmatic stand in the argument: he refused to sanction Berl's anti-violence approach, claiming that violence was evil in principle but useful in certain conditions. On the other hand, his political instincts cautioned him against the possible danger to the party and the Histadrut in the emergence of particularist forces, identified with local militancy. Thus, although his opinions were relatively close to those of the 'Young Turks', his overall grasp of the situation led him to assent to a policy which was acceptable to Berl as well. Ben Gurion revered Berl, although the impression is that Berl felt for Ben Gurion little more than esteem for his qualities as a leader and his talent for action. With Tabenkin the case was different. Berl loved Tabenkin. Their youthful comradeship had blossomed into a profound tie, forged in the Kinneret of the war years. They had been drawn together by their love of Russian political literature, although the one had been influenced more by Herzen and Belinsky and the other by Kropotkin. They began to drift apart when their views on the Russian Revolution diverged. Tabenkin believed in the singularity and independence of the working class, and saw life as a constant class struggle in which the sons of light, the workers, battled against the forces of darkness – the rest of society. He did not subscribe to Berl's views, that in the Yishuv the situation was any different. For Tabenkin, the Betarists were fascists who hated the working class. He did not hold with Berl's attempt to educate the workers in the spirit of national conciliation. Although he opposed violence as it had been employed, for example, against Betar in Haifa, he condoned the Passover clash. In effect, his proposal resembled that of Ben Gurion: the organized use of force, based not on acts of terror but on the strength of the masses, and used only with the sanction of the Central Committee. It was eventually decided to set up a three-man 'command' which included Berl, which would decide when the use of militant action was necessary.

Berl, it will be recalled, had suggested the establishment of a neutral labor exchange, through which the Betarists could find employment without infringing on the rights of Histadrut members. The idea was rejected by the Central Committee, although a tendency to restrict the use of violence in these matters emerged. At the Mapai Council, a month later, Ben Gurion cautioned moderation, whereas Tabenkin favoured militancy. Throughout the meeting, Berl remained silent. That night he wrote in his diary: 'I am a stranger. A black night.'[17] On the third day, he came to the decision that he must resign from the party: 'All my efforts since the Froumine strike and up to Haifa – have been in vain.'[18] Several days later he and Tabenkin had a long talk, after which he noted in his diary: 'A sleepless night. Tabenkin is against the use of violence.' We do not know exactly what transpired between them at that meeting, but it banished his bitter feeling that Tabenkin disagreed with him on a matter which he himself regarded as the substance of the movement. His reconciliation with Tabenkin persuaded him to resume his activities within the party.

But the harmony between Berl and the movement was short-lived. On 8 June 1934, Stavsky was found guilty of Arlosoroff's murder and sentenced to death by hanging. The defense counsel appealed. Prior to the hearing, on 17 July, Berl summoned his friends Rubashov and Beilinson to Arza, his favorite convalescent home (named after Sara Schmuckler), where they worked out *Davar's* editorial policy on the issue. They decided to ask for clemency for the defendant, ostensibly because *Davar* was in favor of the abolition of the death penalty, but more so because they were appalled by the idea that a Jew might be hanged in Jerusalem (the thought of which led many non-Revisionists to support Stavsky). When *Davar's* intent became known, fifty people, led by Ziama Aharonovitch, head of the Tel Aviv Labor Council, burst into the editorial office and threatened to smash the printing presses. As a result, the Political Committee decided to refrain, for the time being, from requesting clemency. A meeting of the Central Committee was convened to discuss whether *Davar* was free to take a positive stand on clemency if the majority in the party opposed it. After a stormy meeting, at which the editorial board threatened to resign, a compromise was reached: the editors could do as they chose, as long as they were aware of the views of their comrades.

At the appeal, Stavsky was acquitted for lack of evidence (there was no reliable evidence corroborating Sima Arlosoroff's identification, and according to Palestine law, two corroborating witnesses were required for a conviction). Berl rejoiced at the verdict: it removed the threat of a hanging while not totally absolving Stavsky of guilt. Berl's colleagues, nonetheless, were troubled by the thought that Stavsky was now free and that his release would trigger public celebrations. On the following Saturday, Stavsky, accompanied by a group of Betarists, went to the Great Synagogue in Tel Aviv where he was honored, as might have been expected, by being called up to read from the Torah. Dozens of workers who usually avoided synagogues, were present at the service and began hooting. Fist-fights broke out and benches were broken, until the police were summoned and Stavsky ascended the platform under their protection. The disturbance was organized by the Tel Aviv Council without consulting the committee set up in order to decide on such matters. This was too much for Berl, and he announced that he was resigning from the Central Committee and from all other posts. But, as had happened before, he was unable to adhere to his decision.

Once the impact of the Stavsky trial had lessened, Mizrahi and the Revisionists began to put out feelers about the possibility of a rec-onciliation between the Revisionists and the Histadrut to end the civil strife in the Yishuv, rampant since the Froumine strike. There was a general feeling of fatigue, of a vain squandering of strength on in-fighting at a time when a concerted effort was needed with regard to immigration and settlement, as well as to political affairs. The High Commissioner, Sir Arthur Wauchope, had once again renewed efforts to set up a legislative council. On 31 July 1934 the Actions Committee of the Revisionist Alliance approached the Mapai Central Committee with a 'peace proposal' – an agreement designed to prevent acts of violence in the Yishuv. The party was deeply divided on the response to the proposal. One faction rallied around the labor council militants in the towns and included some of the members of ha-Kibbutz ha-Meuhad. This faction feared that the negotiations might not remain confined to issues of labor and of violence, but expand to encompass matters pertaining to the Zionist movement, thus ultimately undermin-ing the status of the labor movement. Negotiations with the Revisionists would imply the legitimation of a movement up to now ostracized by labor and considered outside the Zionist pale.

They were countered by a group of front-rank leaders, most of them Second Aliyah veterans, and some prominent Third Aliyah people, such as Golda Meyerson, Eliezer Kaplan and Moshe Shertok, who held important positions on the Zionist Executive. They tried to persuade the Mapai council, which convened to decide on negotiations with the Revisionists, that the Jewish people in the Diaspora and in Palestine would no longer countenance Jews fighting Jews, and diverting atten-tion from the crucial and pressing issues of the Zionist movement – the rescue of Jews in Europe and the building of the country.

The debate between the two camps rapidly turned into a test of con-fidence in the leadership, headed by Berl, who for two years had been trying to stem extremist currents. His speech which, as usual, summed up the discussions at the special party council, was delivered late at night. He tried to allay the fears of a 'sell-out' to the Revisionists. He reiterated his old argument that the greatest damage inflicted on the labor movement by the Revisionists was the infiltration of fascist practices in education, in slogans, in the methods of struggle and in the mood of the movement. He attacked the ugly practice of drawing analogies between Palestine and Germany and called for a return to the conceptual and creative originality of the Palestinian movement. There was a distinctive personal pitch in his speech, which played upon the special affection which his comrades had for him: if the urgent convening of the Council was a manifestation of the lack of confidence of the movement in its leaders, it should replace them. 'It is tragic, but it can be done in a spirit of mutual respect.' He claimed that it was both disgraceful and dangerous for the movement to continue to elect the same leaders while rejecting their policies.

There is no personal bitterness in my remarks. It is possible that our movement is being transformed from what it once was, a movement of national redemption (*geulat-am*) into a movement of blood-feuds (*geulat-dam*). It may be shadowed by the monster of fascism . . . Perhaps it cannot act otherwise. I am willing to bow to this situation. But I am not willing to see the movement make a mockery of itself and of its leaders.[19]

In the 1920s Berl's appeal might have won the day. But this was 1934. When the Council meeting closed, Berl wrote in his diary: 'We have fallen.'[20] The majority at the Council refused to agree to direct negotiations with the Revisionists by responding to the 'peace proposal', as proposed by the Central Committee. Instead, a pamphlet was published addressed 'to all circles in the Yishuv and the Zionist movement'. It called for agreement and for peace, but spared Mapai the act of publicly revoking its boycott of the Revisionists. The Council further agreed that the Zionist Executive should conduct negotiations with all the parties (including the Revisionists).

Berl's defeat reflected the enormous growth of the movement during the 1930s as a consequence of mass immigration. It was a movement with little sentiment for the old-timers. It was composed of people who had become workers because of the conditions prevailing in Palestine and not because of any profound class consciousness. They lacked a socialist education and might just as well have been attracted to Revisionism. The younger leaders, who knew them and their predilections well, saw in the struggle against Betar a cause around which they could be rallied, and a way of preventing desertion to the enemy camp.

The debate on the 'peace proposal' was merely the first round in a fierce battle, which flared up again two months later. In October, Ben Gurion unexpectedly encountered Jabotinsky in London, and to the amazement of everyone involved, managed to arrive at an agreement with him on the issues: the regulation of relations between the Histadrut and the Betar workers' separate union; the prevention of violence; and a solution to differences within the Zionist movement, including the central issue of discipline which had been challenged by the Revisionists. When the agreement became known (on 27 October) it became clear to Berl that its effect would be traumatic. The workers had been taught for years by Ben Gurion that the Revisionists and Jabotinsky were the powers of darkness in Zionism. They were unable to digest the fact that Ben Gurion himself had conducted negotiations with Jabotinsky and added his signature to that of the Revisionist leader. The shock was particularly stunning since the ground had not been prepared either in the Mapai Central Committee or among the rank and file.

Berl regarded the agreements as a sign that Ben Gurion had acquiesced regarding labor relations in the positions advocated by Berl since the Froumine strike. Berl had no intention of abandoning the political fight against the Revisionists, but he wanted to bring the fight in from the streets to the parliamentary sphere and to conduct it according to democratic procedures. A fair system of work allocation appeared to him as a way of ending the sorry situation whereby Jewish workers were fighting Jewish workers.

In the week following receipt of the news from London Berl spoke to Ben Gurion by telephone and congratulated him on his own policy. But within a few days there was a reversal. On 8 November, Berl cabled Ben Gurion:

The movement has been wounded and the danger is very great. What is the point to the miracle if the main instrument of realization [i.e. the party] is broken? Continuation of the negotiations is driving the public towards anarchy and destructiveness. I have always fought for the labor agreement and will continue to do so. But I will not join in ideological and political concessions to the enemy. No reconciliation with fascist Zionism, and Calais [where the Revisionist conference took place which decided on qualified membership of the Zionist movement], with adventurism. Make no binding promises till you come. Expedite your coming, every moment is precious.[21]

Berl sent this cable, which according to Ben Gurion was the most shocking in the flood of cables he received from Palestine for two reasons: first, there was the fear that in his enthusiasm for the negotiations, Ben Gurion might be drawn into a pact with Jabotinsky without ensuring the full and unconditional return of the Revisionists to the bosom of the Zionist Organization and their acceptance of its discipline.

The second reason was his feeling that Mapai was on the verge of a split. When, many years later, people looked back on the annals of the labor movement in Palestine – and on the history of 'greater' Mapai in particular – they recalled a party which united 80 per cent of all of Palestine's workers, and served as the lodestar for wide circles in Palestine and in the Diaspora. That unity which endured for 14 years (from 1930 to 1944) appeared an elusive ideal, which the next generation aspired to regain.

But a closer examination of the history of Mapai during that period reveals that the honeymoon of the united party was short-lived: the first cracks in the wall of unity appeared only five years after it was founded. Considerable emotional and intellectual effort was expended on mending the breaches, but once the idea of a split had been mooted, it created its own momentum. Once the genie was out of the bottle, it could not be replaced. The struggle for and against the Ben Gurion–Jabotinsky pact was a turning-point: for the first time, the possibility of a split became a tangible prospect, and it was mainly for this reason that Berl summoned Ben Gurion back to Palestine. He wanted to salvage the labor agreement and, at the same time, do everything possible to prevent a split in the party.

Months of feverish activity ensued: meetings of the Central Committee took place which lasted till dawn; raw emotions were exposed; and mutual recriminations were the order of the day. The opponents of the agreement consisted, first and foremost, of the urban labor leaders, particularly in Tel Aviv and Haifa, joined by the leadership of ha-Kibbutz ha-Meuhad and a considerable proportion of the kibbutz members. Ben Gurion, on the other hand, was supported by all the founders of the movement, i.e. all the Second Aliyah leaders, excepting Tabenkin.

They were augmented by the Hever ha-Kvutzot and Gordonia*, by most of the former ha-Poel ha-Tzair members and by the three 'brothers-in-law' – Hos, Shertok and Golomb.

Numerically speaking, the urban workers and their leaders constituted the great majority of the opposition. But what concerned Berl was the fact that Tabenkin and ha-Kibbutz ha-Meuhad, the pioneering movement so dear to his heart, were rallied against him. Abba Houshi, Ziama Aharonovitch, Mordechai Nemirovsky, Yosef Kitzis, leaders of the Labor Councils, were to his mind party-machine bosses, expendable and replaceable. Some of them could even be expected to switch sides once it became clear which way the wind was blowing. But the fact that Tabenkin was on their side lent weight and validity to their opposition to the historical leadership: for the first time the group of comrades from Kinneret was seen to be divided. The alliance which had established Ahdut ha-Avoda was disintegrating. In the diary in which he summarized discussions, meetings and sessions of the Central Committee, the only figure in the opposition mentioned by name was Tabenkin. The reader sometimes gains the impression that the controversy on the agreement was conducted exclusively by the three 'grand old men' – Ben Gurion, Tabenkin and Berl.

At the Mapai Central Committee the supporters of the pact were in the majority. As a result, the opposition demanded, from the outset, that the Party Conference rule on the matter. The Committee decided to convene the Conference, but reserved for itself the right to decide on the agreement in an emergency. At this, Tabenkin announced that he was leaving the Central Committee. This seems to have been the first occasion on which a minority imposed its will on the majority of the Party by threatening to secede. Things now began to move rapidly: it was decided to convene the party council and conference. For the first time, elections to the Mapai Conference were based on alternative lists of candidates – the supporters and the opponents of the agreement. In order to prevent clashes within the party, Berl and Ben Gurion agreed

---

* Hever ha-Kvutzot (Kvutzot Association) was the umbrella association of the small kvutzot (as opposed to the large kibbutz); it was based on intimacy and affinity between members, was moderate in its political views and leaned towards the old ha-Poel ha-Tzair outlook. It was smaller than ha-Kibbutz ha-Meuhad. Gordonia was a pioneering youth movement which originated in Eastern Europe; its members started to immigrate during the Fifth Aliyah and served as the manpower reserve of Hever ha-Kvutzot. Its main leader was Pinhas Lubianiker (Labon).

to remove the decision-making process from the party to the Histadrut. On 20 December 1934 it was resolved to conduct a general referendum among Histadrut members on the agreement. It was clear to Berl that the larger the number of voters, the smaller the chances of a positive resolution. Nonetheless he participated in every move aimed at expanding the number of participants in the referendum for reasons of his own: however dear to his heart the labor agreement, the party unity was dearer.

The elections to the Mapai conference revealed that the sides were almost equally balanced. There were no surprises at the conference. People said what had been expected of them, and voted as their mandate indicated. The referendum was held on 24 March 1935 and by the next day it was clear that the agreement had been rejected by the majority of the voters. There was a high proportion of abstentions and Remez claimed that the referendum was incomplete, since not all members of the Histadrut had participated. But his comrades were anxious to bring the unfortunate affair to a conclusion. The agreement to prevent violence was not signed, but, in effect, violence ceased. Mapai ceased using force in its struggle against the Revisionists. Berl's method had triumphed, but only after great delay and painful confrontations with both friends and rivals.

Berl himself summed up the controversy as follows: 'This appears to be the first internal debate in the party, which had not changed things.'[22] This was a particularly sore point with him.

Berl's strength lay in his powers of persuasion, in his talent for achieving direct rapport with individuals and with his audience. This enabled him to change people's opinions and to amend the movement's policies. In the case of the debate on the method of combating the Revisionists he discovered, for the first time, that his words were falling on deaf ears. A wide public was impervious to his arguments. Neither Berl's charm nor his wisdom could break down the barrier erected by the opponents of the agreement. They had made up their minds. People heard him out of courtesy but were not really listening to what he had to say. This was the first time people came to the council and to the conference solely in order to vote. In the early 1930s, the great political debate which raged within the party was decided at the Party Council by force of Berl's persuasive powers. Then people were elected as delegates to the conference on personal merit. This time the delegates were elected to represent a point of view. Their imperviousness to

Berl's logic did not augur well for Berl's standing in the party. Ben Gurion had entrenched himself firmly within the Zionist Executive. Tabenkin had built himself a domain in ha-Kibbutz ha-Meuhad. But Berl, who abhorred institutionalized authority, who was above institutions, began to sense the full measure of his isolation.

The coalition which had established Ahdut ha-Avoda was now divided. The Berl–Ben Gurion alliance was not strong enough or influential enough within the working class to bring about the results they so desired. Nothing like this had happened to the two men since they first met in the days of the Jewish Battalions. The authority of the leaders had been sorely damaged. It became clear in the movement that it was possible to defy Berl and Ben Gurion and to prevail. There were two partners in the triumph: ha-Kibbutz ha-Meuhad and the urban workers' leadership. The former was rooted in the movement, in its pioneering vanguard – and hence its power. The latter drew its electoral strength from its mass membership. This was an accidental alliance, an *ad hoc* partnership, but it portended the future focal points of opposition to the traditional Mapai leadership.

Berl was less harmed publicly by the affair than Ben Gurion, but his inner conviction was that the movement was moving away from him. He was particularly pained by the alienation of ha-Kibbutz ha-Meuhad. When he wrote, 'Those who nod in assent are not important to me, and those who are important to me are not with me',[23] he was referring to the still latent struggle he was conducting with Tabenkin for the hearts and minds of ha-Kibbutz ha-Meuhad members. Berl had devoted most of his time before the referendum to propaganda work in labor settlements. Yet, some two thirds of the members of ha-Kibbutz ha-Meuhad voted against the agreement. Numerically speaking, this movement was insignificant when compared with the tens of thousands of urban workers, and it was not the decisive factor in the outcome of the referendum. But the high percentage of kibbutz people voting against Ben Gurion and Berl made it clear to the latter that he had failed in his fight for the hearts of the people who were most precious to him.

12

THE YOUTH CENTER AFFAIR,
1933–1935

From the late 1920s on, Berl displayed a serious interest in educational activities among the young. While he persistently refused to accept any executive position either in the Zionist Organization or in his own movement, he was quite ready to devote his energies to setting up a 'Youth Center' for the education of Jewish youth in the Diaspora and in Palestine. Whenever the subject came up in the party, he hastened to volunteer his services: first of all, he saw himself as a mentor of the young; secondly, he was not happy with the increasingly dominant role of ha-Kibbutz ha-Meuhad in training young Jews abroad, through the he-Halutz movement.

Berl long feared the consolidation of ha-Kibbutz ha-Meuhad into an independent political force – perhaps even before the movement itself was aware of the process. He was troubled by certain similarities between ha-Kibbutz ha-Meuhad and the Labor Brigade, which had started out as a pioneering movement and ended up as a party, with an organizational, economic and human base in the communal settlements. Berl had apparently hoped that Tabenkin would serve as a buffer against separatist trends in ha-Kibbutz ha-Meuhad. But ideologically Tabenkin was drifting away from Berl, although their friendship was not affected.

Their unacknowledged rivalry surfaced in the controversy over educational methods in he-Halutz. He-Halutz was conceived of as a non-political association of pioneers preparing for immigration, affiliated directly to the Histadrut. This conception of generality was cherished by Berl as a healthy antidote to the sectarianism of the other Diaspora parties and movements associated with Labor Palestine. Ahdut ha-Avoda was too preoccupied with the economic and political struggles in Palestine to devote much energy to he-Halutz. The vacuum was filled first by emissaries of the Labor Brigade and, later, with even greater assiduity, by ha-Kibbutz ha-Meuhad. In 1925 ha-Kibbutz ha-

Meuhad sent its first mission to he-Halutz. It was headed by Tabenkin himself, who spent a year in Poland, laying the organizational and ideological foundations for his movement's activity in he-Halutz. The ha-Kibbutz ha-Meuhad leadership regarded its work in he-Halutz as a task of prime importance, and sent its brightest talents there as emissaries. They raised up a mighty movement in Central Europe, training their own local leadership cadres.

Ha-Kibbutz ha-Meuhad perceived he-Halutz as the reserve force for its ranks in Palestine. The movement preached pioneering Zionism as if it were synonymous with the kibbutz movement, that of ha-Kibbutz ha-Meuhad in particular. A sense of power, superiority and exclusiveness followed naturally.

In 1933 the growth and expansion of the pioneering movement in Poland reached its peak. The grave political and economic plight of the Jews in Central Europe attracted a flood of young people to he-Halutz centres, which offered them some hope of immigration as a solution. From an organization of several thousand members it became a mass movement and it seemed that it would grow and encompass the majority of Jewish youth in the Diaspora.

Although Berl had always been anxious to introduce his own indoctrination and education among the young, and the present growth of the movement's potential increased his sense of responsibility and urgency, he was afraid that any interference on his part in ha-Kibbutz ha-Meuhad's domain – he-Halutz – would adversely affect his relations with Tabenkin. Nonetheless, he finally did take the plunge by deciding to tour Poland. His decision was taken during the Zionist Congress in Prague, in September 1933, and this was why he fought doggedly against any plan to elect him to the Zionist Executive. His choice was to shape both his own future and that of the Palestine labor movement.

His visit to Poland, which was planned to last two weeks but stretched into a month (from 25 September to 27 October) began by way of the border area between Transylvania and Galicia.

In a way, he was returning to the scene of his childhood in the Pale of Settlement, to the way of life of orthodox Jewry, from which he had been severed since coming of age. He traveled through the towns and villages incognito, 'among the poor and dirty Jews, who are nonetheless appealing'.[1] He spent several days in Munkacs and its environs, where his profound emotional ties to Jewish tradition and to Jews as such surfaced. He was immediately able to identify with the Jewish masses and

209

their sufferings: 'From within the poverty and the filth there sometimes shone out at me the glowing countenances of the innocent.'[2] His sense of personal responsibility for the fate of the Jewish people was intensified by this direct contact with Jewish destitution, which he had not encountered since leaving for Palestine. His impressions were highly personal and very detailed. He described the life of Jewish families in the villages, living nine people to a room with two beds: 'and among the rags like little kittens, Jewish children lie concealed'.[3] His emotions were intensified by a sense of urgency: 'All these people will be lost if we cannot rapidly find them a refuge in Palestine . . . and we are still remote from knowledge of how to bring them salvation.'[4] In those 'tumbledown houses' he met and conversed with 'an infant Betarist who wants to go to Palestine'.[5] His visit coincided with the High Holidays, and he visited a Talmud Torah, attended the *selihot* prayers in the *bet midrash* and was invited by the rabbi to attend prayer on the Day of Atonement, which he did. After meeting the rabbi, he wrote in his diary 'A human countenance!'[6] In Munkacs there were groups of young Mizrahi girls and young Mizrahi workers. They sang Palestinian work songs and Berl was greatly taken with them. In contrast, he was unmoved by his visit to a ha-Shomer ha-Tzair group in the town. He read their logbook and defined what he found there as a 'sexual ideology'.[7]

One evening he met the Jewish socialists of Munkacs, apparently Bundists, and described them as 'animals from before the Flood'.[8]

He continued his journey to Galicia, and reached the capital, Lvov (Lemberg), during the Feast of Tabernacles (Succot). The decline of traditional life in Jewish Lvov depressed him: the shops were open during the holiday, the local black market was operating as usual; very few Jews were observing festival customs. He met pioneering training groups from the various movements and discovered that apart from the religious Mizrahi groups, they all worked during the holiday. He also toured the training farms of the smaller groups within he-Halutz. At the farm of ha-Noar ha-Zioni (Zionist Youth) he was distressed by their lack of knowledge of Hebrew. After his visit to the Gordonia group, he noted in his diary that their claim to have developed a unique style – cleanliness and frugality – had not proved itself. He discovered that the boys and girls shared the same dormitory and this disturbed him. Once again he enjoyed his visit to the Mizrahi group: its members knew Hebrew, prayed, studied, observed the Sabbath and worked. They were preparing themselves for life in a *kvutza*. But he was aware that they themselves felt inferior to the secular groups.

At the Lvov railway station Berl bumped into Yitzhak Tabenkin, entirely by chance. Tabenkin was well aware of Berl's intentions to meet he-Halutz groups and was still so strongly attached to him that he did all he could to induce the he-Halutz leaders to accept him. These 20–21-year-olds, who had grown up in Poland (unlike the Palestinian emissaries) proved rather hostile to Berl.

Their views reflected, in a somewhat distorted and magnified fashion, those of their Palestinian leaders, who were suspicious of any 'outsider' who might be trying to curb their control of he-Halutz. Tabenkin spent hours trying to explain to the young activists who Berl was and what he stood for – to little avail.

Berl went on to Warsaw, and spent two weeks holding discussions at the he-Halutz center and touring pioneering training farms (*hachsharot*) in Warsaw, Lodz, and Vohlin. During his tours of the he-Halutz training centers he tried to conceal his identity. Wearing his peaked cap, and speaking Yiddish, he would appear at the gates of the farm and stand there observing the boys and girls. When they asked him what he wanted, he would ask 'innocent' questions: What is this place? What is a kibbutz? What is a training farm? The young people soon responded and he egged them on, inquiring about their knowledge of Hebrew, inspecting the arrangements, the decor, the slogans. He listened to their songs, noted their overt and implied complaints against the leadership, observed their living conditions, the quality of life – cleanliness, hygiene, the kitchen. He inspected the crowded dormitories, with their double-decker bunk beds – and learned that even in those crowded conditions, they were sleeping two to a bed. In some of the farms boys and girls slept apart, in others in the same rooms. He wandered around the centers for hours, and during the working day extracted information from the sick, who were excused from work. The he-Halutz did not permit them to return home to recuperate for fear that they would be lured by the comforts of their former lives and abandon their exacting pioneering ideals. He questioned the young people about their backgrounds, and about working conditions on the *hachshara*, their leisure occupations, the books they read and the topics of their discussions. They succumbed to the charm of the anonymous questioner, and opened their hearts to him, telling him about their attitude to their leaders, voicing their complaints and fears, and sometimes even confessing that they did not intend to live in the kibbutz after reaching Palestine.

At first Berl managed to remain incognito, but word was soon out about the 'spy' who was visiting the branches and training camps. At a meeting of the he-Halutz Center in Warsaw during the course of his travels, his presence did not inhibit the members from airing their differences. Representatives of the youth movements – ha-Shomer ha-Tzair and Gordonia – were ranged on one side, and the representatives of the general he-Halutz, which was in fact, as noted before, affiliated to ha-Kibbutz ha-Meuhad, on the other. The 'talent for haggling' and for 'hair-splitting'[9] displayed by the disputants disgusted Berl.

On 26 October, he completed his tour and returned to Warsaw, again. At the he-Halutz Central Office he engaged in a stormy argument with the emissaries. The topic is unknown, but it was cut short, apparently by Berl 'in a state of rage'.[10] Immediately afterwards he was summoned to London to a conference on German Jewry, during which time he tried to rouse Weizmann to take action to expedite immigration. He continued to Paris, where he visited Jewish refugees from Germany temporarily housed in a barracks. He was shocked by the disintegration of Jewish life and the plight of the displaced persons, all of which strengthened his conviction of the need for direct, educational action, and he returned to Warsaw for additional talks with he-Halutz leaders in an attempt to make peace. Without them he could not carry out his plans.

This time the talk was of longer duration, 'from one night to the next'.[11] Berl kept a tight rein on himself, made no accusations but talked at great length. The he-Halutz members responded, and then Berl took the floor again. He unleashed his powers of persuasion – but his audience remained cool, reserved, and even resentful. When he concluded his remarks, he immediately left to catch a train (in order to return to Palestine) and was accused of having rushed off in order to prevent he-Halutz representatives from answering him – this after twenty-four hours of talk!

Berl returned home even more conscious than before of the complexity of the situation in he-Halutz. Though well aware that he was stirring up a hornet's nest he was determined not to allow matters to continue as they had in the past. He met Tabenkin for a tête-à-tête, and apparently related all his fears and reservations about he-Halutz education. Two days later he attended a meeting of the enlarged secretariat of ha-Kibbutz ha-Meuhad. He spoke at length of his grim impressions of Poland. He focused on three main areas: educational content, the quality of life, and organization. In he-Halutz branches he had seen a slogan on the wall which read: 'The way of the pioneer is cruel in practice and wondrous in essence.' This slogan reflected the educational policy which had been followed at the first kibbutz training center at Klosova in Vohlin, established in the second half of the 1920s, when Palestine was in the grip of an economic crisis and immigration had been halted. The young he-Halutz pioneers were forced by circumstances to turn temporary arrangements into permanent ones. The makeshift camp became their permanent home.

A special way of life and a group spirit emerged. Its members worked supporting themselves, living communally in the camp and preparing for immigration and life in the kibbutz, however distant the longed-for day might be. At Klosova the young pioneers cut themselves off from their parental home, from the bourgeois way of life, adjusting to the rigors of physical labor and the simplicity of communal life. Here they also learned Hebrew. Economic conditions were bad, but they overcame the difficulties through their zealous observance of communal principles, their dedication and youthful fervor. There was an atmosphere of tension, which gave them the strength to endure the years of waiting. In this situation the slogan which Berl quoted was understandable. The cruelty was born out of objective conditions. But as time went by 'cruelty' became part of the ideology, an educational weapon, aimed at maintaining the high pitch of tension. It resembled the practice of self-denial in an ascetic sect both as a test for the individual and as a means of fostering the collective spirit of the community. The educational values of Klosova penetrated the training kibbutzim all over Europe and were not always understood in the same spirit as that in which they were originally conceived. 'Cruelty' became an excuse for dirt, neglect, crude conduct and coarse language. The 'talent for living' which Berl had sought in every social entity in Palestine since the Second Aliyah days found its antithesis in the training farms – not because of a lack of organizational talent, but out of deliberate intent. The physical hardships were compounded by inflexibility, a crude approach to girls, a lack of consideration in personal matters and a disregard for the individual. When Klosova was established, its members voluntarily chose the communal life and the suffering it entailed.

213

But in 1933 the young were not joining training kibbutzim out of inner conviction, but because it was the only way to acquire the longed-for certificate which permitted emigration to Palestine. Berl objected to the theory that 'cruelty' was an educational value. He did not deny the fact that any educational process required a degree of coercion, but he distinguished between the need to establish certain rules and regulations for newcomers to the training kibbutzim, and the absolute authority wielded by the youth movement leaders over the lives of their members. Berl was shocked at the (relative) omnipotence of the central branches: in Palestine, he claimed, no institution wielded such extensive power as did he-Halutz leaders – they had the authority to decide who was ready to immigrate to Palestine, and who should continue to wait in Poland. 'You see a boy, of tender years and wisdom,' he related, 'who holds the authority to decide people's lives.'[12] The tremendous power concentrated in the hands of those who had not yet learned the secret of moderation and patience, had created insufferable attitudes and relationships within the pioneering movement. Berl was particularly pained by manifestations of callous insensitivity. He had remained a nineteenth-century humanist, and the attractions of a mass movement neither dazzled him nor shifted the center of gravity, as far as he was concerned, from man, from the individual: 'When I see that among us as well the human being is sometimes pushed aside by the sacred injunction, I fear for the future of our movement and anticipate danger.'

Berl believed that excessive power not only disrupted relations within the movement, but also engendered fear and hypocrisy. The young men and women who flocked to the training farms were neither highly-educated nor sophisticated. Most of them came from poor, provincial towns. Tabenkin had often said that the young pioneer should be trained for the maximum – for life in the kibbutz; if he could not endure it, then at least he should become a worker. But the young recruits took a literal view of the obligation to live in a kibbutz, and saw it as the condition for receiving a certificate, although some of them had no intention whatsoever of fulfilling this obligation. This was the hypocrisy which Berl abhorred: 'To swear fealty to the kibbutz, to demand of others that they fulfill all the stringent requirements of communal life, and at the same time to breed within your heart other emotions and to conceal them from close friends, with whom you share a bed – this horrifies me.'

'Cruelty', hypocrisy and fear had combined to create a kind of cultural nihilism – a total revolt against their humiliation and suffering which often resulted in a joint decision, aboard ship, not to go to a kibbutz.

Berl was also angered by the utilitarian attitude towards the young: they were seen as a means, the instrument for expanding and glorifying the movement. Such, for example, was the attitude of the Kibbutz to he-Halutz ha-Tzair (Young he-Halutz), conceived as 'the youth movement of, for and by he-Halutz' without any intrinsic value of its own. Berl, on the other hand, stressed the special needs of the young generation as a unique, autonomous society, and not as the mere reflection of adult society. He aspired to an educational method, which would leave more room for adolescent perplexity and self-questioning.

The debate on educational methods was linked to the controversy on relations between he-Halutz and the youth movements. The youth movement graduates came mostly from the urban middle class, and many had completed high school. This was particularly true of ha-Shomer ha-Tzair graduates. On the other hand, those who joined he-Halutz on an individual basis at the age of 18 – called 'just pioneers' – had never been associated with youth movements. They came for the most part from the provinces. Their level of education was inferior, their organization and indoctrination difficult and their commitment to Zionist ideals in general and the movement in particular rather tenuous. He-Halutz's representatives insisted that when boys and girls completed their apprenticeship in the youth movements and wanted to join a training farm, they should join he-Halutz directly, on an individual basis, disbanding their previous homogeneous groups. The intention was to exploit the high-caliber youth movement graduates in educating the thousands coming directly into the pioneering movement. The youth movements, however, refused to disband: they regarded the cohesiveness of their groups, their shared experiences, the esprit de corps as the quintessence of the movement. Politically and organizationally the youth movements constituted the manpower reserve for the various kibbutz movements in Palestine, for whom the presentation of the special training groups was a matter of life and death. Thanks to its domination of he-Halutz, ha-Kibbutz ha-Meuhad had succeeded in accumulating a large manpower reserve while Hever ha-Kvutzot was constantly short of recruits. More than one *kvutza* was forced to ask ha-Shomer ha-Tzair to send it reinforcements and, ultimately, to resign itself to joining Marxist ha-Shomer ha-Tzair's *kibbutz artzi*. Thus, the educational problems were inextricably interwoven with problems of domination and control.

Berl, as we have seen, discovered during his tour of Poland that the rivalry between he-Halutz and the youth movement had become the main issue of the movement. The relations between representatives of the majority in he-Halutz and of the minorities, such as Gordonia and ha-Shomer ha-Tzair, were deplorable. The latter were discriminated against when funds and manpower were allocated, and were in constant fear of coercion by the majority. Berl recognized the validity of the claim of the youth movements, that he-Halutz education was aimed explicitly at directing young people to ha-Kibbutz ha-Meuhad. The solution he proposed was to establish a clear distinction between the training in he-Halutz and indoctrination for kibbutz life. It should be made clear to all, that within he-Halutz there were some groups which planned to join ha-Kibbutz ha-Meuhad, others to join Hever ha-Kvutzot or ha-Kibbutz Haartzi, while others intended to join *moshavim*, as they did not incline to a communal way of life. Ha-Kibbutz ha-Meuhad should proclaim openly that he-Halutz ha-Tzair was its own youth movement, and put it on an equal footing with the other youth movements. This would put an end to the situation whereby it was brandishing the banner of generality while, in fact, it was directing the youth to its own settlements. The Histadrut was in no position to supervise the activities in the Diaspora; and Mapai, which wanted to intervene, was unable to do so, since ha-Kibbutz ha-Meuhad was answerable to the Histadrut alone.

Tabenkin agreed with Berl that in the training farms the quality of life and cultural activities (including the teaching of Hebrew) was deplorable. But he saw no point in revamping the methods of indoctrination employed: all educational processes were relatively coercive, and the education of the masses even more so. He-Halutz was training masses of young people to live together and engage in physical work, and this would not be attained without indoctrination: he considered the elements of self-denial and sublimation to be vital components of mass education. And although he was ready to tolerate the autonomy of the other youth movements on the training farms, he vehemently rejected Berl's proposals to change the organizational structure of he-Halutz and the status of ha-Kibbutz ha-Meuhad within it.

Tabenkin employed the very arguments Berl had once used against the ideological indoctrination of the young. Young people, he said, should be educated on tangible symbols – such as the kibbutz, pioneering, and the Histadrut – and not on political parties. As with Berl, it is difficult to distinguish between Tabenkin's educational and political considerations. He spoke in favor of 'unaffiliated pioneers' as against the 'aristocracy' of the youth movements, and in favor of 'general' party education while insisting on Kibbutz Meuhad control over he-Halutz. Although he had originally gone to the kibbutz as a member of the party (Ahdut ha-Avoda), he ultimately came to identify himself with his power base in ha-Kibbutz ha-Meuhad, and came to consider the interests of one particular sector as those of the entire labor movement.

The debate at the enlarged secretariat of ha-Kibbutz ha-Meuhad changed nothing. Berl appeared there as an outsider, criticizing internal affairs without being cognisant of the difficulties entailed. The fact that he himself did not live in a communal settlement, while not an obstacle with his contemporaries in the leadership, was a definite drawback in the eyes of the zealous young members of ha-Kibbutz ha-Meuhad. Tabenkin found it necessary in his reply to Berl to describe him as 'a man of the kibbutz' although he did not live in one. And Berl, in his rejoinder, noted that Tabenkin had called him an 'insider', apologizing for the fact that his circumstances – the tasks which the movement had imposed on him – had prevented his joining the kibbutz movement.

The debate on he-Halutz dramatized the fact that Berl was ageing. He was now 46, a generation removed from the newly emerging ha-Kibbutz ha-Meuhad leadership and particularly from the he-Halutz activists, who were in their early twenties. The songs, the slogans, the 'cruelty' and poverty – which had shocked Berl so greatly – were more easily tolerated by the young. Their leaders claimed that their *joie de vivre* and *esprit de corps* helped them overcome all hardships. Berl's criticism was that of an older, more sober, subtle and somewhat paternalistic figure.

This was reflected as well in his attitudes on sexual matters. Public discussions of these questions among the young made him uneasy. He objected, for example, to the book on adolescent sex published by ha-Shomer ha-Tzair in Palestine. The veil of discretion which the Second Aliyah drew over these matters was to his taste and that of his contemporaries, but not to that of the young people, who had grown up in the Third Aliyah and after. To a modern eye, the relations between the sexes in the training camps appear quite innocent; but to Berl they appeared as licentious and offensive to the girls.

The debate with ha-Kibbutz ha-Meuhad reflected the extent to which Berl himself had changed. A decade earlier he had shown impatience, even intolerance, towards people and movements who were slow to grasp what he considered self-evident: the historical unity of the Palestinian labor movement or the pragmatic requirements of the Zionist enterprise. Now when the he-Halutz youngsters urged that union be enforced in the youth movements, Berl called for patience and faith in the slow but sure voluntary evolution of the forces of unity. One young man retorted: 'It is impossible to wait' – something that Berl himself might have said ten years earlier.

But in 1933 he regarded 'forcing the issue' as the root of all contemporary evil: 'All the spiritual and political maladies of our day are caused by this "impossibility",' he claimed. 'Everyone who tries to attack us as socialists or as Zionists declares that it is "impossible to wait".'[13] In the early 1920s he had not attributed great importance to democracy; now he was the guardian of the democratic processes and free expression in the movement. As the world went increasingly insane and surrendered itself to the rule of totalitarian tyrants, Berl became more wary of the dangers of ideological coercion. He agreed with Tabenkin that every society imposed certain limitations on its members, but distinguished between practical obligations and coercion in matters of conscience and ideology. 'Without total freedom of conscience', he said, 'no good will come of all our righteousness.' He demanded that the youth movements be permitted free development: 'In our times many believe in the "strong arm", perceive its victories but not its failures. This is not my way. I believe in the value of agreement.'[14]

Berl's stand may also have derived from developments within the party: the more the labor movement became institutionalized and acquired power to exert pressure on the individual, the more Berl tended to voluntarism. His sensitivity to the indoctrination of youth was not a mere pose: he truly feared for the future generation. He compared the contempt for the individual he had observed in he-Halutz with phenomena in the outside world, and was filled with apprehension at the kind of individual the movement might produce.

Berl's tour of Poland had been intended as a preparation for his work among the youth, and indeed, immediately after his return home, the Histadrut Executive met and decided to set up a Department for Youth and Education. It was to be called the Youth Center and would be run by Berl Katznelson with a modest budget of £600 (Palestinian) annually. This was the first time since he became editor of *Davar* in 1925 that Berl had accepted an official position. The man who had shied away from institutionalized authority, whose power had lain in his charisma, now required and accepted official sanction. It could be claimed that without the appointment he would not have obtained the necessary budgets. But it is hard to suppress the thought that Berl's recourse to the authority of a formal appointment attests to his waning personal power and influence. Berl requested the backing of the Histadrut and the party because he sensed his weakness in the face of the organized might of ha-Kibbutz ha-Meuhad.

The strength of ha-Kibbutz ha-Meuhad among the youth derived from two sources: its control of organizational frameworks and, more important, its sway over the individuals capable of implementing the decisions of the 'Youth Center'. Outstanding emissaries who were not affiliated to ha-Kibbutz ha-Meuhad were few and far between: the great majority were educated by ha-Kibbutz ha-Meuhad or inspired by it. Its great appeal lay precisely in the type of individual it produced, the stringent demands it made on the young, the personal example of its representatives, its temperament, activism, dedication and zeal. And Tabenkin himself exercised a fascination on young people eager for action.

Tabenkin publicly declared that ha-Kibbutz ha-Meuhad and its emissaries would cooperate with Berl in the Youth Center. But, at the same time, he continued to maintain that ha-Kibbutz ha-Meuhad and he-Halutz were on the right track and that fostering the idea of communal life was synonymous with fostering a 'general' approach in education. This view conflicted with Berl's argument that the Youth Center was the body authorized to determine the nature of this 'general' education. At the heart of this debate was the struggle for the souls of the young generation in Palestine and in the Diaspora.

On 5 December 1933, Berl submitted a plan of action for the Youth Department to the Mapai Central Committee, and in early January 1934 he explained to the Histadrut Conference its ideological basis and pressing needs. As long as he was dealing with ideological matters, Berl

219

was on firm ground, captivating his audience even when they disagreed with him: he spoke of the giants of the socialist movement who were imbued with both vision and knowledge, comparing them with the following generation who were but a pale reflection. This difference was responsible for the decline in the movement as it appeared today. But he was less successful when he tried to translate his semi-abstract concepts of 'cultural activity' into practical terms. In addition to organizational work in the style accepted by the movement, Berl proposed to concentrate the work of the Center in two main areas – seminars and literary work. The seminars would train emissaries for the Diaspora and cadres for the Palestinian movement. For the emissaries there would be regular annual seminars for 'ideological work'.[15] Once the emissary was trained, he would be sent abroad for two years. Berl hoped to guarantee regular links between the emissary and the Department: the emissary would hold discussions with the Department (i.e., with Berl) before he left, and would consult regularly on ideological and practical questions. For the young Palestinians there would be short, intense seminars. All this would be done through the Histadrut so as to reach young people outside Mapai as well.

He also envisaged wide-scale literary activity – the establishment of a Histadrut institution for the 'development of a consumer market for Hebrew books'.[16] He hoped to attract writers, poets and other artists to the movement through the wide audience it could offer, both in Palestine and abroad. In return for subscription payments, the institution would supply books, pictures and other materials. He apparently hoped that close ties with the Youth Center would bring the various youth movements closer to his sphere of influence. Berl also wanted to establish a publishing house whose central task would be the inculcation of the Second Aliyah heritage to newcomers.

Berl's concept of education was to shape an open-minded independent-thinking young person who would, 'naturally' and on his own, arrive at the 'right' conclusions: a profound attachment to national symbols and values and to the common Jewish destiny, with less emphasis on the international socialist fraternity; an aversion to dictatorship, whether right- or left-wing, including that of the Soviet regime; a belief in democracy and loyalty to Zionist and socialist fundamentalism – without submission to dogma. Tabenkin, on the other hand, wanted to inculcate his views in the young: his national-secular and socialist zeal, his view of the world in absolute terms of good and bad, his theory of the independence of the working class against the rest of society and loyalty to the kibbutz against the rest of the Yishuv. Berl was as zealous as Tabenkin to hand down his views to the young, to mold them in his own image, but his educational methods were different: he favored the Socratic method of inquiry and investigation, of skepticism and questioning. In contrast to ha-Kibbutz ha-Meuhad's uncompromising indoctrination which offered no alternatives, Berl's theories seemed the epitome of open-mindedness and tolerance. The differences derived, above all, from dissimilarities of temperament, level of sophistication and *Weltanschauung*. In the final analysis, if the aim was the same, the question was whose method was the more effective.

Berl favored a 'general' approach: loyalty to the movement as a whole – an approach not commonly accepted, and demanded for himself the role of mentor, instructor and guide of the movement.

Ha-Kibbutz ha-Meuhad insisted on the communal way of life as the acceptable ideal. Berl could only offer the Histadrut, or, at most, the party as inspiration. And what impact could an educational ideal make, when it lacked the personal dimension? The Histadrut had long since ceased to be an ideal, and had become a conglomeration of institutions, scarcely likely to fire the imagination of a young boy or girl. Nor did the party's ideological-political training provide the flavor and vitality of a new, revolutionary and daring way of life.

The Youth Center ultimately confined itself to minor educational ventures, notably the publication of a series of instructional booklets. They were not widely used in Palestine, even less so abroad. The mountain had brought forth a mouse.

The Youth Center was the product of educational motives interwoven with a power struggle, and its failure was related to both elements. Berl himself attributed the failure of the Center to ha-Kibbutz-ha-Meuhad's ambivalent attitude. As noted, Berl envisaged his main activity as the training of emissaries and, subsequently, the supervision of their activities abroad. In theory the emissaries were despatched by the Histadrut. In practice each communal movement chose its own emissaries. The Histadrut Executive served as the rubber stamp and Berl had no say in their choice, their training or their activities. Although they all promised to consult with him before leaving, not many actually did so, and these few were merely discharging what they considered a duty. Berl described how emissaries would come to see him barely an hour before boarding ship. His home was open to any confused young person in search of guidance, but those same young people whom Berl yearned to endow with something of his own wisdom, subtlety, breadth of knowledge did not seek him out. The living current of the movement passed him by, and he was left on the sidelines. The true center was located in ha-Kibbutz ha-Meuhad under Tabenkin.

When Berl planned the work of the Youth Center, he did not yet know what organizational form it would take. He was sure of only one thing: it would *not* be a federative body, representing youth movement emissaries; it would be composed of people whom he himself would select for their personal qualities. Berl wanted to 'rise' above the communal settlement movements (the Hever ha-Kvutzot and Gordonia, on the one hand, and ha-Kibbutz ha-Meuhad, on the other) and above the various youth movements – all in the name of the ideal of 'generality'. It was an expression of his inclination to maintain personal rapport in all his relationships. This is the source of the personal drama entailed in the failure of the Youth Center.

Berl asked Bracha Habas (whom he had known in her youth as a *Davar* reporter) and Israel Galili, to work with him at the Center. Galili was apparently intended to be the mainstay of the Center, implementing Berl's ideas. He was an 'important young man', the term then used for the promising members of the young generation. He was one of the founders of ha-Noar ha-Oved youth movement, and its outstanding leader. Galili was one of a number of youth leaders whom Berl nurtured. But, like many others, he was not indifferent to Tabenkin's charm. Ha-Noar ha-Oved, like ha-Mahanot ha-Olim*, came to identify with ha-Kibbutz ha-Meuhad and accepted its authority. This was a gradual process, possibly inevitable. The Kibbutz ha-Meuhad embodied all the values which the youth movement preached: pioneering, self-realization, physical labor, self-sacrifice. As long as no barriers existed between Berl and ha-Kibbutz ha-Meuhad, the question of divided loyalties did not arise. But as soon as their differences surfaced on the question of he-Halutz and the Youth Center, the competition for the hearts and minds of the talented and loyal younger generation became an open contest. Galili was torn between his loyalties to Berl and to Tabenkin and for two years this hampered his work.

* A youth movement of Palestinian students which developed in the 1930s as an independent movement affiliated to Labor Palestine.

In mid-August 1935, Berl attended the 19th Zionist Congress at Lucerne. For a month he engaged in feverish activity and was in a cheerful and energetic mood. As usual, he refused to join the Executive and successfully withstood the pressure of his comrades. Ben Gurion's slogan, 'Peace in the Yishuv', which was the motto of the new Executive, appealed to Berl. He welcomed the coopting of ha-Mizrahi on to the Zionist Executive and invested considerable effort in persuading members of his own faction to approve this move. This was the commencement of the 'historic alliance' between Mapai and the Mizrahi, an alliance which was to endure for 42 years. He was also gratified by Tabenkin's active participation in the faction's activities.

For a brief moment it seemed that the old Ahdut ha-Avoda alliance might be revived. During the session of the Jewish National Fund Directorate which followed the Congress, the Directorate's Chairman, Ussishkin (one of the first generation of Zionist leaders) asked Berl to visit Poland. Berl was inclined to accept the invitation, but several days later he abruptly changed his mind. To Leah he explained that as a result of fatigue he was reluctant to undertake a speaking tour of Poland. But the truth was that during and after the Congress, meetings had been held in Lucerne among youth movement emissaries, he-Halutz directors and leaders of ha-Kibbutz ha-Meuhad to which Berl was not invited, either in his own right or ex officio. The delegates and emissaries exchanged pleasantries with him, but he was not party to their deliberations. The affront was intolerable. His exclusion implied the curtailing of his influence and he was located as an outsider. His initial response to this rejection was his refusal to go to Poland.

The insult rankled for several days: 'These things pained me like a burn; I was afraid to bring them into the open, and for several days and nights thereafter I talked to myself and not to others.'[17] He made no mention of the affair in his letters to Leah. On 10 September 1935 he joined David Remez on a trip to the glaciers near Lucerne, for a vacation of several weeks. Towards the end of the vacation, as he relaxed on a sunny mountainside, amidst breath-taking landscapes, his equilibrium was restored and he set out to repay those who had slighted him. As usual, he dwelt on the personal aspects of the issue.

In love–hate situations, the first victim is often the go-between: in this case it was Galili. In a long letter to him, couched in eloquent language, Berl made a reckoning of two years of work in the Youth Center. He attributed its failure to the atmosphere of particularism and

separatism created by ha-Kibbutz ha-Meuhad, which had led to Galili's
ambivalence and divided loyalties. This had produced absentminded-
ness, inconsistency and the ineffectuality of his activities. Now, after
Lucerne, Berl had arrived at a final decision: 'I wash my hands of the
Youth Center. Completely.'[18] The gravest charge he leveled at Galili
was that of hypocrisy: 'This institution was founded on error and on
deception. Error on my part, and deception on the part of those with
whom I especially intended to cooperate, those who ostensibly requested
my activity.'[19] He was writing to Galili but appears to have been aiming
at Tabenkin, the person who had assured him of the cooperation of ha-
Kibbutz ha-Meuhad and its emissaries, the person who had encouraged
him to undertake the central task of instruction.

For Berl, the failure of the Center was a threefold tragedy: first, he
had lost his grip on the 'spiritual center' of the movement; secondly, in
the contest for the loyalty of the young leadership, Tabenkin had prevailed; and thirdly, it was evident that there was a rift and a crisis of confidence between him and his beloved comrade from Kinneret.

Berl was hard put to understand Tabenkin's growing estrangement
and the collapse of their profound understanding. It was impossible for
him to believe that the reasons were ideological. They had already had
their differences in the 1920s: Tabenkin had been captivated by the
Bolshevik Revolution, which Berl criticized vehemently. In the Stalin–
Trotsky controversy, Berl had supported Trotsky, Tabenkin had supported Stalin. Although Tabenkin was not then a Marxist, he was more
of a radical socialist than Berl, and his views on the class society, class
struggle and its application to Jewish society, were in conflict with
Berl's views. These disputes also reflected a difference in temperament:
Tabenkin liked to relate how, during their Kinneret days, they would
stroll through the fields around the Kinneret enclosure on the Sabbath.
Whenever they reached a stone fence, Tabenkin would instinctively try
to hurdle it, while Berl chose to walk alongside.

It may be assumed that Berl eventually realized that Tabenkin had
come to identify entirely with his own creation, ha-Kibbutz ha-
Meuhad, and was unwilling to share his intellectual authority there with
Berl. He continued to talk in the old terms of a 'general' approach, but
he was in fact 'partial' – and Berl did not belong to the 'part'. Tabenkin
may have accepted 'generality' on principle, and hence his support for
the Youth Center. But when this support implied forgoing ha-Kibbutz

ha-Meuhad's uniqueness, he was unable to translate principle into practice.

On the other hand Berl observed, with apprehension, that ha-Kibbutz ha-Meuhad was displaying certain of the traits characteristic of the Labor Brigade and he had learned from the Brigade crisis (and the subsequent emigration of some of its members to the Soviet Union) that pioneering ideals alone were not sufficient to assure loyalty to the Zionist vision. According to Berl, the sole antidote to the powerful pull of the left was a profound attachment to the political and ideological authority of a broader labor movement. Ha-Kibbutz ha-Meuhad, however, was becoming increasingly detached from the wider movement, and increasingly caught up in its admiration for the Soviet Union and its revolutionary symbols. Like the Brigade, it regarded itself as the practicing avant-garde of the movement, developing at the same time a sense of its own superiority. Ha-Kibbutz ha-Meuhad claimed that it differed from the Brigade in that it was loyal to the movement as a whole, but it had, in fact, sidestepped movement authority. What remained to protect it against what Berl regarded as destructive trends? Berl used to say: 'I trust Tabenkin's loyalty to socialist Zionism. *He* knows where he is going. But what of his disciples?'

The debate over the Youth Center, in addition to marking Berl's personal failure and his failure as a leader, also represented the failure of the movement against separatist tendencies. And on this issue Berl now went into battle.

13

THE STRUGGLE
TO UNITE THE KIBBUTZ MOVEMENT,
1935–1939

In October 1935, Degania and the entire kibbutz movement celebrated
the twenty-fifth anniversary of settlement on the Um Juni lands. At the
height of the festivities, Berl hurled a time-bomb (which was elegantly
wrapped, naturally, as befitted a birthday gift). He published in *Davar* a
'Letter to My Comrades in Degania' – a document of rare fascination,
representing Berl at his best: the skilled journalist, the historian of the
Palestine labor movement, and the psychologist. He sketched the saga
of the early days of Degania from a very personal viewpoint, that of a
young newcomer to Palestine. With affection and more than a touch of
nostalgia, Berl depicted the singular qualities of Degania and those who
built it, against the general background of the Second Aliyah. He did
not idealize the facts, and sometimes alluded to matters which were better forgotten; but he did so in such a way that only Second Aliyah
veterans could grasp the oblique references. He wrote with the pen of
an artist and the soul of a lover.

His delightful and moving description of the past, however, served
merely as the cover for his main message, which was of immediate
import: the unification of the kibbutz movement. His reasons: first –
despite variations in shades of opinion and style – the movement was
one entity. Secondly, the split in the pioneering sector of the labor
movement hampered its moral and social hegemony over the movement as a whole. The settlement movements – ha-Kibbutz ha-Meuhad,
Hever ha-Kvutzot (which had merged with Gordonia), the *moshav*
movement, and ha-Shomer ha-Tzair were each preoccupied with their
own affairs and not carrying out the function assigned to them: to serve
as the guiding lights of the entire labor movement.

The letter appeared on 25 September 1935 in *Davar* some three
weeks after his 'bill of divorcement' to Galili on the Youth Center. But
Berl did not confine himself to this one appeal. With a vigor reminiscent of days gone by he set out to persuade his comrades, near and

far, of the vital need for union. He toured new and veteran kibbutzim, taking part in the fierce polemic on his challenge, and published further articles in *Davar* during Passover 1936, under the heading 'A Protest against the Status Quo'.

Just as Berl's trip to Poland in 1933 had marked a change in his relations with ha-Kibbutz ha-Meuhad, the 'Protest' now transformed the latent tensions into an acute crisis. The articles condemned the relations evolving in the kibbutz movement between the society and the individual member, among the various sectors of the movement, and between them and the movement as a whole, that is, the party and the Histadrut. Berl regarded the division between the different settlement movements as the root of all evil, gnawing at the heart of the kibbutz movement as a whole and at the entire Palestine labor movement. What he called 'local patriotism' was draining the general institutions of the labor movement of meaning, and any person trying to initiate general action found himself helpless. 'In this case', he wrote, referring to himself, 'individuals unaffiliated to a particular sector, who have a common desire to get something done, may try to rouse our public, but the public does not respond. The spiritual fuse is disconnected.'

But there was more to Berl's 'Protest against the Status Quo': The movements were not satisfied with mere 'tribal' self-interest: they turned on one another, vilifying each other and taking pleasure in the other's misfortunes. As the real differences between them gradually diminished, a more naked rivalry emerged. For as long as Hever ha-Kvutzot built its settlements on the principle of intimate, organic communities, it did not clash with the more broadly-conceived, extensive ha-Kibbutz ha-Meuhad. But once it accepted an expansion of membership as inevitable and even desirable, it found itself in confrontation with them. This clash was reflected in the struggle for control of he-Halutz which, it will be remembered, supplied reinforcements for existing kibbutzim and manpower for new ones. A war was waged for the souls of the young pioneers who, before they had even encountered the country and its customs, were taught to proclaim the virtues of their own movement, and the failings of the others. An ugly atmosphere of mutual vilification was created in the Diaspora, and reverberated in Palestine as well. The individual was judged not according to his talents and qualifications, but according to his movement affiliation – 'friend or foe?'

As the movements became more entrenched in their own exclusivity, their 'collective arrogance' increased. They began to take positions on issues outside the sphere of the *kvutza*. And Berl wrote: 'The *desire* for ideological and political independence existed even before there were any ideas which could justify it. The vessel had to be filled and certain kibbutzim were ready to fill it.'[1]

The process had begun in the Third Aliyah kibbutzim. It was launched by the Labor Brigade, and continued by ha-Shomer ha-Tzair, which formulated its essence as 'ideological collectivism'. This meant that the kibbutz was a collective body whose stand on political and social questions was binding on all its members. Hever ha-Kvutzot and ha-Kibbutz ha-Meuhad had once been strongly opposed to ideological collectivism, but now, Berl claimed, they too were about to embrace it. The Kibbutz had become a party which not only represented its members on economic and social matters, but also served as their political and ideological representatives. Berl thought that this endangered the fabric of *kvutza* life. An individual could decide one fine morning to change his views and leave his party; but this was not true of the member of a communal settlement. If he did not agree to the convictions and tenets held by the *kvutza*, he would be forced to leave his home, his community, his work and his whole way of life. The individual had, as a result, to choose between freedom of thought and ideological collectivism. If the latter, then the kibbutz would have to abandon its proclaimed ambition of creating a new man, and satisfy itself with creating an 'ideological robot'. Berl did not deny the need for a common ideological basis, but he grounded it on general principles: 'the redemption of Israel, the socialist vision, pioneering, the renaissance of the Hebrew language, the unity of the workers'. The rest should be left to the heart and mind of the individual.

In the face of the 'eclipse' which had occurred in the movement because of intramural rifts, Berl called for the unification of the kibbutz movement and the elimination of existing frameworks. He did not formulate a detailed program for arriving at unification. He simply wanted unconditional union, as once achieved in the establishment of Ahdut ha-Avoda: a readiness to break down barriers in a spirit of true comradeship and mutual trust.

The 'Protest' was phrased in general terms, but from the outset it was clear that Berl was addressing ha-Kibbutz ha-Meuhad and Hever ha-Kvutzot and excluding ha-Shomer ha-Tzair – that is, a merger between the kibbutz movements affiliated to Mapai. While ostensibly appealing to both movements equally, he was actually focusing on ha-Kibbutz ha-Meuhad. Hever ha-Kvutzot, which had merged with Gordonia in 1934, was the junior partner, with only about 2,000 members, about a third the strength of ha-Kibbutz ha-Meuhad. Its weakness was the more obvious: the Hever tended to be cautious as regards obligations, and slow to act; it lacked the stormy temperament and relentless drive which characterized ha-Kibbutz ha-Meuhad. Moreover, Hever ha-Kvutzot had never been as close to Berl's heart as ha-Kibbutz ha-Meuhad. It was no chance that Berl's family had chosen to live at Ein Harod, and many of his friends lived there as well. During the Second Aliyah days, Berl had preferred the wide-open atmosphere of Kinneret to the intense closeness of Degania. He was drawn to the bold, dedicated and restless. Few members of ha-Poel ha-Tzair had ever won Berl's affection, and the same was true of Hever ha-Kvutzot, for the same reasons. Berl's alienation from the Hever grew after its merger with Gordonia, and was similar to his relations with ha-Shomer ha-Tzair and the Labor Brigade. Berl never succeeded in establishing rapport with movements which came from the Diaspora complete with a cohesive leadership. Pinhas Lubianiker (Labon), leader of Gordonia, like Yaari of ha-Shomer ha-Tzair, maintained his independence, rejecting the leadership of the Second Aliyah people. Berl, who was both suspicious and skeptical, did not trust the Gordonia 'prodigy'. According to one witness, he described him as a 'brilliant mind in a murky soul'.[2] Although there were similarities between Berl's views and those of Gordonia on such issues as violence, accord with the Revisionists, labor relations and the national consensus, there was no personal affinity between them, a factor more important to Berl than any other.

Berl was well aware that his call for union might succeed, but equally it might – and this was even more feasible – exacerbate visible differences and perhaps even split the party. It was clear to him that the leadership of ha-Kibbutz ha-Meuhad would not accept any edict that went counter to the direction of its development. His public appeal in *Davar* indicates that he preferred to go over the heads of the Kibbutz leaders, to touch off a general debate in the hope that the rank and file of ha-Kibbutz ha-Meuhad would lend support to a scheme which its leaders, entrenched in their positions of power, would reject. Berl knew that he was embroiling himself in a frontal clash with ha-Kibbutz ha-Meuhad's leadership, that he was entering upon a path from which there might be no retreat.

229

Berl's tenacity in the matter stemmed from his very conception of the movement. The rise to power of a party and Histadrut 'machine' was to him a necessary evil without which political bodies could not function, but he was repelled by the kind of people who were now in the saddle, intellectually and, even more, morally. He observed manifestations of careerism and opportunism, obsequiousness and impudence. He believed that the kibbutz movement would provide the party with its future leadership – idealistic men and women, carefully selected and nurtured over the years to receive the mantle of leadership from Berl and the other founders of the movement. In the long run, separatism of the kibbutz movements was counterproductive to this vision. The tendency of ha-Kibbutz ha-Meuhad to self-containment and aloofness from deep involvement in the life of the labor movement as a whole was detrimental to both: without mutual interaction, ha-Kibbutz ha-Meuhad was doomed to sterility, and the party to erosion. It was this ideal reciprocal relationship which apparently inspired Berl when he went into battle. Unity was, for him, the Archimedean lever with which he could move the entire movement. If he failed, the movement would, in any case, disintegrate and wither.

The Kibbutz leadership was hostile to Berl's appeal. Even before the publication of the 'Protest', Tarshish, one of the veteran leaders of ha-Kibbutz ha-Meuhad wrote a letter to Tabenkin on the affair. He described the 'Degania letter' as a declaration of war on ha-Kibbutz ha-Meuhad and called for a calculated response – without 'sentiments'. The secretariat of ha-Kibbutz ha-Meuhad apparently wanted to avoid direct confrontation with Berl, and refrained from any overt reply. Berl again took the initiative: 'If you will not invite me, then I invite you'[3] – but again received no reply. The discussion for which he hoped never materialized. It is possible that the Kibbutz secretariat hoped that the demand would die a natural death if they ignored it. They may have wanted at one and the same time to indicate to Berl their resentment and to avoid a head-on clash with him. Berl disregarded the message and published the 'Protest'. These articles contain some of the best polemic writing which Berl ever produced – clear, the prose simple and unadorned, imbued with personal overtones, and phrased obliquely. He was ironic, without being sarcastic, and surveyed the history of the Palestine labor movement without spilling over into nostalgia. It was a work of art. The controversy, which raged for years afterwards, seems to have added nothing valuable to what Berl wrote.

Several days after the publication of the 'Protest', the 1936 disturbances erupted and diverted public attention from internal movement matters to existential and political issues. Although *Davar* published several articles in favor of unification, the turmoil of Jewish self-defense activities against the Arab Rebellion and measures against the Arab general strike removed the issue from the public agenda. Still, Berl's status within the movement was such that no proposal of his could be dismissed lightly, and the issue continued to arouse a measure of interest, controversy and support, even though official channels of expression were blocked by ha-Kibbutz ha-Meuhad's leadership.

In mid-September 1936, Berl went to London on a political mission (see chapter 14). Several weeks later, ha-Kibbutz ha-Meuhad's conference convened at Kibbutz Yagur. The unification issue was added to the agenda at the last moment, apparently in order to forestall prior debate on the question in the kibbutzim. The Secretariat seems to have hoped for a short discussion, culminating in an almost unanimous resolution against union, thereby crushing the alien growth planted by Berl. At the convention the 'unitarians' in ha-Kibbutz ha-Meuhad – Hayim Ben Asher of Givat Brenner, the writer David Maletz of Ein Harod, Zeev Feinstein of Ayelet ha-Shahar and Eliezer Livenstein of Ein Harod – addressed the assembly. Maletz's remarks were confused, Ben Asher was colorless and unconvincing, while Livenstein harmed the cause of union more than he furthered it by his arrogance, and even more so by the comparison he drew between the Soviet Union and Nazi Germany. In short, the opposition to the Secretariat appeared to be relatively ineffectual. Yet, when their sole proposal was put to a vote – calling for a free and open discussion of the question of unification throughout the kibbutz movement – it mustered one-third of the votes. If we take into consideration the tremendous prestige of the Secretariat, Tabenkin's unique standing, the ineffective way in which the opposition put its case and the brief time allotted to the debate, the vote may certainly be regarded as a partial triumph for Berl! If the leaders of ha-Kibbutz ha-Meuhad had hoped to remove the issue from the agenda, the vote at Yagur indicated that a considerable proportion of members would not allow this to happen. After the Council, Ben Asher, who had undertaken to organize the 'unitarians' in ha-Kibbutz ha-Meuhad, told Beilinson that if intensive propaganda efforts were launched, unity could be achieved within two years.

The year 1937 was crammed with political activity: the Peel Commission, the Partition plan and the resultant controversy, the Zionist Congress at Zurich and its outcome. Berl was close to a breakdown that year because of poor health. He was also too preoccupied with political missions abroad to deal with internal movement affairs, yet he continued to follow events in ha-Kibbutz ha-Meuhad. As had always been the case, comrades often came to him with their problems. Reports reached him of the educational atmosphere prevailing in ha-Kibbutz ha-Meuhad, especially in relation to the Soviet Union. The attitude to the Soviet Union had its ups and downs, fluctuating between admiration, disillusionment and sober appraisal, but it was always a central issue in the outlook of many members of Mapai, particularly in ha-Kibbutz ha-Meuhad. The purge trials against the veteran Bolsheviks, Zinoviev and Kaminiev, were in full swing at that time. *Davar* was highly critical of what it saw as a manifestation of the debasement of the Revolution and the contempt for human dignity, and denounced the Inquisitorial methods being used. Liova Levite from Ein Harod was enraged by this criticism on the part of the workers' paper and wrote that it 'constituted saddening evidence of the decline of socialist and class values among us'.[4] Levite and his comrades were aware of the U.S.S.R.'s anti-Zionist stand; but they hoped that it was a fleeting phenomenon, and that attitudes would improve in the face of the socialist endeavor in Palestine. They saw the Soviet Union as the beacon of liberty and progress in the world, a buffer against the waves of fascism threatening to destroy it. It is difficult for a generation which never put total, unshakeable trust in the Soviet Union to understand the Soviet loyalists of those days, their almost blind disregard for the true course of events in the U.S.S.R., and their blanket rejection of all criticism as hostile and anti-proletarian. 'You can't make an omelette without breaking eggs' was the typical rationalization offered by Levite and his colleagues in the face of despotic Soviet action. The Revolution was more important than the individual, the future than the present. It required 'another ethos', one which deterred more 'fastidious people', by the degree of coercion employed to persuade the public what it was they really wanted.

As far as Berl was concerned, this way of thinking was evidence of the abandonment of humanistic socialism. To his long-standing opposition to totalitarian doctrines, whether right- or left-wing, was now added his apprehension as to the fate of the second generation of ha-Kibbutz ha-Meuhad.

The more ha-Kibbutz ha-Meuhad swore fealty to the Soviet Union, despite its failings, the more Berl moved towards the opposite extreme. And as the spirit of the movement became increasingly dogmatic and closed in upon itself, Berl became more zealous in his concern for democracy and open-mindedness. His controversy with ha-Kibbutz ha-Meuhad, and with Tabenkin, on the unity of the kibbutz movement – which evolved into a debate on humanitarian values, socialism and education – seems to have rounded off Berl's own education, forcing him to state his own credo with definitive clarity. Whereas, in the early 1920s, he had not perceived democracy as a cardinal value, its importance was enhanced for him now that it had been trampled on by both right and left. With a persistence which ignored the prevailing mood – or perhaps because of this very mood – he called for loyalty to a socialism whose objective was the exaltation of man, a socialism which carefully selected its means, considering them as part of the end itself.

Berl was abroad consecutively from February to December 1937, with an interval of three weeks. When he returned home, a series of talks began between the three Ahdut ha-Avoda leaders, Berl, Tabenkin and Ben Gurion (January 1938). Regrettably, Berl made no entries in his diary on these discussions, but one may assume that they revolved around internal party matters, including the unity of the kibbutz movement. The Second Aliyah pioneers were convinced that a 'great controversy', in which various viewpoints were aired, would, in the end, create affinity and mutual understanding among them, resulting in a leadership which acted as one man. This, so it would seem, was the legacy of the Russian revolutionary movement. The discussions among members of the 'troika' – and it was no chance that Sprinzak, the former ha-Poel ha-Tzair leader, who was ostensibly on an equal footing with them, was not included – were held in preparation for the party conference which was to convene shortly after. They had pinned great hopes on the conference, which was perceived as an open debate which would clear the air and bring people closer together. But party dynamics were exerting a pull in another direction. Hints of the dangers entailed in the prospective debate began to surface during the discussions between the three leaders, and, as the issues became more evident, the differences became more blatant. Berl demanded the union of all the kibbutz movements and the merger of the youth movements affiliated with them – ha-Mahanot ha-Olim and Gordonia. Tabenkin

233

reiterated the traditional ha-Kibbutz ha-Meuhad stand: union – yes, but along the lines established by the large and constantly-growing ha-Kibbutz ha-Meuhad movement. Policy should be determined by the vanguard of the movement, not by those bringing up the rear. There were diverse trends within the movement, and heterogeneity was legitimate, even vital, in a wide class party. Ben Gurion dwelt on the organizational aspects of the question: the divisiveness was hampering the capacity of the party to act. While ha-Kibbutz ha-Meuhad demanded jurisdiction over its own followers, Ben Gurion insisted on overall party control and the abrogation of Kibbutz authority over the young generation and over he-Halutz. In the final analysis, he called for the disbanding of the ideological center within ha-Kibbutz ha-Meuhad, which served as the focus of organization in the party, and was undermining unity. Ben Gurion's stand emanated from his conception of the party as an instrument of power, damaged by the presence within it of a rival core of leadership. It is also feasible to assume that Ben Gurion resented the fact that ha-Kibbutz ha-Meuhad had twice led the opposition to his policies – on the pact with the Revisionists and on Partition. To all these reasons was added Ben Gurion's protective instinct towards Berl. The unification of the kibbutz movement had become the crucial issue in Berl's continued activity in the movement, even if this had not yet been spelled out. And Ben Gurion was, in fact, moving into areas remote from his own competence – all in order to appease Berl. But the deliberations of the three former Ahdut ha-Avoda leaders did not bear fruit: each clung to his own position.

Following the failure of the *troika* to arrive at any common position, Ben Gurion attempted to exert direct presure on the Kibbutz ha-Meuhad leaders. Berl embarked on a more sophisticated path of action.

He took every available opportunity of establishing direct contact with the rank and file in all the communal settlements, particularly in ha-Kibbutz ha-Meuhad. His main effort was among the young. He attended youth conferences, seminars and rallies, and indeed an important breakthrough occurred at the conference of ha-Mahanot ha-Olim youth movement at Kibbutz Beit ha-Shita. These young people, who were close in temperament and outlook to ha-Kibbutz ha-Meuhad, and were strongly influenced by their movement leaders, were won over by Berl's catch-phrase of 'unity'. The idealistic youth movements, unlike their elders, could not stomach a compromise between theory and practice. Berl's arguments in favor of the organic unity of the movement and against the contemptible aspects of fraternal strife appealed to them. Several factors operated in Berl's favor. First, ha-Kibbutz ha-Meuhad, after considerable hesitation, had reluctantly appointed Hayim Ben Asher to a leadership position in ha-Mahanot ha-Olim. A man of broad educational horizons, whose thinking was influenced by both Plato and Nietzsche, Ben Asher was successful in nurturing a generation of young leaders of the movement who accepted Berl's views on the labor and kibbutz movements. Secondly, it was only natural for an up-and-coming leadership to seek to emphasize their differences with their immediate predecessors, and acceptance of the principle of unity provided them with a *casus belli*. Moreover, the youngsters of ha-Mahanot ha-Olim preferred the more distant, general authority of the Histadrut to the immediate, and hence oppressive, authority of ha-Kibbutz ha-Meuhad. For these reasons, a call was issued from Beit ha-Shita for the ultimate amalgamation of all the pioneering youth movements – beginning with ha-Mahanot ha-Olim and Gordonia, which were affiliated to the same party, and eventually including ha-Shomer ha-Tzair as well. For Berl, this was most gratifying.

At the same time, he did not relax his efforts to influence ha-Kibbutz ha-Meuhad. He took part in a meeting of its leading members at Kibbutz Givat ha-Shlosha, and was in constant touch with Ben Asher, and Enzo Sereni, both of whom had undertaken to promote the cause of unity in ha-Kibbutz ha-Meuhad. He even went so far as to attend the Passover Seder at Kibbutz Givat Brenner, the bastion of ha-Kibbutz ha-Meuhad. He also maintained his intimate personal ties with Tabenkin, even though they had been weakened. They could still speak frankly to one another.

Berl's mood veered between optimism and pessimism. In the months preceding the party conference (early 1938), he apparently still hoped for an end to factionalism in the party, and the restoration of internal harmony. There was indeed a moment when it seemed that even ha-Shomer ha-Tzair was drawn to the idea of union, and that realization was imminent.

But Berl's hopes were soon dashed. The Mapai party conference took place in Rehovot in May 1938, and up to the very opening Berl was involved in consultations with various comrades. Two days before the opening session, Ben Gurion convened an additional meeting for 'private' consultations with prominent party members, on party and sectoral matters. But despite these efforts, the conference opened without having achieved prior accord.

It was a mass gathering of four hundred delegates, representing 18,000 members. Numerous guests attended in order to bask in the glory of the party which enjoyed hegemony in the Yishuv and within the Zionist movement. According to time-hallowed custom, Berl made the keynote address and in his opening sentence he set the tone: he had come to demand the unification of the party. The plan he proposed was based on the union of the kibbutz movement, the merging of the youth movements and the establishment of a training college for the party's young guard. He had been nursing this idea for some years. Now he linked it to the concept of unity: an educational institution should be set up where people from different sectors and factions would meet and rub shoulders, thus promoting the longed-for unity. He avoided polemics and sarcasm and endeavored to convey his ideas in a moderate and tolerant fashion. As soon as he finished speaking, 120 delegates asked for the floor. The praesidium, under pressure from all those who insisted on having their say, decided to allocate 15 minutes to each speaker. It soon transpired that time was being allocated according to a 'key', reflecting the strength of representation in the towns, colonies, and settlement blocs. The same key was employed in the committees elected by the conference. When a spokesman for the 'opposition' to ha-Kibbutz ha-Meuhad leadership requested the floor, bargaining ensued on the question of how to classify him according to the key, that is, whose time he was using.

Berl's moderation was not emulated by those who followed him. One of the delegates defined the tone of the conference as follows: 'People are greatly exaggerating their self-castigation, which is, in actual fact, castigation of others within the party, whom they see as rivals; the flaws are usually pointed out in others, though ostensibly in the form of self-criticism.'[5] A general free-for-all ensued: members of ha-Kibbutz ha-Meuhad ranted against Hever ha-Kvutzot, urban workers against the communal settlements and among themselves, and in the midst of the bickering, the 'opposition' delegates complained bitterly that they had been cheated of the right to speak or to be elected to the Party Council or Central Committee.

Ha-Kibbutz ha-Meuhad adopted the tactic that the best form of defense was attack. The main ploy was the 'preservation of dignity' and refusal 'to adopt a defensive position'. They claimed that there was no connection between the demand for the unification of the kibbutz movement and the restoration of party unity and health. Where had the party been in the past few years? It was not that the sectors had impinged on the domain of the party and the Histadrut, but that the latter had ceased to deal with the vital issues of the movement. Tabenkin wanted to shift the focus of the discussions from movement affairs – claiming they were not the central issue – to other subjects. He demanded a discussion of political questions: negotiations with Britain and with the Arabs; the economic crisis and its effects on the Histadrut; party democracy in the face of the authoritarian tendencies of its leaders. One frequently reiterated argument was that divisiveness within the movement resulted from the fact that people were deprived of the possibility of an open dialog.

In the same breath the 'authoritarian' party leadership – synonymous with Berl and Ben Gurion – was accused of failure to lead. It was exhorted, at one and the same time, to take a greater interest in movement life and to keep its hands off the settlement movement, the true expression of the '*volonté générale*'.

Another leitmotif in the speeches of ha-Kibbutz ha-Meuhad's representatives was their sense of injury: Huma Hayot, Tabenkin's life companion (the expression then used), and partner in the leadership of ha-Kibbutz ha-Meuhad, described the profound insult she suffered on reading 'A Protest against the Status Quo'. Berl replied: 'What should I do then? . . . Is a man really not to be allowed to express his thoughts in public, because there are sensitive people who see things not as problems but as insults?'[6] Tabenkin took the floor and hastened to defend Huma Hayot, attacking Berl and elaborating upon the issue: an attack on one's commitment and life work was naturally insulting! From then on, ha-Kibbutz ha-Meuhad adopted the posture of righteous indignation in the face of criticism of any kind. Amidst the verbiage, and the constant repetitions, the central problem, as Tabenkin phrased it, was obscured: '. . . the right of the settlement movements to exist within the party, within the Histadrut, not on sufferance, but with pride'.[7] Tabenkin rejected the accusation of separatism – as reflected supposedly in ha-Kibbutz ha-Meuhad's journal, *mi-Bifnim*, in their seminars, in their youth committee, etc., and demanded recognition of the movement as it was, wide in scope and all-embracing in its perception of its tasks. He ceremoniously reiterated their willingness to accept unification of the kibbutz movement and party discipline – on condition that ha-Kibbutz ha-Meuhad be allowed to continue functioning in its own way. His remarks boiled down to a readiness to accept federation with Hever ha-Kvutzot, but not union.

Within the youth movements, however, the mood was different, and Berl hoped that the merger advocated by ha-Mahanot ha-Olim's Council at Beit ha-Shita would create the necessary emotional climate for similar steps among the adults. Discussion on this problem reflected the fact that since 1936, the flood of he-Halutz immigrants from Europe had halted, and the kibbutz movements had begun to seek reinforcements from among the youth in Palestine. Gordonia organized its own youth movement, while ha-Mahanot ha-Olim, an independent and innovative movement of middle-class students, had grown close to ha-Kibbutz ha-Meuhad. Ha-Shomer ha-Tzair had also set up its own youth movement in Palestine. Struggles for the hearts and minds of the young, similar to those Berl had witnessed on his visit to Poland, were now waged in Palestine. Gordonia welcomed the resolution of ha-Mahanot ha-Olim's Council in favor of an unconditional merger, as long as it remained in the sphere of wishful thinking. As the idea appeared to become more feasible, Gordonia gradually retreated. Its leaders could not contemplate relinquishing their own manpower reserve unless the kibbutz movement united in such a way as to solve the overall problem of recruitment of new forces. At first, the leadership of ha-Kibbutz ha-Meuhad was equivocal on the merger but as Gordonia grew increasingly hesitant, ha-Kibbutz ha-Meuhad grew increasingly enthusiastic; it insisted on immediate merger regardless of what transpired among the kibbutz movements.

The conference resolutions ran counter to the nature of the discussions. The conference decided unanimously 'that the time had come to make all necessary efforts to unite the entire kibbutz movement . . .'[8] It welcomed the readiness of ha-Kibbutz ha-Meuhad and Hever-Kvutzot to launch negotiations, and empowered the Central Committee to take an active part in the process. In contrast to the restrained tone of this resolution, the conference decided to 'enjoin' the Party's Central Committee to convene representatives of the youth movements with the aim of amalgamating them. From contemporary evidence it transpires that the first half of the resolution was not mere lip-service, but was a definite injunction, which derived authority from its unanimous endorsement.

The kibbutz movements' assent appears to have confused and perplexed ha-Kibbutz ha-Meuhad leaders who did not attend the conference. The younger leaders were apparently far from gratified by Tabenkin's capitulation at the conference and his acceptance of the unification resolution. And it is in fact hard to explain his move. The explanation may lie in the border area between ideology and psychology: the slogan of unity made a tremendous impact. Tabenkin, who at the time of the establishment of Ahdut ha-Avoda, had been one of the 'unitarians', now found it hard to refute his lifelong beliefs. In years to come, he would claim that it was not unity which was the vital issue but loyalty to one's own path. But during the Rehovot conference he was still enthralled by the slogan of unity. His vote sheds light on his quandary, and possibly also on his difficulties in alienating himself from his friend and rival, Berl.

Resolutions are ultimately measured by their implementation. The resolutions of the Fourth Mapai Conference had little chance of success. While the vote of the Conference seemed to augur a new harmony in the life and structure of the party, the election of the Central Committee and its Council shattered the illusions. After lengthy bargaining, a large Central Committee of 51 members was elected to assure precise sectoral representation, according to the key, as well as a place for people such as Ben Gurion and Berl, who were non-affiliated. This method prevailed in the Council elections as well. Just as Tabenkin had displayed weakness in voting for the unification of the kibbutz movement and the youth movement, Berl too proved irresolute when he acquiesced in the method of elections (on what Ben Gurion termed 'St Bartholomew's Night'). Perhaps Ben Gurion and Berl surrendered because they were not strong enough to reject a proposal accepted by all their colleagues, particularly with regard to the vital interests of the various sectors. Perhaps they feared an open rift, which would have prevented the election of an agreed Council. The length and intensity of the week-long deliberations may also have contributed to their attrition.

In all events, the hoped-for miracle did not occur at the conference. The debate highlighted differences, sharpened hostilities and brought personal and group rivalries to the surface. After the Rehovot conference, the focus of attention shifted from the unification of the kibbutz movement to the very existence of the Party. The conference apparently marked the beginning of a dialog between oppositional circles in the Tel Aviv branch of Mapai – known as Faction B – and members of ha-

Kibbutz ha-Meuhad, which ended in an alliance between them. From then on a rift in the party was only a question of time.

Six months earlier, on 30 October 1937, elections had been held to the Council of the Tel Aviv branch of Mapai. It was a time of economic crisis, unemployment and deprivation. The basement of Brenner House, headquarters of the Labor Council, was the meeting-place for unemployed workers, who found comfort in sharing their frustration and tales of woe. Berl would often slip into the basement unobtrusively, his peaked cap hiding his face, to observe the mood of 'the common people'. This was no polished and responsible public: they were bread-winners unable to support their families, and bitterness had unleashed their tongues. This was fertile soil for both real criticism and unbridled incitement. The criticism was directed against those who were respon-sible for allocating jobs – the Tel Aviv Labor Council. Tales of favoritism, failure to observe the rule of 'first come first served', etc., were eagerly absorbed by the unemployed, many of them new immigrants. At these elections, a minor coup occurred: a group headed by Dov Ben Yeruham captured power, using demagoguery and riding the waves of the hostility of the destitute towards those who were better off and towards the establishment as such.

Yitzhak Ben Aharon, then one of the leaders of ha-Kibbutz ha-Meuhad and the Secretary of the Tel Aviv Labor Council, was not pleased by the populist victory. Their open and refreshingly frank drive for power introduced a new tone into the deliberations between the Party branch and the Labor Council. Ben Aharon frequently noted in his diary his disgust at the methods and language used by the Ben Yeruham group.

But politics make strange bedfellows, and, as noted, the Rehovot conference marked the burgeoning of the alliance between the oppo-sition in Tel Aviv and members of ha-Kibbutz ha-Meuhad, led by Ben Aharon and Joseph Bankover, the Mapai Secretary General.

Although this was a mating of different species, it was an organic alliance, and it revived Berl's nightmares of the Labor Brigade days. The Tel Aviv opposition, fed by the economic and social crisis, but lacking an ideology and high-level leadership, might have constituted a fleeting phenomenon, like previous urban oppositions (some of which had been successfully integrated into the urban establishment and others suppressed by the party machine). But their alliance with ha-Kibbutz ha-Meuhad transformed a chance phenomenon into a permanent fixture. Ha-Kibbutz ha-Meuhad also benefited from the alliance: the Tel Aviv opposition created a focus of dispute in the party, thus diverting attention from the question of the union of the settlement movement. Perusal of the minutes of the Mapai Central Committee deliberations in 1938–1939 reveals the amazing fact that *the* central issue on the agenda of the Party in those fateful years was 'Faction B – Tel Aviv'.

For Berl, this was an alliance between those eager to give and those greedy to take; between the elite pioneering forces that he wanted to guide (in his own way) to leadership and the forces of narrow trade-unionism that he wanted to check. From one point of view, Berl could regard the alliance as proof of the validity of his theory regarding the unification of the kibbutz movement: the very existence of separate blocs had created within the party power centers which inexorably attracted the dissatisfied and served as the foundations for factions, barriers between the party and the individual member. On the other hand, Berl's demand for union had driven ha-Kibbutz ha-Meuhad's leadership into a defensive position, and the alliance with the Tel Aviv opposition was the natural outcome.

The destructive processes at work in the movement, which he had predicted and was now witnessing, seemed to affect Berl's state of health. He had fallen ill, and in the summer of 1938 he moved to Jerusalem, where the heat was less oppressive. Deputations from the youth movements came to visit him there, where he was busy editing an article, 'Bleak Prospects', for *mi-Bifnim*. But his illness affected his ability to work, and he fell into a dark depression, compounded by his general despair.

As for the implementation of the Rehovot resolutions, things seemed, on the surface, to be on the move: two meetings were held with representatives of Hever ha-Kvutzot and ha-Kibbutz ha-Meuhad at which the possibility of unification was discussed at great length and with little enthusiasm.

Berl had meanwhile left for London on a political mission and for medical treatment. The detailed minutes of the discussions persuaded him that his friend, Shaul Meirov, was right in saying that 'the best of our people have invested the best of their intellectual efforts in proving that unification is impossible'.[9] As for the amalgamation of the youth movements, Pinhas Lubianiker of Hever ha-Kvutzot was opposed to the Rehovot resolution, demanding a merger of the kibbutz movements as the condition for amalgamating the youth movements. Ha-Kibbutz ha-Meuhad was in a favorable position, since it was insisting on the immediate merging of the youth movements, without any connection to the unification of the kibbutz movement. And thus the two members of the party Secretariat, Ben Aharon and Lubianiker, each did his share (apparently in a conspiracy of silence) to remove the mergers from the agenda. As Ben Gurion tersely put it: 'One member of the Secretariat made sure that the youth merger would not take place, and the other saw to it that the kibbutz movement would not be united.'[10]

Throughout the months when relations within the party were breaking down, and the Tel Aviv factions were stepping up their fight against one another, both Berl and Ben Gurion were in Europe. They knew of events in Palestine from the minutes of the Central Committee meetings and the Secretariat and from reports from various sources. Berl had recovered his health as a result of treatment in London and his energy was restored (see chapter 14). At the end of November he met Ben Gurion in Paris. Their talk lasted through the night, and they discussed foreign policy and the party. As for the party, Ben Gurion apparently tended to a firm stand against ha-Kibbutz ha-Meuhad, to which Berl objected for fear that it would split the movement. When they returned home, Ben Gurion appeared at the Central Committee like an angry Jupiter, hurling his lightning bolts. Developments in the Tel Aviv branch had infuriated him. He wanted to dissolve the branch, and to send a commissar from the Central Committee to reorganize it from the ground up. Lengthy and tedious discussions on the state of the party followed in which nobody disputed that the party was disintegrating, each bloc blaming the other. Ostensibly the Tel Aviv affair took pride of place, but the true struggle was being conducted between Ben Gurion and Berl on the one hand and ha-Kibbutz ha-Meuhad on the other.

The delegates to the Zionist Actions Committee in London had just returned home. Germany was in turmoil: a young Jewish boy named Hershel Greenspan had assassinated a German diplomat in Paris, and the Nazis retaliated with the Kristallnacht as the world looked on. In London, the Woodhead Commission had proposed the establishment of a Jewish mini-state between Hadera and Rehovot. A confrontation between the Zionist Executive and the Mandatory Government was imminent. And, in the face of the storm brewing in Palestine and in Europe, the Central Committee of Mapai, the ruling party of Jewish

Palestine, was dedicating its energies to mutual recrimination and self-destruction. At one of the marathon meetings, Shaul Meirov commented with amazement: 'During the hours we have been sitting here I awake from time to time in shock and think: Where are we? It is as if we're not living in December 1938 . . .'[11] Berl responded to the absurd situation with pained bitterness:

As for the total confidence I once had in the labor movement as regards itself . . . from this point of view the past few years have roused very great doubts in me. And if a Jewish historian should discover some day what we have been doing these past few weeks – he might find therein some explanation of what has happened to us.[12]

The active members demanded strong leadership, and particularly from Berl. His withdrawal from activity after the Rehovot debacle had deprived the party of the generally accepted, supreme authority, which, it was believed, could overcome the internal confusion and recreate a harmonious fabric of human relations. But Berl had resolved not to undertake the leadership of the party unless it proved itself willing to implement the resolutions of the Rehovot conference. He refused to accept the situation as inevitable. In contrast to Sprinzak (supported by the sectors), who was prepared to accept the status quo in the party but sought to achieve some balance between the warring parties, Berl believed that a revolution, a radical change in the party was the sole path to salvation. As long as he could not discern a willingness on the part of the active section of the party – ha-Kibbutz ha-Meuhad – to accept this change, he saw no point to undertaking the leadership.

Berl had not yet despaired of unification. Processes had been set in motion within ha-Kibbutz ha-Meuhad, which seemed to augur favorably for change.

An opposition emerged within ha-Kibbutz ha-Meuhad, which threatened the dominant leadership. It was relatively complex in construction, and encompassed the veteran opponents to the Kibbutz leadership, led by Maletz, Svorai and Shlomo Lavi of Ein Harod. These people, whom Tabenkin called 'the weary' (i.e. weary of pioneering effort) had always opposed the idea of the country-wide kibbutz which, they felt, did not recognize the limits on the capacity of the commune to expand.

The opposition also included the Nezah group from Kibbutz Afikim, who had maintained partial autonomy within ha-Kibbutz ha-Meuhad – to no small extent thanks to Berl, who had sided with them during the establishment of the Kibbutz (1927). The leadership's hopes of eventually absorbing the Nezah group had been dashed; their group dynamics operated in the opposite direction. Nezah were a group apart within ha-Kibbutz ha-Meuhad with their own leadership and different communal ideal. The ideal of ha-Kibbutz ha-Meuhad was a large settlement – like Yagur – set up by a resolution of the movement's Secretariat and to a large extent contrary to the wishes of the members involved. It was a kibbutz which combined urban work with agriculture and tried to integrate different waves of immigration from different ethnic backgrounds. For the Nezah group, Afikim was the ideal. It was a large and flourishing kibbutz – whose expansion was governed by its 'social absorption capacity'. They felt that this approach had spared them the growing pains which had characterized Yagur. Thus Yagur and Afikim symbolized the two approaches to unification. Nezah favored unity both for its own sake and out of a natural desire to emerge from their relative isolation within the framework of ha-Kibbutz ha-Meuhad and to free themselves of its pressures. Within a united, all-embracing movement, Nezah could be transformed from a suspect and unpopular minority into the central hinge, linking Hever ha-Kvutzot and ha-Kibbutz ha-Meuhad. Paradoxically enough, those who had jealously preserved their autonomy within ha-Kibbutz ha-Meuhad now advocated 'generality' and the unification of the kibbutz movement; while ha-Kibbutz ha-Meuhad, which preached 'generality' to he-Halutz and was traditionally opposed to bestowing rights on particularistic bodies, flatly refused to dissolve its own framework for the sake of a wider one.

This ambiguity was one of the obstacles which hampered ha-Kibbutz ha-Meuhad in the internal debate. Rank-and-file kibbutz members, who had been bred on the slogan of generality, on the organic integrity of the Palestinian labor movement, on the myth of Ahdut ha-Avoda and the constant striving for wider frameworks, found it hard to swallow the arguments of Tabenkin and his comrades opposing unification. Tabenkin emphasized the difference between an association of parties and an association of social bodies, but his arguments seemed forced and hollow. 'I recall the arguments at the Petah Tikva constituent conference and the arguments of Tabenkin, who fought for unity and proved to me and to many others like me, that any framework aspires, by its very nature, to fill itself with content, to sanctify itself and to justify its separate existence.'[13] These remarks by Zeev Feinstein expressed the views of many members of ha-Kibbutz ha-Meuhad, both veterans and newcomers, who found themselves torn between their personal loyalty to Tabenkin and their loyalty to the theories inculcated in them over the years. These were the people whom Berl had convinced of the justness of his claims.

Another important element within the opposition in ha-Kibbutz ha-Meuhad were the immigrants from Germany, who had found their way to the movement through its emissaries – Livenstein, Sereni, Baruch Eisenstadt and Yitzhak Ben Aharon. They were apparently impervious to Tabenkin's charm; their mentors were Martin Buber and Berl. Perhaps the fact that most of the emissaries had been disciples of Berl also had some effect, or perhaps it was the rationalistic education they had received which rendered them more responsive to Berl's sober theories than to Tabenkin's fiery enthusiasm. They may also have been resisting the attempts of the leadership to assimilate them as fast as possible into the kibbutz society. Their identification with the opposition may have been an expression of their desire to preserve their identity and image against the communal crucible.

As a result of the emergence of this opposition, which bolstered Berl's position, the leadership of ha-Kibbutz ha-Meuhad proved increasingly intractable. The movement should logically have been ready to take the risk of unification, since it had three times the number of members that Hever ha-Kvutzot had, and a strong and dynamic leadership. After all, it seemed more than likely that the smaller movement would be absorbed into ha-Kibbutz ha-Meuhad (and, in fact, Hever ha-Kvutzot feared this very possibility). But this hypothesis was valid only as long as ha-Kibbutz ha-Meuhad was monolithic. As the debate on unification became more acrimonious, and breaches appeared in the wall of unity, the leaders became apprehensive at the thought of a merger. They now feared an alliance between the Hever ha-Kvutzot leadership and their own opposition. This would make them a minority in the united movement. If the opposition had not emerged, the leadership might have succeeded in suppressing any internal debate on unification, and did, in fact, do so until the eve of the Na'an conference in July 1939. But the rise of the opposition rallied the leaders who felt that they were under siege and battling for survival. Thus, the fight for the union was self-defeating.

Until spring 1938, ha-Kibbutz ha-Meuhad's leaders were confident of their own strength within the movement, and proponents of unity

245

encountered ridicule and contempt. Even Berl doubted the ability of his supporters to take the lead in ha-Kibbutz ha-Meuhad. This may explain the 'great' – and, it would seem, the last – discussion between Berl and the Kibbutz Secretariat, held on 10 January 1939. The meeting lasted from four in the afternoon until midnight, was continued a week later, and revolved around the twofold issue of Berl's return to active leadership and the willingness of ha-Kibbutz ha-Meuhad to cooperate with him in changing the face of things. Berl was even franker than usual, since the gathering was an intimate one, and the remarks were not for publication. 'It is my opinion that the differences in the party are not ideological; this is a fight for power.' As a result, Berl found it 'hard to breathe in Mapai, in the Histadrut. In this situation I am unproductive. I cannot live in this atmosphere.'[14] Although Tabenkin's remarks were conciliatory, their implication was negative: the demand for unity reflected a desire to disband ha-Kibbutz ha-Meuhad. To this, of course, he could not agree. Berl's impression of the talk was that ha-Kibbutz ha-Meuhad was not willing to alter the status quo. They interpreted any criticism as an attack: 'I feel that there is a barrier between us which prevents us from dealing with the basic questions, and I do not know who constructed it.' But he went on to enunciate what he felt to be the objectives of the merger, even at this moment of crisis: 'The communal enterprise, to me, is the heart of the movement . . . the leadership of the movement comes from the agricultural settlements and I want the leaders to be recruited from the pioneering strata. Otherwise we will have lost our moral influence over the movement.' And in the bitterness of defeat, he added: 'And yet we are accused of dissimulating.' There was nothing left for him but to retire. When he finished, Tabenkin again took the floor. Tabenkin spoke with a warmth and appreciation, and even openness, in contrast to many of his colleagues. He depicted ha-Kibbutz ha-Meuhad's stand as still open to change. Although the crisis was acute, the trend was towards unification. And, finally: 'This group could not bear to be responsible for your retirement, as you seem to conclude.'[15] The old affection was still there and Berl left the meeting encouraged.

In early February 1939 Berl visited London. When he returned in the spring, he found ha-Kibbutz ha-Meuhad in an uproar on the unification issue. Finally, more than three years after his first 'Protest', the debate was in the open. Delegates to the 12th Kibbutz Convention, to be held in July 1939 in Na'an were being elected on the basis of their stand on this question. A number of leading members lost out to less prominent people, elected for the first time on the strength of their views alone.

In the course of the heated controversy, ha-Kibbutz ha-Meuhad's leaders discovered that there was a large bloc supporting merger and the dispute took on the proportions of a life-and-death struggle. Such luxuries as affection or esteem could not be permitted. At the end of April 1939, a meeting of cadres was held at Yagur in an oppressive atmosphere. Tabenkin called the demand for unification a demand for the dissolution of the movement and threatened, in return, to dissolve the party. Berl regarded this speech as 'a declaration of civil war in the party',[16] and finally realized that Tabenkin would never accede to a majority decision to impose unification.

It was clear that his relations with Tabenkin had reached crisis point. The success of the proponents of unification among ha-Kibbutz ha-Meuhad members had undermined his friend's leadership to a point that Tabenkin found unforgivable. Berl had invaded Tabenkin's domain, and the latter, like Berl himself, was not prepared to distinguish between personal and political affronts. On the night after the cadres met at Yagur, Berl contemplated writing a letter to Tabenkin, but he never put his thoughts to paper. Three days later he received the first indication of the depth of the rift. Tabenkin had learned that Berl was to edit a collection of articles on the unification of the kibbutz movement, and hastened to send him a letter, forbidding him to include any of his own writings in the anthology. This was an unprecedented slap in the face for Berl.

The ha-Kibbutz ha-Meuhad Convention, which was supposed to decide the question of unification, was postponed again and again. Meanwhile, Berl harnessed himself to the task of propaganda, visiting kibbutzim, addressing large audiences and conversing with individuals. He was particularly anxious to convince the young people, second-generation kibbutz members, like Moshe Tabenkin and Nehemia Schein, and the youth of ha-Mahanot ha-Olim. Whenever he arrived at a settlement, he was inundated with invitations from 'delegations' of the surrounding kibbutzim. Because he preferred the company of the young to that of the adults, this was an 'hour of grace' for him and his hopes of improving the situation rose. He was delighted by the suc-

247

cesses of the 'unitarians' in ha-Kibbutz ha-Meuhad and he disregarded Tabenkin's letter, whether for lack of time or because he abandoned the task of producing the book. Although they met from time to time at the Mapai Central Committee in the months between the meeting of cadres at Yagur and the Na'an Council, they did not talk personally. Berl's mood improved: for the first time in years he expressed a willingness to join the Party Secretariat (the previous Secretariat, headed jointly by Lubianiker and Ben-Aharon, had resigned in October 1938). The central figure in the newly elected body was Zeev Feinstein, a member of Kibbutz Ayelet ha-Shahar, (affiliated to ha-Kibbutz ha-Meuhad) and one of the advocates of union. The Secretariat treated Berl with the utmost circumspection, for fear that he might again decide to slam the door in their faces. Surprisingly enough, he responded to their cautious overtures, and two and a half months after they approached him, he replied that he was ready to stand for election – though he qualified this statement by adding that this was not to be seen as a commitment on his part.

The Kibbutz Conference was held in mid-July 1939 at Na'an. The elections which preceded the conference stunned the leadership. The 'unitarians' won a majority not only in such 'weary' kibbutzim as Ein Harod, but even in Yagur and Givat Brenner – the crowning glories of ha-Kibbutz ha-Meuhad. The settlements of ha-Mahanot ha-Olim were divided: Beit ha-Shita favored the merger, while Maoz Hayim rallied against it. This division refuted the claim of Tabenkin's supporters that the entire young generation was on their side. In all, the 'unitarians' received 2 per cent more of the total votes than the opponents. The rank and file were rebelling! Ha-Kibbutz ha-Meuhad's leadership behaved as if they were in mourning. This time no mention was made of readiness to accept the decisions of the majority. Instead, open threats of a split were voiced. The debate was conducted in an atmosphere fraught with tension, and efforts were made, not always successfully, to preserve a friendly or at least a 'gentlemanly' approach, since it was generally understood that, after the debate, the disputants would continue to live side by side in the same kibbutz. Many – especially the anti-'unitarians' – felt that the fabric of communal life was being destroyed. The pro-union people took care not to undermine the leadership, both because they accepted its authority on most other matters, and because they feared further exacerbation of the dispute. Outsiders also joined in: Meir Yaari, of ha-Shomer ha-Tzair, lent his support to the opponents of unification as spokesman for those who considered diversity in the communal settlement movement a desirable and encouraging phenomenon. Berl, of course, spoke in favor of unity.

The convention lasted for six days. The time for decision finally arrived, and was influenced by the prior knowledge that the 'unitarians' would not, under any circumstances, split the movement. This fact tied the hands of the majority, and gave the leadership free rein. Instead of proposing an unequivocal resolution on the merging of ha-Kibbutz ha-Meuhad with Hever ha-Kvutzot, the 'unitarians' confined themselves to demanding the election of a committee to clarify the matter. As against this minimalistic demand, Israel Idelson, who had conducted the leadership's campaign with great skill, demanded a reiteration of the old Yagur resolution on the establishment of an alliance of the kibbutz movement; this, he said, did not contradict the demand for union. In the context in which it was presented, however, it was in effect merely window-dressing, designed to gloss over the rejection of unification. The victors were those who adopted the more extreme approach and were prepared to risk a split. The convention endorsed the resolution of the Yagur convention on the Kibbutz Movement Alliance, and another resolution was then adopted to a committee 'to clarify all the possibilities for unification with Hever ha-Kvutzot'.[17]

Despite the moderation of the proponents of union, the leadership of ha-Kibbutz ha-Meuhad emerged from the conference with a profound sense of failure. But the success of the 'unitarians' proved illusory. They were in a psychologically inferior position to the leadership: on the one side was ranged a heterogeneous group, without a closely-knit leadership, representing the 'silent majority' of ha-Kibbutz ha-Meuhad; facing them was an organized, active and resolute minority. What was historically important was what happened after the Na'an Conference ended: had the proponents of unity taken over control of ha-Kibbutz ha-Meuhad's institutions, or at least won a majority in the Council and the Secretariat, things might have turned out differently. But the pro-unity group did not reject the leadership *per se* nor launch an all-out attack on it. They merely opposed its stand on one particular issue. As a result the same leadership was re-elected at Na'an, and after a period of crisis, recovered its bearings and began to work for change. Before two years had lapsed, a reversal occurred, and the majority went over to the side of the 'opponents'.

The amalgamation of the kibbutz movements and merger of the

249

youth movements never took place. Speeches in favor of unification were delivered at Hever ha-Kvutzot's conference at Degania, several days after the Na'an Conference, and a positive stand on the question was adopted. But the key lay with ha-Kibbutz ha-Meuhad.

The controversy shook the very foundations of Mapai. If Berl had intended to jog his party out of its uncritical self-satisfaction, he certainly succeeded. But it transpired in due course that the maelstrom into which the party had been drawn was threatening to drown it. The controversy sharpened rivalries and revived dormant conflicts. The leadership of ha-Kibbutz ha-Meuhad, which found itself in trouble, reacted by strengthening its links with urban oppositional circles, with Faction B in Tel Aviv and later in Haifa. It is not easy to decide if Berl's old claim that separate settlement movements were breeding grounds for new parties was vindicated, or if it was the acrimonious debate which generated the process. The paths of social and political processes are convoluted, and cause and effect are intermingled. But on one point, history would seem to have justified Berl: the introversion of the various settlement movements – one manifestation of which was the opposition to amalgamation – detached the kibbutz movement as a social force from involvement in Israeli society, and determined to a large extent the trade-union character of Mapai's second-generation leadership, and the party's subsequent decline.

For Berl personally, the struggle ended in the breakdown of a lifelong friendship. Tabenkin, it will be recalled, forbade Berl to include his speeches in the book he was preparing. It was the first time that anyone had questioned Berl's status as the movement's undisputed editor and it aroused general amazement. Complaints had been voiced from time to time against *Davar*, but Berl was regarded as the best and most reliable of editors. Tabenkin's injunction implied that Berl was disqualified from serving as the mentor of the entire movement.

On 4 August 1939, the anthology was discussed by the Secretariat of the Histadrut Executive, with the participation of Berl and Tabenkin. 'He sees me as a despot, tormenting him',[18] Berl remarked painfully in his diary. Remez, the Secretary of the Executive, dismissed Tabenkin's obduracy and reprimanded him for his stand. Tabenkin heard him out with bowed head. 'You have the power',[19] he said finally – and left the meeting. But he had no intention of giving up the fight. When he received the galley proofs of the book, he voiced his objections again in a letter to the Secretariat and to Berl. 'I insist on my right not to be

published in the anthology under Berl Katznelson's decisive editorship
on the unification issue.' The selection of material – he claimed –
attenuated the image of ha-Kibbutz ha-Meuhad and 'its members, who
are concerned with its survival, and reject unification'. The book was
aimed at demonstrating 'the conceptual poverty of our members'.[20]
The main brunt of his attack was directed against the 'Protest'. Berl was
depicted in the letter as a man whose own remarks had disqualified him
from appearing in print together with a representative of ha-Kibbutz
ha-Meuhad. More than three years after publication of the 'Protest',
after endless discussions with Berl on its content, Tabenkin was determined to boycott Berl. He could not forgive him for the success of the
opposition at Na'an. Berl finished editing the book, wrote a foreword,
designed the front pages and even gave it a title, *The Kibbutz and the
Kvutza*, and in mid-November 1939, he received a copy of the book.
But it was an aborted effort, since three months before publication Berl
had renounced responsibility for the anthology. To Tabenkin he
wrote:

Yitzhak, I surrender. I will not publish the anthology against your wishes. It is not that
I accept your criticism of me; it is not that I think that any of us has the right to conduct
himself as you have done with regard to me and my work, but I cannot and will not
publish the anthology if you regard it – or the proximity of your words to mine – as an
act of coercion. You or the Executive must decide as you choose – I wash my hands of
the matter.

He concluded the letter with the plea of a disappointed lover:
'Farewell, may our old age not shame our youth.'[21] Berl could not bear
this personal clash with Tabenkin, and in order to avoid a quarrel, he
entrusted the fate of the anthology to the Histadrut Executive Secretariat. Almost a year went by, but Berl made no inquiries as to the fate
of the book. Nobody actually saw it or read it: even the contributors
never received a copy. It was referred to by those in the know as the
'hidden book'. It was never officially decided to shelve the anthology:
its fate reflected Mapai's situation: Remez, Berl's friend and admirer,
who had supported him in the anthology, could not summon up the
courage to go against ha-Kibbutz ha-Meuhad's firm resolve or to stir up
the troubled waters even further.

For Berl, the actual shelving of the book was further proof that the
Histadrut was becoming a federation, in which every act required the
concurrence of all the blocs. He announced his resignation from the
editorship of *Davar*: 'Anyone who is unfit to edit an anthology on a con-

troversial issue – is disqualified from editing the Histadrut paper.'[22]
The cohesion of the group which had built Ahdut ha-Avoda had been
irretrievably shattered. The 'hidden book' marked the end of the road
for Berl and Tabenkin. To political rivalry, and differences of opinion,
was added a personal rift, which was painful in the extreme.

14

HOUR OF PERIL,
1936–1939

In spring, 1936, the Arab Rebellion broke out. Following four years of mass immigration and expansion of the National Home, the Arabs of Palestine took up arms to stem the process which was threatening to turn them into a minority in their own land. The 'disturbances', as they were called at the time, commenced in a way recalling previous periods of violence: assaults on Jewish passers-by in Jaffa, several brutal murders, and the segregation of the populations of mixed neighborhoods into hostile camps. But several days after the first outbursts, the Arab leadership convened and, in an unprecedented display of national unity, established the Arab Higher Committee. The Committee proclaimed a general strike of all Palestinian Arabs, whose duration was contingent upon the fulfillment of three demands: the establishment of a democratic constitution, thus relegating power to the Arab majority; a ban on land sale to Jews and, most vital of all, a halt to immigration. From this point on, the disturbances evolved into a protracted strike which, while accompanied by random acts of violence, was conducted by a political leadership with clearly defined aims. If the 1929 disturbances could have been labelled 'pogroms' – the events of 1936 could not. They reflected the upsurge of a national movement, characterized by both heroism and savagery.

Overnight the Yishuv found itself under siege: travel became dangerous; at night trees were hacked down, barns and fields set ablaze. The labor of years went up in smoke. The Jews were compelled to reorganize their economy on the basis of self-sufficiency – supplying their own vegetables and fruit, eggs and dairy products. Striking Arab laborers were replaced in the citrus groves by Jews. When Arab dockworkers brought Jaffa port to a standstill, the British Government in Palestine gave permission for the construction of a jetty at Tel Aviv which evolved into the first independent Jewish port. Jewish defense formations, neglected since 1929, were now given top priority. A quasi-legal auxiliary Jewish police force under British command (the Notrim) was formed to protect isolated Jewish settlements and to patrol roads.

Together with the fear they inspired and the damage and casualties they inflicted, the disturbances generated a new spirit in the Yishuv – of self-sacrifice and enthusiasm for projects of a scope which would have been unthinkable in quieter times. Withal, the Rebellion triggered an anti-Zionist turn in British policy.

The High Commissioner, Sir Arthur Wauchope, had, from the beginning of his term of office in 1931, won the confidence of the Zionist leadership by his resolute conduct. In 1933, he had harshly suppressed Arab demonstrations which signaled their first political campaign against the British Government in Palestine. For four years he had consistently permitted extensive immigration, which had doubled the Jewish population. Ben Gurion, like Arlosoroff, his predecessor as Head of the Jewish Agency's Political Department, trusted and respected him. Only a few months before the outbreak of the disturbances, Ben Gurion had been earnestly debating with himself whether the time had come to engage the High Commissioner in discussions on the broader questions: the ultimate objectives of Zionism and ways of realizing them. The disturbances changed the direction of his thinking.

Berl had never shared Ben Gurion's admiration for Wauchope. His deep-rooted and intuitive mistrust of Gentiles, particularly those representing imperialist power, rendered him impervious to Wauchope's charm. As early as January 1936, he predicted that the High Commissioner's pro-Zionist period would be followed by a pro-Arab period. Unlike the heads of the Jewish Agency Political Department, who saw the Arab Rebellion as a reflection of a fervent Palestinian nationalism looking for political support to the newly-liberated Arab States, and who perceived the Arabs as the prime factor affecting relations between the Jews and the British, Berl went so far as to suspect the British of merely seizing upon Arab unrest as a pretext for exerting pressure on the Jews. Unlike Ben Gurion, who had since 1929 become aware of the reasoning and contentions of the other side, and could therefore understand Wauchope's motives, Berl regarded any attempt to understand and condone either Arab or British considerations as the first step towards compromise and concession, a luxury the Zionist movement could ill-afford. He chose deliberately to ignore any British or Arab reasoning.

The suspicion and hostility which marked Berl's attitude towards the Mandate Government narrowed his view of Jewish–British relations, and restricted his imagination and flexibility. He found it hard to adapt his patterns of thinking and response to political change: the authorities were again anti-Zionist just as they had been during the Military Administration. Paradoxically enough, Berl's irrational suspicions were vindicated by the irony of history. Although there were short-term fluctuations in British policy, in the long term it became wholly anti-Zionist in orientation. On the eve of the Second World War, the dictum that 'everyone is against the Jew' was borne out by the facts. And Berl, the eternal pessimist where non-Jews were concerned, was not taken by surprise. Moreover, such sentiments were not Berl's alone. As a matter of fact, the Ben Gurion–Shertok line represented a minority in the labor movement. Tabenkin was Berl's staunch ally in this area and tended to regard Berl as representing the movement's firm stand against the compromisers. From now on he was the vigilante, overseeing the Jewish Agency Executive and Weizmann himself.

Berl's political importance was greater now than ever before. 'There was no important political issue discussed in those months,' according to Shertok, 'without Berl's participation.'[1]

Although his views were not shared by the Political Department of the Jewish Agency, he was nonetheless regarded as the voice of Zionist reason: Shertok described him as 'a blend of war-like courage, discretion and clarity',[2] and Ben Gurion agreed. Even when they differed in their evaluation of the positions and tactics of the Mandatory, they found a common language when drawing up plans of action, with the central aim of insuring continued immigration.

Berl's main instrument for shaping public opinion in this period was *Davar*. He himself did not write often, but Beilinson was his faithful spokesman; together they formulated the policy which made *Davar* a fighting paper during those years, the voice of an embattled nation. Ben Gurion and Shertok protested against *Davar's* tendentious anti-British view of affairs, which sometimes obstructed their political efforts. In vain: *Davar* reflected the view of Berl and Beilinson and earned wider public recognition and admiration than it had enjoyed in any other period.

When Ben Gurion returned to Palestine after a session of the Zionist

Actions Committee in Zurich in August 1936, he demanded that Berl be sent to London to invigorate political activity there. Berl flew to London in September.

He was pleasantly surprised by the team he found in the Jewish Agency offices at 77 Great Russell Street in London. They were respectful towards members of the Palestinian leadership, and ready to cooperate with him. Now, as well, he had no official status, and was dependent on his skill at influencing others and operating through them. Although he had mastered English to the point where he could conduct a conversation without an interpreter, his powers of persuasion in that language fell short of his impact in Hebrew and Yiddish. Still, within a few days he sensed that they were responding to him. 'The feeling that I was alien and superfluous has lifted,' he wrote to Leah. 'The people here have been won over to me somewhat, and they take my opinion and advice into account.'[3] This feeling may explain his favorable view of the people in London: he praised Arthur Lourie as a dedicated and self-effacing man, and Zelig Brodetsky for his unflagging zeal. But he was particularly impressed by Lewis Namier and Blanche (Baffy) Dugdale. Namier came from a Polish-Jewish family. He was a renowned historian, whose speciality was British history. A professor at Manchester University, Namier was a stormy and controversial figure. Berl regarded him as the dynamic force in the office, a true political Zionist, who suspected that his mentor, Weizmann, was not entirely reconciled to the strong line of the Executive. His fighting temperament appealed to Berl.

'Baffy' Dugdale, the niece of Lord Balfour, was also a dedicated Zionist. Berl found it hard to digest this unique blend: 'I must admit that I do not approach this woman with an easy heart,' he wrote. But he was finally won over: 'Of all the people with whom I have spoken here – she understood me the best. She asked well, she learned well.'[4]

The central personality in the Political Department in London was still Chaim Weizmann. Berl entertained ambivalent feelings about him. He understood Weizmann and felt affection for the grass-roots element in his personality. Weizmann's humor and Jewish folk instincts appealed to Berl, who saw him as the prisoner of Anglo-Saxon propriety. When Weizmann returned from a visit to the Dutch Jewish community cheerful and lively, Berl noted: 'The numerous meetings, perhaps his Yiddish conversations with Eastern Jews in Antwerp, have restored his spirits.'[5] Weizmann greeted Berl warmly. Said Berl: 'When a patient is gravely ill, they bring him a great professor and he does what he can. But by the professor's side stands a Jew, a poor relation, and he too does what he can – he recites Psalms. I have come to recite Psalms by the professor's side.'[6] This parable indicates something of the problematic nature of his relationship with the great statesman. Berl believed that Weizmann needed constant stimulus and constant supervision. On the other hand he knew that Weizmann could not function if he felt that he was being coerced. Weizmann responded negatively to pressures from Palestine. Disgruntled and resentful, he would go to the Colonial Office; but, because of his reluctance, his effectiveness was impaired. Weizmann's changing moods were of national significance, since, despite his faults, nobody could present the Zionist cause to the British with such skill. Berl gained the impression that Weizmann was wearied by the incessant struggle, the constant need to press and urge, and hence he sought a subtle way of infusing him with a fighting spirit. 'The trouble is that he is clever enough and sensitive enough not to be deluded by the guise of adulation with which we camouflage our battle with him.'[7]

The Peel Commission was about to arrive in Palestine and the Zionist leadership was considering various possible Jewish counter-proposals to the schemes the Commission was expected to broach. Namier had become enthusiastic about the idea of parity and tried to persuade the other members of the Zionist Executive to further the cause by appealing to Ormsby-Gore, the Colonial Secretary. Weizmann too was enthusiastic about the idea. But Berl, who had originally been one of its advocates, had recently abandoned it, and he found an ally in Ben Gurion. To advocate parity now seemed a step liable to harm the Jewish cause; if it served as the starting-point for Jewish–Arab–British deliberations, it would inevitably lead to further Jewish concessions. Berl also feared that the idea of parity would be grasped as implying numerical equality – and would lead to restrictions on immigration and the sale of land, which the original parity scheme had tried to avoid. Berl now believed, as had Arlosoroff, that the British would not understand the scheme, for which there was no precedent in their own imperialist tradition.

Similarly to Ben Gurion, Berl was ready, within the framework of a round-table conference with the Arabs, to assent to the restriction of immigration to the 1935 annual rate (62,000), the highest ever achieved. But, more cautious than Ben Gurion, he opposed a Jewish initiative on the subject – for the same reason which led him to oppose Jewish initiative on parity, and also because he had little faith in Weizmann's steadfastness on the issue: 'To open the sluice gate on this matter could flood our fields. We know our own people.'[8]

By virtue of their common East European background, Berl resembled Weizmann in many ways, but they differed drastically in their Zionist outlook. This disparity was reflected in an exchange between the two when Weizmann was preparing for his appearance before the Peel Commission. As 'inspiration' he took with him an English translation of the works of Ahad ha-Am. He also sent the book as a gift to the Commission's Secretary. 'You are laughing at me,' he said to Berl. 'I knew you would laugh. That is why I showed it to you. This is still the best book. It is still relevant.' Berl replied:

Ahad ha-Am is an important writer, but in English translation he is dangerous. Between the writing of this work and Hitler, not thirty but three hundred years have passed. Ahad ha-Am was a great optimist. He believed in constitutional monarchy in Russia and in equal rights, and in the prospect that educated Jewish businessmen would set up a Hebrew school and publishing house.

'At these last remarks,' Berl continued, 'he nodded, but how remote he is from all this. It would not occur to him to see how relevant Herzl is.'[9] Just as Weizmann kept faith with Ahad ha-Am, the teacher he admired, and with minimalist Zionism, so Berl was loyal to his youthful beliefs.

Politically speaking, this was an interim period between the struggle which preceded the ending of the Arab strike, and the visit to Palestine of the Peel Commission (November 1936). In Great Russell Street, Berl found a staff weary from the long months of battle. He was a Palestinian, an intruder in a small, exclusive group, who had gone through difficult times together. He was apparently made a party to consultations, and was considered 'in' enough to receive classified information, but he left no special mark.

Berl took advantage of his stay in London to strengthen his ties with the Anglo-Jewish 'aristocracy', with Israel Sieff and Henry Melchett. Somewhat out of place in his careless and certainly non-formal attire, he still found ample opportunity to express his views, and if the ties he established did not bear immediate fruit, they could be considered a long-term investment.

Of particular significance were his links with prominent people in the Labor Party. These were the sole direct contacts he made with non-Jews in England (excluding his talks with Blanche Dugdale). Berl summoned up the courage to try to renew the ties established in the 1920s between the British and Palestinian labor movements. He attended the Labor Conference in Edinburgh. (He noted that Weizmann, 'who displays great tenderness and warmth towards me', had warned him that the city was very cold and he would be well advised to take an overcoat.) In Edinburgh he observed a labor movement in all its strength and its weakness, and was highly impressed by the leadership. They were neither bureaucrats nor narrow-minded party officials, but 'people of character and soul'. They were humanists and their view of the problems of the world was colored by their concern for peace and for the workers. 'I do not know', he said, 'if there exists anywhere else in the world a group of people who consider themselves responsible for saving civilization, as do those I saw there.'[10] The involvement and personal integrity he observed at Edinburgh won his heart more than the intellectual gifts of the great socialist theoreticians he had met in Austria. He was captivated by George Lansbury, the 80-year-old pacifist who, upon hearing that the fascists were planning a march through Whitechapel, immediately left the Conference and travelled overnight to London to stand guard there. Berl's report to Mapai's Central Committee on the unique human qualities he had found in the British Labor leaders seemed to reflect his wish that his own party might continue to boast of such a leadership.

Berl also witnessed the Jarrow hunger march of thousands of unemployed dock-workers from northern England, who trudged the 280 miles (450 km) to London with their families to protest to the Government. The demonstrators took pains to present their demands in non-political terms. They spoke clearly, simply, reasonably, and it was evident that they were confident of being heard, that theirs was a national issue. Berl was moved: 'The meeting', he noted in his diary, 'is the afterglow of a great civilization.'[11]

At the same time, Berl was quite aware of Labor's weaknesses: 'A movement which has no hope of prevailing, which does not believe that it can win . . . a movement disintegrating from within.'[12] The leadership was divided between the pacifists and those who wanted Britain to arm in the face of the threats of Europe's dictators. Even on the issue of the Spanish Civil War, the Conference did not succeed in passing an unambiguous resolution in support of the Republicans. The

Spanish delegation, however, was given a royal welcome and was granted special permission to address the delegates, a privilege denied to other foreign delegations. Berl, who did not speak at this forum, wrote in his diary: 'I would not like to change places with them. I feel good as I am.'[13] Berl sensed at the conference that the world of the pacifists and humanists had been shattered. The trade unionists, led by Bevin, representing the views of the rank and file, claimed that British civilization must be defended against Hitlerite barbarism and that rearmament should be supported.

They were opposed by most of the leadership and the younger generation, who were attracted to the Soviet Union. Berl gained the impression that the young had abandoned the Labor Party's once characteristic pragmatism. They wanted intervention in Spain, yet opposed rearmament, and they refused to reconcile themselves to the existence of the Empire. 'The extreme radicalism of the younger generation cannot find positive political outlets',[14] he said. They did not respect the humanist intellectuals like Susan Lawrence and Hugh Dalton, who had built the Party. Perhaps Berl was thinking of his own movement when he said: 'Actually, the younger generation is not concerned even for the unity of the movement.'[15]

Labor had become a party hampered by factionalism. Berl met Attlee, and had an unrewarding conversation with him on Palestinian affairs. It was his impression that Attlee was of minor importance and that he had been chosen among more talented men to lead the party because he threatened no one. Again, the analogy with his own party was clear.

Berl's trip to Great Britain marked the onset of the illness from which he never recovered. The maladies of leaders are often unnamed, and this was particularly true of the Second Aliyah leaders, who guarded their private lives zealously from the public eye. Most of Berl's generation had grown up in conditions of poor hygiene and deficient nutrition. The years of wandering and the harsh conditions in Palestine – physical toil in the blazing sun, poor food and bouts of malaria – undermined their health even further. Berl often complained of fatigue, and spent long days at home, working in bed. Often, at meetings, he reclined on a bed or on a rug, the others sitting around him. Leah attributed his health problems to insufficient rest, and urged him to take more frequent holidays. In the early 1930s, short periods of recuperation had sufficed to restore his health, but this was no longer so. The bouts of depression and debility confined him to bed with increasing frequency. He felt that his ability to work, his energy and will were draining away, and for a man whose work was his life this was a bitter realization.

During his stay in London Berl's condition deteriorated. His movements were leaden. He could scarcely muster the energy for essential meetings. When he finally consulted a physician, his malady was diagnosed as a thyroid deficiency. Its treatment is relatively simple: tablets supplying the missing hormone are ingested. Within several days, the patient's condition improves, and several months later the improvement is evident in his outward appearance as well.

The doctors insisted that he remain in London another two weeks for tests, treatment and observation. Berl hesitated, as a result of the cables he received from Palestine, and asked the doctors to shorten their probe to one week. But even this brief period sufficed to improve his condition: his step became lighter, and his drive was restored somewhat. He continued to meet Labor leaders, browsed in bookshops and even attended a lecture by A. Cust – a former Mandatory official – who proposed solving the Palestine problem by dividing the country into cantons. (Berl was not impressed.) He flew to Paris, where he met an old friend, Ben Adir, saw a Russian film, visited the Louvre. He returned to London, and on 13 November 1936, he left for Palestine. His renewed interest in life was in remarkable contrast to his apathy before the treatment.

Recovered and reassured, he arrived at Haifa port on 19 November. He was met by loyal Berl Repetur, who tried to divert his attention from the death announcements posted up in the port, and prevent him from glancing at *Davar*. But Repetur's expression betrayed him and when Berl pressed him, he told him that Beilinson was very ill. The truth soon emerged: Beilinson had died of a heart attack. 'I was too late',[16] Berl wrote in his diary.

It was a staggering blow for Berl, his greatest loss since the death of Brenner. And, as after the deaths of Brenner, Sara Schmuckler and his father, he experienced feelings of guilt and remorse. Beilinson was Berl's right hand at *Davar* and had taken care of the chores which Berl found wearisome. It was not Berl but Beilinson who had exhorted, consoled, condemned and raged in 1929 and again in 1936. As long as Beilinson was there, Berl knew that his newspaper, his weapon, was in good hands and would be navigated according to his own wishes. Of all his friends, Beilinson served as Berl's 'eyes and ears' when he was abroad. The thought that, had he come home a week earlier, he might have prevented Beilinson's death, pursued Berl for a long time.

At the beginning of February 1937, the Mapai Central Committee learned that during Weizmann's testimony before the Peel Commission, Professor Coupland, the most active and prominent member, had asked for his opinion of the idea of partitioning Palestine into two independent states – Jewish and Arab. Excited and enthralled by the vision of an imminent Jewish state, Ben Gurion submitted to the Committee a plan of his own for a Jewish state to be established in part of Western Palestine.

Berl had agreed with the idea that the Jews should be 'seduced' into accepting a plan such as Ben Gurion's: they should not, however, preach it on their own initiative – else it would be doomed to failure. He urged that the Jews continue to insist that the terms of the Mandate be respected; if a state was offered to them within reasonable boundaries, they could agree to discuss the offer.

After the Central Committee meeting Berl and Ben Gurion met privately, and apparently agreed on the tactics to be adopted by the Zionist Executive.

Berl's doctors in Palestine did not accept the diagnosis of the London doctors and, on their orders, he stopped taking the thyroid tablets. As a result he suffered from constant headaches and bouts of vertigo. His poor health was known to his friends and became the problem of the entire movement. It was suggested by his comrades that he go again to London for treatment, and, at the same time, supervise the staff at Great Russell Street. But Berl submitted (halfheartedly) to the opinion of the Sick Fund doctors, confirmed by a distinguished specialist, that what he needed was complete rest. In other words – they had found nothing wrong with him! So instead of going to London, Berl left on 12 February, 1937 for Egypt, then considered the ideal place for a cure, with its dry, crisp air, warm winter climate and peaceful atmosphere – far from the turbulence of Palestine.

What is a man to do when his physicians claim that he is healthy, but he lacks the stamina to converse with other human beings, or even to write a letter? Berl sought explanations for his condition, and seized on Beilinson's death as a cause: he was not strong enough – he claimed – to carry the load and bear the tension alone. The more he thought about life without Beilinson, the more dejected he became. It never occurred to him to seek a physiological cause for his condition.

Leah was anxious about him, but showed no great resourcefulness or common sense. She suggested that she join him in Egypt. At first he flatly refused – as if he were seeking a refuge from her, as well as from all his other mundane cares. But after he had rested, he agreed that she might join an organized tour of Egypt, and visit him at the same opportunity. Still he tried to persuade her that the place was boring, that the tour was pointless and tiring and that the whole plan was not worthwhile. When he realized that she had been hurt by his rejection, he tried to explain to her what he himself did not understand: 'The difficulty with my present situation is that the part which hurts me – is my brain, and therefore I feel that I must be very careful. But my good friends' – referring to her – 'do not understand this. I may lose my equilibrium at any moment.'[17] On 17 March 1937, more than a month after he had arrived in Egypt, Leah came to visit him. Their reunion was not a success. Berl was cold and distant, introspective and reserved. During the two weeks she spent with him, he neither confided in her nor explained his conduct. Only after she left, hurt and uncomprehending, did he write to her of his fears that his nerves and his mind were deteriorating.

Meanwhile, political pressures were building up in London, and Dov Hos, who was there, insisted that Berl be sent over. Berl's friends, Eliyahu Golomb, Dov Hos and others, had apparently reached the same conclusion as Leah, namely, that Berl's troubles resulted from an incorrect diagnosis. Dov Hos's wife, Rivka, undertook to deal with the formal arrangements for Berl's trip to London, and Eliyahu Golomb succeeded in persuading him to go. For a time Rivka thought that Leah intended to accompany him. 'I think that would be a grave mistake', she wrote to her husband. 'But who can interfere and express an opinion?'[18] But Berl found no difficulty in intimating to Leah his desire for solitude, and at the beginning of April 1937 he left for London without her.

Berl left by ship, and Golomb, concerned for his comfort, purchased him a first-class ticket, but Berl did not enjoy the luxury. Most untypically, he did not try to make new acquaintances on board, but kept to himself. He shared a table with a German professor and his wife, who ordered various dishes at each meal, in order to sample from one another's plates. Berl, wrapped up in his own troubles and the predicament of his people, noted: 'It seems that one can live differently in this world.'[19]

In London he stayed with his physician, Kunin, who had taken him under his wing, and began to take his thyroid tablets regularly again. Within two weeks a dramatic improvement took place in Berl's condition. His energy was restored, and he began to take an interest in the world around him: he registered at a language school in Oxford Street for English lessons, attended a dog-race, visited the theatre and the galleries and particularly enjoyed the Rembrandts at the National Gallery, which he visited with Kunin. During this period he checked the proofs of a book on the disturbances which Bracha Habas sent him, and resented her proposal that his name be included among the editors of the volume 'for commercial reasons'. 'What am I – one of those professors who signs his name to a paper by a young researcher, merely because he contributed advice or made a suggestion?'[20] he wrote to her. However, he wrote the foreword and made one comment: noting that the party affiliation of the Revisionist victims of the riots had not been mentioned, he wrote: 'To my mind this is a grave injustice. We do not ignore people's Histadrut or political affiliation. And why should we discriminate against our own brethren just because they belong to a detested party?'[21]

He was restless and troubled by his failure to tackle the political mission the party had charged him with. The Peel Commission was meanwhile writing its report. Its deliberations and resolutions were confidential, and the members of the Political Department at 77 Great Russell Street received only snippets of information from the Cabinet and the Commission itself. Rumors were rife: the Commission would include Galilee within the territory of the Jewish state – no, it would exclude Galilee; Jewish Jerusalem was included – no, it was not, and so forth. Weizmann, Ben Gurion, Moshe Shertok , and the 'Britishers' – Namier and Baffy Dugdale – all supported partition. Their contacts with British leaders had led them to the conclusion that the Arab Rebellion would be followed by restrictive measures aimed against the National Home. The fact that the British Mandate in Palestine was the sole remaining Type A Mandate strengthened their belief that there was no escape from changes in the status quo. They assumed that immigration and land purchase would be curtailed severely, and that other changes inimical to the Zionist cause would be introduced. The proposal of partition and the establishment of a Jewish state appeared to be a breakthrough: a Jewish state could supervise immigration and free itself of the stifling patronage of the British administration. Development would be stepped up within a few years. As far as they were concerned, the partition scheme was not intended to provide the conclusive answer to the Palestine question. And, just as they were ready to accept a five- or ten-year agreement on the rate of expansion of the Yishuv, they were also willing to accept partition as the solution 'for the time being'.

Berl took a different view of the situation. His comrades were basing their assumptions on the restrictive decrees which had followed the 1929 riots, while he attached greater weight to the achievements of Zionist policy in 1930–1931, which had in effect voided the Passfield White Paper through its interpretation in the MacDonald Letter. Berl advocated a wide-scale Zionist campaign on behalf of an 'amended Mandate', i.e., unrestricted Jewish immigration on an unparalleled scale. Zionist willingness to cede parts of Palestine would have implications for generations to come, and would be very difficult to reverse. This would not apply to decrees which the Zionist movement refused to endorse.

While Berl's opposition to the partition scheme was colored by an irrational element – a blend of mysticism, historical ties and love of every corner of the country which had been sanctified by Jewish sweat -- his protests were concrete and political in nature. He believed that a Jewish state within the confines the British would propose would be a mere caricature: neither a state nor Jewish. His reservations related to borders, relations between the two proposed states, and particularly to the question of the transition period between the proclamation of partition and the actual establishment of the sovereign states. He feared that war and international conditions would nullify the scheme after it had been adopted. In this event the Zionists would be two-way losers: after having ceded most of Palestine, they would be left without even the prop of the Mandate. In short, Berl preferred to stand fast on what he considered the firm ground of the Mandate rather than to plunge into the icy waters of a new political situation. In answer to those who claimed that the Mandate was fragile, that there was no prospect of amending it or carrying it out to the full, he claimed: 'I presume, and it is a simple Jewish assumption, that those same factors which will forestall any good alternative will also work against a good partition.'[22]

He was alone among Zionist leaders in London to resist partition and his position forced him onto the sidelines. It was only when Golomb reached London in early June that Berl, Ben Gurion and Golomb settled down to practical talks, and were joined later by Dov Hos. Ben Gurion wanted to arrive at accord with Berl, but not at the price of giving up what seemed to him the essence of Zionist policy at that time – the chance of establishing a state. What appeared to Berl a mirage, seemed to Ben Gurion a unique historical opportunity. Having arrived at an understanding of the British and their way of thinking in the course of years of political activity, he believed that the alternative to partition was not an improved mandate, nor the strict implementation of the existing terms, but restrictive legislation. On the other hand, he thought, a Jewish state would open up unlimited opportunities for immigration and development. Ben Gurion felt that history was tapping them on the shoulder; Berl was oblivious to its presence.

For tactical reasons, Ben Gurion adhered to the stratagem which had been decided on when the first rumors of partition surfaced: to fight for the implementation of the Mandate, while maintaining a reserved attitude towards partition and depicting it as a British scheme. But in the course of the Commission's deliberations, the representatives of the Zionist Organization were asked, both directly and obliquely, what boundaries they would prefer; and thus they found themselves discussing partition without having been empowered to do so.

After perusing the minutes of the Mapai Central Committee session in early June 1937, at which Yitzhak Tabenkin, Shaul Meirov and Moshe Shertok criticized the policy being followed in London, Berl discovered that he was not alone in his objections to partition, and that it was within his power to rally a considerable proportion of the party around him. This discovery marked his return to political activity. Whereas the question of the merger of the kibbutz movement had created a breach between Berl and Tabenkin, the partition issue divided Berl and Ben Gurion. Tabenkin and ha-Kibbutz ha-Meuhad were passionately opposed to partition, and *ipso facto* Berl's allies.

On one question Berl and Ben Gurion were in agreement, namely, the need to 'create hard facts', to accelerate the establishment of new settlements at key points in the country – the Beisan Valley, the area between the Jezreel Valley and Zikhron Yaakov, the Gaza region, the environs of Jerusalem and the north of the country. Berl tried to get Weizmann to raise funds from prosperous Jews, and particularly from The Family (Sieff–Sacher–Marks) for this project. Weizmann was not enthusiastic: 'I cannot tear myself to pieces,' he claimed, and despatched Berl and his comrades to do the work. The money, the drive and the manpower materialized, and some fifty 'tower and stockade' settlements were established.

At the beginning of August 1937, the World Council of the Union of Poalei Zion (Z.S.), the umbrella organization of Mapai and its sister organizations in the Diaspora, was convened in Zurich. Immediately afterwards (in fact almost simultaneously) the 20th Zionist Congress was held there. Not since the Sixth Zionist Congress in 1903, the 'Uganda' Congress, had the Zionist movement been gripped by so strong a sense of portentous urgency. The partition issue divided factions, ruptured old friendships and created new alliances. Some of the delegates were euphoric, particularly those from Eastern Europe: others were haunted by a sense of impending catastrophe.

In his speech at the Congress, Berl cautioned against partition but refrained from a blanket rejection of the idea. He recalled what a simple Jew from Palestine had once said: 'When a bankrupt debtor tells you that he is willing to pay back part of his debt – do not turn him away; but don't accept payment in promissory notes. Ask for cash.'[23] The 'hard cash' which Berl wanted was a definition of the sovereignty of the new state, the conditions for its defense, and its immigration rights. Simultaneously he recommended that the Mandate should not be repudiated by the Zionist Organization until a Jewish state was established.

Berl's tone was ambivalent and so, apparently, was his stand. During the Congress, a cartoon was published showing two groups engaged in a tug-of-war; the last member of both teams was Berl. He feared two things: a split in the labor faction and a rift in the Zionist Organization. But he was, as well, essentially opposed to the adoption of a clear-cut resolution in favour of partition, which would place the Jews in an inferior bargaining position *vis-à-vis* the British. Once the Zionist Organization openly acquiesced, it would no longer be able to play the coy bride, to be courted and pursued with gifts until she surrendered. If the movement intended to fight for better terms than those proposed by the Peel Commission – and there was no argument on this point between the moderate advocates, such as Shertok, and the moderate opponents, such as Berl – it must adopt a prudent stand half-way between total acceptance and total rejection. Berl wanted a resolution, acceptable to all. By its very nature it would circumscribe the authority of the Zionist Executive.

The first stage in this obstacle course had been to obtain a resolution at the World Council of the Poalei Zion Union, which would be binding on the Labor delegation at the Congress (the largest delegation attending). The Council deliberated for six days – up to the very opening of the Congress. The moment of truth arrived on Thursday morning, 5 August. The Congress was scheduled to open at 10.30 – but the saving formula had not yet been found.

It was then that Berl drew up a draft resolution, which was accepted by most of the delegates. It proposed empowering the Zionist Executive to conduct negotiations to clarify 'the content of Government proposals on the establishment of a Jewish state in Palestine',[24] the conclusions to be submitted for scrutiny to a specially convened Zionist Congress, which would then decide on future action. The delicate balance achieved in this resolution between the Executive's authority to negotiate and denial of its right to make binding decisions, satisfied both sides, and restrained the negotiators from displaying excessive enthusiasm, which was what Berl feared most of all.

Although numerous impressive speeches were made at the Congress, it was basically an anticlimax. The main clauses of the resolution adopted six days later bore a strong resemblance to the resolution of the Poalei Zion Union Council.

Berl's stand at the Council and, even more so, the position he adopted at the Congress itself, surprised and disappointed the opponents of partition. They found it hard to understand his readiness to sanction Executive authority to negotiate, and his refusal to reject outright the concept of partition.

Moshe Shertok offered a highly sophisticated interpretation of Berl's conduct at the Congress in a letter to his wife, Zippora. He attributed to Berl tactical skill of the first order – winning the confidence of the opponents of partition while placating its champions until they arrived at a joint formula at the Union Council. This, according to Shertok, had been a wise step which prevented the adoption of too emphatic a resolution in favor of partition, which could have been politically harmful. Furthermore, he went on, had it not been for these tactics, it was doubtful whether a two-thirds majority could have been mustered: Weizmann, moreover, was clearly in favor of partition, as was Ben Gurion, who was moreover in a state of considerable tension. Thus, Shertok concluded, it was Berl who galvanized the Congress and found the way to preserve both the unity of the labor movement and that of the Zionist movement as a whole.

Berl emerged from the Congress – and perhaps this was his greatest achievement – equally popular with both the pro- and the anti-partition camps. Both Ben Gurion and Tabenkin exerted heavy pressure on him to join the Executive. He, too, acknowledged that the political situation required his involvement in steering the Zionist ship of state. But now, for reasons other than those that had influenced him in the past, he was reluctant to accept political posts: Berl felt that his days were numbered.

During the Congress, he felt better than at previous Congresses, although he worked harder. But he was convinced that time was short and he had not yet carried out his mission. 'I have begun to take pity on my years',[25] he wrote to Leah. He wanted the solitude of his room, his desk, the discipline of meticulous editorial work, in order to devote himself to matters he regarded as personally mandatory. First and foremost among them was the editing of the works of Beilinson (the first anniversary of whose death was close). He also wanted to edit the works of Nachman Syrkin, one of the fathers of Zionist socialism, for whom he felt abiding affection. He hoped to return to *Davar*, which was without direction. He also felt that he had a great deal still to give in the educational sphere, and dreamed of setting up a memorial for Beilinson which would be the movement's supreme educational institution. 'I dream of such an institution in the heart of the agricultural sector, where I can gather around me the best of our young people and hand down our heritage to them. This is the profoundest need which impels me in my public activities.'[26]

Before and during the Congress, Berl spent every free moment trying to raise funds for the Beilinson memorial. He pinned his hopes on £20,000 (Palestinian, more or less equivalent to pounds sterling) for dormitories, a library, lecture halls and classrooms. But despite some initial successes, the project never got off the ground and eventually petered out.

Berl did not join the Executive, but when a London-based advisory political committee was set up, he could not evade membership. In the month following the Congress, he traveled extensively through Europe. In Holland he visited museums and spent time in Spinoza's country house perusing the philosopher's Hebrew books. He was greatly impressed by the sea reclamation work in the country and called it 'a Zionist scheme'.[27] In Paris he discovered Moses Hess's archive, and found it hard to tear himself away from the documents relating to

269

the early days of Zionism. In conversing with a German Jew who was working on Lasalle's papers, he was struck by the fact that the young Lasalle's belongings included his father's phylactery case. In the Hague Berl visited Nehemia de Lima, who was the benefactor of the International Institute for Social Research, which contained the German S.D. archives and the papers of various personalities. Berl asked for his assistance in an exchange of books between Palestine and the Institute, and tried, in particular, to interest him in land purchase, all to no avail. De Lima, one of the first Western European Jews to become a Zionist, after the Balfour Declaration, had withdrawn from activity. Berl described him in his diary: 'old, embittered, ruined, acerbic'.[28]

Berl remained in Europe because of his membership in the advisory committee, (the other members of which were Rabbi Meir Berlin and Stephen Wise). Their function was to supervise the negotiations which Weizmann was to conduct in London with the British Government. But the negotiations were postponed. 'All the doors here are locked against our statesmen. Freezing fog',[29] he wrote, and while he waited, inactive, for the negotiations to commence, a trip to America was forced on him. Ben Gurion had returned from a visit to New York with a draft agreement between Mapai's American movement (Poalei Zion – Tzeirei Zion) and the Chairman of the Jewish Trade Unions Committee, on the coopting of trade unionists into the Zionist Organization. The prospect of recruiting one-quarter of a million new members in the United States was highly attractive and Ben Gurion, among others, urged Berl to go to the States to see if the scheme was feasible. Simultaneously, he was to raise funds to promote strategic Jewish settlement in Palestine and to attempt to improve relations with the Brandeis group.

Berl sailed aboard the luxury liner, *Queen Mary*, and managed to embarrass his hosts even before he disembarked. The party notables who came to greet this important leader from Palestine, looked for him in the first-class section of the ship – in vain. He was finally run to earth in the third-class section. They were astounded and 'regarded this "folly" almost as an insult to the honor of the movement'.[30]

Berl complained of the numerous time- and energy-consuming trips, meetings and social obligations, organized for him. But this intensive activity seemed to help him to emerge from his depression. He attended the Poalei Zion Conference, the Hadassah Women's Conference, the J.N.F. Workers' Council. He spoke at various functions and apparently with greater success than 16 years before, either because of his repu-

270

tation, or because he was now a more experienced speaker. As for the trade union agreement, it was impossible during the first weeks of Berl's stay in America to bring the sides together for serious negotiations (the New York municipal election campaign was at its height). When they did eventually meet, it became clear that Ben Gurion's optimism had been excessive. As disciples of the profound anti-Zionist Bundist tradition, the trade unionists objected to participating in the Zionist Congress. And thus the hoped-for union of all Jewish workers in the United States under the banner of Zionism came to naught. Berl noted, sardonically: 'I came, I saw – and I did not conquer.'[31]

In contrast to his previous visit to the United States, the doors of the Zionist establishment were now opened wide to Berl. He was warmly received by that most important and respected of Zionist leaders – Justice Brandeis. Berl tried to persuade him to take an active interest in land purchase, the consolidation of new settlements and the solution of the unemployment problem in Palestine. Brandeis lent a sympathetic ear, but did nothing. Berl took the opportunity to acquaint him with his pet scheme – the educational center – and Brandeis's positive response gratified him. He met Justice Frankfurter, and after the meeting, Frankfurter wrote to Wise: 'I enjoyed a pleasant meeting with Katznelson yesterday. What a wonderful group they are, these Palestinian Jews! Whenever I see them, they convince me that one way or another they will overcome all obstacles, even the most difficult.'[32]

The partition controversy and its corollaries pursued him to America. Berl was greeted with considerable suspicion: the advocates of partition regarded him as the emissary of their opponents; the opponents, particularly the Hadassah Women, saw him as the clandestine emissary of the Zionist Executive, despatched to soften their opposition. The internal dispute aroused mutual hostility and affected the operative capacity of the Zionist movement, and particularly the United Jewish Appeal. Except within his own party, Berl did not succeed in reconciling the opposites.

The trip to the United States was a brief intermezzo in Berl's life. When he returned home, he was immediately plunged into a maelstrom of quarrels and controversies. Mapai was engaged at that time in the stormy conflict which preceded the Rehovot conference, and after it the controversy on the unification of the Kibbutz movement gathered momentum. Here, it will be remembered, Berl and Ben Gurion were ranged against Tabenkin. Simultaneously, Berl and Tabenkin found themselves at loggerheads with Ben Gurion on partition. The delicate balance achieved on this issue at Zurich had been upset. The 'opponents' had the impression that their representatives were not being made a party to the negotiations or the internal consultations. Their apprehensions and sense of frustration, stirred by the explicit support for partition on the part of members of the Executive, such as Nahum Goldmann and Yitzhak Gruenbaum, revived the internal debate. The Zionist Actions Committee was about to convene in London on Ben Gurion's initiative. It was clear to Berl that the debate on partition would start again at this session, although the time for a practical decision had not yet arrived: the British had not yet had their say. He decided to forestall the controversy, which would generate superfluous tension, and at the same time to indicate to Ben Gurion and the propartition group that the 'opponents' would not remain passive in determining policy. To this end, he organized a boycott of the Actions Committee session by the anti-partitionists.

Berl continued to walk the tightrope between non-rejection of partition and the struggle to preserve the Mandate. When the Woodhead Commission arrived in Palestine, and the 'opponents' requested permission to give evidence separately from the Zionist Executive, Berl sided with the pro-partitionists, objecting to separate testimony. He did not believe that the Commission would decide the fundamental issue of partition, but assumed that it would propose the establishment of a state – 'and therefore,' he said, 'I want to obtain from it the best possible document relating to the Jewish state, if this can be done.'[33] Berl used the anti-partitionists to pressure the Executive into adopting a circumspect policy. It did not occur to him to split the movement over an embryonic scheme. Tabenkin, for his part, saw partition as a question of principle, liable to cause a split. He could not sanction the idea of partitioning Palestine, which he saw as indivisible; Berl, on the other hand, was ready to compromise under certain conditions.

After the stormy Mapai Conference at Rehovot and the subsequent frantic political activity, Berl spent the summer of 1938 in Jerusalem. In early September he left for London, to await publication of the Woodhead Commission report. His physician had also insisted that he come for tests and further treatment.

In London, Berl found Ben Gurion tense and spoiling for a fight. Ben Gurion still believed that the Zionist Executive should continue to fight for favorable partition. 'Leave that alone', said Berl. 'We must now fight for our very survival and we must unite the people for this battle.'[34] Berl did not believe that the partition plan had any chance of materializing and he felt that it was of supreme importance to rally all forces for the imminent political struggle. And, in fact, only ten days later Weizmann and Ben Gurion met with the Colonial Secretary, Malcolm MacDonald, who made it abundantly clear that the British Government had abandoned the partition plan, and was about to impose severe restrictions on the National Home.

Political etiquette was still observed: ostensibly nothing had been decided, and the Colonial Office was still awaiting the recommendations of the partition commission: but a cold wind was blowing in the corridors of power. Negotiations were underway between Chamberlain and Hitler on the fate of the Sudetenland. Weizmann deluded himself that now that war threatened again, the British would court the Jews as they had in 1917. Berl had no such illusions: it was clear to him 'that they will want to win the loyalty of our neighbors and the price is our heads'.[35] He was impressed by something said by Jan Masaryk, son of the founder of Czechoslovakia and Czech Ambassador to London. Masaryk proposed to Weizmann, with bitter sarcasm, that he purchase a three-story building in London: the first story would house Haile Selassie, the Emperor of Abyssinia, who had been expelled from his country by the Italians. He, himself – he said – would live on the second floor. The third would be reserved for Weizmann. Berl regarded the British efforts to conciliate the Arabs as part of their appeasement policy towards Hitler, and was not aware of the anomaly of his theory: in actual fact, the efforts were directed at recruiting the support of the Arabs for the forthcoming war against Hitler. But in those dark days of Munich it was hard to discern this fact.

Berl witnessed the war scare in London on 27 September 1938. On the night of 1 October, when the German forces invaded Czechoslovakia, the Zionist activists in London, including the three Palestinians – Locker, Ben Gurion and Berl – met in Weizmann's home. Late that night, Jan Masaryk joined them. Vera Weizmann and Baffy Dugdale embraced him mournfully. Then they all listened at length to the tale of betrayal and of the dissembling of British politicians who had abandoned their ally. Baffy Dugdale thought that the Czechs had erred: they should have fought and not surrendered without a battle. Berl had similar thoughts. He wrote in his diary: 'Jan Masaryk came and took revenge on the British in words.'[36]

In the early days of the negotiations with MacDonald, in September 1938, Berl came to the conclusion that, under a smokescreen of friendly and soothing statements, the Colonial Office was preparing unprecedentedly stringent restrictions against the Yishuv. He thought that preparations should be made for a world war, on the one hand, and a struggle against the Mandatory Government, on the other.

As a first step, he urged that the movement abandon the debate on partition and unite 'around the one trouble and the one war'.[37] 'Certain matters which once appeared to us as lofty mountains', he wrote to Tabenkin, 'now wane in value. We must think of one thing: how to navigate our vessel through this flood, when all the sluicegates have disappeared.'[38]

There were two focal points in his plan: settlement of the Negev and the organization of illegal immigration, both as fast and as energetically as possible.

Berl had been an advocate of illegal immigration ('Aliyah Bet') for many years. As far back as 31 July 1934, he witnessed the arrival of the first 'illegal' ship. He then wrote in his diary: 'All night on the beach. Greeting the first boat. Splendid and horrific. The capsized boat: two drowned. Early morning, with Galili.'[39] 1934 was, however, one of the peak years for *legal* immigration. Relations between the High Commissioner and the Zionist Executive were extremely cordial and Ben Gurion and Shertok opposed any clandestine action which could endanger cooperation with the Mandate authorities. Berl was not troubled by the law on this issue. He lent his full support and authority to Shaul Meirov, Berl Repetur and their comrades who organized illegal activities. Ben Gurion fumed – and officially his wishes prevailed. But activity continued under cover, and Berl did not hesitate to circumvent the movement's formal policy. In the light of the anticipated change in British policy, the time had come for partisan activities to emerge from underground and be recognized as an additional mode of action sanctioned by the movement. 'The Zionist movement once conducted itself in purely legal fashion', he said. 'Now it must adapt itself to a dual policy.'[40] He himself found it very easy to adapt: this policy compensated for the impotent rage he felt for the way in which the Great Powers were toying with the fate of the Jewish people. 'Illegal' action was defiance – a refusal to accept passive surrender, as the Czechs had done. At the same time, illegal immigration embodied the alpha and omega of Berl's Zionism – immigration and settlement.

274

As usual when he was engaged in schemes close to his heart, Berl summoned up endless energy and resourcefulness. At the time of Munich, he began raising funds for Aliyah Bet, and no sum was too small to be accepted. He sought ways of contacting Jewish philanthropists, both Zionists and non-Zionists. Polish Jews were being expelled from Germany overnight. The Kristallnacht cast a lurid light on the predicament of the Jews of Germany under Hitler. The problem of Jewish refugees was of concern to all the countries of Europe. Ghost ships wandered from port to port but there was no refuge for a Jew without a homeland or a passport. The Evian Conference, which was intended to find a solution to the plight of the refugees, merely revealed the naked shame of civilized nations which balked at offering shelter to the Jewish wanderers. Now that the rest of the world was barred, Jews, who until then had looked askance at Zionists, had to recognize the facts, and to open their hearts and pockets to the Aliyah Bet workers. Thousands of pounds were raised, and in early January 1939 the ships began to sail. Illegal immigration was now legal as far as the movement was concerned, and Ben Gurion too supported it. But there was still a difference between him and Berl: Ben Gurion attributed importance to the demonstrative aspect and to world public opinion. For Berl the supremely important fact was the rescue of Jews. He calculated that clandestine action would be more effective than demonstrations, which might endanger the immigrants.

It was to Berl that Aliyah Bet agents turned with both small and vital questions, and it was he who undertook responsibility. This role suited him perfectly, while those holding formal office found it difficult to function in the shadowy world of semi-legal activity.

In early February 1939, Berl returned to London for the St James's Palace talks between the Jews and the British, on the one hand, and the Arabs and the British on the other. In addition to the Zionist Executive, headed by Weizmann and Ben Gurion, a Jewish panel attended the talks. It consisted of a delegation from the Yishuv, representatives of Zionist and non-Zionist parties and public bodies, and representatives of British Jewry – several of them titled English Jews, some of them non-Zionists.

St James's Palace was an appropriate background for the events. The main participants appeared in morning coats. Berl made do with his old black suit. 'The outcome which the Government is preparing for us', he commented 'does not justify my dressing more elegantly in its honor.'[41]

The British delegation, led by MacDonald, expounded the Arab stand to the Jews, 'and it does so better than the Arabs'. Berl was impressed by the political courtesy of the British partners: they listened patiently and with a pleasant smile to all the Jewish claims and complaints, and responded to biting criticism 'with a laugh of concurrence and enjoyment of the "witticisms" of our people'.[42] 'On the face of it, insignificant and colorless young fellows,' he marveled, 'but in political conduct and negotiations, they are truly sharp, *durchgetribben* ["crafty" in Yiddish].'[43]

Despite the anxieties and the sense of helplessness, Berl also experienced moments of gratification at the St James's Palace deliberations. He had opposed Jewish participation because he felt that the Zionist stand was insufficiently resolute. But, miraculously enough, the talks proved to be the finest hour of Jewish unity: Jewish peers listened respectfully to Ben Gurion and his comrades and accepted their authority. The anti-Zionist Rabbi Moshe Bloi of Agudat Israel shook Weizmann's hand with emotion and congratulated him after a successful speech.

The 1939 White Paper had not yet been published, but its recommendations were mostly known: restriction of immigration to 75,000 Jews over a five-year period following which immigration was to be conditional on Arab consent; restrictions on land purchase by Jews; and, above all, the establishment of an independent Palestinian state within ten years. The Yishuv responded with demonstrations, strikes and street riots. Berl was pleased by this defiant reaction. 'The Government must be made to feel that it is dealing with a public, without whom no regime can be imposed on the country', he wrote.[44] But he doubted the impact of demonstrations and strikes. In the era of Hitler – he claimed – they would intimidate nobody, and could only cause harm to the Yishuv itself. It should emulate Gandhi, who found the means of struggle appropriate to his national objectives and the nature of his people. 'Constructive resistance'[45] was the policy he favored. The foremost measure, as far as Berl was concerned, was illegal immigration. At the same time he emphasized that the political aim was secondary to the very act of rescuing Jews: 'We are after something essential: Jews in Palestine. Therefore I am not enthusiastic about clashes. I don't want conflicts. I am not pursuing the romantic aspect of the matter. I want *takhlis* ["the real thing"]: Jews. But I will not hesitate, if Jewish immigration clashes.' If the British opened fire on immigrants, if ships were sent back – never mind! 'This is the Jew's battle for his country.'[46]

The other face of 'constructive resistance' was land purchase and settlement. During the disturbances, fifty 'tower and stockade' settlements were established in various parts of the country, the fruit of tremendous efforts by the national institutions and the settlement movement. Berl wanted to exploit the time left before the promulgation of the regulations in order to buy as much land as possible. The assumption was that once the land had been purchased, the Government would not, in the end, be able to prevent Jewish settlement there.

For Berl, as usual, practical and educational aims went hand in hand: the rescue of Jews and the redemption of land, on the one hand, the education of a young generation ready for battle and for sacrifice, on the other. Thus, he became increasingly involved in Hagana affairs – here too in a most practical manner: buying arms, raising money and preparing operational plans. As in the case of Aliyah Bet, Berl held no official position in the Hagana, but the commanders considered him their mentor, the man who delegated the movement's authority to them.

The summer of 1939 passed and the White Paper was published. Ships continued to arrive, ha-Kibbutz ha-Meuhad held its conference at Na'an, and the internal debate reached a crescendo. Berl completed the editing of the anthology *The Kibbutz and the Kvutza*, and in Tel Aviv the factions in Mapai continued to quarrel. People seemed to be operating on two levels: on one they were preparing for an emergency and doing all that was necessary to face the bitter times ahead. On the other, it was 'business as usual' – as if there were no Hitler in the world and no White Paper. The squabbles within Mapai, and between Mapai and other sections of the Yishuv continued, draining the energies and minds of the best people.

On 16 August 1939, the 21st Zionist Congress was convened in Geneva. This was Berl's last appearance at a Congress, although nobody could have imagined this to be so at the time. It was also his most impressive performance at any forum outside Palestine. Weizmann delivered an effective opening speech, utterly rejecting British policy, and hinting at the possibility of continuing the work of developing Palestine even under prevailing conditions, in the spirit of gradualism which the Zionist Organization had always advocated. This point was taken up and accentuated by Rabbi Solomon Goldman of Chicago, who enjoined his listeners to restrain their feelings, to be patient and to continue their constructive endeavors. The culmination was the call by Dr Abba Hillel Silver of Cincinnati to refrain from any action liable to bring about a clash with the Mandate Government. He argued that the British Government would not be able to maintain its policy. That change was likely, and that the time had not yet come for a confrontation. 'I appeal to you to refrain from desperate acts of opposition, from civil rebellion, from non-cooperation',[47] he said. His remarks were interrupted by questions from the floor about illegal immigration. He responded with open criticism, predicting that it would drag the movement into an overall struggle with the Government, prematurely, and unwillingly. It was in the Zionist interest to insure peace and security in Palestine and not to undermine them. He concluded with a call for patience, tenacity, strong will and faith. The next day (20 August), Berl took the floor to attack this line. He did not beat about the bush or try to camouflage the differences of opinion. He launched an all-out offensive on the optimistic and amateurish view of the White Paper, which considered it merely 'another' decree. 'Remarks have been made by people in very responsible positions', he said, referring to Weizmann, 'which prove that they have not even begun to comprehend what the White Paper is.' The gradualism of the Zionist movement – *dunam* after *dunam*, slow and dogged practical work – could no longer suffice under the new conditions. The brunt of his attack was directed against Silver: '[and] from this podium remarks were made yesterday by Rabbi Silver, which I cannot permit myself to ignore. It was as if he cast a stone at our refugees on the high seas, and stabbed Zionist policy in the back.'[48] 'There is immigration which is denoted "illegal" ', he said ironically. 'Everything in this legal world is legal. Legitimate governments, legitimate conquest, legitimate documents, even legitimate violations of promises. Only the immigration of Jews, on the basis of the ancient mandate of the exodus from Egypt, is not legal.' And, as if he had been afforded a glimpse of the years ahead, he went on to describe the future: 'Every idea seeks its own social element, people who will serve as its instrument all their lives.' First it was the shopkeeper of Hibat Zion, who undertook the task of realizing Zionism; then the Jewish student and intellectual; then the worker battling for Jewish labor. 'Now', he went on, 'the Jewish refugee heads the fight, and we must all join his ranks [*protracted applause*]. He will not permit the conscience of the world to rest; the Evian Conference was convened on his behalf; because of him Jewish peers cannot rest easy.' To those who doubted the power of the refugees to shatter convention and frustrate the schemes of great powers, he replied. 'I know that sometimes even a great nation may be helpless in the face of the troubles and suffering of masses of people . . . if you will it or not, if you help or hinder, the afflictions of the Jewish people will drive the boats out to sea.'[49] He concluded his speech with a call to close Zionist ranks around the nucleus of forces which had grown up in Palestine.

When Berl completed his hour-long speech, the audience rose to its feet and applauded at length. Emotions ran high. Members of rival parties, from the Mizrahi rabbis to Moshe Erem (the representative of leftist Poalei Zion, who had returned to the bosom of the Zionist movement at this Congress), all hastened to congratulate him and shake his hand. 'Even ha-Kibbutz ha-Meuhad people made their peace with me for the moment', he wrote to Leah.[50] A young man who was unknown to him came up to say: 'When I heard you, I was proud of being a member of the Histadrut.'[51] Weizmann told him that it was one of the best speeches ever delivered at a congress. At the same time he was furious. His first response to the speech was: 'It will do no good.' Weizmann did not want to expose to the world the duality of Zionist policy, operating both within and beyond the law. It was a delicate situation, and Berl's remarks had been remote from the spirit of diplomatic prudence. Weizmann's critical comment was made to Ben Gurion, who sat beside him during the speech, and Ben Gurion replied spontaneously: 'The best Zionist speech made here'.[52] This exchange enraged Weizmann – to the point where he threatened to resign from the Presidency of the movement, and was dissuaded only with great difficulty.

The minor incidents and more weighty events of the Congress were overshadowed two days later by word of the non-aggression pact signed on 22 August between the Soviet Union and Nazi Germany. Darkness descended on the Congress. Against the prospect of war, everything else paled into insignificance. Through sheer inertia, the routine work went on for another three long days, and the gathering closed with a touching ceremony. Weizmann made a brief and moving speech. Addressing the delegates from Poland, he expressed the hope that their fate would not resemble that of their brethren in Germany, and concluded:

My heart is overflowing. I cannot find fitting words to greet each of you. You all know that at such moments, words do not suffice. Auf Wiedersehen [*protracted applause*] . . . There are things which cannot fail to materialize, without which the world cannot be conceived. The remnant will continue to work, to fight, to live, until better times come, and I wish you all better times: may we meet again in peace![53]

He embraced his colleagues on the podium, the aged Ussishkin and Ben Gurion, as if he found it hard to take leave of them. Many of those present shed tears. There was a sense that night had fallen. The delegates hastened back to their countries and their families. Many of them would never meet again.

The Palestinian labor delegates convened in an anteroom late at night. The vital question was whether the emissaries to he-Halutz in Poland, the Balkans, Germany, Austria and Czechoslovakia should return to their tasks, or go home to Palestine. The emissaries rose one after another and protested against the very suggestion: precisely because the danger was so great, they must stay at their posts. Berl reclined on a bench, seemingly half asleep. From time to time he opened his eyes and gazed at this scene of simple dedication, and an expression of gratification lit up his tired features for a moment.

Now that the die had been cast, and war was inevitable, Berl was calm. The fear which had seized him during the Munich crisis did not return. He observed the panic-stricken atmosphere at the Congress like a bystander. He was confident that whatever happened he would succeed in reaching Palestine – and was in no hurry. From Geneva, Shaul Meirov summoned him to Paris for urgent consultations on Aliyah Bet and Hagana affairs. But at this point his plans changed. 'Today I met a man, an old acquaintance and persistent adversary,' he wrote to Leah, 'and he begged me to come to London for a fundamental discussion with him.'[54] It was Jabotinsky. Berl went to see him in his hotel, where they spoke briefly. Jabotinsky urged Berl to come to London, since he himself was unable to remain in Paris long enough for a serious conversation. Berl decided that he could not refuse.

The issue which impelled Berl to undertake the burden of talks with Jabotinsky at a time when the conflagration had begun was the use of terror as a weapon in the Zionist struggle. From the outbreak of the 1936 disturbances, and, actually, even before that, the question had been sharply debated in the Yishuv.

Berl had been opposed to acts of vengeance from the outset, and not necessarily out of purely moral considerations. This was the official stand of the Zionist Executive, who hoped that Jewish respect for law and order would fortify the Government against the political demands of the Arabs. They claimed that the British should not reward the aggressors and must defend the law-abiding. Moreover, they wanted to deny the British the possibility of depicting the disturbances as a clash between the two peoples. Berl was adamant in resisting pressures within the Hagana for retaliation against Arab terror. When Shaul Meirov claimed that he could not withstand the pressures of his comrades-in-arms, Berl replied that if this was so, he should resign. But after the murder, in August 1936, of two Jewish nurses, who had been treating Arabs in Jaffa, Berl gave the green light for retaliation. During the incident which followed, Arab women and children were injured and Berl, horrified, reverted to the policy of self-restraint (*havlaga*) and never again permitted any deviation. He could not stomach acts of terror. His ethical code was different – that of the first Russian Revolutionaries who avoided shedding innocent blood, even while risking their own lives in combat. He did not, however, endorse a policy of inactivity, and welcomed the establishment of the 'Night Platoons' which anticipated Wingate and his Special Night Squads. Zionist activity combined with defense, as embodied in the 'tower and stockade' settlements, for example, was Berl's idea of the most fitting response to terror.

What aroused his particular concern was the grave fear that a civil war might erupt between Jews. This dread, which had plagued him since the early days of the struggle between the labor movement and the Revisionists, now returned to haunt him. The Irgun Zvai Leumi (created through the secession of activist elements from the Hagana, and now the military arm of the Revisionist movement) refused to abide by the policy of self-restraint. The terrorist outbursts undermined the security situation in Palestine and destroyed the inner fabric of Yishuv life. 'After terror by Jews against Arabs,' he prophesied, 'terror inflicted by Jews on Jews will surely follow.'[55]

The Mapai Central Committee – in full agreement with Berl's position – passed a number of sharply worded resolutions condemning terror and its perpetrators. They proposed that a wedge be driven between the terrorists and the wide sections of the Yishuv which were now providing them with refuge and funding. The resolutions included a clause calling for efforts to scotch planned acts of terror. In summer

1939, during the struggle against the White Paper, a new wave of terror commenced. It evoked no small measure of sympathy among the young, among them youth from the labor movement as well, disillusioned with the British. Berl addressed the youth on 'the purity of our struggle'. He also signed a 'Manifesto against Internal Terror' (the only labor movement leader to do so); among the signatories were Henrietta Szold, Avraham Halevi Frankel, S. Y. Agnon and Professor Hugo Bergman. On visits to kibbutzim he expounded his views over and over again. At the Geneva Congress he extolled restraint: '*Havlaga* means: may our weapons be pure! We study arms, we bear arms, we face those who attack us. But we do not want our weapons to be stained with the blood of the innocent.'[56] He cautioned against provocation which could lead to unforeseen consequences and did not shrink from openly accusing Jews of dangerous and superfluous adventurism.

While maintaining an uncompromising stand on terror, Berl also sought ways of arriving at a dialog with the Revisionists, haunted as he was by fear of fraternal strife. It is not surprising, therefore, that he was unable to refuse Jabotinsky's invitation.

The meeting was held at Jabotinsky's home in London on 31 August 1939, and lasted from 10.15 in the morning till seven at night. In his diary, Berl wrote: 'I was reduced to despair and total exhaustion.'[57] But on the following day Jabotinsky came to see him, and the dialog continued. They met four times in all. Berl encountered a bitter, despairing and disillusioned leader. He sensed Jabotinsky's unhappiness, his rootlessness, his feeling of being an emigrant. (Jabotinsky had been refused re-entry to Palestine by the British in 1930.) When Berl complained of the deplorable acts of terror perpetrated by the Irgun, Jabotinsky replied that he had no right to judge people in the thick of it, people prepared to go to the gallows for their actions. Berl discovered during the course of the conversations that Jabotinsky believed Mapai members to be Zionists in the spirit of Ahad ha-Am, i.e., advocating selective immigration and the establishment of a spiritual center, indifferent to the plight of the Jewish masses. It was because of his fear for the Jewish people, that Jabotinsky displayed hostility towards the Yishuv. 'For me, Zionism is the concern of those Jews who are not living in Palestine',[58] he said.

The difference of opinion between the two encompassed all the spheres of Zionist action: defense, terror, settlement and immigration. When they tried to formulate their views in writing, it became clear that there was a yawning abyss between them. Towards the end of the talks, Jabotinsky commented: 'I am greatly saddened by your remarks. I see that you do not appreciate us at all . . . you want me personally to be in the Zionist movement, but you want us only in order to rid your-selves of our "nuisance value".'[59] He had deduced from Berl's remarks that Berl believed that his own movement knew more than the Revisionists about political activity, Zionist policy, defense and settle-ment – 'then why should you need us?' It was a difficult moment, since Jabotinsky had pinpointed the labor movement's evaluation of the Revisionists. Berl's reply revealed his own singular qualities and humane intelligence: 'When I see an opponent, I want to know *why* he opposes me – and although I am usually convinced that I am right, I tend to assume that it is some flaw in me and in my movement which encourages and nurtures my opponent . . . you exist because of some deficiency in us.' This was his approach to both right- and left-wing movements tainted – he believed – by the spirit of false messianism. The Revisionists, he explained, had concentrated solely on political action. Perhaps the labor movement, because of its numerous practical preoccupations, had not given sufficient attention to this aspect, and had therefore been punished. On the other hand, Revisionist emphasis on political activism alone had led them inevitably 'along the blind road to false messianism'.[60] Were the Revisionists to return to the living body, they would redeem themselves, and mutual enrichment would result.

The main question of the talks was the authority of the Zionist Organization. All Jabotinsky's bitterness and suffering had fueled his hostility towards the Organization and made him contemptuous of his rivals, although he still had some affection for his Mapai comrades from the Jewish Battalion days. When Berl reminded him how *Tat*, the Irgun journal in Poland, had slandered Eliyahu Golomb, he was somewhat abashed. But he went on to claim that if a popular Jewish congress were to be held, in which voters were not required to purchase the Zionist shekel,* his movement would win a majority. Until such a congress was convened – he said – he would not return to the Zionist movement. As far as he was concerned the Zionist Congress was purchased with money. Berl did not believe that a non-committed assembly of populist sympathizers, such as Jabotinsky demanded, would be capable of

---

* i.e. a voucher received for paying one's dues to the Zionist Organization; it enabled the recipient to vote in elections to the Zionist Congress.

Zionist action, which required financing. But after the second talk, he made a suggestion: if the Zionist Organization decided to convene a special congress after the war, to be elected on the basis of the shekel – but the shekel would be distributed gratis to whoever signed a Zionist declaration of faith – would the Revisionists consent to return to the movement? Jabotinsky was impressed. On the following day he telephoned Berl and informed him that he would agree to return to the Zionist Organization under such terms.

Berl did not repeat Ben Gurion's mistake: he signed no documents, made no commitments. The talks were conducted on a personal basis, between two prestigious leaders of rival movements. Berl seemed more sympathetic than Ben Gurion to Jabotinsky's pain as an exile. But, unlike Ben Gurion, he was not overpowered by the personality of his companion. His personal esteem and affection for Jabotinsky could not compensate for the conflicts of the past and the apprehensions of the present. There was mutual admiration, there was a sense of affliction – and over the meeting lurked the specter of the imminent destruction of Polish Jewry. On the eve of Berl's return to Palestine, they met again. Jabotinsky said sadly, and bitterly: 'You have won. You have America, the rich Jews. I had only poor Polish Jewry, and now it is gone. I have lost the game.'[61] For Berl and the labor movement the loss was no less significant than to Jabotinsky. The sources of immigration, the power reserves of the pioneering movement, had been choked off by the outbreak of the war in Poland. In the face of the catastrophe of Eastern European Jewry, both the Revisionists and the labor movement stood defeated.

In mid September 1939, Berl sailed home on the *Marco Polo*. He arrived in Haifa on 21 September 1939, and never again left the shores of Palestine.

15

WITH OUR BACKS TO THE WALL,
1939–1944

The eye of the storm

Although the war had long been expected, its actual outbreak was still a shock, exposing the weakness and vulnerability of the Yishuv. Withal, the Jewish community of Palestine lived in relative tranquility. It is true that the Italians bombed Haifa and Tel Aviv several times, killing and injuring a number of people, and that until 1942, the Yishuv was in the throes of an economic slump and people were actually starving. But, in comparison with England, not to speak of continental Europe, the Yishuv seemed to be located at the quiet eye of the storm. If its prospects for survival seemed dim, and there were moments when it seemed that the Jews of Palestine might share the fate of European Jewry, life nonetheless went on as usual. The war was at one and the same time near at hand – and yet remote.

This duality may explain the conduct of the Yishuv and its leaders at this time, a mixture of anxiety and calm, of heroism and commonplace deeds. There was a state of constant tension hovering over all, but when danger lacks the tangible element, people tend to ignore its existence out of sheer weariness and escapism. The instinct for survival clings desperately to reassuring routine.

There was a tragic paradoxicality in the relations between the Yishuv, the Zionist movement and the British authorities: after the fall of France in spring 1940, Britain alone bore the burden of the war against the Axis Powers. The Jews were eager to play a part in the struggle against the Hitlerite foe, but their natural ally, Great Britain, treated them as a superfluous and troublesome burden. The British continued to do battle against the Jewish refugee ships, and those immigrants who managed to reach the shores of Palestine were imprisoned in the Atlit detention camp. The authorities clamped down on the Hagana and confiscated all the arms they found. And when the

Jews requested the establishment of a Jewish brigade within the framework of the British army so that they could fight under the Jewish flag – a privilege granted to the Czechs and the Poles – they were given evasive replies.

When the war started, Ben Gurion coined a resounding phrase: 'We will fight Hitler as if there were no White Paper, and the White Paper as if there were no Hitler.' As a slogan, it served its purpose. But when the Jewish community was called upon to implement it, the difficulties became apparent. How could one fight the White Paper and its edicts without hampering the war effort? Would it not be better to wait until the war ended?

The promulgation of the Land Regulations (1940) aroused bitter internal controversy, and brought Mapai to the verge of a split. The 'men of action', led by Ben Gurion, Berl, Eliyahu Golomb and ha-Kibbutz ha-Meuhad, feared that their failure to react strongly would be interpreted by the British as compliance, and result in even harsher restrictions. They demanded a policy of non-cooperation with the authorities in all spheres of life: vehement opposition to the disarmament of the Yishuv; mass demonstrations against Government policy and a readiness to clash with the police. They hoped to maintain a constant state of unrest, in order to clarify to the British that the ability to undermine security in Palestine was not confined to the Arabs.

Against these 'men of action' were ranged the moderates. Within Mapai, they consisted mostly of the former members of ha-Poel ha-Tzair, headed by Sprinzak, and some former members of Ahdut ha-Avoda, led by Remez. They considered the activism of Berl and Ben Gurion to be both foolish and dangerous. White Paper policy, they claimed, was dictated by Britain's needs on the eve of war, and it was pointless to fight it when it would in any case be canceled out by a British victory. Moreover, the Jews should rally to the Allied cause, since it was their cause as well. They also feared that Britain might react with force to Jewish rebelliousness, or, alternatively, introduce economic measures which could completely stifle the Yishuv. If Britain should decide, for example, not to defend the Yishuv against its Arab neighbors, the very survival of the Jewish people would hang in the balance.

At this stage, the moderates carried the day. In April 1940, Ben Gurion found himself in a minority in the Jewish Agency Executive on this issue, and resigned. The Executive refused to accept his resignation, and Ben Gurion retracted. He had received a cable from Weizmann, expressing confidence in him. Shortly afterwards he left for the United States.

Berl was the most influential of the activists left in Palestine, and his was the voice of the Hagana rank and file. When France fell, he delivered a speech to them entitled 'With our Backs to the Wall', in which he emphasised the necessity to expand the Jewish defense forces. This was important in those bitter war days when doubts had been expressed as to the ability of so small a force to influence the fate of the nation. Berl, it will be remembered, held no official position in the Hagana command, but was considered its supreme civilian authority. The Hagana chief, Eliyahu Golomb, was Berl's source of information and the channel through which Berl conveyed his reactions and opinions to the commanders. Most of them regarded him as a fount of wisdom, consulting with him on every issue. This was true to the day of his death.

The debate between the activists and the moderates reached crisis point at the end of 1940, when three illegal ships – the *Milos*, the *Pacific* and the *Atlantic* – reached the shores of Palestine.

The authorities refused to grant immigration certificates to these immigrants from 'enemy countries' on the pretext that the Germans might exploit this way of infiltrating spies and fifth columnists into Palestine. The term encompassed all the countries overrun by the Axis powers, i.e. most of Europe. Thus the sole immigration which continued throughout the war was defined as illegal. Consequently, even the meager quota of certificates at the disposal of the Jewish Agency under the White Paper was not exploited to the full.

When the *Milos* and the *Pacific* anchored at Haifa, word reached the Jewish Agency that the High Commissioner planned to despatch the immigrants to the British-ruled island of Mauritius, some 500 miles east of Madagascar in the Indian Ocean. Until then the Government had always detained illegal immigrants in the Atlit camp, releasing them in a slow trickle and deducting their numbers from the quota. This new act was intended as a slap in the face for the Yishuv, and was in fact interpreted as such. The High Commissioner hoped in this fashion to put an end once and for all to illegal immigration. After several weeks in Haifa, the immigrants were transferred to the *Patria* which had been fitted out for the voyage to Mauritius. On 20 November 1940, a general strike was organized in protest. Evidence was provided that the fears

287

that fifth columnists might be aboard were baseless: the immigrants included organized groups of pioneers, relatives of families living in Palestine, well-to-do persons who had transferred their assets to Palestine before the war, and a number of refugees. But all the attempts of the Jewish Agency Executive, the leaders of the Vaad Leumi and other public bodies proved futile. Even Weizmann, in London, was not able to overcome the obduracy of the Government.

Several days later, Berl received word from Haifa that the *Patria* had blown up and was sinking. Immediately afterwards Shaul Meirov and Berl Repetur arrived from Haifa to talk to him. Though there is no direct evidence of this, Berl had probably been privy to the plan, and was now informed that it had gone wrong: a Hagana member had smuggled explosives onto the ship, with the intention of damaging it and postponing its departure, in the hope that in the interim the authorities could be persuaded to alter their decision. The old and ramshackle vessel responded to the explosion to a degree which had not been anticipated: a gaping hole appeared in its side and within a few minutes it began to sink. The extent of the catastrophe was revealed only later: some 250 people were drowned. The British conducted themselves in exemplary fashion during the rescue operations, and thanks to their dedicated efforts 1,500 passengers were saved. As a result of the tragedy the British Cabinet overruled the High Commissioner and decided that the surviving immigrants should be allowed to remain in Palestine, and reckoned as part of the immigration quota.

Another illegal immigrant vessel, the *Atlantic*, was also brought to Haifa around this time. An epidemic had broken out aboard and the British decided, for humanitarian reasons, to transfer the *Atlantic*'s human cargo temporarily to Atlit for treatment and recuperation. The ruling on the *Patria* passengers, however, was not extended to the *Atlantic* immigrants and they were condemned to exile in Mauritius. In a lightning operation, a large force of British policemen transported the immigrants from Atlit to Haifa. The immigrants resisted fiercely, and the British had to use force to load them onto the trucks which were to take them to the port. Heart-rending scenes took place, which so affected some of the British that they were unable to carry out their duties effectively. The evacuation took the Yishuv and the Hagana by surprise. Haifa was deserted when the trucks drove through because the siren had been sounded, and it was only after the event that the leaders of the Yishuv learned what had happened.

The Yishuv was now split into those who accused the initiators of the *Patria* bombing – including Berl and the activists – of shedding innocent blood, and those who blamed the moderates for the disgrace of the unopposed evacuation of the *Atlantic* immigrants. Berl, like many of the latter, was outraged that the Jews had neither risked their lives nor demonstrated along the roads leading to the port, trying to stop the evacuation. Speaking at the Histadrut Council on the night after the Atlit evacuation (9 December 1940), Berl took issue with the moderates, though he also severely denounced the British. The theme of his speech was summed up in the following sentence: 'No nation can give up its fight for liberation, without terrible consequences.'[1] Certain good Jews, he said, referring to Sprinzak and his colleagues, appeared now to regard immigration as an issue of second-rate importance, one which did not justify disturbing the British Cabinet, and which could be postponed till after the War. But the Yishuv, he continued, could not allow any interest to take precedence over the Jewish interest. Had the movement displayed more tenacity at an earlier stage, there would have been no need to resort to such desperate measures as the blowing up of the *Patria*. 'Readiness to take risks', he exclaimed, 'can sometimes save us from danger.'[2]

On 17 December 1940 the Council of the World Union of the Poalei Zion movement convened at the Ayanot agricultural school. Among those attending were public figures from Jewish communities all over the world, who were now refugees who had run for their lives. The gathering mirrored the fate of the Jewish people in Europe, their haplessness and helplessness. On the one hand, echoes were heard of the horrors of the Nazi occupation of Poland, of the Nazi take-over of Rumania and the resultant horrors; on the other hand, a picture was drawn of national and cultural suicide in the Russian-occupied areas: Jewish institutions had been obliterated overnight, Jewish schools closed, and Zionism and Hebrew condemned to extinction. Those who had succeeded in reaching Palestine, displayed no greater courage or resourcefulness than the Jewish masses in the occupied territories: the dimensions of the catastrophe seemed to have numbed them. At the gathering, a heavy indictment was drawn up against the movement in Palestine, which had not summoned up the energy, the dedication and the resolve to make contact with members of the Jewish resistance in either the German- or the Russian-occupied areas. Nor had the Palestinians even sent financial assistance to he-Halutz cells in Poland, which were still operating.

The gathering veered between the abysses of the unfolding Jewish tragedy and the shallow waters of petty human conduct, marked by ineffectuality, verbosity, and failure to rise to the challenge. Sprinzak, who presided, symbolized – by his good-humored behavior and innocuous witticisms – the prevailing atmosphere which was, in fact, void of the tension and discontent which impel to action. Only three people disturbed the placid mood by their remarks: Zalman Rubashov delivered a gloomy diatribe on the post-war world, predicting that the progressive world would move away from nationalism, and that Zionism would be perceived as running counter to the forces of progress in the world. Ziama Aharonovitch sketched possible methods of clandestine operation among Jews in the Diaspora and in Palestine and hinted at possible schemes for the post-war period, such as the demand for reparations from the German people for plundered Jewish property.

The third was Berl. It seemed that there had never been so great a distance between him and his colleagues in their perception of the present, and vision of the future, as at that gathering at Ayanot. His comrades continued to talk in terms of the era which had gone, summoned up visions of Jewish communities which would come to life again after the war, and engaged in polemics on 'Zionist work' in the Diaspora, as if Jewish life in Europe were continuing unchanged. Berl did not deceive himself with thoughts of this kind. With unwavering acuity which his colleagues found hard to stomach, he spoke of the war as the end of European Jewry: 'The essence of Zionist awareness must be that what existed in Vienna – will never return, what existed in Berlin will never return, nor in Prague, and what we had in Warsaw and Lodz – is finished, and we must realize this!' He continued in this same tone: 'Why don't we understand that what Hitler has done, and this war – is a kind of Rubicon, an outer limit, and what existed before will never exist again.' The starting-point of any serious Zionist discussion, as far as he was concerned, was the destruction of European Jewry. Even if Jews survived – and he doubted this – they would not want to live in places steeped in Jewish blood. 'And I declare,' he reiterated with great emphasis, 'that the fate of European Jewry is sealed, not because I wish it to be so, but because cruel destiny has so determined.'³ To say such things in December 1940 was a revolutionary turn. Political Zionism had been accompanied from the outset by a catastrophic view of the future of the Jewish people. But there was a great difference between Herzl's apocalyptic vision and the statement of the brutal, immediate facts as the basic hypothesis for a plan of action. Berl's incisive logic did not permit him to take refuge in illusions. Hence, he could not believe, as did many of the best and the brightest in the Zionist movement, that just as the First World War had given the Jews the Balfour Declaration, the present war would produce a British political reform with regard to Palestine: the torn and bleeding Jewish people, spiritually and physically destroyed, would not be able to come forth on the day of victory to enjoy its fruits. He drew one sole conclusion from his vision of the world: if Zionism wanted to be the future force of the Jewish people, it must prepare to solve the Jewish question in all its scope. And therein, according to Berl, lay the connection between the fate of European Jewry and the Zionist plan of action: an end to previous policies, no more petty deeds! Berl, the Second Aliyah veteran, the constructivist, who cherished even the smallest deed more than the most sweeping of political achievements, had deduced that practical Zionism, based on slow and gradual development, had reached the end of the road. Further development of the National Home under the prevailing political conditions would be foiled by the British, and even if it were possible, it would be woefully inadequate for post-war needs. For Berl, the war had spelled the end of old Zionist policy. Truths which he had accepted before the White Paper and before the war, had become outdated overnight – and he did not hesitate to alter his views. The conclusion he drew was: 'We must raise the banner of solution of the Jewish question, of a *Jewish state*',⁴ he said. If the Zionist movement did not learn how to present its demands openly through a mighty mustering of national forces, nobody would present them on its behalf.

In the late 1930s Ben Gurion had claimed that there was no further room for the expansion of the National Home within the Mandatory framework, while Berl had been convinced (and his view was later vindicated) that a viable Jewish state could not be established at that time. Now there was once again a meeting-point between the two. Berl proclaimed the Jewish state as the objective of the Zionist struggle more than a year before Ben Gurion did so at the Biltmore Conference.

Berl's open avowal that the state was the Zionist goal was based on belief that once the Peel Commission had broached the idea, it could never again be shelved. In 1931, during the Basle Congress, the labor movement had denounced Jabotinsky's demand that the 'final objective' of Zionism be proclaimed. But now that the state was being mooted by non-Zionists, the Zionist movement could no longer deny its aspirations. Otherwise, it would be accused of deceit, or would be considered to have abandoned all political intentions and to have reconciled itself to the existence of a Jewish minority within an Arab Palestinian state. The demand for a Jewish state would disperse the mist which had befogged Zionist policy since the White Paper, and pinpoint the war objectives of the Jewish people. In 1931 this demand had been premature; now its time had come.

As he expressed his thoughts on the future of Palestine, Berl sketched the outlines of a possible solution to the Arab problem. He saw no way of conducting a dialog with the Arab national movement in Palestine. Like Ben Gurion before him, he offered the Arabs aid in establishing a pan-Arab federation in return for their assent to the transformation of Palestine into a Jewish state, although he assumed that such a program would be unacceptable to them. One may surmise that this proposal was based on Berl's assumption that when the 'heavens opened up' after the war and each national movement was required to state its objectives – the Zionist movement would be expected to respond on the Arab question. But the scheme which apparently appealed to Berl as the ideal solution was the idea of population exchange (which had been advocated by the Peel Commission). He saw in it a core of historical truth and the means of a long-term solution. As an example, he cited the transfer of Greeks and Turks in Asia Minor after the First World War, which had solved painful problems for both populations. He had been gratified when the British Labor Party conference reasserted the party's support for the Zionist movement and cited population transfer by peaceful means and by mutual consent as part of the proposed solution of the Palestine question. Berl believed that the immediate post-war period would be ripe for changes which, in more orderly times, would seem wildly unrealistic. His attitude to the transfer question was marked by the same unrestrained candor which characterized his analyses of Jewish and Zionist reality.

Berl's vision was rejected by his comrades, and particularly the veterans of ha-Poel ha-Tzair. Their picture of the future was peaceful, lacking the sense of urgency which colored his outlook, and his demands died a natural death: the majority simply ignored them. His attempt at the Council of The World Union to effect the adoption of operative resolutions failed: Sprinzak passed over his proposals and wound up the meeting without adopting any resolutions. Berl's remarks at the Mapai Central Committee on the same issue suffered a similar fate.

The body which shared Berl's views was ha-Kibbutz ha-Meuhad. Like Berl, Tabenkin was haunted by a presentiment of catastrophe. Tabenkin and Berl were in full agreement on the need for the Jews to take an activist, independent stand: to fight for the right to immigration and settlement without taking into account the war and the interests of the British. Both recognized Jewish isolation in an indifferent world and stressed their conviction that the Jews could influence the fate of the Yishuv and of Zionism, however limited their means might appear. In almost all the spheres in which operative political decisions were required, they were in accord. But there was one basic difference as regards their political orientation: whereas Berl pinned his hopes on Western democracy, Tabenkin trusted in the Soviet Union.

Paradoxically, despite his activism, Berl was less anti-British during the war than he had been since the murder of Brenner in 1921. To his mind, the Western powers fighting Hitler, despite their weaknesses, represented the hope for a better future, and the sole prospect for the Jewish people. His ambiguous attitude towards the British was shared by Ben Gurion, Eliyahu Golomb and Dov Hos. But Tabenkin, a considerable section of ha-Kibbutz ha-Meuhad and all of ha-Shomer ha-Tzair believed otherwise. Their anti-British sentiment was the converse of their sympathy for the Soviet Union.

When word of the Molotov–Ribbentrop pact was received in 1939 during the Zionist Congress at Geneva, Soviet sympathizers greeted the news with skepticism and dismissed it as hostile propaganda. When the facts were verified, they split into two camps: those whose world had collapsed about their ears, and those who sought ways of justifying the Soviet move. The latter blamed the pact on the vacillating two-faced stand of France and Great Britain, which had driven the Soviet Union to seek alliances elsewhere, out of fear that the Allies were about to do the same.

Most of the pro-Soviet forces in the Zionist camp in Palestine – in Left Poalei Zion, ha-Shomer ha-Tzair, ha-Kibbutz ha-Meuhad and Faction

B in Tel Aviv – remained steadfast even after the Molotov–Ribbentrop pact. They flatly rejected the Soviet attitude to Zionism, which they considered a historical error. But this did not prevent them from regarding the Soviet Union as the homeland of the Revolution, a beacon of light in the dark night of fascism, and humanity's hope for a better world. In the merger negotiations conducted at the time between Mapai and ha-Shomer ha-Tzair, the latter demanded, *inter alia*, that the principles of class warfare and the dictatorship of the proletariat be accepted as basic tenets of the united party. It also demanded a 'positive attitude' towards 'socialist construction in Russia'. Within Mapai itself there was a considerable group, headed by Tabenkin, whose approach to the Soviet Union was close to that of ha-Shomer ha-Tzair.

This may explain why Berl wrote a series of articles against ha-Shomer ha-Tzair in *Davar*, entitled 'Smiling through Tears', marked by trenchant polemics, bitter irony and irate pain. The question of the movement's attitude to the Soviet Union gave him no rest. When Russia invaded Finland, Tabenkin and his comrades justified the move. At a meeting held on the first anniversary of the outbreak of war, they continued to defend the Soviet position, and Berl wrote: 'I have discovered that there is no act, however despicable, which can tarnish Stalin's name. Indulgence is due him in advance.' And he quoted ironically the phrase used by the apologists: 'Those in charge know best.'[5]

The event which highlighted the cleavage between the two positions was the return of he-Halutz emissaries from Russian-occupied Poland. It will be recalled that on the night the Geneva Congress ended, the Palestinian emissaries to he-Halutz in Central and Eastern Europe – most of whom were affiliated to ha-Kibbutz ha-Meuhad – decided unanimously to continue their work in those countries for as long as possible. A bare three months later, they returned to Palestine via the Soviet Union, and several months after published a book called *In the Time of Holocaust*. The book was an account of their experiences in Poland and Russia *en route* to Palestine, in which they had nothing but praise for the Russian occupation and the exemplary attitude of the Red Army towards the civilian population. Their impressions of the Soviet scene were highly favorable: a new type of human being was being fostered as were new social and organizational patterns, and the standard of living and quality of life were improving. These effusions aroused at least one sarcastic reaction: 'They saw the backview of the Red Army, one Russian *kolkhoz* and maybe something else, a hasty glimpse in troubled times – and lo and behold – a weighty essay full of conclusions and assumptions on the whole endeavor, and on the "new man" who had come into being.'[6] The emissaries' report was contrary to all information received in Palestine from other sources, according to which the Soviet authorities had arrested all active Zionists in the occupied areas, closed Hebrew centers, dissolved all the parties and deported activists to Siberia.

On their return, the emissaries were invited to a meeting of the Histadrut Executive Secretariat, and Berl, surprisingly, took the trouble to attend. He listened at length and in silence to Liova Levite's laudatory description of conditions in Russian-occupied Poland. People behaved with circumspection in the presence of the emissaries: it was difficult to voice the questions which were on everyone's mind: Why did you return, and in such haste? What of the oath you took several months ago? But who had the right to judge a comrade for displaying weakness in such times? Finally Remez asked diplomatically why the emissaries had not considered leaving one of their number in the occupied area, for at least another two or three months, if only in order to provide up-to-date information on what was happening there. The emissaries held Palestinian-British passports and the risks they were taking were not beyond the bounds of reason. No clear-cut answer was given to Remez's question: one of them claimed that only underground illegal work could be effective and that they had not been willing to take this step. Another said apologetically that he-Halutz leaders in Poland had insisted that they leave at once and avoid risks. But the true answer apparently lay elsewhere: 'We all have a homeland, families and children, and it is not so easy or so simple for us to tear ourselves away . . .' If they had confined themselves to this simple and human explanation, Berl might have accepted it. But Levite's remarks in praise of the Soviet Union had enraged Berl and his outburst embarrassed all those present. Berl was contemptuous of the emissaries' precipitous return, even ridiculing them. 'They were very cautious,' he said, 'I would have liked to see ten emissaries fall martyrs to the cause in the occupied countries.' Berl considered their return another moral defeat for the Zionist labor movement in Poland since the outbreak of war: 'The movement in Poland . . .', he cried, 'has not displayed a single instance of self-sacrifice, has not said to itself that there is something sacred worth dying for.' And he added: 'I am haunted these days by a sense of terrible

shame, which I have never felt before. I did not know that our movement was capable of such baseness.'[7] In his diary he wrote: 'In all of
Vohlynia and Galicia, where are Hanna and her seven sons?'[8] Berl was
the disciple of Narodnaya Volya, nurtured on the tradition that
revolutionaries were prepared to risk their lives. He wanted to imbue
his movement with a fierce sense of national leadership, with Zionist
socialist fidelity, and he was sorely disappointed when the hour of trial
came. He suspected that the hesitation of the emissaries to go
underground in the Soviet Union was motivated by fear that such an act
would imply disloyalty to the Land of Revolution. For Berl, fidelity to
the Soviet Union was synonymous with fidelity to a false messiah, long
after the deception had been exposed.

For Berl, however, the central issue was not the justness of the Soviet
Union, but the war against Hitler. 'What good is it to me, if there exist
other forces which are totally just but are not fighting him?' he
exclaimed in response to Ben Aharon's pro-Soviet remarks. Berl
understood the origins of the idol-worship of the Soviet Union. Ben
Aharon's was a generation which had witnessed the decline of the
European socialist movement, had watched the destruction of idealistic
innocence in the Spanish Civil War and had seen the great democracies
adopt a policy of appeasement to Hitler, Franco and Mussolini. His
generation was seeking new gods and had seized on them with all the
force of despair; they believed in the Soviet Union as the country in
which a socialist regime was being constructed. This faith fulfilled some
elemental psychological need for many, and it was no accident that it
was so prevalent in the Yishuv, which was geographically remote from
the Soviet Union and relatively peaceful.

The pro-Soviet orientation was an additional bone of contention in
Mapai. The outbreak of war, the danger of extinction hovering over
European Jewry and the challenges facing the Yishuv, had not deflected
the party from its self-destructive course. In January 1940, Ben Gurion
addressed his comrades in the party's Central Committee, exhorting
them to forget old rivalries and to re-establish mutual trust, so as to prepare for the difficult days ahead. He took great care to suggest that the
blame was universal, even though in his heart of hearts he was not
entirely convinced of this. Ben Aharon hastened to interpret this to
mean that Ben Gurion and Berl were to blame. The conciliatory mood
which Ben Gurion seemed to have established evanesced, and the con-

troversy flared up again. The minority, which cohered around ha-Kibbutz ha-Meuhad, vehemently rejected Ben Gurion's proposal that the airing of differences be postponed until after the war for the sake of a united and concerted effort: 'It is precisely the war', they claimed, 'which obliges us at this difficult time to air these serious questions which have taken on added gravity, and we can not act until we have clarified matters and decided together.'[9] They were all weary of pointless discussions but, nonetheless, it was argued again and again that matters had not been 'clarified' sufficiently, and as long as this was so – the party was paralyzed.

The main battlefield of the Mapai opposition was the Histadrut. The economic crisis in Palestine continued unabated until 1942. There were numerous unemployed, families went hungry – and no solution was in sight. The efforts of the Zionist movement in the United States to raise money were unsuccessful: people were cautious about giving money in wartime. The Histadrut Executive Secretariat did its utmost to collect funds to help the unemployed, first and foremost from among workers who still held jobs. But the money raised was only a drop in the bucket.

The Secretariat was headed by Remez; Golda Meyerson was responsible for social assistance and the running of 'Mishan', the workers' social security fund. The Faction B attacks were directed against 'the Histadrut leadership' in general. Incitement is not difficult in times of economic plight, and the Histadrut leaders, who were constantly vilified, were in an intolerable situation. The feeling was that the Histadrut was on the verge of collapse. Perhaps the dispute could have been settled by building up a new Mapai branch from scratch in Tel Aviv, in line with Ben Gurion's old proposal. But the party was effectively barred from doing this, since ha-Kibbutz ha-Meuhad was ranged behind Faction B; rumor had it that there was now a countrywide Faction B, which had not yet been openly acknowledged. The expulsion of the Faction B leaders in Tel Aviv from the party was liable to split Mapai. On the other hand, ha-Kibbutz ha-Meuhad's leaders were forced to sanction acts of Faction B which, in more normal times, they would probably have condemned. As a result, they often resorted to arguments in the famous 'but' style: it is true that such and such was not as it should be, *but* there are greater wrongs in the party: failure to observe democratic procedures, lack of respect for the opinions of certain members, corruption in the Tel Aviv Labor Exchange, etc. All these were taken to explain, and even justify, irresponsible and unacceptable conduct.

The dispute between the two Mapai trends in Tel Aviv appears to have been the source of the hostility between the party's leaders. They were locked in relentless fraternal strife. The members of the Mapai Central Committee did not grasp the source of the differences between the two factions. It was apparently a struggle between two groups of party workers for positions of power. Naturally enough, the group which advocated change was depicted as the soul of integrity, social concern, class fervor, etc.; while the group under attack was obliged to defend itself against various charges of misconduct, some of them true, and found it hard to counter-attack since, apart from accusing its rivals of demagoguery and uncomradely behavior, it had nothing to say.

This was the situation throughout 1940. The fall of France, Italy's entry into the war, Nazi victories – none of these changed the atmosphere. One of the many tedious discussions of Histadrut affairs was cut short by the heavy Italian bombardment of Tel Aviv (9 September 1940) but none of those present saw the writing on the wall. Berl attended most of the debates (Ben Gurion was abroad), and listened in silence. He despaired, feeling that he was witnessing a deepening and irreversible process of division. He was still firmly convinced that there were no real differences of opinion between the two poles, but could find no way to bring them together.

On 20 October 1940 all the members of the Mapai Central Committee convened at Ayanot for a special meeting, which someone described as a 'conclave'. It was a desperate endeavor to settle matters in order to overcome the malaise which had infected the party. But the attempt did not succeed.

The atmosphere was not conciliatory and the dialog, instead of mitigating differences, gave them a sharper edge. The accusations were vague, but the underlying hostility was clear. Like Cato, stubbornly reiterating his demand that Carthage be destroyed, Berl returned again and again to the non-implementation of the Rehovot Conference resolutions on the merger of the kibbutz and youth movements: 'A party can operate', he said, 'when its members require it to operate. But if a certain member has private means of fulfilling party needs – what need has he of the party?' The decline in the party's power to decide – according to Berl – was caused by the divided loyalties of its members.

As always, Berl did not hesitate to employ emotional blackmail, and spoke with pain about the task of educating the young generation, which was no longer within his domain: 'I am a man without a party within Mapai, and therefore have no place where I can educate the young . . . I am thus dependent on the mercies of party bosses . . .'[10] Several days previously Berl had completed a series of lectures to ha-Mahanot ha-Olim youth leaders, and was still under the strong impression that his influence was now limited. He was now ready to join the Party Secretariat on condition that, first, the youth question be solved – apparently by revival of the abortive Youth Center – and, secondly, that the party be reorganized.

But his emotional–personal appeal fell completely flat. A storm erupted after his speech, and he was attacked on all sides. His comrades accused him of dictatorial tendencies. At the same time all those present demanded that Berl, Tabenkin and Sprinzak join the Secretariat as the essential condition for the party's rehabilitation. If there had previously been some prospect that Berl might accede, the attacks rang down the curtain on it. Berl needed to feel loved, admired, or at least accepted, in order to function. There may have been some truth in Sprinzak's claim that if Berl had worked for the merger of the Kibbutz movements in gradual stages, without honing the issue, he could have carried it through. But Berl did not believe that negotiations and agreements could overcome the feuds. Only a wave of enthusiasm could sweep away the acrimony of the past. The greater the opposition to his wishes, the stronger his sense of righteousness. He did not respond by launching an implacable struggle to achieve his goals, but chose to retire from party activity.

The lengthy debate changed nothing. Berl may have acted capriciously, even childishly, when his unconscious appeal for the affection of his colleagues was rejected, but his basic argument was valid: in a divided party a leader who lacked a base in one of the all-powerful blocs, was unable to act effectively. His presence in the Secretariat could make no difference to the internal rift as long as the blocs refused to surrender some of their power. Moreover, since he had written his 'Protest', the central issue had changed: it was no longer the unification of the kibbutz movement, but the party's authority over its parts. The various blocs, and particularly ha-Kibbutz ha-Meuhad, could exercise their veto whenever resolutions were not congenial to them. The majority refrained from decision-making, fearing dissension. Without a guarantee, beforehand, of the cooperation of all the groups, Berl's activity was doomed to failure from the outset. If he had been an organizer by nature, he could perhaps have joined the Secretariat and built up a power base within the party machines, gradually imposing his will on the party. But he was incapable of this by nature. He disliked work of this kind and hated the kind of person with whom he would have been required to cooperate. Having been pampered since the Ahdut ha-Avoda days by his comrades, who trusted him unreservedly and considered him their final arbiter, he now suffered from a crisis of confidence. 'What hurts me in the attitude of the society around me is not lack of consent but the absence of trust', he wrote in his diary. 'I do not ask for assent in advance, but I have the right to demand trust in advance, *before* the need for opposition is revealed.'[11] But the party was in a precarious situation and no longer able to give its unlimited trust to any one member.

Vested party interests marked the limits of trust, and beyond lay mutual suspicion. The party had lost its point of gravity, and Berl, its living symbol, felt that he had forfeited his capacity for action.

December 1940 was a traumatic month in other ways: the *Patria* and the *Atlantic* incidents took place; the World Union Council convened at Ayanot, and on top of all this, Dov Hos and members of his family and friends were killed in a road accident. Yet amidst all these events, in which Berl was profoundly involved, two schemes came to fruition which were to occupy him fully for the next few years: the publishing house and the 'study month'.

Berl had been dreaming of setting up a publishing house for some years. From time to time he published a book under the *Davar* imprint, without authorization. On the tenth anniversary of *Davar* (1935), the Histadrut Executive decided to establish a publishing house, to be run by Berl. The scheme had been approved unanimously and even ha-Shomer ha-Tzair gave it its blessing at the time. But the plan was shelved because of the economic slump and the disturbances which occurred shortly after. Now David Remez, Chairman of the Executive Secretariat, decided to revive the scheme to culminate the twentieth-anniversary celebrations of the Histadrut. At first Remez broached the plan at the Central Committee, proposing that the publishing house be set up 'within *Davar* and according to *Davar*'s system',[12] and that Berl be granted the same unlimited powers of editing, selection and choice of staff that he had enjoyed as editor of *Davar*. The Committee welcomed the idea in general and nobody voiced objection to Berl's becoming editor. But some did object to his being solely and exclusively in charge. Now that the party was coming apart at the seams, the 'grace of his youth' was forgotten. Ha-Kibbutz ha-Meuhad still remembered the affair of the anthology, which, in their eyes, disqualified Berl for the task of sole editor. It goes without saying that the great majority of the Central Committee voted for the establishment of the publishing house and endorsed Berl's special status: but if Berl had required additional proof of his waning status, this was it.

At the discussions on the publishing house held by the Histadrut Executive and then at the 42nd Histadrut Council, ha-Shomer ha-Tzair and Left Poalei Zion delegates voiced their objections on the matter. The former had recently set up their own publishing house, Sifriyat ha-Poalim, with initial success. They strongly opposed lending the Histadrut's name to a publishing house which would, in fact, be affiliated to Mapai. Such a large and prosperous party could afford to establish its own publishing house, they claimed, and cited *Davar* as an example: the Histadrut paper had many good qualities, and was skillfully edited, but the minority groups in the Histadrut had always felt that it discriminated against them, allotting them insufficient space. They demanded 'active tolerance', i.e. an opportunity to present their views in such a manner as to enable them to swing public opinion. If a daily paper, which dealt with everyday matters, discriminated against them, then books, which were lasting treasures, undoubtedly would do so. Left Poalei Zion did not object to the concept of a publishing house, recognizing that only the Histadrut possessed the required funds for a project of this scope (nor did they have a publishing house of their own); but they emphatically demanded that an editorial board be established, and that the *Davar* model of one all-powerful editor, should not be repeated, since it treated the minorities as historical 'accidents'. The left-wing parties in the Histadrut had never forgiven Berl for some of his acrimonious anti-Soviet articles.

The speakers, and particularly Yaari and Hazan of ha-Shomer ha-Tzair, carefully avoided slighting Berl. They did not accept his authority, they refused to succumb to his charm; but they recognized his great talents, his broad approach, and his unique suitability for the project. Opposition to endowing Berl with 'dictatorial' powers as editor was not confined to the left-wing parties. Within his own party, many were disgruntled: on the left, Faction B and on the right, the former ha-Poel ha-

Tzair members. The brief interval between the discussions and the voting was filled with feverish backstage activity. The resentment at Remez's proposal reached such dimensions, that Berl's supporters sought a way of placating the opposition. On the other hand, they were well aware that if Berl was not granted the freedom of action to which he was accustomed, he would resign, as was his wont when displeased with the course of events.

In the end, the Mapai majority in the Council outvoted the left-wing parties, setting up the Histadrut publishing house, and choosing Berl Katznelson as editor. But at the same time, they established a kind of token directorate, representing all the trends and parties in the Histadrut, whose powers were confined to receiving reports and making plans. All other authority rested with Berl; it was also decided, however, that the publishing house would be subordinated to the Histadrut Executive, and that in the event of differences of opinion between the editor and the directorate, the Executive would be the final arbiter.

Berl was now at the crest of one of his cyclical waves of vigor and resourcefulness, and while drawing up the plan for the publishing house, he also dedicated a good deal of effort to organizing a 'study month' for Histadrut members.

A synthesis between manual labor and intellectual pursuits had been one of the cornerstones of the second Aliyah ideology, inspired by the ideas of the Russian populists. The dissemination of culture among the working masses was to replace intellectual and cultural elitism. Berl conceived of the 'study month' as a fitting way to put the idea into practice among the intellectually aware members of the Palestinian working class, that is, mainly among members of the communal settlements.

The idea was broached in the early 1930s, but at the time Berl failed to raise the necessary funds. Now he decided to attempt the scheme with the modest means at the disposal of the Histadrut. The timing was somewhat surprising: the world was in flames, Hitler had launched an offensive in the Balkans and reached Crete; the Yishuv lived in dread of the consequences of the war; Palestine was still in the throes of a severe economic crisis, and a storm was raging in Mapai. Still Berl was eager. At his speech at the opening session of the 'study month', he said that internal invigoration, 'reinforcing ourselves', was a task of vital importance, precisely in such troubled times. He spoke of 'summoning all our inner strength' to provide an answer to the question of the future image of society and the nation when the war ended. But this was largely hyperbole. In fact, the study month was probably part of the struggle he was waging in order to win back the best of the young generation in his fight against pro-Soviet trends in the movement, and to re-establish himself as a mentor and teacher.

Controversy erupted even before the 'month' began. Just as Am Oved (the publishing house) had been represented as a general Histadrut project, so the study month was intended to be a supra-party endeavor, stressing the basic unity of all Palestinian workers. Berl wanted to create a framework, within which people of different opinions could meet for discussion and debate without turning it into a political arena. He selected themes which were not directly related to current affairs, and participants according to his own subjective criteria: a tête-à-tête which had impressed him, an interesting letter he had received, or a stimulating comment overheard. The selection was random and personal, including people he had encountered all over the country, particularly in the kibbutzim. What he sought was intellectual liveliness, open-mindedness, idealism. He refused to concede to the custom, now widespread in the movement, of running everything according to a rigid party key. The leaders of ha-Kibbutz ha-Meuhad perceived this as an attempt to undermine their authority. Most of the invitations were sent to kibbutz members on an individual basis, and ha-Kibbutz ha-Meuhad was not given the opportunity of intervening. Berl had not consulted them on the program or on the lectures, and not one of the Kibbutz's regular lecturers (except Tabenkin himself) was invited to take part. What Berl regarded as the only way of guaranteeing high standards and open debate was seen by them as an onslaught on their authority.

The Kibbutz Secretariat chose its own method of retaliation. Young people who had responded eagerly to Berl's invitation withdrew, after 'comradely discussions' in their kibbutzim in which Berl's motives were 'clarified'. Several even wrote to Berl complaining against his method of selection, his disregard for the wishes of the kibbutzim, and the fact that he had chosen mainly advocates of the merger of the kibbutz movement. He replied that the candidates were not emissaries, but merely students, and that, in most cases, he had not been aware of their views on the merger. The more letters he received in this spirit, the more slighted he felt. His replies took on a sarcastic note, rather incongruous in an exchange between a great leader and the young members of his movement. Berl was hurt by the fact that these young people, whom he regarded as his disciples, had succumbed to the pressures of their kibbutzim, thereby risking the loss of his affection.

Although it was conducted within the Histadrut framework, the study month actually turned out to be a Mapai seminar. Berl had handled ha-Shomer ha-Tzair's leaders with kid gloves to ensure the participation of their members. He allowed them to select both the speakers and the students from their own ranks, on the ground that he was not acquainted with their members. At first, they apparently agreed to participate, but once they discovered that Faction B, and particularly ha-Kibbutz ha-Meuhad, were against the idea, they too canceled their participation.

The 'month' took place in April 1941 in Rehovot and was attended by 138 people from all over the country. The great majority came from communal settlements and only 20 per cent from towns. Close to seventy invitees failed to come, most of them because of the objections of their movement institutions. Those attending were between 20 and 35 – for the most part – with secondary or university educations. The C.I.D. took a great interest in this seminar for youth leaders, and asked its Rehovot branch to provide a list of lecturers and students, and to find out whether it was not, in fact, a camouflaged Hagana gathering.

Study was organized into three major and several minor fields of interest. The first major study group, headed by Golda Meyerson, surveyed Histadrut projects, and the overall picture presented was very impressive, perhaps the appropriate answer to the harsh attacks on the Histadrut by Faction B. Lectures on Hebrew literature were given mainly by Rachel Katznelson. The writers chosen for study were Berl's favorites, all of them representative of the revolt against the rule of reason: Feierberg, Berdichevsky, Brenner. The third study group was devoted to cultural matters, to problems which had always preoccupied Berl: how to preserve national traditions and symbols at a time when religious values and belief were being discarded.

The curriculum also included lectures on Jewish history (Zalman Rubashov on immigration to Palestine in the Middle Ages, Ben Zion Dinaburg on the Emancipation, and Gershom Sholem on his initial research on Shabbetai Zvi).

The controversial lectures were those devoted to socialism and contemporary politics. Here Berl tried to point to various paths to socialism, giving pride of place to national democratic socialism.

Berl had invested all his educational skill in organizing the program. He was not fond of frontal lectures, and preferred independent study by the students. He had tried to arrange study groups with a limited number of participants, with access to a well-equipped library. This was particularly successful in the Hebrew literature and Jewish history groups. The 'cultural' studies were conducted by the students themselves, without a teacher or instructor.

Berl was happier at the 'study month' than he had been for some time. His good spirits infected all the participants, and fostered an atmosphere of camaraderie and creativity. The most impressive part of the seminar was the informal Friday and Saturday evening get-togethers, where the participants would recount their own experiences. One day Berl asked for the floor and, with unique candor, told the story of his life up to the time of his immigration. He called his story 'My Road to Palestine'. He described his confusion as a young boy from the Pale of Settlement, torn between Zionism and socialism, between the pain of the Jewish people and the lure of the liberating revolution, and his dilemma in wandering from party to party – until his final decision to immigrate to Palestine. His account was distinguished by a sincerely, unflagging search for truth even when the facts did not reflect well on him.

Berl was speaking off the record, but Golda Meyerson had concealed a young stenographer named Sara Zayit behind a curtain, and she took down Berl's story. Her presence at the 'study month' was no accident. Since the end of 1939, a special relationship had grown up between her and Berl, a relationship which endured until his death.

The passage of time had not improved relations between Berl and Leah. As they aged, prematurely, in their early fifties, they found less and less in common. He was attractive to women, and his radiant charm and warm personality drew people to him. He liked women, but his moral principles were inflexible and puritanical, and his sense of obligation to Leah, who had shared the storms and the torments of the Sara Schmuckler affair, never wavered. As a leader, whose conduct was observed by the public at large, he lived in a glasshouse, and this fact as well explains his reluctance to carry mutual attractions beyond platonic ties. Women poets and writers often visited his home, seeking his advice, support – and perhaps more. Leah, increasingly left out of his world, was a bitter and weary woman. Even in her youth she had never been particularly tender or affectionate, like Sara Schmuckler. Now she devoted herself largely to her sisters and their children. She worried about Berl and was desperately jealous where he was concerned, hostile to any woman who showed an interest in him. After his death, she went through his diaries and letters and erased any references to other women. She hated the role of housewife and refused to regard the care of her husband as her life-work. She tried to escape into social work, but even there she failed to find satisfaction.

Sara Zayit was twenty-eight years old and Berl fifty-two when their friendship blossomed. Born in Kovno, Lithuania, into an educated and observant Zionist family, Sara was an unusual and highly independent woman. After graduating from the Tarbut school, she spent six years in France, where she studied philosophy, literature and art. She immigrated to Palestine in the late 1930s, and found work as a shorthand typist at the Histadrut Executive, where she was highly regarded. Sara was very different from Berl and from his former women friends. Dark-haired, attractive and well-built, she was not beautiful in the conventional sense, but always aroused attention. Her taste in clothes was highly individual, and her appearance always striking. She was open and friendly and an avid conversationalist. Her name was linked with that of more than one man, but she never married. A born city-dweller, she was never attracted to rural settlement and agriculture, and lacked the idealistic dedication which characterized Sara Schmuckler, Leah and other women whom Berl befriended. Nor did she have any predilection for public life. When her relations with Berl became known, one of his disciples puzzled as to what his teacher had found in the Histadrut clerk, whose lifestyle differed so much from that expected of a labor movement leader. Perhaps it was that very contrast which attracted Berl. Few details are available on Berl's 'autumn love'. Sara Zayit was killed in 1953 when an El Al aircraft was shot down over Bulgaria. Berl's letters to her have been lost, and with them the secret of their relationship. Sara was highly discreet and Berl, too, guarded his privacy jealously. They were rarely seen together in public. Their friendship seems to have been important and unique to both of them.

There was a certain amount of gossip about them, although less than might have been expected in the light of Berl's public standing. Her work at the Histadrut was a convenient excuse to meet: she accompanied him to party gatherings all over the country as a stenographer, a fact that explains her presence at Rehovot.

The 'month' was an educational success but no more. No great leaders emerged from among the participants. There are those who claim that Berl erred in selecting the candidates; others blame the kib-butzim which did not allow the seminar graduates to take up public duties. There is probably some truth in both arguments and perhaps the very question is irrelevant, since the qualities Berl was seeking in young people – sensitivity, openness, the desire for wider horizons – were not necessarily the traits of leaders. They were common among the group of comrades from Kinneret, but it is to be doubted whether they were suited to a party which had become institutionalized.

Berl hoped to nurture a new generation of leaders, educated, broad-minded and idealistic, detached from the party apparatus. He preached tolerance, but was himself not tolerant nor did he respect the views of his rivals. There was constant tension between the values he strove to inculcate and the fanatic element in him. He did not in fact permit his disciples to choose their own path, but tried to persuade them to see the world through his eyes. When the skepticism which he advocated led people to reject his views, he felt that he had failed. In short, he did not teach them how to break free of him and did not endow his disciples with intellectual and emotional independence. Herein may lie the key to an understanding of the weakness of the generation bred in Palestine, which never produced first-rank leaders. There was something sterile in the handing down of theories from one generation to another without mutual struggle, without an overhauling of values, without the consolidation of the collective persona of the new generation. Because they continued the way of their mentors, they never succeeded in extricating themselves from their patronage.

Ben Gurion returned to Palestine in February 1941, having been away for a year, and plunged straight into party life, with all its squabbles and factionalism, with one aim: to change it. He drew up a plan for the approaching party conference: consolidation of a centralistic party, based on a limited leadership, a small and efficient Central Committee, which would report to the annual party conference. The main point of this program was that the party's representatives on various bodies should be elected by all the members, and each elected officer should be responsible directly to the party, and not to his own bloc. But, con-trary to Ben Gurion's plan, a Faction B list – made up of Faction B in Tel Aviv and ha-Kibbutz ha-Meuhad – took part in the elections to the party conference, appearing for the first time on a national scale.

Concomitantly with the elections, Ben Gurion demanded that a referendum be held among party members in order to settle organizational questions. According to the main clause of the referendum: 'The directorate and the Council should not be composed of representatives of blocs and factions, but should be elected by all the delegates to the conference, each of its members to bear responsibility to the entire movement.'[13] Berl moderated the text of the referendum here and there, but in the main he supported it. The question is to what extent he believed in the power of a referendum to solve the party's basic problems. The Party Council, held on 27 April 1941, discussed the statutes for elections to the conference and the referendum. Ben Gurion presided with an iron hand, and did not permit the opposition to argue with him. Berl remained silent, having drawn up the resolutions according to Ben Gurion's guidelines.

May 1941 was a difficult month in Palestine. In the Western Desert Rommel was continuing his triumphant advance eastward. An abyss was opening up beneath the Yishuv, but the strife continued. Faction B was growing. When Berl talked to Israel Galili, who had joined it, he asked him where the party was going, but Galili could offer no reply. A few hours before he joined the Faction, he told Berl, he had not known that he was about to do so. On the Saturday, Berl attended a discussion at the Petah Tikva branch of the party and witnessed a squabble between the factions. After having delivered a speech in the stifling heat, he returned to other realities. In his diary he wrote: 'Shaul [Meirov] came. We talked of what awaits us tomorrow and the next day.' 'At Ben Gurion's. With Shaul, Moshe [Shertok], Eliyahu [Golomb]. On the same subject. Unable to face tomorrow.'[14]

For the next few weeks they were buffeted between the heroic and the grotesque: elections to the party conference were held in those anxious days, and the Central Committee debates revolved around electoral issues.

For all his authority, Ben Gurion was unable to impose his will on the party. When the referendum was held, the great majority voted against the continued existence of the factions, but the party Secretariat decided to shelve the results. It was agreed that the first session of the newly elected party assembly would be devoted exclusively to political themes, and that the party institutions would be elected there; organizational questions, however, would be postponed to the second session. There seems to have been tacit agreement between the former ha-Poel ha-Tzair supporters and Faction B on organizational matters. None of them were overjoyed at the thought of a centralist party without the traditional 'key' which had guaranteed ha-Poel ha-Tzair's standing in the party since Mapai was established. In the face of this alliance, it was hard for Ben Gurion to function. But the main reason for the general assent to postponement was Rommel's North African offensive, which had brought him to the Egyptian border and aroused an evacuation panic among the British. The conference was held in the shadow of Rommel, and a permanent committee was elected, its task being to nominate candidates for positions on the Secretariat and the Central Committee (this had formerly been done by the blocs); Berl was a committee member. But he discovered soon enough that he was being out-maneuvered: the list of candidates to the Central Committee was submitted and approved in his absence. When he protested, he found himself isolated: nobody could summon up the strength to launch a bitter debate on the last day of the conference, when all eyes were on the events in the Western Desert. The principle of allocating a third of the seats on party institutions to Faction B was approved almost clandestinely. The results of the referendum were never brought up for discussion. Berl wrote in his diary: 'I am a stranger to all this.'[15]

Ten days after the Mapai conference, Germany invaded the Soviet Union. In his diary Berl passed over the event in silence. Several days previously he had noted a small-scale British withdrawal from Marj-Ayun, but of this world-shaking event he made no mention. Since the end of June, he had been in a depression again, suffering from fatigue. The energy which had marked his actions in the past six months had abated.

He spent the summer and autumn of 1941 in Jerusalem and at the Arza convalescent home, which he dearly loved, returning to Tel Aviv only at the end of January 1942. During this time he had withdrawn almost completely from public activity. Only the 'brothers-in-law' (Shaul Meirov and Moshe Shertok) continued to visit him from time to time, reporting on happenings. This was a period of unparalleled loneliness: Ben Gurion was in the United States, Berl had lost contact with ha-Kibbutz ha-Meuhad, and most of the young generation had shifted away from him. For his own party, he felt very little sympathy.

In autumn 1941, the Mandate Government responded to the Jewish Agency request and permitted a special radio broadcast from the Yishuv to Soviet Jewry. Berl was asked to deliver the message of the Palestinian labor movement. He spoke Yiddish, and opened with the words 'Jewish brothers', rather than 'workers'. He made no reference whatsoever to the Soviet regime; only once did he use the actual words 'Soviet Union' – in the context of that country's alliance with the great democracies. He offered neither praise nor encouragement to the birthplace of socialism, choosing to speak only of common Jewish destiny, of the brotherhood of suffering, of the joint battle against Hitler and the hope of defeating him. His remarks angered Aharon Zisling, whose reaction was apparently typical of ha-Kibbutz ha-Meuhad: how could he address Soviet Jewry for the first time after so many years without first consulting the party and the Histadrut!

The months of illness passed. Leah visited him from time to time, as did Sara Zayit, but he spent most of his time alone. Lying in bed, he planned his last great project, the Am Oved publishing house. As usual when he was engaged in a task close to his heart, he summoned up inner resources of energy and creativity, which may also have accelerated his physical and emotional recovery.

Zalman Rubashov once compared the Berl of the Second Aliyah and Moses of the *midrash* tale who, when he saw that judgment had been passed on the world, drew a circle around himself, and tried to annul the sentence from within. He felt that Berl had withdrawn into his circle during the Second World War, despairing of altering facts. Berl, however, saw his new project otherwise. It was not the caprice of a beloved and vulnerable leader, whose comrades had acceded to his 'eccentric' love of books. He regarded Am Oved as a vital instrument in fashioning the new Jewish society. 'For a brief moment I succeeded in inducing the Histadrut – consciously or otherwise – not only to join this publishing project, but also to undertake responsibility for the fate of Hebrew literature and the working conditions of the Hebrew writer.'[16] No more and no less. Just as Hevrat ha-Ovdim undertook responsibility for building the country, Am Oved accepted responsibility for shaping the intellectual life of the people.

Ever since the Second Aliyah, Berl had supported various writers. He never considered literature to be a luxury which could be indulged in only when conditions were favorable. He perceived it as a vital and integral part of the Jewish national movement. As was his wont, he translated great ideas into simple and everyday language. Having seen how Brenner was prevented from devoting himself to creative work by the need to make a living, he understood the problems of the struggling writer. Once he became a known public figure, he fostered contacts with people able to subsidize needy writers. He did not shrink from courting philanthropists in order to obtain the 'knipelach' ('bundles') which rescued more than one writer from destitution. As the years went by this task became increasingly difficult: 'All the financial institutions which I helped found, cost me less in personal effort than my little "onslaughts" on friendly philanthropists.'[17] He now felt that one of the central tasks of Am Oved was to release writers from philanthropic patronage and to bring them to the attention of a wide reading public.

Am Oved started operations during an economic slump. Berl was flooded with requests from writers and poets. He was forced to reject many of them outright, and this aroused hostility and led to accusations of favoritism. His standing as a publisher revealed to Berl some of the less edifying aspects of literary creation: a certain writer harassed him incessantly with appeals for work; another was dissatisfied with the modest fee Berl obtained for him; a third was never content unless he saw other poets discredited.

Berl found himself playing the joint role of father confessor, psychiatrist, philanthropist and editor. He differed from more prosperous patrons of the arts in that there were no barriers between him and the writers who flocked to his home. Supplicants had always flocked to his open doors, and now their number rose alarmingly.

On 1 April 1942 *Davar* published the first Am Oved prospectus. Berl launched it with sweeping vision and flair, with four initial series of books: la-Dor (For this Generation), for adults; Shaharut, for the young; la-Yeled, for children; and Min ha-Moked (From the Flames), on wartime problems. He wanted to guide the workers and their families in filling their bookshelves. In selecting books for children and young people, he sought those works which would enlighten the young and help them 'understand the truth'.[18] Many of the books he proposed dealt with Jewish life in Palestine and in the Diaspora, with Jewish history and pioneering sagas. It was only his own good taste which prevented the series from crossing the borderline of propaganda literature. Bracha Habas was in charge of the series for children and for youth. Her own book *Our Little Heroes* is typical of the kind of works published in these series intended not to entertain but to indoctrinate. In Berl's defense it should be noted that the selection of Hebrew children's literature available to him was small, as was the number of writers writing for children. *Davar* had published *Lubengulu King of Zulu* by Nahum Guttman, but

311

there were few shining talents of this kind at the time. Berl deliberately subordinated his aesthetic sense to his educational aims. He left the works of imagination and adventure, as well as the classics, to commercial publishing houses, and confined himself to those books which preached patriotism, love of Palestine and 'the pioneering spirit'. Thus the Shaharut and la-Yeled series are inferior in quality to la-Dor.

In the la-Dor series Berl gave free rein to his literary taste, although here too he set himself limits. He did not publish the translations of his favorite writers – the giants of Russian literature – or any other of the classics. His task was to promote Hebrew literature.

After bringing the public the best of the modern Hebrew writers – Hazaz and Agnon, Dvora Baron, Kabak and Fichman – Berl chose for translation mostly non-fiction, particularly political writings with a sociological bent. He wanted to publish Gandhi's autobiography, regarding him as one of the great personalities of his time. He also selected *School for Dictators* by Ignazio Silone (with whom he was friendly); he produced Arthur Rosenberg's book on the German Republic, and was happy to publish a book by his boyhood friend, Yaakov Leshchinsky, on the Jews of the Soviet Union.

In selecting political literature, Berl worked on two assumptions: one, that the books were earmarked for workers who had little leisure for reading and the other, that the publishing house should select their reading matter for them. In the first Am Oved prospectus he announced his intention of publishing two anthologies, one containing examples of the modern British socialist thought, the other a compendium of the best political thought from ancient Greece to modern times. He also planned an additional anthology introducing American thinkers to the Hebrew public. Berl hoped in this way to create a barrier against the romantic pro-Soviet literature, so popular among large sections of the Palestine labor movement. 'I did not undertake to supply what the public wants, but what I think they need.'[19] He flatly refused to succumb to the pressures exerted on him by the left, and rejected criticism that he had not published the writings of the founding fathers of socialism. The *Communist Manifesto*, he argued, could certainly be produced in Hebrew, but not as a document in itself; it should be accompanied by footnotes, explanations and a foreword, setting it in its historical context, revealing which parts were still relevant and which were now outdated. After the publishing house had established itself, he conceived the plan of publishing the writings of several of the early socialists, disregarding those who were awarded pride of place in the bookcases of ha-Shomer ha-Tzair kibbutzim and some of ha-Kibbutz ha-Meuhad's settlements. Not all of Berl's preferences were distinguished by their intellectual methodology, but they were original and humanistic thinkers: Rousseau, Herzen, Proudhon, Kropotkin, Hess, Mazzini and Gustav Landauer.

It was a militant library and all the fears of the Histadrut opposition, that he would use it as a weapon in the fight for his political views, were realized. He deliberately ignored works which he considered a threat to his own socialist Zionist truth. The Left Poalei Zionists were infuriated when he published a volume of Borochov's works, edited by Zalman Rubashov, which presented a different Borochov from the schematic and one-dimensional figure depicted by those who considered themselves his disciples and heirs.

Berl devoted a special series to the works of the fathers of socialist Zionism. He had started this project before Am Oved was established, when he published some of the works of Nahman Syrkin with his own lengthy foreword. He did the same with the writings of Moshe Beilinson, to which he also appended an extensive introduction. There were those who taunted Berl with inflating their importance. But as far as he was concerned, the decisive factor was his own emotional affinity with them.

Berl further wrote introductions to the works of E. Yaffe and S. Lavi, as if he did not trust the Hebrew reader to appreciate for himself the unique qualities of these men. When an old friend, Mordechai Kushnir, asked him if the Hebrew reader had gone down in his esteem, he replied with his typical candor: 'Not gone down. I would say moved away, moved away from us. Our generation is not his . . .' 'What we see as the intoxicating present – is the distant past for him . . . I envy those who do not feel this way,' he added. 'I live with it.'[20] When David Zakai asked him why he had addressed his introduction to Lavi's book to 'the stranger', he burst out, as if he had been awaiting the opportunity to unburden himself: 'I will answer you frankly . . . the present is foreign to me.'[21]

Berl was a meticulous editor, who attended to the infinitesimal details of publishing. He took great pains over uniform spelling and clean proofs, and introduced partial voweling, to aid the reader. Am Oved employed a professional proofreader and a style editor. According to Berl, this was the first Hebrew publishing house which permitted itself such 'luxuries'. Towards the authors he adopted the role of critic: he analyzed their works, pointing out flaws and good points, noting anomalies in the characters and the plot; but in the final analysis, he allowed the author to have his own way. The writers often felt that he had grasped what they were trying to say but had had difficulty in expressing. His editorial touch was particularly evident when he edited anthologies or published selections from the writings of fellow-members of the movement. He tried to cut out wounding expressions used in the heat of the debate, but was careful to avoid bowdlerizing, lest the nature of the controversy be obscured. 'I shied away from cosmetics, from false respectability. And I debated with myself a great deal while editing.'[22]

In matters of literary taste he was without sentiment. Having been inundated with appeals from writers and poets since the early *Davar* days, he had learned to reject inferior work decisively and had reconciled himself to the idea that he would always be accused of favoritism. Nor did he recognize 'class' preferences where culture was concerned. He did not attribute less importance to Uri Zvi Greenberg as a poet because of his extreme right-wing views. When the Ohel theater was in difficulties and the directors asked for Histadrut support, they argued that Habimah (the national theater) was a bourgeois theater while the Ohel was the theater of the workers. Berl rejected this argument outright. It was not a question of class, he said. The Ohel's right to exist must derive from its unique qualities, its originality – and not from its proletarian origins.

Though Berl was entrenched in his early tastes, he began, as time went on, to open up to other European literature. He admired Kafka, and, possibly under the influence of Sara Zayit, read Stendhal and included *The Charterhouse of Parma* in the Am Oved list. Michael Assaf brought him works by Arab writers, which had been translated into European languages and though he was not impressed, he did publish Tewfik el Hakim's book *The Diary of an Egyptian Village Prosecutor*. The sole Egyptian work which aroused his admiration was the autobiography of Tah Hussein. Modern literature did not appeal to him, and this may be why he showed no interest in contemporary English or American literature. Over the years he recognized the fact that he had been left stranded at some point. As regards Russian literature, nothing written after the Revolution seemed to interest him. The same was true for Yiddish literature. Finally, he felt no affinity with modern Hebrew poetry. Berl was not among those who accused the young poets of being incapable of writing for a wide public. 'I have come to see', he wrote, 'that in these matters as well, age counts in this world.'[23]

Though writers could publish their works in several literary journals or in other papers and publishing houses, *Davar* and Am Oved were of decisive importance on the Palestinian literary scene. Thus, even if Berl was not the final arbiter of literary life, he was no doubt aware that he occupied a very sensitive position in the network of relations that stretched between the broad reading public and the intelligentsia dependent on it.

Berl's attitude towards writers depended on whether he considered them 'only' professionally or expected from them a total commitment. With some of the former – Agnon and Gershom Sholem, for example – he was personally very friendly. With others, such as Yitzhak Behr and the young Nathan Rotenstreich, he was editor, publisher, and lover of literature. He never tried to involve them in the life of his movement, or in the affairs of the publishing house. His attitude towards them was liberal. His comments, literary or otherwise, derived from the needs of a publisher, producing books for a wide reading public – and nothing more.

But he adopted a different attitude to those from whom he expected total commitment. In his heart of hearts he hoped that the writers, poets, essayists and authors of children's books with whom he came into contact would feel towards Am Oved as he did; that they would identify with the project, regarding it as their life-work. It was this devotion he sought – and rarely found. The literary people with whom he was closely associated, and particularly the more talented among them, Dov Stock, Leah Goldberg, Yatziv and others, did not regard *Davar* and Am Oved as their whole world, and retained their independence as creative artists. He revealed something of his disappointment in a letter to David Zakai, which he never sent. The pretext for writing it was the resentment expressed by *Davar* veterans, headed by Zakai, at the fact that Berl had excluded them when setting up Am Oved. In his reply he conducted a reckoning with Zakai and the *Davar* staff, and wrote, *inter alia*:

All my life, in Zionism and in agriculture, I have set my sights on highly talented people, I have knocked on their doors, aroused them to the best of my ability . . . and when the gifted did not respond, or responded for only a brief time and then kicked over the traces again – I went down a rung and worked with those who were available, people like me, neither highly gifted nor highly knowledgeable, but people who put their shoulders to the wheel, for whom the failure of *Davar* would have seemed a personal failure, as it would have to me.

The intellectuals whom he referred to in his letter did not consider themselves partners in the project but rather free-lance employees. Berl added:

And I could never work with hired employees. I was a member of a communal group. It was thus that I perceived *Davar*; anyone who wanted to work with me – had to bring all of *himself*, his wholehearted participation and desire to bear responsibility for every drawback. It is such people, and not necessarily those blessed with talent, that I sought when I established *Davar*, and it is such that I require in Am Oved.[24]

Berl demanded absolute loyalty. He was particularly pained by the fact that some of the contributors to *Davar* and Am Oved published their best works in other journals under other imprints. He wanted total dedication; he wanted proud and independent writers who, at the same time, would commit themselves wholly to the project. He both loved and was irritated by those who refused to submit. The practical outcome was that Berl was forced to work with second-rate people, in whom he found the loyalty which the more talented withheld from him.

These 'lesser souls' oscillated between adoration and constant frustration. They recognized Berl's greatness, his unquestioned talent, his literary taste, his rare knowledge, subtlety and unflagging ability to dedicate himself to a task. At the same time he aroused their resistance and rebellion. These emotions were sometimes the outcome of the struggle of writers who wanted to preserve their own personality and unique qualities but found themselves swept away by him. Many of those who submitted to him found themselves rejected at times: when Berl was absorbed in a project, he paid scant attention to the niceties of human relations. He was impervious to the feelings of those who worked in close proximity with him day after day. Personal indebtedness was not important to him when he came to select his companions in some creative endeavor. He offended people and was not aware of having done so. When the *Davar* staff informed him that they had been hurt by the fact that for a whole year he had run the Am Oved publishing house in the *Davar* offices, and yet bypassed many of his lifelong colleagues from the paper, he treated their complaints as a sign of their aging, an indication that his contemporaries were now hungry for prestige and honor, whereas formerly they had placed the good of the cause above everything else. It is possible that he disregarded them because he was engaged in a race against time; the same patience and etiquette which in former years had concealed his true impatience with those who no longer interested him, now fell away because of his eagerness to make haste and carry out his plans while there was still time.

In its first year, Am Oved published 36 books. It launched a subscription campaign and acquired 9,000 subscribers for the la-Dor and Shaharut libraries. In 1942–1943, some 150,000 copies of books were distributed. There were then 450,000 Jews in the Yishuv; this figure speaks for itself. Am Oved's was a success unparalleled by any other Hebrew publishing house. The books were sold throughout Palestine, sent to Palestinian soldiers in the Western Desert and in Europe and to he-Halutz emissaries abroad. Aliyah Bet agents in Constantinople, who were trying to maintain contact with the Jews of the Balkans, smuggled the books across borders. Copies were sent to Ben Gurion working in the U.S.A. on the Biltmore Program, to Hagana men and Lehi ('Stern Group') prisoners in Acre jail and elsewhere. Years later, Nathan Yelin-Mor, one of the Lehi leaders, recalled the encouraging and friendly response of the Am Oved editor to an appeal from Lehi prisoners for books – a response which contrasted sharply with the Yishuv's hostile attitude towards them. Am Oved ended its first year of activity with a profit of £3,000 (Palestinian), a respectable sum in those days. As he toured the country, Berl knew the heady taste of success: wherever he went he was congratulated on the success of his project. And he, who ostensibly was unmoved by public opinion, was now deeply gratified. This was the sole sphere where he found satisfaction in those difficult years.

The bitter years

These were in fact bitter years. His illness, which was becoming more severe, forced him to retire from active life for months at a time. Lying in bed at Arza, in Jerusalem, or at his home in Ramat Gan, he corrected manuscripts, wrote introductions and made footnotes. Sara Zayit came to visit him often. The ties between them had grown closer: she took the minutes at Am Oved meetings, and to her he entrusted letters which he wanted to pigeonhole until the right occasion presented itself. At the same time, he reverted to romantic nostalgia for his distant past.

As the young generation moved away from him and towards Tabenkin,

he immured himself in the conviction that this was not his generation,
nor was this his time. As he returned to memories of the Second Aliyah
and its heroes, he was, as usual, excessively harsh with himself. The
unattainable ideal of himself which was ever before his eyes was the
leader by grace, holding sway over the souls of his followers. The truth
was, of course, that he still exerted influence over young and old,
friends and foes, simple people and public leaders.

The cycles of depression and elation which affected him were caused
by physiological processes as well as by external events, though it is difficult to establish the extent to which his illness was responsible for the
gloom which was his constant companion in his later years. At the same
time, there were certain circumstances which intensified his misery and
his seclusion – above all, the news from Europe. At a very early stage,
and well before his fellow-leaders, he sensed the coming Holocaust. It
will be recalled that at the World Union Council at Ayanot in 1940, he
spoke in terms of total destruction, of a Rubicon, of the end of a chapter for Eastern European Jewry. There lingered in his mind a sketch he
had read, containing a conversation between some women in the
marketplace, in which one old woman said: 'It's not good that the
blessed Lord is lingering and not sending us the Messiah! What will
happen if the Messiah comes, and finds none of his Jews left?'[25] Berl did
not doubt that the Nazis intended to execute their extermination
scheme. At the Histadrut conference on 19 April 1942 he recalled the
remark of one of the leaders of the Reich that the sole solution for the
Jewish problem was the graveyard, and added: 'And they mean what
they say.'[26] Before 1943, the Zionist and Yishuv leaderships tended to
regard events in Eastern Europe in terms of the First World War:
hunger, epidemics, deprivation, humiliation, refugees and pogrom-
scale slaughter. Not so Berl. He was haunted by the feeling that the
Jewish people was being wiped out, that they would no longer exist
when the war ended: 'Will we have the perseverance to reach the
end?'[27] he asked. His dread that redemption would come 'to a world
which has become a graveyard for the Children of Israel'[28] never left
him. Even later, when the dimensions of the catastrophe and its
significance were common knowledge, Berl remained unique in his
awareness. Yoel Palgi, one of the parachutists sent from Palestine to
establish contact with the besieged Jewish communities, described the
meeting of the parachutists on the eve of their departure with 'the people
who were the symbol of our chosen course'. To the young men and

women who asked what their assignment was, Eliyahu Golomb answered: 'to teach the Jews to fight'; Ben Gurion answered: 'that Jews should realize that Palestine is their country and their fortress'; 'Save Jews', said Berl. 'All the rest will come later. If no Jews remain, then Palestine and the Zionist endeavor will also be destroyed.'[29]

Berl did not talk much on this matter. It seems to have been too painful a subject to discuss in the old worn phrases used for times of trouble. He seemed to carry the burden of Jewish suffering, the torment of human beings, as sharply and vividly as if he were himself experiencing it. His wanderings as a boy in the Pale of Settlement and his encounter with the degradation of Jewish life in the alleyways of Jewish Vilna, had generated a Zionism inspired by profound pessimism as to the future of the Jewish people in the Diaspora. Now that his nightmares were coming true, he felt no surprise. And in this he differed from his colleagues, whose path to Zionism had been an easier one, illuminated by hope. They found it hard to digest the events in Europe, and blocked out knowledge even when the facts were blatantly obvious. It was hard to live with this reality. His merciless realism did not permit him to find respite from the horrors around him, and his total identification with the fate of the Jewish people burdened him with a sorrow and dread, which threatened to break him.

A bitter personal note was added to his grief. Yitzhak Katznelson, the poet and principal of the Hebrew high school in Lodz, and a relative of both Berl and Tabenkin, had been in Poland when war broke out. Berl learned that Yitzhak was in danger because of his public standing. For two years nothing more was known of the fate of Katznelson and his family. In June 1942 a rumor reached Palestine that he had safely arrived in Switzerland. Berl hastened to send him a congratulatory cable, but the report proved false. In November 1942, the first group of Holocaust survivors reached Palestine: women and children with Palestinian certificates, who had been exchanged for German civilians. For the first time the Yishuv and its leaders were confronted with living, first-hand, testimony of the extermination, its scope and the methodicalness with which it was being carried out. The women told of the death camps, and the deportations, facts which had been known before from telegraphic reports, stories and rumors, but rejected as war propaganda or the imaginings of people driven out of their wits by the horrors they had undergone. When one of the women described what she had witnessed during the years of Nazi occupation, Eliyahu Dobkin,

319

member of the Jewish Agency Executive, tried to calm her, and said: 'You must be exaggerating. Perhaps it wasn't exactly like that. It can't be.' The woman rose, went over to Dobkin, and slapped him on both cheeks. Later Dobkin was to say that the slaps had opened his eyes and shown him the nightmarish reality. Berl had never for a moment doubted the veracity of the stories.

In August 1943 Berl was informed that Yitzhak Katznelson and his sole surviving son had acquired South American passports and been transferred to a civilian prisoners' camp at Vittel in France as enemy aliens. There was now some hope of saving him. Contact was established by letter through the Red Cross, in Geneva. Berl sent him regards, a letter and a parcel and apparently even received a letter from him. In early 1944 it appeared that the Rescue Committee in Geneva had succeeded in conveying a Palestinian passport to Katznelson and that he would be able to leave occupied Europe through one of the civilian exchanges. But in mid-1944 the Germans discovered that the alleged South American passports held by the prisoners were not recognized by the governments which were supposed to have issued them, and several months before the liberation of France they sent some of the Vittel detainees to death camps. Among them were Yitzhak Katznelson and his son. Shortly afterwards an exchange of civilians took place, and Ruth Adler, who had been incarcerated at Vittel with Katznelson, arrived in Palestine. The poet had entrusted his writings to her, and she brought them with her, concealed in the handle of a suitcase. In the presence of the silent and distressed members of the family gathered at Berl's home, Ruth Adler produced the manuscripts. 'Only you and my cousin [Tabenkin]', wrote Yitzhak Katznelson to Berl, 'will read this elegy on the murder of our entire people, with its babes and children in their mothers' arms . . .'[30] The poet requested that this last elegy, 'The Song of the Murdered Jewish People', should be published only after the kingdom of evil had been vanquished from the face of the earth, and entrusted the execution of his literary legacy to his relatives, Berl and Tabenkin.

As on previous occasions, Berl was haunted by feelings of guilt. These emotions were apparently also fed by other, deeper wellsprings. He had seen with what detachment the Yishuv received the reports of the Holocaust, going on with their normal lives. Before the facts were confirmed, all knowledge of the Holocaust had been held at bay. When the radio reported world events, everyone listened attentively. When it turned to the plight of the Jews, attention wandered. 'The lack of attention to our people's suffering, the inability to face it is frightening', [31] he said.

Berl was not seeking outward manifestations of grief. He recalled the days following the death of his father: though he had felt something akin to relief at his death, his figure had visited him nightly in his dreams. But he had come to realize that the absence of outward grief did not necessarily conceal a deeper level of emotion; it rather reflected apathy and acquiescence, alienation and dismissal. Am Oved's special series Min ha-Moked (From the Flames) was devoted to the war and its horrors. The series on London during the Blitz was popular, but 'Letters from the Ghetto', containing 250 excerpts from letters from the Jewish underground, from he-Halutz behind the ghetto walls, were not in demand. 'I do not think', Berl deduced, 'that these terrible events, which we are all consciously aware of, are being experienced on the personal level, as part of our own destiny.'[32] The generation bred in Palestine identified with partisans, both Gentile and Jew, and with those who joined in the ghetto rising. They were discussed at length in the youth movements, admired and idealized. 'I fear', said Berl, 'that there may be a great falsehood involved here.'[33] A new tribe of Jews had emerged in Palestine, with qualities of their own, but lacking roots in the history of their people, strangers to the instinctive Jewish feeling that 'All Israel are responsible for one another.' These young people could relate to the 'disturbances', to the achievements of ha-Shomer and Trumpeldor, to the adventures of Wingate and the Night Squads. They could identify with the Hasmoneans or Bar Kochba. But not to the history of their people through two thousand years of exile, to the annals of Jewish trials and suffering, sacrifice and martyrdom. Their identification with the ghetto heroes relieved the guilt they felt at their revulsion from Jewish suffering in the ghetto. For Berl a tale of the martyrdom of the brother of the Gur Rabbi – who, in the death camp, asked for a little water, to enable his fellow-victims to wash their hands before setting out on their last journey – was more significant in his eyes as a Jew than the ghetto uprisings, and he recognized that Palestinian youth understood neither the doer nor the deed 'because we do not experience the Jewish world, because we are different'.[34]

Berl did not absolve himself of responsibility for this alienation. As the mentor of the movement, who had left his indelible stamp on its consciousness through lectures, seminars and talks, he had shared in

321

creating it. The denial of the Diaspora, which implied, on the one hand, rejection of the Jewish way of life in the Diaspora, and, on the other, denial of the possibility of the continued existence of the Jewish people there, was one of the underlying tenets of Zionism. It had, however, been interpreted by both teachers and students as a rejection of the *Jewish people* in the Diaspora, thus, inevitably enhancing the specific value of the new tribe growing up in Palestine. This had not been the intention of the Second Aliyah teachers. In their revolt against their own past, their home towns and villages had appeared to them as the epitome of ugliness and degradation. They were well aware, however, that this was not the whole truth, and even while attacking their own background, they had remained inextricably bound to it, and through it to the fabric of Jewish life. The young generation in Palestine did not regard their origins in the same fashion. Their associations lacked the existential dimension, absorbed with mother's milk, with Sabbath and festival rituals, with the dread of pogroms, with the grief which followed in their wake. For them, identification was an intellectual process, in the course of which the Jewish people was weighed and found wanting. For the young the Diaspora was everything against which their parents had rebelled. The denial of the Diaspora in Berl's generation implied the duty to rescue the Jewish people; for young people bred in Palestine it meant the severing of the link binding them to the Jewish people and to Jewish history. In his twilight years Berl witnessed the utter failure of the education of 'the children of Zionism'. The estrangement between the new Jewish people in Palestine and the suffering Jewish people elsewhere was a constant reminder to him of his own failure.

This sense of culpability may have helped him to suppress a more profound and burdensome guilt: a year after Berl's death, Rabbi Benyamin published an article in which he took issue with Berl as if he were still among the living. Berl, he said, had not devoted his energies in troubled times to rescuing Jews. Instead, he had dedicated himself to his publishing house. This critique aroused a storm of protest, since he was attacking a dead man, unable to defend himself. But the question remains: Why was Berl not more active in initiating rescue operations?

He could not hide behind the excuse that he was not aware of what was happening. Some of the things he said confirm his great sensitivity and intuitive understanding. His sensibility was that of a poet rather than of a political leader, and yet he did nothing. Of Ben Gurion it may be said that he was occupied with political work, which he regarded at the time as the crux of Zionist action, and had no time or energy for rescue work. Ben Gurion also lacked the warm human qualities which were universally acknowledged in Berl. Hence it is not surprising that Ben Gurion was able to shut himself off from events in Europe and to continue his exertions for the establishment of a Jewish state. But Berl was not engaged in any vital political task, and was certainly incapable of ignoring Jewish suffering. Perhaps common sense told him that there were no ways of action open to him. But he was never a cold-blooded realist, measuring his actions on the basis of profit and loss, and had often undertaken tasks which seemed hopeless. Anyone acquainted with Berl's past history might have expected him to summon a select few colleagues, ensure that they were free of other obligations and persuade them to put together an unconventional organization for rescue work, untrammeled by party and policy considerations, or problems of legality. But the man who was capable of galvanizing his movement into action through a series of articles in the press, did not protest against 'things as they were' with regard to the rescue of Jews. Berl's silence on the Holocaust was almost total. This is a puzzling question, and will probably remain so, since neither Berl nor any of his close associates ever explained it.

On 4 August 1942 Berl wrote to Ben Gurion about Am Oved. His letter opened with the words: 'David, you may laugh at me: of what do I write to you at this time (from this you may learn what remains to me in our community life).'[35] This may be the key to Berl's actions and omissions during the war years. He was above all a man of the movement. His capacity for action was conditional on the reciprocal ties between him and the movement. The bitter polemics within Mapai had deprived him of the ability to act and to impel others to act: 'To see all that is most dear to me disgraced and to know that I am unable to help.'[36] He saw himself as a leader without followers, and found refuge in Am Oved, shutting himself up with his books and manuscripts. Thus weighed down by a sense of isolation, he was unable to summon up the reserves of energy and stamina required for effective action.

October and November 1942 were fateful months. The British Eighth Army was rallying in the Western Desert under Montgomery for a counter-attack on Rommel at El-Alamein, and the German forces, massed on the threshold of Palestine, were defeated. The threat of annihilation was averted. At that very time, just as Montgomery's forces were going into battle, the third session of the Fifth Mapai Conference was held at Kfar Vitkin (25–29 October 1942). The Mapai elders later reckoned the split in Mapai from that conference, although the official split occurred only in 1944. From the point of view of historical veracity, as distinct from chronology, they were correct, since the patterns of future developments were established at Kfar Vitkin.

The turning-point had been the election campaign to the fifth Histadrut Conference, in December 1941. The attempt to unite the party and to consolidate it for the struggle to maintain hegemony in the Histadrut inevitably exacerbated the differences which were to find expression at the Kfar Vitkin conference. Mapai feared the elections because of ha-Shomer ha-Tzair's participation as the 'Socialist League', a Zionist-constructivist left-wing party, which was likely to win the support of many of the new voters who had joined the Histadrut. In anticipation of the elections, therefore, the Mapai leaders tried to rally all their supports, and to this end arrived at an agreement with the opposition within. Ha-Kibbutz ha-Meuhad was promised a third of the seats won by Mapai in all Histadrut institutions. This decision was taken in the knowledge that the party had no choice but to reconcile itself to the fact that it was a federative body. Official sanction was thus given to a situation which had long existed but had never been so openly and decisively acknowledged. Sectoral affiliation was recognized as the key to personal and political loyalties.

The Histadrut election results were highly satisfactory for all active party workers: Mapai won more than two-thirds of the votes (61,128 out of 88,198). Ha-Kibbutz ha-Meuhad regarded itself as a major partner in the achievement and demanded the promised third of Mapai seats on the Executive Secretariat, a fair share in running the Tel Aviv and Haifa labor councils, and other Histadrut institutions, such as the contracting office, and Hevrat ha-Ovdim. A six-man committee drafted an agreement, according to which at least one representative of Faction B would serve on the management of each central Histadrut body. But if the Mapai leaders had hoped that these concessions would reunite the party, they were sadly mistaken: several days after the Histadrut conference, Faction B emerged as an independent group, holding its own national convention.

Berl was not active in the party, although he delivered the keynote address at the Histadrut conference and infuriated the left wing of the

Histadrut, which had gone all out in defense of orientation on the Soviet Union and 'the forces of tomorrow', against Great Britain and the feeble 'formal' democracies. His speech was a work of art, the credo of a proud Palestinian socialist, fighting to preserve the singular character of his movement from the tidal wave of Soviet idolatry which had engulfed large sectors of the party in the wake of Stalingrad. For many, support of the Soviet Union, which was battling desperately against the Nazis, was a basic tenet of faith. Berl mocked their belief that the U.S.S.R. would change its position with regard to Zionism. His remarks did not enhance his prestige in the eyes of his fellow party-members from Faction B and the young generation. More than twenty years before, during the First World War, Berl had made a similar keynote address and though his remarks had been somewhat vague, high-flown and complex, his audience had heard him out with bated breath. Now his remarks were crystal clear and precisely phrased – and they fell on deaf ears.

Life within the party had become intolerable. The dispute among the Mapai representatives on the executive of the Tel Aviv labor council had flared up again, and now the catch in the agreement on the seat allocation came to light: in a vote taken on an issue related to the contracting office, Faction B representatives voted with the Socialist League and Left Poalei Zion, and Mapai found itself in the minority. Mapai representatives on Histadrut institutions could not be deposed between elections, and hence Faction B could constantly obstruct party resolutions in Histadrut institutions. The party leadership was powerless when faced with a minority which voted as the spirit moved it. As Faction B crystallized as a separate entity, it began to unravel the ties which bound it to the party. Its relations with the Mapai majority came increasingly to resemble relations between two rival parties – without the customary courtesies observed between strangers and waived between close associates.

The composition of the emerging country-wide Faction B was not really clear-cut. Not all members of ha-Kibbutz ha-Meuhad joined the Faction. First of all, those who had supported merging the kibbutz movements and regarded Berl as their leader, maintained their earlier position. Secondly, not even all ha-Kibbutz ha-Meuhad members who supported their leadership were enthusiastic at the idea of an alliance with the urban workers and many apparently hesitated to join. The urban Faction had nothing to lose in a life-and-death struggle, and a split could only enhance their standing and prestige in any new party. The Kibbutz, on the other hand, a complex social and economic structure, burdened with assets and obligations, would be rent internally by any shock to the party. And since many of their members represented the party in the Histadrut, the Hagana, Aliyah Bet, and other national institutions, a split from Mapai could have far-reaching implications for them.

Tabenkin feared the schism more than others. Although he did not join Faction B he was not indifferent to the fact that it provided an outlet for previously unrepresented sectors of the urban working class. Although their style was alien to him, he recognized their right to self-expression. But as schism became more likely, Tabenkin sought a way out. For him, it would mean a rift with the people with whom he had worked to build the Palestinian labor movement, a lifelong alliance, born in Poland and consolidated in the days of Ahdut ha-Avoda and the Histadrut. And despite recurring periods of controversy and estrangement, the bonds were still strong. True, Tabenkin was not ready to transform ha-Kibbutz ha-Meuhad to Berl's conception of the kibbutz. He wanted to maintain it as an economic, spiritual, social, and certainly political, movement, cohering around a central leadership. On the other hand, he wanted to remain in Mapai and a split seemed to him an act of lunacy, unjustified from the Zionist and socialist viewpoints.

In early October 1942 Ben Gurion returned to Palestine. Only two weeks before, Berl had written in his diary: 'I am weary to death of meetings.'[37] Now he suddenly enjoyed an upsurge of energy, and began to travel the country and organize meetings with people from the Moshav Organization, Hever ha-Kvutzot, the youth movement and the opposition members within ha-Kibbutz ha-Meuhad, grouped around Kibbutz Afikim. On 23 October 1942 Berl, Ben Gurion and Golomb, Meirov and Shertok went to Haifa for a last pre-conference talk with ha-Kibbutz ha-Meuhad representatives: Yitzhak Tabenkin, Berl Repetur, and Aharon Zisling, veterans of the Jewish Battalions and Ahdut ha-Avoda; Israel Galili, the 'junior' member of the leadership; and Batsheva Haikin, a heroine of the socialist Zionist underground in the Soviet Union, a wise and cautious woman, the only representative of the Fourth Aliyah. No former members of ha-Poel ha-Tzair were invited to the fateful meeting – they sat on the sidelines, witnessing the self-destruction of the former Ahdut ha-Avoda leaders. The ten who met in Haifa were all activists, and maximalist Zionists: in their constant thirst for action and fervor they were alike. Yet the greater the similarities, the wider the gap between them. 'In personal relations we have come up against a blank wall. We neither listen to one another nor understand each other', was Shaul Meirov's observation. Ben Gurion presented an ultimatum: either Faction B accept party authority and disband, or the conference would end in a split. There was a full fifteen minutes of silence, followed by a painful discussion, reflecting the communications breakdown between the participants. Tabenkin enumerated the instances in which he had felt that the party was discriminating against him, rendering him ineffective. He read Ben Gurion's ultimatum as a demand for the dissolution of ha-Kibbutz ha-Meuhad, and responded to it with counter-accusations. Yet when he concluded, it was in dread: 'I am terrified of a split . . . I don't know what to do. What will become of me? It is the degeneration of the entire movement.'[38] Although old political scores were broached in the course of the discussions, a sincere effort was made to re-establish lines of communication and arrive at a useful dialog. Old friendship and mutual esteem were not easily effaced. But Galili, the last of the Kibbutz participants to speak, was not of the 'old guard' and he made it abundantly clear that any hopes that the Kibbutz would be a partner to abolishing the Faction were ill-conceived. The last speaker, as usual, was Berl. Although he had promised not to rake up old accounts, he did not keep his word. A remark of Tabenkin's implying that he was 'a dictator in the party' had wounded Berl deeply. Unlike Ben Gurion, he did not try to tone down the points of contention. There were fundamental differences between them on socialism, on the nature of relations between the working class and the people as a whole, and on their conception of the kibbutz and of the kibbutz movement. At times it seemed that he was addressing Tabenkin over the heads of the others in a bitter and trenchant rejoinder. Yet, withal, there were undertones of sorrow, even despair, in his remarks. The discussion continued till four in the morning but it was, ultimately, a dialog between two deaf people.

The Kfar Vitkin conference was decisive and yet inconclusive: on the one hand, a formal resolution was passed abolishing factions in the party and emphatically stating the obligation of every member to accept party discipline. Statutes were drawn up, detailing the nature of the member's affiliation to the party and the punitive measures to be enforced in case of obduracy. On the other hand, no explicit mention was made of Faction B. Members of the Faction were present at the discussions, as delegates to the conference, as the majority heaped abuse on them and called for an end to factionalism. However, in accordance with their previous decision, they took no part in the proceedings. At the conclusion of the conference, Zisling read out a statement on behalf of the Faction which merely added fuel to the fire. He presented his Faction as a persecuted minority. The majority had done everything possible to undermine the Faction's standing and to prevent it from ever prevailing in the party. 'We refuse to live as forced converts in the party', he declared. 'You cannot repress or fetter us with statutes or with the threat of Bolshevization. We will fight for living space, for the right to grow . . .' One particular remark of his was not forgiven or forgotten for many years: 'I want to say to you: Mapai will not survive without us. Mapai can exist only with us.'[39] The arrogance displayed by ha-Kibbutz ha-Meuhad was regarded as a searing insult, and Ben Gurion responded two weeks later: 'There are two traits which characterize Faction B today: they are at once the self-righteous elect and the harassed victims.'[40]

Despite the verbal pyrotechnics, Faction B averted a final break. Although they rejected the majority resolutions, specifically the abolishing of factions, and refused to serve on the party institutions subsequently set up, they continued to insist that they subscribed to the unity of the labor movement and were part of the party. Their reasoning was not hard to fathom. Were they to split the party, Ben Gurion would carry out his threat to split ha-Kibbutz ha-Meuhad, a threat he was eminently capable of carrying out.

An uneasy truce prevailed in 1943: the countrywide Faction B was consolidated and showed signs of independence, though it continued to observe its formal affiliation to the party. What began as a refusal to take part in the Kfar Vitkin proceedings, continued as a policy of non-cooperation in party life, in the hope, as Zisling put it, of paralyzing the party. But they were proved wrong. The party Secretariat elected at Kfar Vitkin began, at the initiative of Ben Gurion and Berl – who for the first time since 1938 returned to active party work – to reorganize the party.

In anticipation of the split, Ben Gurion dedicated his energies to enlarging the party membership through the formal registration of previously unaffiliated supporters. His plan was to call a conference of these non-party people who would join the party *en bloc* and provide it with a broad enough public backing to offset any possible secession.

Even if the split did not occur – this bloc would still tip the balance in favor of Ben Gurion and Berl. Ben Gurion wanted to prove to the Faction leaders that he was determined to annihilate them as a separate body in the party even at the cost of a split. And, indeed, during the year following the Kfar Vitkin conference, 1,400 new members swelled the ranks of the party.

Party activity was conducted at the expense of the Histadrut, where Faction B exercised its veto in collaboration with ha-Shomer ha-Tzair and Left Poalei Zion. Important questions were gradually transferred from the Histadrut Executive to the party center. Ben-Gurion's intentions were clear to Tabenkin and his comrades – but they were powerless to do anything about it. Tabenkin expressed his feelings when he said: 'There is no way out for me.'[41] In the prevailing situation, he could see no objective reason – social, economic or ideological – for dividing the party in two – into a reformist and revolutionary party. 'There is no comparison', he said, 'between a split at a decisive function, a split which is historically inevitable, and a split at the core of a people and a class which has not yet been fully formed.'[42] Tabenkin realized that his influence was greater inside the party than outside it: within the party, he and ha-Kibbutz ha-Meuhad could mobilize close to half the votes. But outside, he would be isolated, cut off from potential supporters, sources of manpower and funds. He did not feel himself at liberty, however, to act on the basis of his own inclinations. It was his young comrades who pressed for a decision: either a return to full activity in the party, or a total rift. Under pressure from Faction B in Tel Aviv, Tabenkin appeared to feel that he had lost control of the situation, that he had become enmeshed in a pattern of relations which had created its own momentum, and was dragging him unwillingly towards schism.

Ben Gurion and Berl did not share Tabenkin's perplexity. Despite their differences, both seemed to have concluded, by the second half of 1943, that there was no avoiding a rift. Neither of them was happy at the thought, but as long as Faction B would neither accept the majority resolutions nor disband, the party could not function effectively. Berl did not play an active part in forcing the issue: he, who had united the labor movement, found it highly painful to take the decision to split it. But his capacity for facing facts, however unpalatable, prevented him from deluding himself with hopes of reconciliation. Like Tabenkin, he did not perceive the rift as the necessary outcome of ideological or political differences, and again like Tabenkin, he was pained at the

329

thought of the loss to the movement as a result of fraternal strife. He had realized as early as 1938, like Tabenkin in 1943, that the ship was about to founder and that he was powerless to rescue it. The bitter sensation of being helplessly swept towards a yawning chasm, as a result of a political-psychological process which was gradually widening the breach between close associates, was shared by both men. Although he knew that there was no way back, he could not bring himself to offer active support to Ben Gurion in his activity. But Ben Gurion, having come to a decision, acted forcefully. 'In my heart I have taken the decision', he said at a meeting of his party's Central Committee on 23 September 1943.

The next problem was tactical. Neither side wanted to appear responsible for inflicting the *coup de grâce*. The myth of unity was, after all, still sacrosanct. Ben Gurion, in consultation with Berl, drew up the following plan: he demanded that elections be held to the Histadrut conference. This would place Faction B in a quandary, since if it remained in the party and failed to appear as a separate list in the elections, it would lose a large proportion of its representatives in the Histadrut institutions. If it chose to secede from the party, it would be clear to all that they were responsible for the split. Concomitantly, Ben Gurion organized his conference of the former non-affiliated party supporters.

The Mapai Council was convened in Jerusalem on January 1944, in order to endorse this far-reaching step. On the eve of the meeting, Yitzhak Tabenkin visited Berl. At first they spoke of their mutual relative, Yitzhak Katznelson, and then turned to party matters. 'Woe to our old age which is shaming our youth',[43] wrote Berl in the wake of this conversation, recalling the sentence with which he had concluded his letter to Tabenkin on the 'hidden book'.

Berl attended the Council meeting in Jerusalem with the feeling that the fate of the party had been sealed, but there was still life in the party: at the last moment most of the members drew back, and asked for one more chance to attempt to reconcile the differences. A committee of 'elders' was set up, consisting of the Second Aliyah stalwarts, augmented by Israel Idelson, and with Yosef Sprinzak, former member of ha-Poel ha-Tzair, as mediator. At the first meeting of the committee it appeared that the torn threads could be rewoven and that the old camaraderie had been revived. Tabenkin had proposed the gradual abolition of Faction B within a given period of time; that in the meantime Faction B members renew their activity in the party; that the pre-Kfar Vitkin status –

the famous one-third allocation – would be restored, and efforts made to arrive at federative union with ha-Shomer ha-Tzair. But when the committee convened for a second time in March, Tabenkin seemed to have retreated from his basic willingness to disband the Faction, probably under pressure from his comrades.

Berl said little during these long meetings. He had no illusions and very little hope that verbal maneuvering could alter a process which was by now beyond control. He was firmly resolved to abolish the Faction – at any cost. 'I am willing to concede on any issue, but the abolition of the factions must be the basic tenet of any negotiations',[44] he stated. In the course of the discussions held between the party council in Jerusalem in January and its continuation in March, he fully backed Ben Gurion's efforts to convene the non-affiliated supporters.

In mid-January the Kibbutz ha-Meuhad conference was held at Kibbutz Givat Brenner, on a conciliatory note. Berl met with ha-Kibbutz ha-Meuhad's opposition group on the eve of the conference, but maintained silence during the sessions. A critical speech, he feared, would be interpreted as an attempt to torpedo the negotiations of the Committee of 'elders', and he could not bring himself to deliver any 'heartfelt greetings'. Guests at the conference were struck by Ben Gurion's creative vigor and Bel's torpor. Ben Gurion was on the platform in high spirits; Berl huddled in one of the back rows, looking suddenly old.

While at Givat Brenner, Berl met a young girl of whom he wrote in his diary: 'With Hanna from Caesaria, who is leaving on a dangerous mission.'[45] This was his only meeting with Hanna Senesh before she was parachuted into Hungary, a mission from which she never returned. He attended an arts exhibition at the kibbutz and spent time with Sara Zayit, who had accompanied him to the conference. His silence reflected his despair: the time had passed when Berl could sway people by the force of his words and personality. The positions were now predetermined, and there was no bridge between the two camps.

The blow-up occurred at the Histadrut Executive meeting on 23 February 1944. The subject on the agenda was a proposal to send a Histadrut delegation to the T.U.C. conference, due to convene in London in summer 1944. Opinions were divided on the political program the delegation was to present. Mapai proposed an identical platform to that decided on at Kfar Vitkin, including the Biltmore Program, which

331

demanded that the gates of Palestine be opened for free immigration and that the Jewish Agency be granted jurisdiction over immigration, the development of the country and its consolidation as a Jewish 'commonwealth'. Ha-Shomer ha-Tzair objected to the Biltmore Program on the grounds that the proposed plan did not include a solution to the Arab problem, while it advocated an independent Jewish state. Tabenkin was also against the Biltmore Program and offered counter-proposals, calling for an international mandate over Palestine (see below). When the members reassembled, after an interval in the discussions, it transpired that consultations had been held between Faction B, ha-Shomer ha-Tzair and Left Poalei Zion, and that the three bodies were presenting a joint draft proposal. This proposal omitted the Jewish state in the Mapai proposal and watered down all the demands relating to the future standing of the Jewish Agency. A vote was taken, and the result was 21 for the draft proposal of the three bodies, and only 24 for the Mapai proposal (actually identical with the program of the Zionist Executive). This was a blow for Ben Gurion, as it was now publicly evident that his own movement did not accept the political line he had formulated. Furthermore, while ostensibly negotiating for return to full and loyal activity in the party, Faction B had conspired with the minority parties in the Histadrut to sabotage Mapai's proposal and infringe party solidarity. This was the last straw.

Years later it was claimed that the Biltmore Program was the basic cause of the split: Tabenkin was vehemently opposed to partition, which he believed the Biltmore Program would further (this was in fact what happened); as a result, he was driven to the extreme step of making an alliance with ha-Shomer ha-Tzair in order to foil it. The view of Palestine as one, indivisible country was undoubtedly the fundamental principle in Tabenkin's Zionist philosophy. At the same time, it is questionable whether this was in fact the issue which led to the rift.

Contemporary sources, which are both abundant and detailed, do not confirm this hypothesis. After attending the St James's Palace Conference (1939), Berl, it will be recalled, had concluded that Great Britain did not intend to honor its obligations under the Mandate and could not be forced to do so. Thus, it was essential to adopt a maximalistic Jewish policy, which could serve as the focus for the consolidation of Jewish political forces in Palestine and abroad, and emphatically voice Jewish demands *vis-à-vis* Palestine. Speaking at Ayanot on the war objectives of the Jewish people, Berl had openly advocated a Jewish state, and his remarks had been accepted without question by ha-Kibbutz ha-Meuhad. Berl cast his whole weight in support of Ben Gurion in his battle to obtain the support of the Zionist movement for the Biltmore Program, which was essentially identical with his demands. In November, 1942, a few days before confirmation was received of the dimensions of the Holocaust, a session of the Inner Zionist Actions Committee was held in Jerusalem, and Ben Gurion requested that the Zionist Organization approve his plan. His main opponent was Meir Yaari, the leader of ha-Shomer ha-Tzair. As against Ben Gurion's vision of mass immigration (two million Jews within two years), Yaari called for a more realistic approach, which, he felt, required a continuation of the slow pace of settlement and particularly of selective immigration. As for the desperate Jewish war refugees, uprooted from their former homes, he proposed that they be returned to their countries of origin; the mass immigration of broken human beings – he claimed – would be a catastrophe for the Yishuv. Jewish immigration should be planned for a period of 10–15 years, and meanwhile Jews should be 'repatriated' to Poland. Yaari also expressed his opposition to the independent Jewish state called for in the Biltmore Program, which would entail ruling over Arabs or transferring them from Palestine. This question, which had not, in fact, been seriously studied by the Zionist Actions Committee, was of vital concern to ha-Shomer ha-Tzair. Yaari broached the idea of a bi-national state in Palestine and the surrounding countries under international supervision. The practical implication of his proposal was the postponement of an independent Jewish state. Berl responded to these proposals with trenchant and biting sarcasm. Referring to the idea of selective immigration and repatriation he retorted: 'It is said that there is another program: repatriation, that they should be sent to a health spa. Poland will be their spa; there they will convalesce, and then we will begin to prepare them for Zionism.' And he added, 'I could perhaps understand these remarks, if they had been made by Zionists from these countries which the war has not touched, who see the Zionist problem in other ways, who have not experienced pogroms. But when this is said by a pioneer, who had traveled this road – what has happened here?' As for the Arab problem, he sharpened the issue: 'It is possible', he said, 'that the desire to be the majority in a country which already has a national majority is morally reprehensible, and that therefore we are to be deplored. But Yaari has confessed that he too harbors this idea.' Hence he too was not to be absolved of the thought of dominating the Arabs. And as for the claim that the idea of a Jewish state smacked of utopianism – it was no more utopian, said Berl, than the idea of a bi-national state. There was no guarantee of either. When the Jewish people expressed the desire for a state, it was proclaiming its own aspirations, while bi-nationalism called for partners, and the prospective partners had shown no eagerness to join in: 'I would like to ask all good Zionists', he said, 'not to try to sell us goods which are not their own.'

As for the main issue, the formulation of post-war Jewish demands, Berl welcomed the Biltmore Program, although he considered it late in coming: 'In every war victory has been preceded by a clear statement, the raising of a standard, an expression of the wishes of the people.' In the aftermath of war, the status quo is disturbed, 'the heavens open up',[46] and the map of the world is redrawn. This is the moment to make great demands. He adhered to this view to the day of his death.

Never had Berl supported Ben Gurion and his policy as emphatically as he did in 1942–4. As Berl became increasingly aware of his own weaknesses, he came to respect in Ben Gurion those qualities he himself lacked, namely his iron resolve and tenacity in carrying out his plans. Berl could still restrain Ben Gurion when his ardor swept him beyond what Berl considered practical. But now, more than ever before, he saw Ben Gurion as history's gift to the Jewish people, the man who was destined to bring the Jewish state into being.

Like Ben Gurion, Berl wanted the Biltmore Program to become the manifesto around which the great majority of the Jewish people would rally. But unlike him he was not anathema to the opponents of partition, who still trusted him. Berl's support for the program rendered it acceptable to many people, including the opposition group in ha-Kibbutz ha-Meuhad. Berl did everything possible to ensure that the Biltmore Program would not be identified with partition. In this he was trying to achieve a twofold aim: he did not want the proponents of an independent Jewish state to be divided into supporters and opponents of partition. On the other hand, as negotiations were at hand, he carefully avoided formulating objectives which the Zionist movement would consider minimalistic. His approach remained pragmatic: 'Not one of us', he said, 'has proclaimed that his political stands are immutable.' But he had argued consistently since 1937 that if the Jews adopted 'partition' as their slogan, they might be maneuvered in negotiations into accepting a state as defined by Woodhead, perhaps even without absolute sovereignty. He therefore urged the Zionist Actions Committee to instruct the Zionist Executive to 'prevent the possibility of talk on our part of partition'.[47]

Comparison of the views of Berl and Tabenkin on political questions reveals an amazing similarity: Tabenkin was an enthusiastic advocate of mass immigration, and was not deterred by the prospect of the influx of millions of Jewish refugees into Palestine. Ha-Shomer ha-Tzair had argued that the immediate transfer of half a million Jews was identical with the old Revisionist scheme and was a fascist scheme. Tabenkin reminded ha-Shomer ha-Tzair that the workers' delegation to the 1920 London conference had also welcomed such a plan: 'Why is the transfer of half a million Jews fascism?' he asked them. Tabenkin also disagreed with ha-Shomer ha-Tzair's assumption that the demand for Jewish rule over Palestine was neither just nor feasible: 'It is possible and it is just,' he said. He rebelled against the concept of a bi-national state with every fiber of his being. Making his last speech as a member of Mapai, at the somber March 1944 Mapai Council, he noted: 'We never spoke of bi-nationalism.' And, half-jokingly, he confessed: 'I can't get my tongue round the words.'[48] Like Berl he felt that the main issue was not the Arab problem but the Jewish problem, and did not believe that the rivalry between the two nations could be overcome through successful phrasing. He too regarded the aim of a Jewish majority in the country as the focal point of the conflict, and assumed that the consolidation of a viable Jewish entity would eventually reconcile the Arabs to the situation. He welcomed the idea of a population transfer, as long as it was voluntary, and also cited the historical example of the transfer of Germans from the Volga provinces to Siberia during the War (he was apparently unware of what this transfer had involved). To these similarities should be added their common views on activism in immigration, settlement and defense activities.

There are those who claim that Tabenkin was able to cooperate with ha-Shomer ha-Tzair because of their common opposition to the Biltmore Program. This theory is questionable: the differences between Tabenkin and ha-Shomer ha-Tzair were infinitely more acute than his differences with Berl and Ben Gurion. It could be argued that the bi-national state was not yet an immediate prospect, and thus that there was still room for cooperation between ha-Shomer ha-Tzair and Tabenkin. However, one could say the same of the dispute on partition; this, too, was not yet on the cards but was only implied in the Biltmore

Program (which Berl did his best to gloss over). Tabenkin could easily have found the basis for joint political action with his fellow party-members, thus postponing the crisis. When the problem had been raised in 1937, Tabenkin and his associates had chosen to work for a joint resolution in order to avoid a schism. No similar effort was made in 1944. Moreover, the pro- and anti-partition camps in Mapai cut across Faction B *and* the majority: most of the Faction in Tel Aviv enthusiastically supported partition and the Biltmore Program. The opposition group in ha-Kibbutz ha-Meuhad, on the other hand, were ambivalent and tended to support Berl's complex stand. Tabenkin's prospects of establishing a serious opposition to partition were greater inside the party than outside it, and Tabenkin was aware of the facts even when his supporters tended to delude themselves.

A rift in the party was liable to weaken the activist camp, which Tabenkin wanted to bolster. The battle against the White Paper, Aliyah Bet, reinforcement of the Hagana, and so on, would suffer without Tabenkin's support for the Berl–Ben Gurion alignment against the moderates – Sprinzak, Eliezer Kaplan, Lubianiker, and the others. These open questions suggest that political issues were not the root of the dissension. Tabenkin and his comrades subsequently blamed it on political differences, since these were considered more 'respectable' reasons, than contests for power within the party. But this appears to have been *ex post facto* rationalization.

For Ben Gurion, the Biltmore Program and his ability to function as the leader of a consolidated party were inextricably bound up together. Since 1937 the struggle for a Jewish state had been the focus of Ben Gurion's life, and a disciplined party was vital for his functioning in the Zionist Executive. He paid scant attention to Tabenkin's ideologies but immediately took up arms when he discovered that party discipline was being undermined, and that he could no longer rely on the backing of party representatives in the Histadrut and the Zionist Executive. He did not see the party as a debating club, but as a militant body, in which organizational questions were of great moment. It was no accident that Ben Gurion styled the existence of factions within the party 'moral corruption'. Since most of the party members supported his stand, he regarded himself as the embodiment of the will of the party. Anyone who prevented him from running it in his own way, was eroding inner democracy, using organization ploys to hamstring the majority. It was this train of thought which provided Ben Gurion with the moral legitimization for splitting the party.

One of the problems which was not discussed at length during the deliberations, but frequently alluded to, was the attitude of Faction B to the Soviet Union. Ben Gurion, however, was not disturbed by the growing adulation of the U.S.S.R. as long as discipline was preserved. Berl, on the other hand, was afraid that the best of the young generation would be attracted to the alien ideal, but did nothing about it. Faction B, for their part, did not consider their attitude to the Soviet Union to be a reason for seceding from the party.

During the lengthy deliberations at the Jerusalem Council, the general feeling, then, was that there was no ideological basis for a split.

Modern psychosociologists would probably say that the arguments were attempts to rationalize instincts and urges beyond reason and beyond human control, a view which Berl shared. In the grievous months after the split, the last months of his life, he reiterated constantly his belief that the true causes of the split were concealed from his contemporaries. He wrote and spoke of a mental illness which had afflicted them. 'All the rational explanations', he said, 'explain nothing, if in the name of activism they secede from David [Ben Gurion] and in the name of family unity, they abandon me.'[49] He also rejected the division into 'left' and 'right' in the party, into 'democrats' and 'non-democrats'. Nor could he swallow the sociological theory that this was a generation struggle between 'fathers' and 'sons'. 'I myself tend to think that the true cause lies outside our field of vision', he explained. '*I do not think that in the historical sphere people have a clear perception of their progeny, and I do not think, that the arguments people proffer (and in which they believe) necessarily guide their actions* [present author's italics] . . . It is possible that it is not we who choose positions, but they which choose us and force themselves on us.'[50] Thus Berl came full circle. Outwardly, since the mid-1920s, he had been the symbol of a rational leader seeking a firm practical basis for all his convictions. His strength lay in his lucid mind and considered opinions. But underneath, Berl had remained the loyal disciple of Berdichevsky, who believed that irrational, hidden and uncontrollable instincts were the true arbiters of human action. Towards the end of his life, he came to see man as the plaything of unconscious drives. This was a pessimistic outlook, in total contrast to his fervent belief (here again inspired by Berdichevsky) in human will-power, creativity, voluntarism. There is an analogy here with Freud's 'death wish': whereas 'unity' reflects the optimism of youth and the belief in the triumph of the forces of light and of life over the forces of destruction, the split represents the triumph of the self-destructive urge over the creative force. Having rejected historical determinism all his life, Berl in his twilight years arrived at an outlook which could be described as psychological determinism.

It is interesting to note that throughout the entire controversy, Berl ignored Faction B in Tel Aviv, focusing his attention exclusively on ha-Kibbutz ha-Meuhad. Without dwelling on the objective importance of the faction, one can state emphatically that the Mapai leadership, as reflected by Ben Gurion and Berl, attributed no importance whatsoever to the Tel Aviv group. It regarded the Kibbutz leadership as the focal point of the problem, both because of its power of influence in the party struggle and the quality of its people. The discussions in early 1944 were held almost wholly between the leaders of ha-Kibbutz ha-Meuhad and the Mapai leaders. Faction B may have acted behind the scenes to stiffen the resistance of the Kibbutz representatives, but they were not granted the privilege of attending the various discussions of the 'elders'.

In spring and summer 1944 Berl fought a desperate battle for the hearts and minds of the younger generation. His health was deteriorating, and between periods of rest and recuperation, treatments and tests, he attended the party seminar at Rutenberg House in Haifa, and delivered his last great series of lectures on the history of the labor movement. There was a sorry contrast between the Berl of 1928, who had lectured to the 'Socialist Youth' on the Second Aliyah with abundant confidence on the road of an increasingly-united Palestinian labor movement, and the ailing skeptic whose disrupted movement had gone off course. His subject was the international labor movement since the beginning of the century, but in fact he spoke of the history of his own movement, contrasting the iron conviction which had characterized it at the outset, when its leaders believed that the socialist revolution was inevitable, with the disappointing historical developments, which had shown that fascism was a possible alternative. He concluded:

One lesson should be learned: that in society there is no certainty, no room for complacency; terrible dangers always lurk in waiting, dangers inherent in human nature, in man's failings and flaws, in that something which is lacking in him: *and there is no guarantee whatsoever that reason is likely to rule us tomorrow, for dark forces always break out from various sources and they conquer us and we become their slaves* [present author's italics].

And out of the depths of his despair, he added that 'in social matters we must always be on guard ... not against others, but against our own selves'.[51]

He frequently visited ha-Kibbutz ha-Meuhad settlements with the evident aim of winning over the irresolute. He also attended party meetings in the Jordan Valley, but took little part in mass meetings in towns. Nor was he active in the intensive election campaign which Ben Gurion organized throughout the country. Eye-witnesses gained the impression that he was depressed and there were tragic overtones to his remarks. His speeches at the kibbutzim encouraged the opposition, and they repeatedly urged him to visit them more frequently. But by mid-July 1944 Berl was totally exhausted and went up to Jerusalem to rest and recuperate.

He was absent from the final stage of the election campaign and attributed Mapai's victory mainly to Ben Gurion. The last session of the Mapai Central Committee which he attended was held on 10 July 1944 in Jerusalem. He never returned to Tel Aviv and stayed with friends, spending most of his time resting and writing. He planned to publish a book on the Second Aliyah, and in the last week of his life sent a circular to 'the Second Aliyah Stalwarts'.

Elections to the Asefat ha-Nivharim (Elected Assembly) of the entire Yishuv, were held on 1 August, and to the Histadrut Conference five days later. Mapai won 37 per cent of the seats in the first, and 53 per cent at the second. Together with the support of the delegates of the general Zionist Workers and the Religious Workers (6 per cent of the total), Mapai enjoyed an overwhelming majority in the Histadrut. Le-Ahdut ha-Avoda (For the Unity of Labor), the party founded by Faction B, won about 19 per cent and the Socialist League established by ha-Shomer ha-Tzair won 20 per cent. Dependence on Faction B's one-third was now a thing of the past. This was Ben Gurion's great hour of triumph.

Word of the success reached Berl in Jerusalem but did not console him. On the following Friday evening he visited the home of his friends Gershom and Fania Scholem. He was in the habit of arriving without prior notice, in the late evening hours. Wearing his embroidered Russian shirt (*rubashka*) and his peaked cap, he would peep in through the door and ask: 'Have you gone to bed already? Never mind, get up and make me a glass of tea.' The Scholem household was a perfect refuge for him: Scholem was not involved in politics and Berl could converse with him to his heart's content on current affairs, art, writers and literature, the university, Jewish tradition, Kabbala and Hassidism, the labor movement and the Yishuv. At the Scholems' he found the warmth, affability, and mutual affection so sadly lacking in his own home life. In his latter years, when public life was particularly enervating for him, he had no real home, in the more profound sense of the word. Leah, grim of countenance and jealous by nature, did not succeed in making a pleasant and attractive home for him. Their modest apartment lacked distinction, apart from Berl's bookcase and desk. The stylelessness of the apartment reflected Leah's personality. The tea and empathy he found with the Scholems restored his spirit. And thus he came to visit his friends on the last Friday of his life. The house was filled with guests. Berl, in good spirits, soon became the center of attention. As midnight approached, the guests left one by one, but Berl stayed behind. He inquired about the people he had met, and then began to talk about the elections and the split. 'I now believe that there are historical processes', he said, 'in which men take part without understanding the reasons for their own actions. For example, here I am, splitting the party without wanting to, and believe me: I don't know why, and nor does Tabenkin.' The conversation went on until 2.0 a.m., when Fania Scholem reminded him that it was time to go to bed. 'You always throw me out! Are *you* tired?' he asked lightly, but soon admitted: 'I am really exhausted.' Again they spoke of the elections and of Ben Gurion, and finally he left, saying to Fania: 'Tell me, how does one rest? I don't know how.'[52]

Leah joined him in Jerusalem that weekend, and they stayed with friends in Rehavia. The Sabbath passed slowly; he spent hours talking to Eliezer Kaplan. In the afternoon he met two young men, Zeev Sherf and Teddy Kollek. It was his last conversation.

At 8.30 in the evening he suffered a brain hemorrhage. Doctors were summoned, but he died within half an hour, aged 57. In Tel Aviv Sara Zayit suddenly glanced at her watch, and a premonition gripped her: she hastened from her home to the *Davar* offices. Just as she arrived, news of Berl's death came through.

The radio reported the news late on Saturday night, 12 August, and from all over Palestine people began to flock to the modest apartment in Jerusalem. David ha-Cohen received a telephone call from friends in Tel Aviv informing him that Berl was dead. He was asked to inform Ben Gurion, then holidaying in Haifa. It was very late when ha-Cohen arrived and Ben Gurion had been asleep. The two men sat on his bed, and ha-Cohen said: 'Berl is gone.' Ben Gurion – according to ha-Cohen – 'started up like a tightly-coiled spring, fell backward and his head struck the wall. He sat up again facing me as if he were turned to stone. He covered his head with a sheet, moaning like a wounded animal, and banged his head on the mattress, muttering: "Berl, without Berl, how?, without Berl?" '[53] With a grim frozen countenance he joined ha-Cohen on the night drive to Jerusalem, taking his wife and son with him. They reached Jerusalem at dawn and Ben Gurion hastened to the room where Berl's body had been laid out. He gazed at his friend's still face, and fainted. When he revived, he asked to be left alone with Berl. For hours he sat there by himself, and when he came out, said to his son: 'That was the only true friend I ever had.'[54]

In the following week, Berl's death competed for headlines with the news of the forthcoming liberation of France. The Hebrew press was unanimous in its adulation. Over his coffin in the courtyard of the Jewish Agency offices in Jerusalem, his beloved sister, Hanna Nesher, made a pathetic appeal for the reunification of the movement and in fact a new series of talks was launched between Mapai and le-Ahdut ha-Avoda. They petered out, but the very fact that they were held at all attests to the sense of collective guilt which all his comrades felt at his death. After the end of the seven days of ritual mourning, special councils of Mapai and the Histadrut were convened in his memory. The mourning lasted until the end of the official thirty-day period, but with waning intensity. The war had reached a decisive stage; the annihilation of the Hungarian Jewish community had commenced; Lehi activity had been stepped up, and the death of the beloved leader gradually faded from the headlines.

On the first anniversary of his death, a special trainload of mourners traveled up to his grave on the Kinneret shore. *Davar* devoted an issue to his memory. His death was still commemorated publicly on the fifth anniversary, but the number of those attending had dwindled.

It was related that Berl's picture was the only one Ben Gurion kept on his desk, and years after Berl's death he remarked to a friend: 'Not a day passes when I do not miss his conversation.'[55] Golda Meir (Meyerson) venerated his memory, as did Moshe Sharet (Shertok) and Shaul Avigur

(Meirov). The pioneer settlements remained loyal to his memory and so did people from the Mapai party machine, including the younger generation, which often referred to him to prove either side of an argument. As the years passed, and the controversy died down, he was again accorded pride of place in the hearts of ha-Kibbutz ha-Meuhad veterans and even among its younger leadership, now growing old. After a lapse of thirty years, ha-Shomer ha-Tzair's leaders recognized his greatness and found in his writings a fresh humanist socialist Zionist approach.

But as the years went by, his image became less vivid: instead of the living, battling Berl, there emerged an idealized paternal figure, a source of nostalgia among his surviving colleagues, who in every crisis would ask themselves: 'What would Berl have said?' His name was perpetuated in educational projects, streets were called after him and his photograph hung on the walls of offices of people who never knew him. He became a symbol and ceased to be a human being. In Israel, as the years transformed its social makeup, he became alien to the majority of the population, and his name lost meaning.

Sixteen years after Berl's death, Abba Ahimeir wrote an article about him, summing up a saga of love and hate which had endured for more than twenty-five years:

. . . they have all forgotten him. All, apart from a few 'old codgers' including the present writer. Ben Gurion, who in Berl's lifetime, stood before him as a disciple before his master, no longer mentions him. It seems that his absence troubles nobody. They get along quite well without him. Berl! You are not missed by your friends in the party. I miss you. Has the dialog between us really ended?[56]

16

STRENGTH AND WEAKNESS

On the eve of his fateful mission to Nazi-occupied Northern Italy, Enzo Sereni sent a letter to 'Berl, David, Yitzhak – my mentors and comrades: I hope we will soon meet again', he wrote, 'and if not, farewell to you and my gratitude for all you have given me in life, for the way you have illumined my path.' He added a final word: 'Farewell – and don't fight along the way!'[1] Sereni's note is emblematic for a whole generation.

Berl, Ben Gurion and Tabenkin were fashioned from the same clay from which Gandhi, Lenin and Trotsky were made: men of action and ideological force, who set their seal, for better or worse, on their disciples and colleagues and on the world in which they lived. It was these three men who shaped the unique reality of the Palestinian labor movement in particular and Israeli society in general.

There were, of course, others who contributed to the fabric of the nation and the state. But these three were unequaled in the scope of their influence.

Theirs was the generation of the great leap: their parental homes were pervaded with religion, with innocent faith and hallowed custom; the homes of their children were detached from Jewish tradition, rooted in a secular life style and alienated from the Jewish past. They themselves were affected by the ambivalence which comes from being bred in one society and living in another. Wherever they went and whatever they did, they were influenced, consciously or unwittingly, for better or worse, by the society from which they emerged. Those born in the Pale of Settlement identified naturally and instinctively with the Jewish people, its existential experience, and its destiny. All three cast off the burden of Jewish religion at an early age. Berl was unique among them in his love of Jewish learning, his profound involvement in Jewish tradition and history. The way in which his comrades leapt across the 2,000-year gap between Bar Kochba and early Zionist pioneering, did not appeal to him. His nationalism was inspired by Jewish suffering. He experienced two thousand years of Jewish history with every fiber of his being, and the concept of Jewish martyrdom (*kidush ha-Shem*) appealed to him. It was not the biblical heroes he admired but those who 'anticipated the coming of the Messiah', the victims of pogroms and persecutions. Unlike several of his more famous comrades, he felt no shame or unease with regard to Jewish life in exile. In his last years, he came to the conclusion that a national culture could not survive without traditional symbols and customs, and here too he differed from others in his movement.

They all grew up in a compact Jewish world, always on the defensive against the strong and threatening Gentile world, and none of them felt really at home there. Ben Gurion taught himself over the years to accept the non-Jewish world with which he had to maintain contact. Tabenkin was never exposed to the outside world and his grudge against it was reflected in his suspicious and hostile attitude towards the British. He nurtured a special fondness for the Russian revolutionaries and seemed to exempt them from his reservations towards the non-Jews. Although Berl was exposed to many Gentiles, he never tried to understand them; he may have made contact with some non-Jewish writer or statesman, but he never sought or attained real intimacy. He did not exclude the heroes of the Revolution from his alienated attitude towards all non-Jews. As the years passed, he adopted a cautiously positive attitude towards the democratic and humanistic West. But it was merely theoretical approval, related to ideas and images and not to people.

Tabenkin was involved, from his youth, in socialist Zionist work, as a member of Poalei Zion in Warsaw and a comrade of Borochov. Ben Gurion was drawn into the turmoil of socialist Zionist activity almost by chance, and rapidly found his place there. Both he and Tabenkin had been raised in Congress Poland, somewhat removed from the storms of the Revolution, and they never wavered in the Zionism they had absorbed in their childhood homes. Borochov's theories, in which Zionist and socialist inevitability were combined, inspired them with a positivist and powerful belief in the future of human society in general and of the Jewish people in particular. In due course Tabenkin moved away from Borochovism, admired Kropotkin, and leaned towards anarchism – but he eventually returned to the Marxist theories of his youth. Ben Gurion's Marxism, on the other hand, never became an integral part of his ideology, and as his public career progressed, he shed it unconsciously, almost casually.

Berl, in contrast, plunged into the cauldron of Russian revolutionary life before and after the First Revolution. His travels over White and Southern Russia brought him into contact with the diverse groups emerging in Russian society in general and in the Jewish world in particular. The death of his father, when he was only twelve, precipitated a crisis of identity, reflected in his bitterness against the society in which he lived and resistance to the ideas accepted within the revolutionary world into which he had been drawn. Party after party disappointed him, and he found satisfaction in none of the movements which emerged in the Jewish community. His adolescent crisis lasted ten years, during the course of which he rejected the Hibat Zion of his father, even dabbling in anti-Zionist activity. He finally found the synthesis between the instinctive Zionism of his home and the revolutionary world he knew and had come to love. The kind of socialist Zionism which he adopted repudiated hard and fast truths and beliefs. It was the outcome of a process of self-questioning and the examination of ideas in the light of reality. It was marked by an excess of doubt and constant criticism. Withal, there was an element of optimism in it, inspired by the anti-Marxist Narodnik conceptual outlook and their activism, or, as Berdichevsky called it – will; it was the very opposite of Marxist historical determinism. The voluntarist element in Berl's thought was, from the outset, the antithesis of cohesive theories, of prediction, and of the confidence in the future which Marxism bestows. This may have been the secret of his independent development, his tendency to examine every issue on its own merits. 'This man sees everything with his own eyes. Have you met many people who can see with their own eyes?'[2] Arthur Ruppin once said of Berl.

Berl's emergence as the leader of the Second Aliyah is shrouded in obscurity, and contains something of the element of revelation, as in the case of certain charismatic leaders. When he arrived in Palestine, he was known to few people. But soon afterwards an unknown laborer recounted that he had entered into conversation with Berl, and became convinced that the drudgery in which he was engaged had some significance. Brenner singled him out from all the others. One moonlight night, on the shores of Lake Galilee, the young Agnon came – permanently – under his spell, as did Zalman Rubashov, on a visit to Palestine. Berl was not distinguished by the quality of his work, by courage or by any heroic qualities. Yet he emerged – enigmatically – at the end of the First World War as *the* acknowledged leader of that group of stubborn hopefuls, the remnants of the Second Aliyah, to whom he preached his vision in 'Facing the Days Ahead'. On his comrades from Kinneret and on those Second Aliyah pioneers who never joined either of the workers' parties, he exerted an inexplicable fascination which Aliza Shidlovsky, one of them, tried to define at his graveside: '[He was the] bearer of a fervent vision of the Jewish worker, the Hebrew village, the fraternity of all workers, the Hebrew language, the Hebrew book.'[3] Berl gave utterance to their hopes, their criticism of institutionalized Zionism and their thirst for action. His dream of a united labor movement, emerging from the everyday realities rather than from any preordained ideology, was the rock on which the Palestine labor movement was to be founded.

For Berl the idea of unity was an organizational principle, elevated to the level of an ideology of intrinsic value in itself. Its origins can be traced to his youth, when he wearied of the excessive ideological verbiage of Jewish intellectuals in the Pale of Settlement. He yearned for heroic deeds, like those of the Russian revolutionaries. He believed that redemption lay in the drive for action and the spirit of self-sacrifice, which, he found, were lacking in the Jewish public, whether socialist or Zionist. Once he came to the conclusion that Palestine would be built up through agricultural labor settlements, he began to regard them and their concomitant social and educational ideals, as the natural ideological program for Palestinian Jewish workers. 'Unity' was the catchphrase for realizing the potential of these workers who, divided among various parties, squandered their energies on squabbles. The call for unity implied that all ideologies originating in the Diaspora should be subordinated to convictions born out of Palestinian conditions. The movement in Palestine was capable of containing a wide divergence of views, from idealism to materialism, for those who held them believed also in a common destiny and a common goal for themselves and the Jewish people.

The unity of the labor movement was a source of strength in a period when the focal point of Zionism shifted from theoretical debate to the ideology of action and the hope of rapid Zionist achievement in Palestine, following the Balfour Declaration and the British occupation. Berl's praxis preceded the voluntaristic trends of the Third Aliyah, and provided an ideological and organizational framework for the immigrants in advance of their arrival. The broader and more flexible the framework, the greater its scope of action and appeal.

Berl recoiled from movements which brought with them to Palestine their own preconceived ideologies, complete with a built-in leadership. He felt that they constituted a threat to his central ideology, undermining his leadership and authority. To accept the principle of the historic unity of the movement, and the harmony of contrasts it entailed, was, in fact, to accept Berl Katznelson's supreme and charismatic authority.

Max Weber defines charismatic authority as that which derives neither from position, law nor bureaucratic power, a definition particularly appropriate to Berl's unique authority over his comrades. He was an institution unto himself. He shunned official status and delegated authority, with their inherent limitations. Had he been asked, he might have explained that he evaded official positions because they did not appeal to him, and this too was partially true. But, above all, he wanted to reach as wide a public as possible in the most direct fashion. Berl expected unanimous assent and the loving acceptance of his authority from others and interpreted any resistance as the result of his own shortcomings or those of his adversaries. His absolute conviction that he was right prevented him from recognizing the legitimacy of other systems of values and leadership. Like all charismatic leaders, he was authoritative, intolerant and fanatic in his own way. He was jealous of his beliefs and of his authority. When he felt that he had been slighted, he withheld the grace of his leadership from the movement, expecting his followers to placate him and to beg him to take his place among them again. And he did not hesitate to wield his authority, and to impose his views on a hesitant public. This pattern of relations was conditional on the love and devotion which others felt towards him, and could function only as long as they believed in him. During the 1920s none questioned his code, but in the 1930s and 1940s his repeated appeals to the devotion of others were interpreted as emotional blackmail and he was even accused at times of dictatorial tendencies.

His leadership was accepted unreservedly by Ahdut ha-Avoda. His wisdom, shrewdness, and particularly his eloquence, singled him out and elevated him above others. In a revolutionary movement, where the word is father of the deed, Berl's strength lay in his incisive analysis of social and political processes, his formulation of objectives and his program of action. He never preached in the abstract; his message was

347

always pragmatic: what were the priorities and how to implement them organizationally. The Association of Agricultural Workers, ha-Mashbir, the Workmen's Bank and Aliyah Bet were his brain-children no less than *Kuntres*, *Davar* and Am Oved. Although he was blessed with the talent for moving the masses, he preferred to act through his comrades and disciples, whom he infected with his own enthusiasm. Logical, rationalistic in his approach to plans of action and in his instruments of analysis, he also radiated enthusiasm, which infected those who worked with him and won them over to his will.

Charismatic rule is, by its very nature, opposed to the existing order, but for efficacy it requires, in the final analysis, institutionalization and bureaucratization. Tabenkin, who was also charismatic, soon confined his authority to ha-Kibbutz ha-Meuhad and its social and organizational frameworks. Ben Gurion followed an opposite course: lacking charisma and personal charm, he built up his authority in the corridors of power, first as Secretary of the Histadrut, then in the Zionist Executive. Over the years and by force of his official positions, his leadership and authority grew. But it was only after his political and military triumphs with the establishment of the State and the War of Independence that Ben Gurion acceded to charismatic leadership, acquiring – especially in the eyes of the new immigrants – the image of the 'Father of his Country'.

Berl did not follow Tabenkin's example, but claimed leadership of the entire labor movement, or at least of all of his party. Nor did he rely on the bureaucratic system, since to be dependent on it would have conflicted with his self-image as an outsider to accepted authority. By nature Berl was incapable of fostering the relations customary between leader and bureaucracy, based on give and take. His attitude to other people was based on personal esteem, irrespective of their roles in the system. He was capable of taking an unknown but potentially impressive young man and pushing him into the front ranks of the party leadership. Berl displayed a cool and correct attitude (at best) towards those in the party who did not live up to his personal criteria. Members of the party and the Histadrut apparatus received short measure from him, and most of them reciprocated. In the 1920s, members of Ahdut ha-Avoda allowed him to select candidates for office in the party and the Histadrut because of his talent for judging people and because of their acceptance of his right to mold the movement's future leadership. But he never acquired a power base, a regular group of supporters. In the 1930s, after Mapai was established, joining together various forces and blocs and people, some of whom had rejected his authority as far back as the Second Aliyah days, he was deprived of his exclusive authority to decide. It was still hard for an ambitious young man to advance if Berl was against him. But as the party became more institutionalized, and the blocs consolidated, Berl's sphere of influence shrank.

As noted, his authority flourished in open frameworks, where he could wield his personal charms. But in a large movement, based on pressure groups and power struggles, his influence was not felt. Thus, when he went to battle for the unity of the kibbutz movement, or the 'generality' of the party and the Histadrut, he was fighting for his own authority, as well as for the future of the movement. Any attack on the concept of unity, was also an attack on his standing in the movement, since he was the living symbol of unity. What had formerly seemed self-evident was now regarded as an indication of his lust for power. His attempts to consolidate support around him from within the various sectors encountered the bitter opposition of those who wanted to preserve the loyalty of their comrades. What led him to feel most miserable and abandoned was his desertion by the younger generation on whom he had pinned all his hopes.

One of the bludgeons used against him in the party was the slogan of democracy. The man who had preached liberty and the rule of the people was now being attacked as anti-democratic. Democracy was the catchword of both the pressure groups and the apparatus: all of them wanted to base their influence on rational, objective and measurable criteria, such as numbers of votes and delegates. Berl's authority was incompatible with the democracy he preached, since he stood outside the regular network of relations. In theory he accepted the view that *vox populi vox dei*, but in practice he denied it: he refused to support workers' demands when he thought them unjustified; he rebelled against the decisions of the movement when he considered that they were not consistent with moral criteria. In the same spirit, he rejected the principle that the electoral weight of various bodies, urban or communal, should determine the leadership of the movement. He saw himself as expressing the *volonté générale* of the movement in its historic mission, as against those who merely represented the democratic count.

In accordance with the principle of generality and unity, Berl aspired to a movement which would encompass the widest possible social strata and as many public bodies as possible. Essentially, however, his type of authority was suited to a body of limited scope, based on personal, even intimate ties. As the movement grew, it became increasingly institutionalized and required the formal rules of the democratic game. Hence, the idea of unity with which Berl's authority was identified was the immanent cause of his decline.

Berl was a man of contrasts. One might say, paradoxically, that his weaknesses as a man gave him strength as a leader, and his weaknesses as a leader sprang from his superior human qualities. He had a predilection for criticism both of society and of self. He vigorously maintained a set of stringent moral principles for both. Berl was not deterred by the thought of punishing rioters or spilling blood in the course of a struggle. Nor did he hesitate to send young people on missions from which he knew they might not return. But he did everything in his power to check violence and prevent it from becoming an accepted weapon in the political life of the Yishuv – as, for example, during the campaign against the Revisionists, or in his unequivocal stand in favor of self-restraint in relations between the Yishuv and the Arabs.

He was not alone in his insistence on the importance of integrity, frugality, simplicity and mutual aid; but in his case, nobody ever doubted his right to exhort others to these values. He established them as norms in the conduct of an entire generation of leaders and if some of them sometimes 'faltered', he was there as a living reproach.

Tabenkin and Berl, and many of the other protagonists of the Second Aliyah, were the spiritual children of Russian revolutionary ferment, but when their Russian teachers tried to translate their values into practical terms, they failed and vanished from the stage of history. In Palestine, however, under totally different conditions, their philosophy became the foundation of a society and a nation under construction: an inflexible morality, an opposition to terror which does not distinguish between the innocent and the culpable, profound personal involvement, a thirst for action, and self-realization. Out of it was fashioned an optimistic outlook, based on the desire to build a new society, free from despotism, coercion and injustice, practicing equality, and securing the weak and the needy. This was Berl's fundamental *Weltanschauung*, even if his optimism abandoned him towards the end of his days. His repeated denial of the claim that 'the end justifies the means', a claim sometimes accepted by Tabenkin and Ben Gurion, accentuates the depth of his humanism.

At the same time he was basically a pessimist and a skeptic. It was as if he lived in two worlds: the domain of the present, in which one had to proceed with prudence and adopt all the necessary precautions against imminent dangers, and the domain of the future, perceived as a positive and radiant universe. Berl was automatically suspicious of everyone he met until their innocence was established. This fundamental pessimism intensified as the years went by, and clashed with his faith in mankind.

The conflict between the two domains was only one aspect of his contradictory nature. He preached democracy, open-mindedness, tolerance, a humane socialism, but at the same time he guarded his standpoints no less zealously than his rivals. His instincts, and the petty and aloof elements in him, contrasted with the breadth of his horizons and with the convictions he held so wholeheartedly. The zealot in him often wrestled with the teacher, and, there was often a contradiction between what he preached and his own profounder feelings. For example, his world was divided sharply into Jews and Gentiles. To the former he offered dedication, tenderness and love, profound concern and a great tolerance of failings. Towards Gentiles, on the other hand, he displayed hostility, deep suspicion and intolerance. He apparently never tried to put himself in the place of an Englishman or an Arab when a concrete problem was involved. When he spoke theoretically, however, his world was sophisticated and variegated, unlike Tabenkin's black-and-white world. Berl avoided the use of stereotypes to explain social and national relations. Anyone who divided the world into 'us and them' was, in effect, advocating a life-and-death struggle between the two. Tabenkin, naturally enough, preached revolution, but Berl denied the justification of acts of violence and aggression in a world where innocence and guilt were mingled. Within the Yishuv, Berl strictly practiced what he preached. But when discussing the non-Jewish world, he often spoke in black-and-white terms.

The sophistication of Berl's vision of the world as against the simplicity of Tabenkin's was the source of Berl's weakness and Tabenkin's strength. Berl dismissed all-embracing ideological explanations. He once defined himself as follows: 'I have never labeled myself a realist or an idealist, and if I were forced, Heaven forbid!, to do so, I would consider myself close to the school of realism as regards my choice of a slow pace in the work which lies ahead, but would depart from them in my refusal to rely solely on reason.'[4] He claimed that the world was moved by both rational and irrational forces; hence there was a limit to the analytical ability of human reason, and certainly to the ability to predict social, political and economic processes. Berl did not believe that dialectical materialism was capable of illuminating the future, nor did he see in historical materialism the sole, or even the main, explanation of past phenomena. After his youthful crisis, he was little attracted to social theories which claimed to offer comprehensive solutions to the ills of mankind and of society. This weakened his position in the Yishuv: the revolutionary, risking his life or living in penury and deprivation, would like to believe that his suffering in the present will be recompensed by some future reward. Moreover, the division of the world into good and bad is convenient for revolutionaries at such times. It delineates the enemy clearly, simplifies thought and decision and makes group identifications easier. Tabenkin gave his disciples the simple and unequivocal answers they sought. Berl did not. He never pointed out the route to a better world and never promised that Utopia would be achieved. As he moved onward from the 1920s, he took a pitiless view of the world, which left scant room for hope. His own conclusion was Brenner's defiant 'nonetheless', but for most of the young generation, this was an unsatisfactory answer.

The emergence of a revolutionary leader usually entails a process of detachment, an impersonalization of human relations. The leader comes to attribute greater and greater importance to ideas and goals and less and less to human relations, enabling him to act without the restrictions of interpersonal ties.

A study of Ben Gurion's rise to national leadership reveals how he deliberately freed himself of burdensome emotional ties to his family, and gradually put a psychological distance between himself and his fellow party-members until he let them feel that he had no need of them, that he was an autonomous personality with no room for such pointless considerations as love and enduring personal commitment. Berl seems to have been one of the only people in the party for whom Ben Gurion felt something like love. His esteem for Berl derived primarily from recognition of his intellectual powers. For Ben Gurion, Berl was a law unto himself and did not threaten him; rather they complemented one another wonderfully. Ben Gurion's tendency to protect Berl attests to the fact that he never saw him as a rival.

Berl too underwent a process of impersonalization, but it was ambiguous and had only partial results. All his life he retained profound emotional links to his family. He deferred to his aged mother and supported her. The death of his sister's infant children caused him profound distress. His affection for children was evident in every encounter with them. He had a need for comradeship which was always unsatisfied. Berl remained loyal to old friends: the group of comrades from Kinneret were close to his heart all his life, and every meeting with them was a celebration. He nursed affection for his former colleagues in the Russian Z.S., and never despaired of persuading them to accept Zionism. Human plight affected him, and the general public sensed this. People appealed to him for work and for assistance in immigration, or with complaints against individuals and institutions; they told him of injustice and corruption in high places and arbitrary conduct. And he responded to the best of his ability.

As the years passed, he wearied of people who no longer interested him. Although he had many political and intellectual friends, there was no one person whom Berl considered his intimate friend. Although Beilinson appeared to fulfill the role, in actual fact the relations between them were those of leader and follower. Within his own movement, his relations with his followers were based on mutual ties, as between mentor and disciples. He took an interest in their personal problems, crises of belief, family problems and ailments and tried to help. His attitude was in dramatic contrast to that of Ben Gurion.

More problematic were his relations with his equals. His life in Palestine is strewn with partings from comrades because of ideological differences: Eliezer Yaffe, A. D. Gordon and Tabenkin, among others. When he was forced to choose between his convictions and a dear friend, he always chose the former. He loved Eliezer Yaffe deeply, but did not hesitate to part from him when he decided to set up Ahdut ha-Avoda. It was even more difficult to tear himself from A. D. Gordon, whom he adulated, and with whom he had shared a rush-mat at Ein Ganim, but when Gordon opposed the unification of the labor movement, Berl tormented himself at having grieved his friend; however, it did not deter him from going his own path.

The most dramatic and painful of his partings was from Tabenkin, against whom he had to defend the unity of the movement. When he traveled to Poland in 1933 he knew that he was endangering their friendship, but pressed on regardless. It was he who fired the first volley in the debate on the merger of the Kibbutz movement, backed the opposition in ha-Kibbutz ha-Meuhad in order to restore unity. On the eve of the Mapai split, Berl found it very hard to associate himself with it. He was desperately unhappy at the thought of parting from beloved colleagues but ultimately gave Ben Gurion his full support.

It should be noted that whenever Berl sacrificed emotional ties for principles, it was the unity of the movement that was involved. Unconsciously, of course, he was also operating to defend his authority.

Berl's emotional vulnerability resulted from the blend in his makeup of excessive sensibility and obduracy. He hungered for esteem and affection, and was hurt to the depth of his being by charges of hypocrisy, deception or malice. To protect himself, he became a master in the use of irony and sarcasm. He analyzed the statements of his rivals and exposed their emptiness to the light. Merciless in his polemics, he did not differentiate between worthy and ineffectual adversaries. Nor could he forgive. He claimed that 'the bitter suffering, the insults, malice and mistrust that I have encountered *since my youth* have helped me to find myself; through them I have become impervious to certain spiritual tortures'.[5] His insistence on his imperviousness suggests that the opposite was true.

In a peculiar way Berl's humanity, stringent moral code and breadth of vision worked against his leadership. Ben Gurion has been compared by his contemporaries to a blinkered horse, intent only on the immediate road ahead. When Ben Gurion dedicated himself to a task, he saw it as the be-all and end-all of his own and the nation's life. This approach characterized him as Secretary-General of the Histadrut, as Chairman of the Jewish Agency Executive, and later as Prime Minister, and Defense Minister. He never engaged in idle conversation, never read fiction, never took an interest in art or in other human beings. Nor did he pay attention to happenings within his own movement, except when they threatened his ability to function as its authorized spokesman. Berl was interested in a multitude of subjects: politics, settlement, mores, philosophy, art, *belles-lettres* and poetry. There was no limit to his curiosity and his capacity to absorb new experiences and make new acquaintances. In no period of his life – excluding, perhaps, his work on the Kinneret vegetable farm – did he dedicate himself utterly to a single interest. He divided his energies between political activity, economic enterprises, journalism, educational work, intellectual exchanges, voracious reading, and simple human intercourse. Nothing human was alien to him. As a leader, this abundance of understanding and erudition was to his detriment. He left his stamp on many projects and countless people, but lacked the single-mindedness and obduracy to stick to one work to the end.

He despised routine work. He would commence new projects with great though concealed enthusiasm, going into the minutest of details. But once the novelty wore off and the fervor abated, he would abandon it and seek another challenge. This hampered his ability to cooperate with bureaucrats, whose strength lay in their pertinacity.

Berl's diversity contrasted with the dogged perseverance which characterizes single-minded 'professional' revolutionaries, for whom nothing exists but the revolution. Just as he refused to content himself with impersonal relations with his colleagues, he also refused to act solely as the instrument of the revolution.

Berl wanted to do those things which interested him, which helped him to fulfill himself as an individual, irrespective of what his contemporaries considered important or respectable. He considered himself to be the movement's educational light. He wanted to bequeath his legacy to the next generation, and his failure in this sphere was a tragedy for him, because of the great significance he attributed to it. The failure also indicated that the attempt to hand on his authority and perpetuate his charisma was unsuccessful.

He sought consolation in the other sphere which had always interested him – literature. Am Oved compensated Berl for his disappointments, especially the decline in his influence as leader of the movement. Many wondered how, in those nightmare years in which the Jewish people were perishing and the labor movement was in crisis, Berl could permit himself the luxury of devoting himself exclusively to a publishing house. The question was out of place, since Berl had always preserved a private domain. His often impulsive flights from the public to the private and back again appear almost as a leitmotif throughout his life. It was for him a question of where he could be most efficacious at the moment. His unbroken personal relations with writers and scholars were one manifestation of that private, closely-guarded sphere.

Berl was a perfectionist. He was the most exacting judge of himself and of others, pedantic in the extreme. By its very nature, this tendency slackens momentum. Yet at the same time, Berl was always strongly impelled to act. He was possessed of endless enthusiasm for innovating, setting things in motion, activating other people. He loved translating ideas and objectives into practical schemes, devising 'short cuts', attaining the possible. It was this quality which prevented him from becoming himself a member of the literati, or a scholar. The combination of the intellectual and the man of deeds created in him a constant tension between his critical instinct and his drive to action. Among other things, this often caused him to associate with people of inferior intellectual caliber in undertaking social, cultural or political projects and no doubt contributed to his dissatisfaction with himself and with his surroundings.

One might perhaps draw an analogy between Berl and the three stages in the life of King Solomon: the young lover of the *Song of Songs*, optimistic, romantic, imbued with hope, faith and the burning vision of a new society – this was Berl of the Second Aliyah and early 1920s; the author of Proverbs, a deliberate man, guiding his people and measuring his steps logically, a man who had attained equilibrium between the desire to act and the capacity for action – this was Berl between 1925 and 1935; and then Ecclesiastes, the man whose ship was adrift and rudderless, whose world was in ruins, and who retired into a corner, mumbling: 'Vanity of vanities, all is vanity.' If the truth be told, Berl never arrived at this nihilistic conclusion, but a profound despair and sense of purposelessness embittered his last years. 'Sad, you say', he wrote to a veteran *Davar* contributor, Yitzhak Yatziv. 'Yes. I never knew fifteen years ago that the steam-roller would crush us like this. And former generations will say to us: "Art thou also become weak as we? Art thou become like unto us?" '[6]

Tabenkin once sketched the focal points of the three leaders of Mapai as follows: 'My quandaries, Ben Gurion's storms and Berl's tragic wisdom.'[7] The tragic element in Berl's wisdom lay in his ability to share in events while taking a critical, outsider's view of them. He was able to look ahead while in the thick of events and to grasp where the movement was going, and his clear vision deprived him of the consolations of incomprehension. On the cover of his diary for 1942, he jotted down a verse from a poem by Shin Shalom 'Together we are all alone'.

Where charismatic leaders are concerned, we often find it difficult to assess wherein their great strength lay. The secrets and fascinations of the personality cannot be gauged by a historian, and elude definition.

As a thinker, Berl left no ordered ideology behind him. He never tried to summarize his views in writing – probably because he never summed them up for himself. When he lectured on the history of the labor movement, his views were implicit in the content. But he had nothing in common with the socialist theoreticians. He preached a simple Zionist and socialist fundamentalism, untrammeled by dogma: mass immigration, a working nation, pioneering settlement, self-fulfillment, love of Israel and national accord. How self-evident, even simplistic, these values appear today, now that they smack of political manifestos and catch-phrases. But the apparent triteness of his ideas should not obscure his singular contribution to socialist thought in a period when obeisance to the 'world of tomorrow' being constructed in the Soviet Union was the cornerstone of socialist thought. His was a national and humanistic socialism. Berl may be considered one of the progenitors of that school of thought which recognized the inalienable right of each nation to arrive at socialism independently, and in accordance with its own lights.

His sophistication, diversity and open-mindedness, once regarded as failings, endow his remarks in retrospect with a relevance lacking in the writings of his contemporaries. The unequivocal truths, which make a tremendous impact in heroic eras, sound hollow and meaningless later. In Berl's singular doubts, perplexities and soul-searching, there is something modern and fresh, anti-dogmatic and democratic – and yet, imbued with a social and national pathos.

In the period between the two world wars, two attempts were made to build a socialist society – one in the Soviet Union, the other in Palestine. In both, a deliberate attempt was made to realize a utopian image. Russia chose the route of coercion, establishing institutions and living patterns and imposing them on the people from above. In Palestine, although there were clear Bolshevist tendencies, the process was essentially voluntaristic, and was implemented within the boundaries of a pluralistic society: socialist forms of life evolved side by side with a capitalistic economy and bourgeois styles of life.

The architect of Palestinian socialist society was Berl. This was not a one-man venture, however elevated his standing may have been, but rather a collective endeavor, in which parts were played by leaders and ordinary people, laborers and intellectuals, as in all social movements, borne along by subterranean currents, although those who observe them see only the foam on the surface. And yet it still seems that Berl, more than any other man, deserves the title of master-builder. There combined in him several qualities which singled him out from his comrades: his all-embracing vision of social processes, his ability for long-term thinking and planning, his talent for discerning in the tiny seed the future tree. Berl was uninterested in the constitutional aspects or the idea of a 'state'. Although it was dear to his heart as proof of Jewish independence, it did not have the same irresistible fascination for him as for Ben Gurion. Ben Gurion sought to define things according to accepted legal and political convention. His clear and uncomplicated aim was the establishment of an independent Jewish State. Berl sought a more elusive and multidimensional target: he wanted to shape the image of Jewish society in Palestine in the spirit of the socialist ideals he had absorbed from his youth, from the men of the First Revolution. He sought his goal in a thousand and one ways: through public activity, talks with simple workers, the establishment of *Davar* and Am Oved, the struggle to unite the kibbutz movement, the dream of educating the young. His thought was not formally structured, but sought answers to fundamental questions, such as the quality of life, patterns of conduct, scales of values, the human quality of the movement and its leaders and the ability of a people to function cohesively in quest of its aims.

One of the questions – still unanswered for many – which pre-occupied the fathers of the labor movement, was whether the Jewish people, by its very nature, was capable of becoming a state-building nation. The history of the era of the Second Temple, the specter of a nation torn by fraternal strife at the height of a war of annihilation loomed before them and they repeatedly asked themselves whether a motley group of people from different countries of origin, a variety of social classes and different cultures, speaking a babel of languages, could find a common tongue, a common basis, and create national accord. Berl did not confine himself to asking the question, but set about to create those qualities which distinguish a nation from a random collection of people. The tolerance towards different groups which he tried to inculcate in his followers, stemmed from his conviction that the labor movement was the leader and guide of the Yishuv as a whole. Perceiving his movement as a kind of *noblesse de la robe*, he believed that the quality of its leaders, their moral standards and dedication to the common good, were national issues of the first rank.

Careful scrutiny reveals that each of Berl's deeds and projects added to the mosaic of construction of the Palestinian labor society. For better or worse, he left his indelible stamp on the Yishuv which grew into a state. People sensed this intuitively and the way in which they escorted him to his last resting-place at Kinneret was a demonstration of their love for Berl – teacher, molder and architect.

Since Berl's death no leader has emerged in Israel capable of making the quality of the society and its leadership the central issue of his life. Ben Gurion tried to fill Berl's place, occasionally firing the imagination of the young state with catch-phrases about 'the chosen people' or 'the settlement of the Negev'. But he lacked the subtle attentiveness to what was going on within the human heart, under the surface. The same was true of the others, immersed as they were in the tasks of building the state, consolidating it, absorbing immigrants and other everyday concerns. Berl had a talent for standing aside and scrutinizing the throng in the parade of daily events, thinking and dreaming and carrying out small plans, which coalesced into great schemes. This talent had no heirs.

Perhaps Berl could have no heir: the Yishuv had changed, the idealistic elements were now but a tiny minority, who closed in on themselves and became preoccupied with their own interests. Berl's gloomy prediction that the divided and strife-torn communal settlement movement would forfeit its influence over the labor movement and the country as a whole, detaching itself from social and political commitment, became reality. It was the hour of the bureaucracy. In an organized and institutionalized state, ruled by a hierarchical leadership and by pressure groups, turning a blind eye to questions of moral and cultural quality, what place could there have been for a man who all his days sought human beings?

NOTES

PROLOGUE

1. M. Dorman, 'El Mul Demuto' (Confronting his Image), *le-Ahdut ha-Avoda* Newsletter, 18 August 1944.
2. Alexander Sened.

1 THE ROAD TO ZION, 1887–1909

1. Berl Katznelson, 'Darki la-Aretz' (My Road to Palestine), *Collected Works*, Tel Aviv, 1946, Vol. 5, p. 316.
2. Berl Katznelson, 'ha-Yesh Miflat me-Hitporerut ha-Tenua ha-Tziyonit?' (Can we escape the Disintegration of the Zionist Movement?), *Collected Works*, Vol. 6, pp. 184–5.
3. Berl Katznelson, 'le-Lo Hitgalut' (Without Revelation), *Collected Works*, Vol. 4, pp. 246–7.
4. Berl Katznelson, 'Darki la-Aretz', *Collected Works*, Vol. 5, p. 312.
5. Ibid., p. 314.
6. Ibid., p. 316.
7. Berl Katznelson, 'le-Lo Hitgalut', *Collected Works*, Vol. 4, p. 264.
8. Berl Katznelson, 'Azkara she-Nitahra' (Too Late a Memorial), *Collected Works*, Vol. 3, p. 351.
9. Berl to Druyanov, 6 May 1931, Berl Katznelson Archive, Beit Berl. Hereafter referred to as BKA, BB.
10. Berl to Israel Katznelson, Passover 1907, *Letters*, Tel Aviv, 1961, Vol. 1, p. 48.
11. Berl to Israel Katznelson, Vilna, 25 January 1908, *Letters*, Vol. 1, p. 58.
12. Berl to Hanna Katznelson, Ben Shemen, 5 June 1912, *Letters*, Vol. 1, p. 388.
13. Abba Ahimeir, *le-Ahar ha-Ahava, le-Ahar ha-Sin'a* (Beyond Love, Beyond Hatred), *Selected Writings*, Vol. 4, Tel Aviv, 1974, pp. 176–7.
14. Berl to Hayim Katznelson, Bobruisk, 5 September 1908, *Letters*, Vol. 1, p. 69.
15. Ibid.
16. Berl to Israel Katznelson, Bobruisk, 6 April 1909, *Letters*, Vol. 1, p. 86; 'ha-

Em Mesaperet' (The Mother Recalls), *Al Berl Katznelson*, ed. Mordechai Snir, Tel Aviv, 1952, p. 29.
17. Berl to Hayim Katznelson, Odessa, 24 August 1909 *Letters*, Vol. 1, p. 87.
18. David Zakai, 'me-Reshito' (About his Early Days) *Al Berl Katznelson*, p. 26.
19. B. Dinaburg, 'Reshito' (His Origins), *Al Berl Katznelson*, p. 267.
20. Ibid., p. 256.

2 DISCOVERY AND SELF-REVELATION, 1909–1914

1. Y. H. Brenner, 'Bein Mayim le-Mayim' (Between the Waters), *Collected Works*, Tel Aviv, 1924, Vol. 4, p. 42.
2. Berl Katznelson, 'Darki la-Aretz', *Collected Works*, Vol. 5, p. 325.
3. Ibid.
4. Berl to Sara Schmuckler and Leah Miron, 25 September 1909, *Letters*, Vol. 1, p. 112.
5. Berl to Sara Schmuckler and Leah Miron, 30 September 1909, *Letters*, Vol. 1, p. 118.
6. Ibid.
7. Ibid., p. 120
8. Berl Katznelson, 'le-Haverai ba-Ohel' (To My Comrades in Our Theatre), *Collected Works*, Vol. 2, p. 202.
9. Berl to Sara Schmuckler and Leah Miron, 30 September 1909, *Letters*, Vol. 1, p. 120.
10. Berl to Sara and Leah, 25 September 1909, *Letters*, Vol. 1, p. 111.
11. Brenner to A. Beilin, Jerusalem, 7 July 1909, Brenner, *Letters*, Tel Aviv, 1941, Vol. 2, p. 19.
12. *Al Berl Katznelson*, ed. Mordechai Snir, Tel Aviv, 1952, pp. 145–6.
13. Brenner, *Collected Works*, Vol. 7, p. 277.
14. Brenner, *mi-Kan umi-Kan* (From Here and There), *Collected Works*, Vol. 4, p. 233.
15. Berl to Sara and Leah, 30 September 1909, *Letters*, Vol. 1, p. 119.
16. Ibid.
17. Berl to Hanna Katznelson, after Passover, 1910, *Letters*, Vol. 1, p. 141.
18. Berl to Hayim and Israel Katznelson, 6 September 1910, *Letters*, Vol. 1, p. 144.
19. Berl Katznelson, 'Mikhtav le-Haverai be-Degania' (Letter to my Comrades in Degania), *ha-Kibbutz veha-Kvutza*, Tel Aviv, 1940, p. 4.
20. Berl to Israel Katznelson, 29 August 1910, *Letters*, Vol. 1, p. 176.
21. Berl to Israel and Hayim Katznelson, 6 September 1910, *Letters*, Vol. 1, p. 142.
22. Ibid., p. 144.
23. Berl Katznelson, 'Mikhtav le-Haverai be-Degania', *ha-Kibbutz veha-Kvutza*, p. 2.

24. Ibid.
25. Brenner to David Shimovitz, 28 August 1910, *Letters*, Vol. 2, p. 52.
26. Berl to Israel Katznelson, 29 August 1910, *Letters*, Vol. 1, pp. 175–6.
27. Minutes of Berl's Lectures, in stencil, 1935, p. 34.
28. A. Ruppin, *Pirkei Hayai* (My Life and Work), Tel Aviv, 1968, Vol. 2, p. 56.
29. Mamashi, 'ha-Shvitah be-Kinneret' (The Kinneret Strike), *Ha-Poel ha-Tzair*, 31 March 1911.
30. Berl to Israel Katznelson, Kinneret, 19 March 1911, *Letters*, Vol. 1, pp. 205–6.
31. Berl to Hanna Katznelson, 4 July 1912, *Letters*, Vol. 1, p. 388.
32. Berl Katznelson, 'be-Havlei Adam' (In Human Bondage), *Collected Works*, Vol. 5, p. 256.
33. Berl Katznelson, 'be-Shulei Dvarim' (Marginal Comment), *Collected Works*, Vol. 5, p. 176.
34. S. Y. Agnon, in *Al Berl Katznelson*, p. 146.
35. Minutes of Berl's Lectures, p. 61.
36. Berl Katznelson, 'mi-Toch ha-Avoda' (Within Labor), *Collected Works*, Vol. 1, p. 35.
37. Ibid., p. 37 (present author's italics).
38. Ibid., p. 38.
39. Berl to Noah Naftulsky, 6 June 1912, *Letters*, Vol. 1, p. 368.
40. Berl to Sara Schmuckler, Ben Shemen, 1 March 1913, *Letters*, Vol. 1, p. 500.
41. Berl to David Zakai, Ben Shemen, 21 September 1913, *Letters*, Vol. 1, p. 543.

3 KINNERET, KINNERET

1. Ben Zion Israeli, *Ketavim u-Dvarim* (Articles and Speeches), Tel Aviv, 1956, p. 62.
2. Berl to Leah Miron, Ben Shemen, 4 December 1912, *Letters*, Vol. 1, p. 423.
3. Aliza Shidlovsky, 'Beit ha-Almin shel Kinneret' (The Kinneret Cemetery), *Al Berl Katznelson*, p. 420.
4. Rachel Katznelson-Shazar, *Masot u-Reshimot* (Essays and Articles), Tel Aviv, 1946, p. 217.
5. Aliza Shidlovsky, ibid., p. 420.
6. Rachel, 'Al Sfat ha-Kinneret' (On the Kinneret Shore), *Davar*, Second Aliyah Supplement, 1 April 1929.
7. Berl, *Letters*, Vol. 2, p. 268.
8. Ben Zion Israeli, *Ketavim u-Dvarim*, p. 75.
9. Berl Katznelson 'Hotza'at ha-Sefarim shel ha-Histadrut' (The Histadrut Publishing House), *Collected Works*, Vol. 5, p. 133.
10. Rachel Katznelson-Shazar, *Masot u-Reshimot*, p. 247.
11. Shmuel Dayan, 'Ledato shel ha-Mashbir' (The Birth of ha-Mashbir), *Davar*, 24 June 1956.

12. Sara to Berl, undated (apparently beginning of 1918), Sara Schmuckler Archives.
13. Leah to Sara (apparently beginning of 1918), Sara Schmuckler Archives.
14. Sara to Berl, Merhavia, undated, Sara Schmuckler Archives.
15. Berl to Hanna Katznelson, Jerusalem, 24 October 1917, *Letters*, Vol. 2, p. 389.
16. Berl to Sara, Jaffa, 27 July 1912, *Letters*, Vol. 1, p. 399.
17. Berl to Sara, Jerusalem, 24 October 1917, *Letters*, Vol. 2, p. 393.
18. Berl, work manual, 29 October 1917, *Letters*, Vol. 3, p. 521.
19. Rachel Katznelson-Shazar, *Al B.K.*, p. 224.
20. Berl, work manual, 3 April 1918, *Letters*, Vol. 3, p. 546.

4 FACING THE DAYS AHEAD, 1918–1919

1. Italics in original. Micha Yosef Bin Gurion, *Ma'amarim* (Articles), Leipzig, 1922.
2. Berl Katznelson, *Collected Works*, Vol. 1, p. 19.
3. Berl Katznelson, 'le-Tenuat he-Halutz' (To the he-Halutz Movement), *Collected Works*, Vol. 1, p. 53.
4. Berl Katznelson, 'Li-Krat ha-Yamim ha-Baim' (Facing the Days Ahead), *Collected Works*, Vol. 1, p. 66.
5. Ibid., p. 68.
6. *Collected Works*, Vol. 1, p. 75.
7. Ibid., p. 76 (present author's italics).
8. Berl to Mordechai Kushnir, Jerusalem, June 1918, *Letters*, Vol. 2, p. 529.
9. Ibid.
10. Ibid., p. 530.
11. Berl to Hayim Katznelson, Jaffa, 30 April 1919, *Letters*, Vol. 3, p. 265.
12. Berl to Hanna Katznelson, October 1918, *Letters*, Vol. 3, p. 64.
13. Berl to Sara Schmuckler, Legion camp, 13 December 1918, ibid., p. 99.
14. Berl to Mordechai Kushnir, Jerusalem, June 1918, *Letters*, Vol. 2, p. 530.
15. *Ahdut ha-Avoda*, Jaffa, 1919, p. 1.
16. Ben Gurion, *Zikhronot* (Memoirs), Vol. 1, Tel Aviv, 1971, p. 110.
17. Yitzhak Ben Zvi, *ha-Gedudim ha-Ivri'im* (The Jewish Battalions), Jerusalem, 1969, p. 48.
18. Berl to Sara Schmuckler, Jaffa, 4 January 1919, *Letters*, Vol. 3, p. 112.
19. S. Y. Agnon, *Al Berl Katznelson*, p. 147.
20. Sara to Berl, 15 March 1919, Sara Schmuckler Archives.
21. Berl to Hayim Katznelson, Jaffa, 30 April 1919, *Letters*, Vol. 3, p. 269.
22. Letter from Leah to Berl, written by Sara's grave.
23. Berl to Leah, Mikveh Israel, 25 July 1919, *Letters*, Vol. 3, p. 502.
24. Berl to Leah, 25 July 1919, ibid.
25. Berl to Leah, Rafah, 29 July 1919, ibid., p. 511.

26. Berl to Leah, Stockholm, 4 October 1919, *Letters*, Vol. 4, p. 50.
27. Berl to Leah, Tel Aviv, 29 December 1919, ibid., p. 76.
28. Berl to Leah, Vienna, 21 August 1920, ibid., p. 139.
29. Letter from Leah to Berl, written by Sara's grave.
30. Ibid.
31. Berl to Leah, undated, BKA, BB.

5 REVOLUTIONARY TIMES, 1919–1921

1. Berl, 'Harugei Malkhut' (Martyrs to the Cause), *Kuntres*, 16 April 1920.
2. Berl's address to the Ahdut ha-Avoda Council, Jaffa, 9–11 December 1919, Labor Archives (LA) IV 404, File 18.
3. Berl to Ahdut ha-Avoda Executive, London, 14 September 1919, *Letters*, Vol. 4, Tel Aviv, 1970, p. 30.
4. Berl to Ahdut ha-Avoda Executive, London, 7 July 1920, *Letters*, Vol. 4, p. 116.
5. 'Min ha-Veida ha-Tziyonit' (From the Zionist Conference), *Kuntres*, 6 August 1920.
6. Berl to Leah, London, early July 1920, *Letters*, Vol. 4, p. 110.
7. Berl, 'Me-Rahok' (From Afar), Mikveh Israel, *Kuntres*, 1 July 1919.
8. Berl to the Ahdut ha-Avoda Executive, Vienna, 24 August 1920, *Letters*, Vol. 4, p. 127.
9. Berl to Ben Gurion, Jerusalem, 2 June 1920, ibid., p. 99.
10. Minutes of Ahdut ha-Avoda Executive, 14 October 1920, LA IV 4040.
11. Berl, 'M. J. Berdichevsky', *Collected Works*, Vol. 2, p. 307.

6 MISSION TO THE UNITED STATES, 1921–1922

1. 'Yoman America' (American Diary), 19 November 1921, *Letters*, Vol. 5, Tel Aviv, 1973, p. 106.
2. Ibid.
3. *Der Tag*, 20 December 1921.
4. Berl to David Zakai, Cleveland, Ohio, 22 February 1922 (apparently), BKA, BB.
5. Berl to Leah, New York, 2 December 1921, *Letters*, Vol. 5, p. 28.
6. Berl to Hanna Katznelson, New York, 20 November 1921, BKA, BB.

7 THE THIRD ALIYAH CRISIS, 1923–1925

1. Berl to Hanna Katznelson, Jerusalem, 10 January 1923, BKA, BB.
2. Ibid., 31 January 1923.
3. Ibid., 10 January 1923.
4. Ibid., 29 November 1922.

5. Ibid., 10 January 1923.
6. Ibid.
7. Berl to Eliyahu Golomb, Borochov Quarter, 2 April 1923, BKA, BB.
8. From a notebook, BKA, BB.
9. Rivka Hos to Moshe Shertok, September 1920, Dov Hos Archives.
10. Berl to Moshe (Shertok), 2 May, 1923, BKA, BB.
11. Draft of letter from Berl to Leah, Karlsbad, 6 August 1923, BKA, BB.
12. Berl to Hanna Katznelson, Karlsbad, 7 August 1923, BKA, BB.
13. Ibid.
14. Conference Minutes, published by Ahdut ha-Avoda Executive, Tel Aviv, 1925, pp. 6–7.
15. Ibid., p. 116.
16. Ibid., p. 117.
17. Ibid., p. 127.
18. Ibid.
19. Ben Gurion, *Memoirs*, Vol. 1, p. 281.

8 *DAVAR*, 1925

1. *Ha-Poel ha-Tzair*, 16 January 1925.
2. 11th Histadrut Council, January 1925, LA IV 207, File 12.
3. 11th Histadrut Council, op. cit.
4. M. Beilinson to Dov Stock, Beilinson Moshe letters, National and University Library, Jerusalem 401072.
5. Berl Katznelson, 'Bein *Davar* le-Korav' (Between *Davar* and its Readers), *Collected Works*, Vol. 7, p. 407.
6. A discussion on *Davar* 1930 (apparently), BKA, BB.
7. Berl to Rachel Katznelson, 1939 (apparently), BKA, BB.

9 IN TRANSITION, 1925–1929

1. Berl Katznelson at the Third Conference of the Histadrut, *Collected Works*, Vol. 3, p. 109.
2. Berl to Kurt Blumenfeld, Trieste, 7 October 1927, BKA, BB.
3. Kurt Blumenfeld to Berl, Berlin 21 October 1927, BKA, BB.
4. Berl Katznelson 'ha-Congress ule-Aharav' (The Congress and its Aftermath), *Collected Works*, Vol. 2, p. 177.
5. Berl to Leah, Berlin 14 September (1927), *Letters*, Vol. 5, p. 242.
6. Berl Katznelson, 'be-Moetzet he-Halutz be-Danzig' (At the he-Halutz Council in Danzig), *Collected Works*, Vol. 3, p. 193.
7. Ibid., p. 191.
8. Leah to Berl (undated, apparently 1930), family archives.
9. Leah to Berl (undated, apparently 1930), family archives.
10. Berl to Leah (undated, apparently 1930), family archives.

10 FIRST POLITICAL BAPTISM, 1929–1931

1. Minutes of the Fourth Conference of Ahdut ha-Avoda, Tel Aviv, 1926, p. 35.
2. Berl to Hugo Bergman, 30 June 1925, 401502 Bergman, ARC, National and University Library, Jerusalem.
3. Ibid.
4. Berl Katznelson, 'Al ha-Mevukha' (On Confusion), *Collected Works*, Vol. 4, p. 288.
5. Berl to Moshe Beilinson (2–3 January 1930), *Letters*, Vol. 5, p. 290.
6. Berl to Leah, London, 30 January 1930, *Letters*, Vol. 5, p. 310.
7. Berl to Mapai Secretariat, London, 14 February 1930, *Letters*, Vol. 5, p. 323.
8. Undated letter from Beilinson to Berl (Summer 1930), BKA, BB.
9. Berl to his comrades, London, 31 October 1930, BKA, BB.
10. Berl to Leah, London, 11 December 1930, *Letters*, Vol. 5, p. 367.
11. Berl to colleagues on *Davar* editorial board, London, 11 December 1930 *Letters*, Vol. 5, p. 360.

11 THE LEADER AND HIS PARTY, 1931–1935

1. M. Beilinson, *Davar*, 3 May 1928.
2. Berl to Mapai Central Committee, London, 31 October 1930, BKA, BB.
3. Berl to Leah, Vienna, 28 July 1931, during the Socialist Congress, BKA, BB.
4. Berl to Leah, Vienna, 4 August 1931, after the Socialist Congress, BKA, BB.
5. Berl to Leah, ibid.
6. Berl to the Party, Vienna, 27 September 1931, BKA, BB.
7. Ibid.
8. M. Beilinson to Berl, 22 March 1933, BKA, BB.
9. Minutes of Histadrut Executive session, 28 March 1933, Histadrut Executive Archives.
10. Mapai Central Committee minutes, 20 April 1933, BB, 23/33.
11. Ibid.
12. Berl to Dov Stock, BKA, BB.
13. Mapai Central Committee minutes, 20 April 1933, BB, 23/33.
14. Berl to Leah, 20 August 1933 (eve of Prague Congress) BKA, BB.
15. Berl to Matussis, 17 April 1944, BKA, BB.
16. Mapai Central Committee minutes, 31 January 1934, BB, 23/34.
17. Berl's diary, 21 March 1934, BKA, BB.
18. Berl's diary, 23 March 1934, ibid.
19. Mapai Council minutes, 24–26 August 1934, BB, 22/8.
20. Berl's diary, 25 August 1934, BKA, BB.
21. Berl to Ben Gurion, BKA, BB.
22. Mapai Council, 4–5 January 1935, BB 22/10.
23. Berl to Dov Stock, 1933, (apparently) BKA, BB.

12 THE YOUTH CENTER AFFAIR, 1933–1935

1. Berl to Leah, 18 September 1933, BKA, BB.
2. Berl to Leah, Lvov, early October 1933, BKA, BB.
3. Ibid.
4. Ibid.
5. Berl's diary, 3 October 1933, BKA, BB.
6. Ibid., 1 October 1933.
7. Ibid., 30 September 1933.
8. Ibid., 2 October 1933.
9. Ibid., 11 October 1933.
10. Letter from Ya'akov Eshed, Warsaw, 17 November 1933, Ha-Kibbutz ha-Meuhad Archives, Section 15a, Box 15, File 67b.
11. Ibid.
12. Minutes of session of wider ha-Kibbutz ha-Meuhad Secretariat, 24–26 November 1933, ibid. Section 5, Container 1, File 6.
13. Ibid.
14. Ibid.
15. Mapai Central Committee minutes, 5 December 1933, BB 23/33.
16. Ibid.
17. Berl to Israel Galili, Mt St Vigilius, 30 September 1935, *Niv-ha'Kvutza*, September 1953, p. 740.
18. Ibid.
19. Ibid.

13 THE STRUGGLE TO UNITE THE KIBBUTZ MOVEMENT, 1935–1939

1. B. Katznelson, 'Ir'urim Al ha-Matzav ha-Kayam' (A Protest against the Status Quo), *ha-Kibbutz veha-Kvutza, Yalkut le-Berur She'elat ha-Ihud* (The Kibbutz and Kvutza, an Anthology), Tel Aviv, 1940.
2. Moshe Sharett, *Diary*, Tel Aviv, 1978, Vol. 3, p. 672.
3. Berl to ha-Kibbutz ha-Meuhad Secretariat, 26 March 1936, ha-Kibbutz ha-Meuhad Archives, section 6, file 46.
4. Minutes of the 11th convention, Yagur, 2–7 October 1936, Ein Harod, 1937, p. 122.
5. Letter from Ephraim Reisner to his wife, 6 May 1938, Private Archives.
6. Minutes of Fourth Mapai Conference, Rehovot, 3–9 May 1938, BB 21/4.
7. Ibid.
8. Resolutions of the Fourth Mapai Conference, ibid.
9. Minutes of the Mapai Central Committee, 15 December 1938, BB 23/38.
10. Ibid.
11. Ibid.
12. Ibid., 7 December 1938.

13. 12th convention of ha-Kibbutz ha-Meuhad, Na'an, ha-Kibbutz ha-Meuhad Publishing House, p. 201.
14. Talks on unification of the kibbutz movement, ha-Kibbutz ha-Meuhad Archives, Efal, Box 2, File 10b.
15. Ibid.
16. Berl's diary, 29 April 1939, BKA, BB.
17. 12th convention of ha-Kibbutz ha-Meuhad at Na'an, p. 339.
18. Berl's diary, 4 August 1939, BKA, BB.
19. Ibid.
20. Letter from Tabenkin to Histadrut Executive Secretariat, ha-Kibbutz ha-Meuhad Archives, Section 15a, File 33.
21. Berl to Tabenkin, 13 August 1939, ibid., file 51.
22. Berl to Remez, 31 July 1940, BKA, BB.

14 HOUR OF PERIL, 1936–1939

1. Mapai Central Committee Minutes, 11 August 1936, BB 23/36.
2. Ibid, 11 August 1936.
3. Berl to Leah, 2 October 1936, BKA, BB.
4. Berl to Mapai Central Committee, London 28 September 1938, ibid.
5. Ibid.
6. Ibid.
7. Berl to Moshe Shertok, 16 October 1936, BKA, BB.
8. Berl to Ben Gurion, London, 24 October 1936, ibid.
9. Ibid.
10. Mapai Central Committee minutes, 9 December 1936, BB 23/36.
11. Berl's diary, 1 November 1936, BKA, BB.
12. Mapai Central Committee minutes, 9 December 1936, BB 23/36.
13. Berl's diary, 6 October 1936, BKA, BB.
14. Mapai Central Committee minutes, 9 December 1936, BB 23/36.
15. Ibid.
16. Berl's diary, 19 November 1936, BKA, BB.
17. Berl to Leah, Helwan, first letter, March 1937, BKA, BB.
18. Rivka Hos to Dov Hos 22 March 1937, Hos family archives.
19. Berl to Leah, Messina, 3 April 1937, BKA, BB.
20. Berl to Bracha Habas, 1 May 1937, ibid.
21. Berl to Bracha Habas, London, 8 June 1937, ibid.
22. Berl to Mapai Central Committee, London, 13 June 1937, ibid.
23. 20th Zionist Congress, stenographic report, Jerusalem, p. 79.
24. 'Al Darkei Mediniyuteinu' (On our Policy), Tel Aviv, 1938, p. 219.
25. Berl to Leah, Zurich, after the vote, BKA, BB.
26. Berl to Leah, Zurich, 23 August 1937, ibid.
27. Berl's diary, 3 September 1937, ibid.

28. Berl's diary, 5 September 1937, ibid.
29. Berl to Leah, London, 1 October 1937, ibid.
30. Berl to Leah, 20 October 1937, ibid.
31. Mapai Central Committee minutes, 29 December 1937, BB 23/37.
32. Stephen Wise to Berl, 17 November 1937, BKA, BB.
33. Mapai Central Committee minutes, 17 May 1938, BB 23/38.
34. Berl's diary, 10 September 1938, BKA, BB.
35. Berl to Eliyahu Golomb and Sahul Meirov, 28 September 1938, ibid.
36. Berl's diary, 1 October 1938, ibid.
37. Berl to Golomb and Meirov, 28 September 1938, ibid.
38. Berl to Yitzhak Tabenkin, undated, apparently October 1938, ibid.
39. Berl's diary, 31 July 1934, ibid.
40. Mapai Central Committee minutes, 7 December 1938, BB 23/38.
41. Berl to Leah, 20 February 1939, BKA, BB.
42. Berl to Leah, 14 February 1939, ibid.
43. Ibid.
44. Berl to Leah, London, 6 March 1939, ibid.
45. Berl Katznelson 'le-Ahar London' (After London), *Collected Works*, Vol. 9, pp. 30–57.
46. Ibid., p. 45.
47. 21st Zionist Congress, Jerusalem, p. 35.
48. Ibid., pp. 147–9.
49. Ibid., pp. 149, 152.
50. Berl to Leah, Geneva, 24 August 1939, BKA, BB.
51. Ibid.
52. Norman Rose, *Baffy: The Diaries of Blanche Dugdale, 1936–1947*, London, 1973, p. 145.
53. 21st Zionist Congress, p. 223.
54. Berl to Leah, Paris, 29 August 1939, BKA, BB.
55. Berl to Dov Stock, 28 July 1938, ibid.
56. 21st Zionist Congress, p. 145.
57. Berl's diary, 31 August 1939, ibid.
58. Berl's report on his talks with Jabotinsky, Mapai Central Committee, 21 September 1939, BB 23/39.
59. Ibid.
60. Ibid.
61. Ibid.

15 WITH OUR BACKS TO THE WALL, 1939–1944

1. 41st Histadrut Council, 9 December 1940, LA IV 207.
2. Ibid.

3. Minutes of World Union Council, 17 December 1940, BB 22/40.
4. Mapai Central Committee Minutes, 9 January 1941, BB 23/41.
5. Notebook 63, BKA, BB.
6. Mordechai Kushnir to Berl, 14 June 1940, BKA, BB.
7. Histadrut Executive Secretariat Minutes, 29 November 1939, LA File 368/4.
8. Berl's diary, 29 November 1939, BKA, BB.
9. Mapai Central Committee Minutes, 11 January 1940, BB 23/40.
10. Mapai Central Committee Minutes, 20 October 1940, ibid.
11. Notebook 63, BKA, BB.
12. Mapai Central Committee Minutes, 25 December 1940, BB 23/40.
13. Mapai Central Committee Minutes, 14 April 1941, BB 23/41.
14. Berl's diary, 9 May 1941, BKA, BB.
15. Ibid., 13 June 1941.
16. Berl to David Zakai, 8 June 1943, ibid.
17. Ibid.
18. Berl Katznelson, 'Am Oved', *Collected Works*, Vol. 12, p. 161.
19. Ibid. p. 169.
20. Berl to Mordechai Kushnir, 23 April 1944, BKA, BB.
21. Berl to David Zakai, 8 May 1944, ibid.
22. Berl to Mordechai Kushnir, 23 April 1944, ibid.
23. Berl to Dov Stock, apparently 1943, ibid.
24. Berl to David Zakai, 8 June 1943, ibid.
25. Berl Katznelson, Introduction, Report of Study-Month Secretariat.
26. Minutes of Fifth Histadrut Conference, 19–23 April 1942, Tel Aviv, 1942, p. 44.
27. Ibid.
28. Berl Katznelson, Introduction, Report of Study-Month Secretariat.
29. Yoel Palgi, *Ruah Gedola Ba'ah* (A Great Wind was Blowing), Tel Aviv, 1977, p. 17.
30. Yitzhak Katznelson to Berl, BKA, BB.
31. Minutes of Fifth Histadrut Conference, 19–23 April 1941, p. 44.
32. Berl Katznelson, 'be-Ikvot Siha al ha-Gola' (Following a Talk on the Diaspora), 6 June 1944, *Collected Works*, Vol. 12, p. 218.
33. Ibid., pp. 222–3.
34. Ibid., p. 223.
35. Berl to Ben Gurion, 4 August 1942, BKA, BB.
36. Berl to Shlomo Lavi, 13 October 1942, ibid.
37. Berl's diary, 23 September 1942, ibid.
38. Last comrades' discussion before the split in Mapai, ha-Kibbutz ha-Meuhad Archives, Efal.
39. Minutes of Fifth Party Conference at Kfar Vitkin, Third Session, Tel Aviv, 1944, pp. 174ff.

40. Minutes of regional Mapai assembly, Ein Harod, 13 November 1942, BB, 15/2/42.
41. Tabenkin's remarks, 'Seven protocols on Faction B', ha-Kibbutz ha-Meuhad Archives, labor parties sector.
42. Ibid.
43. Berl's diary, 3 January 1944, BKA, BB.
44. Mapai Bureau Minutes, 13 January 1944, BB, 25/44
45. Berl's diary, 15 January 1944, BKA, BB.
46. Minutes of Inner Zionist Actions Committee, 10 November 1942, Central Zionist Archive S25/294.
47. Minutes of Inner Zionist Actions Committee, 1 September 1943, CZA S25/301.
48. Minutes of Mapai Council, Jerusalem, 6 March 1944, BB 22/22.
49. Berl to unknown person (spring 1944), BKA, BB.
50. Berl to Dov Stock, 23 July 1944, ibid.
51. Berl Katznelson 'le-Toldot Tenuat ha-Poalim' (On the History of the Labor Movement), *Collected Works*, Vol. 11, p. 9.
52. Gershom Sholem, 'ha-Layla ha-Aharon' (The Last Night), *Al B.K.*, pp. 138–140.
53. David ha-Cohen, *Et le-Saper* (Time to Tell), Tel Aviv, 1974, p. 85.
54. Michael Bar-Zohar, *Ben Gurion*, Tel Aviv, 1975, Vol. 1, p. 484.
55. Testimony of Zeev Scherf.
56. Abba Ahimeir, *le-Ahar ha-Ahava, le-Ahar ha-Sin'a* (Beyond Love, Beyond Hatred), pp. 240–1.

16 STRENGTH AND WEAKNESS

1. Enzo Sereni to Berl, 4 May 1944, BKA, BB.
2. S. Y. Agnon, *Al B.K.*, p. 149.
3. Aliza Shidlovsky, 'le-Yad ha-Aron be-Kinneret' (By the Coffin at Kinneret), *Al B.K.*, p. 418.
4. Berl to Dov Stock, London, 24 April 1939, BKA, BB.
5. Berl to Rabbi Avraham Hen, 1943 (apparently), ibid.
6. Berl to Yitzhak Yatziv, 1944 (apparently), ibid.
7. Talks on Biltmore with ha-Shomer ha-Tzair, Minutes of seven meetings of Faction B supporters in Mapai (1943), ha-Kibbutz ha-Meuhad Archives, labor parties sector.

GLOSSARY

ha Adama (The Soil) Literary journal of Ahdut ha-Avoda, 1919–1921, edited by Yosef Hayim Brenner.

Agudat Israel (Association of Israel) Orthodox religious party, founded in 1912, which opposed Zionism as the solution to the Jewish problem.

ha-Ahdut (Unity) Poalei Zion journal, founded in 1910, during the Second Aliyah period.

Ahdut ha-Avoda (Unity of Labor) A socialist Zionist association. The central party in the Palestinian Jewish labor movement, 1919–1930.

Aliyah (Immigration) (**First, Second, Third, Fourth**) Successive waves of Jewish immigration to Palestine, in 1882–1903; 1904–1914; 1919–1923; and 1924–1926 respectively.

Aliyah Bet (lit. 'Immigration B') 'Illegal' Jewish immigration into Palestine, i.e. in violation of British regulations.

Am Oved (Working Nation) The publishing house founded by Berl Katznelson in 1942.

ha-Aretz (The Land) Liberal paper, founded in 1920 (first Hebrew daily in Palestine).

Asefat ha-Nivharim (Assembly of Delegates) Central representative body of the Palestinian Jewish community, established in 1920.

ba-Avoda (At Labor) An anthology published by the Agricultural Workers' Union, 1918, edited by Berl Katznelson.

Betar Revisionist youth movement (the name is an acronym of Hebrew 'Joseph Trumpeldor Alliance').

bet midrash (house of study) Academy of religious studies.

Brit Shalom (The Covenant of Peace) An association of Jewish intellectuals 1925–1933, led by Arthur Ruppin, aimed at bringing about Jewish–Arab accord. Most of its members were of Central European origin.

Bund (Yiddish 'Union') Jewish socialist party, founded in Eastern Europe in 1897, of great influence in Russia till 1917; in Poland till 1939.

Doar ha-Yom (Daily Mail) Palestinian Hebrew daily, founded in 1920, with views to right of center. Somewhat sensationalist.

372

Glossary

dunam A unit of land measurement, equivalent to 1,000 square metres.

Gemarrah *See* **Talmud**.

hachshara (pl. hachsharot, lit. 'training') Pioneering training farms.

Hagana (Defense) A clandestine defense organization, set up in 1920.

he-Halutz (The Pioneer) A non-political association of pioneers preparing for immigration, affiliated to the Palestinian labor movement via the Histadrut.

havlaga (restraint) A policy of self-restraint adopted by the Zionist Executive and the Yishuv during the Arab Revolt, 1936–1939, which refrained from acts of retaliation against Arab terror.

Hazit ha-Am (The People's Front) Journal of extremist circles in the Palestine Revisionist Party, 1932–4.

heder (lit. 'room') Religious elementary school, often situated in one room in teacher's house.

Hever ha-Kvutzot (Kvutzot Association) Founded in 1928.

Hevrat ha-Ovdim The constructive arm of the Histadrut, an association of all the labor settlements, economic institutions and mutual aid associations. Founded 1923.

Hibat Zion (Love of Zion) A movement, started in 1881 in Eastern Europe, which advocated the return of Jews to Zion. The progenitor of the First Aliyah.

Histadrut (General Federation of Jewish Workers in Palestine) Founded in December 1920, it encompassed almost all Jewish workers in Palestine.

ha-Horesh (The Plowman) Association of Galilean Jewish workers, set up during the Second Aliyah.

Kaddish (Aram. 'sanctification') Mourner's prayer recited by bereaved son.

Kapai An acronym for Palestinian Labor Fund, started by Poalei Zion during the Second Aliyah. It lasted until 1925.

Keren ha-Yesod (Foundation Fund) Established in 1920 by the Zionist Organization to raise the funds required for the development, and particularly settlement, of Palestine. Met with limited success.

kibbutz artzi (nationwide kibbutz) Organization uniting numerous *kvutzot* or kibbutzim all over the country under single authority and leadership.

ha-Kibbutz ha-Meuhad (United Kibbutz Movement) A kibbutz movement, founded in 1927. It was a *kibbutz artzi* which soon encompassed more settlements and people than any other movement.

kiddush ha-Shem (sanctification of the Name) The concept of Jewish martyrdom.

Knesset The Israeli parliament.

kvutza (pl. **kvutzot**, lit. 'groups') Communal way of life, based on a small group of people, closely acquainted with one another. Its size is restricted by the principle of social capacity to absorb new members. First established in Degania in 1909.

J.C.A. (Jewish Colonization Association) Established in 1891 to encourage Jewish agricultural settlement all over the world.

373

Glossary

J.N.F. (Jewish National Fund) Established by the Zionist Organization in 1901 as a financial institution for purchase of land for Jewish settlement in Palestine.

ha-Mahanot ha-Olim (The Ascending Camps) Youth movement for student youth in Palestine, organized in the 1930s.

Mapai An acronym for Palestine Workers' Party, founded in 1930 through the amalgamation of ha-Poel ha-Tzair and Ahdut ha-Avoda. Was the dominant party in the Yishuv and, from 1933, in the Zionist Organization. Pivotal party in Israel till 1977.

ha-Mashbir (The Provider) Consumer cooperative institution, founded during the First World War to supply cheap food to workers. Became one of the most important economic institutions of the labor movement.

matmid Diligent student of religious studies.

melamed Infant teacher.

mi-Bifnim (From Within) Journal of ha-Kibbutz ha-Meuhad, founded in 1927.

mi-Kan umi-Kan (From Here and There) Novel by Yosef Hayim Brenner, describing life in the Second Aliyah, which appeared in 1911.

Mishan (Support) Workers' Social Security Fund.

Mishnah *See* **Talmud**.

Mizrahi Religious Zionist party, founded in 1902.

moshav Cooperative form of settlement, based on individual plots of land and individual households; contrasting with **kvutza**, which advocated communality.

Narodnaya Volya Movement of revolutionary Russian youth, which emerged in the 1870s with the aim of 'going to the people'. Composed basically of intellectuals, marked by purity of motive and great dedication.

ha-Noar ha-Oved (Working Youth) The movement of Jewish working youth in Palestine, established in 1925.

ha-Noar ha-Tzioni (Zionist Youth) Youth movement of the liberal Zionist Centre, founded in Central Europe in the early 1930s.

Non-Affiliated Group The manifestation of a trend within the labor movement which grew out of the Agricultural Workers' Union during the First World War, led by Berl Katznelson. One of the two political bodies which founded Ahdut ha-Avoda in 1919.

Notrim (Guards) An auxiliary Jewish police force under British command, formed in 1936.

P.C.P. (Palestine Communist Party) Founded 1921. Most of its members were Jewish but it was oriented towards the Arab *fellahim*. Extremely anti-Zionist

Pinkas (Notebook) Organ of the Histadrut, 1922.

Poalei Zion (Workers of Zion) Marxist-Borochovist party, established in Russia in 1906. Those of its members who immigrated to Palestine were active during the Second Aliyah.

ha-Poel ha-Tzair (The Young Worker) Populist party, established in Palestine in 1906, joined Mapai in 1930.

374

Glossary

poskim Literature on questions of *halakha* (Jewish law).

Revisionist Party Founded in 1925 by Zeev Jabotinsky, it demanded a revision of Zionist policy and greater activism. Based on the lower middle class; right-wing tendencies.

selihot Penitential prayers.

S.D. (Social Democracy) Socialist parties in Europe which opposed communist dictatorship and denied the need for revolution as a means of reforming society, believing that this could be attained through democratic means.

Seder Ritual observed on first two nights of Passover.

ha-Shomer (The Watchman) Jewish guard organization, founded by a group of Poalei Zion members in Palestine in 1909; symbolized the image of the 'new Jew'.

ha-Shomer ha-Tzair (The Young Watchman) Zionist youth movement established in Central and Eastern Europe towards the end of the First World War. Its members immigrated to Palestine from 1919 on and set up a kibbutz movement (ha-Kibbutz ha-Artzi ha-Shomer ha-Tzair). Left of Mapai.

Sifriyat ha-Poalim (Workers' Library) The publishing house founded by ha-Shomer ha-Tzair.

S.R.P. Social Revolutionary Party, founded in Russia at the beginning of this century, spiritual heir of Narodnaya Volya. Oriented towards the Russian peasantry; advocated terror as the instrument of political struggle.

S.S.R.P. An acronym for Zionist Socialist Labor Party. Founded in Russia in 1905, in the wake of the Uganda controversy, with a territorialist program.

Succot Feast of Tabernacles.

Talmud Summary of oral laws evolved by the sages in Palestine and Babylon. Its two main components are the Mishnah, a book of *halakha* (law) in Hebrew, and the commentary on it, the Gemarrah, in Aramaic.

talmud torah (study of the Torah) Religious school.

Tat 'Irgun' journal in Poland.

Torah The law of Moses.

Tzeirei Zion (Young Zionists) Socialist Zionist movement set up in Eastern Europe after the First World War. Its left wing became affiliated with Ahdut ha-Avoda and the right with ha-Poel ha-Tzair.

Vaad Leumi (National Committee) Executive body of the Asefat ha-Nivharim.

yeshiva Academy for study of Talmudic subjects.

Yishuv The Jewish community in Palestine before the establishment of Israel.

zaddik Righteous man, saintly figure.

Z.S. (Zionist Socialist Party) Zionist socialist movement which existed clandestinely in the Soviet Union in the 1920s. Some of its leaders immigrated to Palestine and joined Ahdut ha-Avoda, where they displayed outstanding organizational ability.

BIBLIOGRAPHICAL NOTE

Surprisingly enough, with the exception of a few articles (the outstanding among which is Israel Kolat's 'Berl Katznelson: Ish u-Nevo Lo' (A Man and his Vision), *Avot u-Meyasdim* (Fathers and Founders), Tel Aviv, 1975, pp. 85–113), this is the first biography of Berl Katznelson attempted so far. Historical research into the history of Zionism in general and the annals of the Israeli labor movement in particular is in its youth – dating back only twenty years. Most of the studies in this sphere have been published in the course of the past decade. This explains why the present bibliography is not abundant in secondary sources.

On the other hand, I was fortunate enough to have access to rich archival sources. When Berl died, his friends and disciples collected his letters in a special archive (BKA), which constitutes a special section of the Israel Labor Party Archives, housed in the educational institution which bears his name, Beit Berl (Berl's House). To Berl's extensive correspondence were added the diaries he kept in the last decade of his life and the files which he accumulated over the years.

The Labor Party Archives (BB) contain material from 1930 (the year in which Mapai was founded) to the present. Filed here are the minutes of meetings of all the Party's institutions (conferences, councils, the Central Committee, the Secretariat, the Bureau) and the minutes of informal gatherings; also housed here are the archives of Mapai's sister parties in the Diaspora – the World Union of Poalei Zion.

The Labor Movement Archives (LA) in Tel Aviv contain archival material on workers' associations, from the Second Aliyah (1904) to the present. Available here are the minutes of the Histadrut conferences and councils, as well as the archives of Ahdut ha-Avoda, Mapai's parent party. The Histadrut Executive Archives, containing the minutes of meetings of the Executive and the Secretariat, are located at the Executive headquarters in Tel Aviv.

Additional important material is housed in the Kibbutz ha-Meuhad Archives at Yad Tabenkin. It includes, *inter alia*, Tabenkin's archives and his correspondence with Berl.

The National and University Library in Jerusalem contains two private archives of vital importance to our subject: those of Dov Sadan (Stock) and of Hugo Bergman. Particularly rewarding is the correspondence between Berl and Sadan.

The Central Zionist Archives in Jerusalem (the archives of the Zionist Movement

376

Bibliography

and the Zionist Organization (CZA)) hold the minutes of all the Zionist congresses, and of Zionist Actions Committee meetings, as well as varied archival material relating to political activities, to the Vaad Leumi, the Jewish National Fund, etc.

The Genazim Archives in Tel Aviv, the archives of the Israel Writers Association, contain the private archives of writers and political essayists such as David Shimoni, Shlomo Grodzensky and others, which were of assistance to me in my work.

Berl's brother-in-law, A. M. Slutzkin of Kibbutz Ein Harod, placed at my disposal family archives and the archives of Sara Schmuckler, which have been in his possession since her death in 1919.

Dov Hos's daughter, Mrs Tamar Gidron, permitted me to peruse her father's archives.

Unless otherwise stated, all the books and articles listed are in Hebrew.

I BERL'S WRITINGS

Berl was a very prolific writer and an enthusiastic correspondent, as can be seen from the scope of his collected works and letters.

Collected Works, Vols. 1–12, Tel Aviv, 1945–1953
Letters, Vols. 1–3 (1900–1919), Yehuda Sharett (ed.), Tel Aviv, 1961–1976
　Vols. 4–5 (1919–1930), Yehuda Erez (ed.), Tel Aviv 1970–1973
ha-Mashbir, Tel Aviv, 1924 (booklet)
Rashei Perakim le-Toldot Tenuat ha-Poalim be-Eretz Israel (Brief History of the Labor Movement in Palestine), stenographic record of lectures, Nov. 1928, second edition 1935 (in stencil)
Arakhim Genuzim (Hidden Values), Ephraim Broide (ed.), Tel Aviv, 1957 (Berl's collected lectures)
Berl Katznelson (ed.), *ba-Avoda* (At Work), Jaffa, 1918 (booklet)
　ha-Kibbutz veha-Kvutza, Yalkut le-Berur She'elat ha'Ihud (The Kibbutz and Kvutza, an Anthology), Tel Aviv, 1940
　ba-Kur (In the Crucible), a contemporary anthology, Tel Aviv, 1941

II INTERVIEWS

In order to round out the picture, I interviewed some thirty of Berl's colleagues and rivals, whose testimony was a vitally important source of information and insight.

III NEWSPAPERS AND JOURNALS

ha-Poel ha-Tzair
ha-Ahdut

Bibliography

ha-Adama
Kuntres
Davar
mi-Bifnim
ha-Aretz
ha-Olam
Niv ha-Kvutza
Hazit ha-Am
Yediot ha-Tenua le-Ahdut ha-Avoda
Be'ayot

IV SELECTED BIBLIOGRAPHY

This bibliography lists those books which served as direct sources for the present work.

Snir, Mordechai (ed.), *Al Berl Katznelson* (On Berl Katznelson), Tel Aviv, 1952 (an anthology of the reminiscences of Berl's contemporaries)

On his Eastern European roots

Primary sources
Ahad ha-Am, *Kol Kitvei* (Collected Works), Tel Aviv–Jerusalem, 1961
Bin Gurion (Berdichevsky), Micha Yosef, *Ma'amarim* (Articles), Leipzig, 1922
Dinur, Ben Zion, *be-Olam she-Shaka* (In a World that Disappeared), Jerusalem, 1958
Katznelson-Nesher, Hanna, *Ah ve-Ahot* (Brother and Sister), Tel Aviv, 1978
Shazar, Zalman, *Zion ve-Zedek* (Zion and Justice), Tel Aviv, 1971
Slutsky, Yehuda (ed.), *Bobruisk*, Vols. 1–2, Tel Aviv, 1967
Zilberfarb, M., *Roiter Pinkes, Ershter Zamelbuch* (Red Notebook, a First Anthology) (Yiddish), Warsaw, 1921
    Sotzialistisher Territorialism, Ershter Zamelbuch (Socialist Territorialism, a first Anthology), Paris, 1934 (Yiddish)

Secondary sources
Frankel, Jonathan, *Prophecy and Politics: Socialism, Nationalism and the Russian Jews, 1862–1917*, Cambridge, 1981 (English)

On the Second Aliyah period (1904–1918)

Primary sources
Ben Gurion, David, *Zikhronot* (Memoirs), Vol. 1, Tel Aviv, 1971
    Igrot (Letters), Vol. 1, Tel Aviv, 1971

Bibliography

Brenner, Yosef Hayim, *Ketavim* (Collected Works), Vols. 1–2, Tel Aviv, 1978
   Igrot (Letters), Vols. 1–2, Tel Aviv, 1941
Golomb, Eliyahu, *Hevyon Oz* (Hidden Strength), Vols. 1–2, Tel Aviv, 1950
Habas, Bracha (ed.), *Sefer ha-Aliyah ha-Shniya* (The Second Aliyah Book) Tel
   Aviv, 1947
Israeli, Ben Zion, *Ketavim u-Devarim* (Articles and Speeches), Tel Aviv, 1956
Katznelson-Shazar, Rachel, *Masot u-Reshimot* (Essays and Articles), Tel Aviv, 1946
Kushnir, Mordechai (ed.), *Y. H. Brenner, Mivhar Divrei Zikhronot* (Selected
   Reminiscences by his Friends), Tel Aviv, 1944
Ruppin, Arthur, *Pirkei Hayai* (My Life and Work), Tel Aviv, 1968

Secondary sources
C'naani, David, *ha-Aliyah ha-Shniya ha-Ovedet ve-Yahasa la-Dat vela-Masoret* (The
   Second Aliyah Labor Movement and its Attitude to Religion and Tradition), Tel
   Aviv, 1977
Frankel, Rafael, 'Yosef Bussel, ha-Kommuna ha-Haderatit ve-Hivatzrut ha-Kvutza'
   (Yosef Bussel, the Hadera Commune and the Creation of the Kvutza),
   ha-Tziyonut, No. 4, Tel Aviv, 1976, pp. 44–71
Gorni, Yosef, 'Shinuyim be-Mivneh ha-Aliyah ha-Shniya' (Changes in the Structure
   of the Second Aliyah), *ha-Tziyonut*, No. 1, Tel Aviv, 1970, pp. 204–47
Slutzky, Yehuda, *Sefer Toldot ha-Hagana* (The History of the Hagana), Vol. 1, Tel Aviv,
   1963
Teveth, Shabtai, *Kinat David* (The Zeal of David, a Biography), Vol. 1, Tel Aviv,
   1976

Kolat, Israel, '*Ideologia u-Metziyut be-Tenuat ha-Poalim ba-Aliyah ha-Shniya*' (Ideology
   and Reality in the Labor Movement in the Second Aliyah), unpubl. Ph.D thesis,
   Hebrew University, Jerusalem, 1965

On the history of the Palestinian labor movement

Primary sources
Al ha-Saf (On the Threshold) Jerusalem, 1918
Ben Gurion, David, *Zikhronot* (Memoirs), Vols. 1–2, Tel Aviv, 1971–1973
   Igrot (Letters), Vols. 1–3, Tel Aviv, 1971, 1974
Ben Zvi, Yitzhak, *ha-Gdudim ha-Ivri'im* (The Jewish Battalions), Jerusalem, 1969
Repetur, Berl, *le-Lo Heref* (Unceasingly), Vols. 1–2, Tel Aviv, 1973
Tabenkin, Yitzhak, *Devarim* (Writings), Vols. 1–3, Tel Aviv, 1967, 1974
Yalkut Ahdut ha-Avoda (Ahdut ha-Avoda Anthology), A–B, Tel Aviv, 1929–1932

Secondary sources
Bar-Zohar, Michael, *Ben Gurion, biografia* (Ben Gurion, A Biography), Vol. 1, Tel
   Aviv, 1975

Bibliography

Gorni, Yosef, *Ahdut ha-Avoda, 1919–1930, ha-Yesodot ha-Ra'ayoni'im veha-Shita ha-Medinit* (Ahdut ha-Avoda, 1919–1930, The Ideological Foundations and the Political Methodology), Tel Aviv, 1973

Kolat, Israel, 'Ahdut ha-Avoda: mi-Hevrat Avoda le-Mifleget Ovdim' (From a Workers' Society to a Labor Party), *Asupot*, October 1969, pp. 3–23

'Poalei Zion bein Ziyonut le-Communism' (Poalei Zion between Zionism and Communism), *Asupot*, November 1971, pp. 30–52

Shapira, Anita, *ha-Ma'avek ha-Nikhzav* (A Futile Struggle), Tel Aviv, 1977

'he-Halom ve-Shivro' (The Dream and its Meaning), *ba-Derekh, Givat Haviva*, No. 3, December 1968, pp. 34–63; No. 4, August 1969, pp. 33–54

Shapira, Jonathan, *Ahdut ha-Avoda ha-Historit* (The Historical Ahdut ha-Avoda), Tel Aviv, 1975

Teveth, Shabtai, *Kinat David* (The Zeal of David), Vol. 2, Tel Aviv, 1980

The labor movement and the Revisionists

Primary sources

Ahimeir, Abba, *Ketavim* (Collected Works), Vols. 1–4, Tel Aviv, 1966, 1974

Golomb, Eliyahu, *Hevyon Oz* (Hidden Strength), Vols. 1–2, Tel Aviv, 1950

Jabotinsky, Zeev, *Ketavim* (Collected Works), Jerusalem, 1947–1959

Yevin, Yehoshua Heshel, *Yerushalayim Mehaka* (Jerusalem Waits), Jerusalem, 1939

Secondary sources

Ophir, Y., *Sefer ha-Oved ha-Leumi* (Book of the National Worker), Tel Aviv, 1959

Schectmann, Yosef, *Zeev Jabotinsky, biografia* (Jabotinsky, a Biography), Vols. 1–3, Tel Aviv, 1957

Shapira, Anita, 'ha-Vikuah be-Mapai al ha-Shimush be-Alimut, 1932–1935' (The Debate in Mapai on the Use of Violence, 1932–1935), *ha-Tziyonut*, No. 5, Tel Aviv, 1978, pp. 141–81

Shavit, Ya'akov, *me-Rov li-M'dina* (Revisionism in Zionism), Tel Aviv, 1978

The polemics with ha-Kibbutz ha-Meuhad

Primary sources

Dan, Hayim (ed.), *Sefer Klosova* (The Book of Klosova), Tel Aviv, 1958

Mishpat ha-Shivah (Trial of the Seven), Tel Aviv, October 1942

Yerah ha-Iyun (Study Month), Report of the Study-Month Secretariat, publ. by the Histadrut

Secondary sources

Utiker, Israel, *Tenuat he-Halutz be-Polin, 1932–1935* (The he-Halutz Movement in

Bibliography

Poland, 1932–1935), Tel Aviv, 1972

Harel, Yehuda, *Mekoroteha shel Siya Bet be-Tel Aviv* (The Origins of Faction B in Tel Aviv), M.A. thesis , Tel Aviv University (in stencil)

Zionist policy

Primary sources

Al Darkei Mediniyuteinu (On our Political Path), Council of the World Union of Poalei Zion, 29 July – 7 August 1937, full report, Tel Aviv, 1938

ha-Cohen, David, *Et he-Saper* (Time to Tell), Tel Aviv, 1974

Locker, Berl, *me-Kitov ad Yerushalayim* (From Kitov to Jerusalem), Jerusalem, 1977

Rose, N. A., *Baffy: The Diaries of Blanche Dugdale, 1936–1947*, London, 1973 (English)

Sharett, Moshe, *Yoman Medini* (Political Diary), Vols. 1–5, Tel Aviv, 1968–1979

Secondary sources

Cohen, Michael J., *Palestine: Retreat from the Mandate. The Making of British Policy*, New York, 1978 (English)

Eilam, Yigal, *ha-Gdudim ha-Ivri'im* (The Jewish Battalions), Tel Aviv, 1973

Margalit, Elkanah, 'ha-Vikuah be-Tenuat ha-Avoda be-Eretz Israel al Ra'ayon ha-Medina ha-Du Leumit' (The Debate in the Palestine Labor Movement on the Idea of the Bi-National State), *ha-Tziyonut*, No. 4, Tel Aviv, 1976, pp. 183–258

Porat, Yehoshua, *Tzemihat ha-Tenua ha-Leumit ha-Arvit ha-Palestinait, 1918–1929* (The Emergence of the Palestinian–Arab National Movement, 1918–1929), Jerusalem, 1971

mi-Mehumot le-Medina: ha-Tenua ha-Leumit ha-Palestinait, 1929–1939 (From Riots to Rebellion – the Palestinian Arab National Movement, 1929–1939), Tel Aviv, 1978

Slutzky, Yehuda, *Sefer Toldot ha-Hagana* (Hagana Book), Vols. 1–2, Tel Aviv, 1963

Sefer Toldot ha-Hagana (Hagana Book), Vol. 3, Tel Aviv, 1972

The Holocaust

bi-Yemei Shoah (In time of Holocaust), testimony of he-Halutz emissaries, ha-Kibbutz ha-Meuhad

Palgi, Yoel, *Ruah Gedola Ba'ah* (A Great Wind was Blowing), Tel Aviv, 1977

INDEX

Abramovitch, Zeev, 127
ha-Adama, literary journal of Ahdut ha-
Avoda, 111; Berl helps produce, 137
Adler, Ruth, 320
Afikim kibbutz, 244; Berl and, 243, 326
Agnon, S. Y., 24, 27, 32, 282, 312; Berl's
friendship with, 142, 143, 170, 315, 345;
describes Berl, 49, 91
agricultural colonies, colonist farmers, 6n,
28–9, 38–9, 62; Berl's attitude to, 52
agricultural education, Berl advocates, 51,
63
agricultural workers, Jewish, 38–9, 41–2,
50, 52; compared with Arab workers,
28–9, 103; regarded by Berl as nucleus
of Palestinian society, 52, 54, 75
Agricultural Workers' Union, 50, 51, 64,
79, 88, 89; Berl's work in, 53, 78, 83,
85, 150, 155
Agudat Israel, 102n, 146n, 276
Ahad ha-Am, 12, 70, 126, 171, 282; Berl's
assessment of, 258
Aharonovitch, Yosef, 24, 25, 39, 51, 138,
193; asked by Berl to contribute to
Davar, 142
Aharonovitch (Aran), Zalman (Ziama), 152,
290; Berl's relations with, 191, 192, 200,
205
ha-Ahdut, Poalei Zion journal, 45
Ahdut ha-Avoda, 65, 82–90, 100, 102, 126,
137, 151–2, 167, 208; Berl addresses
Fourth Conference of (1924), 133–6;
Berl's part in establishment of, 82, 84,
85, 88, 90–1; Berl's status and role
within, 101, 114–15, 126, 128, 132, 151,
152, 153, 154, 347, 348; delegation to
World Zionist Congress (1927), 157–8;
dissension within, over settlement issues,
155–6; financial difficulties, 111–12;
leadership of, 114, 155; merger with ha-

Poel ha-Tzair, 159–61; relations with
Poalei Zion, 89, 90, 107, 108, 109–10,
132, 134, 135–6; structure of, 154; and
Third Aliyah, 112, 113, 114
le-Ahdut ha-Avoda party, 339, 341
Ahimeir, Abba, 188, 194; Berl's feelings
about guilt of, in Arlosoroff murder
case, 195, 196, 197; writes about Berl,
19, 145, 342
Alexander II, Tsar, assassination of, 10
Alexander III, Tsar, treatment of Jews
under, 1, 11
Aliyah, see Aliyah Bet; First Aliyah; Second
Aliyah; Third Aliyah; Fourth Aliyah;
immigration
Aliyah Bet (illegal immigration), 285, 287–
9, 317, 336; Berl's involvement in, 274–
5, 276, 278, 288, 348
Allenby, General Edmund, 68, 98, 99
Am Oved publishing house: Berl's editorship of, 300–2, 310–17, 323, 348, 355;
books published by, 311–13, 314, 317,
321
American Jewry, see United States
Anglo-Jewry, 179–80, 275; Berl's links
with, 175–6, 258
Anokhi, Zalman Yitzhak, asked by Berl to
write for Davar, 142
anti-Semitism, 12, 98, 183; see also pogroms
Arab Higher Committee, 253
Arab literature, Berl's attitude to, 314
Arab Rebellion (1936), 231, 253–4, 264
Arab riots of 1929, 166–7, 170, 174, 177,
183, 186, 265
Arabs, Palestinian: Berl's attitude towards,
134, 167–8, 169–71, 178, 254, 257, 333–
4; Berl's encounter with Arab plowman
('the day of Ibrahim'), 68–9; Berl's
solution to problem of, 168–9, 180–1,
292–3; British attitude towards, 98, 177–

382

Index

Index

Ben Gurion, David (*cont.*)
Ahdut ha-Avoda, 89, 92, 114, 155; Marxist approach to socialism, 84, 107, 344; pact with Jabotinsky, 197, 203–6, 207; and parity proposal, 257; and Poalei Zion, 77, 78, 84, 85, 87, 89, 109, 111, 135–6; receives news of Berl's death, 341; relations with Berl, 90, 114–15, 136, 139, 160, 199, 234, 255, 269, 334, 352; and Revisionists, 189, 190, 191, 203–4, 284; and rift within Mapai, 296–7, 307–9, 326, 327, 328–39 *passim*; at St James's Palace talks, 275–6; and scheme to coopt American Jewish workers into Zionist Organization, 270, 271; stand on Arab problem, 167–8, 178, 292; stand on use of force, 199; supports partition, 264, 265–6, 268, 272–3; and unification of kibbutz movement, 233, 234, 235, 237, 239, 242; and unification of labor movement, 85, 87–8; and Weizmann, 102–3, 173, 279, 280; Zionism of, 8, 25, 86, 266, 291, 336, 344, 358; on Zionist Executive, 197, 207, 223, 274
Ben Shemen: Berl addresses Third Conference of Judean workers at (1912), 51–2; Berl represents workers of, at Second Conference of Judean workers (1911), 50; Berl works at plant nursery in, 49, 53, 54, 55
Ben Yeruham, Dov, 240
Ben Zvi, Yitzhak, 24, 25, 77, 78, 83, 90, 96, 107, 109, 167; describes Berl's attitude to unification of labor movement, 84–5
Benyamin, Rabbi, 142; accuses Berl of failure to rescue Jews, 322
Berdichevsky, Micha Yosef, influence on Berl, 70, 71, 72, 73, 79, 84, 116, 337, 338, 345
Bergman, Hugo, 171, 282; relations with Berl, 139, 142, 168, 170
Berlin, Rabbi Meir, 196
Berlin, Berl's visits to, 172; as delegate to Congress of Labor Palestine (1930), 178–9; as delegate to Sixth Conference of Poalei Zion Alliance (1923), 132
Berman, Moshe, manager of Kinneret farm, 42, 43, 44, 45, 59
Betar, Betarists: Berl's attitude to, 186–7,

190–1, 192, 193, 194, 199, 202; relations between Histadrut and, 189–203 *passim*; *see also* Revisionists
Betzer, Israel, 47
Bevin, Ernest, 260
Bialik, H. N., 141; poem 'In the City of Slaughter', 14
Biltmore Program, 291, 317, 331–2, 333, 334, 335–6; Berl welcomes, 333, 334, 335–6
Bilu colony, 58
Blaustein, Rachel, 25
Bloch-Blumenfeld, Ephraim, 101, 107
Bloi, Rabbi Moshe, 276
Blumenfeld, Kurt, 171; Berl's anger at, 158–9
Bobruisk, Russia, 1–2, 15, 40, 58, 91, 123; Berl teaches at Bobruisk school, 16–17; Berl works in Yiddish library, 11, 21; Berl's childhood in, 1–11; Jewish intelligentsia in, 7, 8, 10–11
Bolshevik Revolution, 73; Berl's attitude to, 106–7, 110, 174, 184–5, 193, 199, 224, 344; impact on Jewish labor movement, 86, 105–6, 107, 113, 198; Zionist Organization and, 109
Borochov, Ber, Borochovism, 13, 15, 83, 88, 134, 344; Berl and, 38, 84, 108, 313
Brailsford, Henry Noel, Berl meets, 176
Brandeis, Louis, 98, 270
Brenner, Batya, 58, 60
Brenner, Yosef Hayim, 17, 24, 25, 69, 111, 112, 137, 143, 304, 310, 352; Berl and, 31–3, 34, 37, 40, 70–1, 115, 261, 345; describes Berl, 32; *mi-Kan umi-Kan*, 32; murder of, 100
Brit ha-Biryonim, 195
Brit Shalom, 146, 167, 172, 178; Berl's attitude to, 170–1
British Labor Party, 76n, 179, 292; Berl's contacts with, 176, 258–60
British Zionist Federation, Berl's speech at 1930 conference, 175
Brodetsky, Zelig, Berl praises, 256
Buber, Martin, 113, 245
Bund, Bundists, 7, 17; American, 86, 118, 119, 120, 271; Berl meets Polish, 210; Berl's early contacts with, in Russia, 8, 16
Burla, Yehuda, asked by Berl to contribute to *Davar*, 142

Index

Index

Eretz Israel, Berl's early awareness of, 6–7
European Jewry, Berl's vision of extinction of, 290–1
Evian Conference (1938), 275, 279
'externists', 11–14, 18; Berl as one of, 11, 12–13, 14

Faction B: alliance with ha-Kibbutz ha-Meuhad, 239–41, 250, 297–8, 325–6, 338; allocated one-third of seats on party institutions, 309, 325, 331; Berl and, 241, 308, 329–31, 338; and Biltmore Program, 332, 336; emergence as independent group, 239, 307, 324, 325; non-cooperation policy in party life, 325, 327–30; opposition to Berl, 301–2, 304, 325; pro-Soviet orientation, 293–4, 337; see also le-Ahdut ha-Avoda party
fascism, fascists, 187, 188, 199, 232, 259, 335; Berl and, 186, 202, 338
Feigin, Rivka, 196–7
Feinstein, Zeev, 231, 244, 248
Feisel, Emir, later King of Iraq, 98, 99
Fichman, Yaakov, Berl publishes works of, 312
Filastin, Arab paper, 171
Finland, Russian invasion of, 294
First Aliyah (1882–1903), 6n, 29; Berl hears about as a child, 7; relations with Second Aliyah, 24–5; see also agricultural colonies
First World War, 57, 291; Berl and, 78–9; Jewish involvement in, 75–6
Flakon, Leib, boyhood friend of Berl, 19
Flexner, Bernard, 121
Forverts, 118, 119, 120, 124
Fourth Aliyah (1924–6), 156, 326; Berl and, 152, 154
France: fall of (1940), 285, 287, 298; liberation of, 341; occupation of Syria by, 186
Franco, Francisco, 296
Frankel, Avraham Halevi, 282
Frankfurter, Felix, 271
Frankfurter Zeitung, 143
Freud, Sigmund, 113, 338
Fridland, Benny, describes Berl's arrival in Palestine, 22–3
Froumine factory strike, Jerusalem (1932), 189–90, 201
Fula settlement, 42

fund-raising campaigns for Palestine labor movement, 156, 158, 297; Berl's part in, 115, 117–24, 266–7

Galicia: Berl visits pioneering training farms in, 210–11; Poalei Zion in, 135
Galilee: agricultural colonies in, 25, 39; Arab raids in Upper (1920), 99; Berl in, 55, 57, 92, 125; Berl's description of, 34, 36–7; communal experiments in, 24, 39, 42–3; Sea of (Lake Kinneret), 58, 59; Second Aliyah pioneers' view of, 41–2; siege and British capture of, 67, 72, 76, 77, 81; see also Galilee Workers' Union
Galilee Workers' Union, 49–50; Berl active in, 47, 63, 65; Berl attends Um Juni conference (1911), 46–7
Galili, Israel, 274, 326, 327; relations with Berl, 222, 223–4, 308
Gandhi, Mohandas Karamchand ('Mahatma'), 343; Berl's admiration for, 276, 312
Gaza region, 266
Gedera, 58
Geneva: Berl attends 21st Zionist Congress (1939), 277–80; Rescue Committee in, 320
Germany, 183, 202, 309; Berl's relations with Zionists in, 158, 171, 172, 176; Berl's visits to, 132, 164, 171–2, 178–9; Jewish immigration to Palestine from, 245; Jewish resistance in areas occupied by, 290; Jews in, 242, 275; non-aggression pact with Soviet Union, 279, 293; Social Democratic party of, 198, 270; see also Nazis
Ginsburg, Shimon, friend of Berl in Bobruisk, 11
Givat Brenner kibbutz, 231, 248; Berl visits, 235, 331; Kibbutz ha-Meuhad conference at (1944), 331
Givat ha-Shlosha kibbutz, Berl visits, 235
Gluecksohn, Moshe, 140
Golda, manager at Kinneret farm, 45
Goldberg, Leah, 315
Goldman, Rabbi Solomon, 278
Goldmann, Nahum, 272
Goldsmith, O. d'Avigdor, 175
Golomb, Eliyahu, 205, 265, 283, 308, 319, 326; attitude to British, 286, 293; and Berl, 89, 114, 127, 163, 191, 193, 263,

Index

287; and Haganah, 76n, 287; status in labor movement leadership group, 89, 152

Gordon, Aharon David, 57, 60, 62, 64; idealistic view of 'conquest of labor', 33, 38–9; relations with Berl, 31, 33, 34, 39, 90, 353

Gordonia, 205, 238; Berl's attitude to, 222, 226, 229, 233, 235; Berl's tour of groups in Poland, 210, 212, 216

Gorky, Maxim, 143; Berl meets, 174

Great Britain, British, 111, 117, 281, 309, 344; anti-Zionism of, 98–9, 177, 178, 254–5; and Arabs, 98, 177–8, 181, 273, 275–6; Berl advocates policy of 'constructive resistance' towards, 276–9, 286–7, 289; Berl's attitude to, 99–101, 147, 178–9, 185, 254–5, 273, 293; Berl's visits to, 164–5, 172–7, 179–80, 212, 246, 256–61, 263–4, 269–70, 272–3, 275–6; military administration of Palestine, 98–9, 100; occupation of Palestine, 67, 69, 71, 72, 75, 99; proposal for establishment of Jewish state in East Africa, 13–14; relations between Yishuv and, 75–6, 98–101, 147, 177, 285–8, 325; White Paper (1939), 276, 277, 278, 282, 286, 336; Zionist movement in, 101, 173, 175, 177; see also Anglo-Jewry; Balfour Declaration; British Labor Party; Hope-Simpson; legislative council; London; Macdonald, Ramsay; Mandate; Passfield; Peel Commission

Greenberg, Uri Zvi, 188, 189; Berl and, 142, 314

Greenspan, Hershel, 242

Gruenbaum, Yitzhak, 272

Guttmann, Nahum, 311

'gymnasists', see Herzliya Gymnasium

Haan, Jacob Israel de, Berl's attitude to murder of, 146

Habas, Bracha: Berl and, 222, 264; *Our Little Heroes*, 311

Habimah Theater, 314

Hadassah Women's Conference, Berl attends, 270. 271

Hadera commune, 34, 58; Berl works as woodcutter at, 35–6

Hagana, 117, 167, 281, 285, 288, 304, 317, 326, 336; Berl's special relationship with, 175, 277, 280, 287; establishment of, 76n, 100, 186

Hague, the, Berl visits, 270

Haifa, 250, 285, 287, 326; Ahdut ha-Avoda conference in (1920), 113–14; Berl attends party seminar at Rutenberg House (1944), 338; Labor Council, 198, 204, 324

Haikin, Bat-Sheva, 152, 326

el Hakim, Tewfik, *The Diary of an Egyptian Village Prosecutor*, Berl publishes, 314

Halamyia training camp, Egypt, Berl sent to, 80

he-Halutz, 99, 107, 108, 112, 208, 223, 227, 244, 290, 321; Ben Gurion and, 234; Berl's contempt for returned he-Halutz emissaries, 295–6; Berl's letter 'To the he-Halutz Movement', 67, 71–2; Berl's reservations about ha-Kibbutz ha-Meuhad's educational methods in, 160–1, 208–9, 212–18, 219; Berl's tour of groups in Poland, 209–12; Conference in Danzig (1927), 159, 160; he-Halutz ha-Tzair, 215; immigrants in Palestine, 112, 238; Palestinian emissaries to, during Second World War, 280, 294–6, 317

Harzfeld, Avraham, 157, 158

Hashin, Alexander, 78, 109

Hayot, Huma, 237

Hazan, Ya'akov, 301

Hazaz, Hayim, works published by Berl, 312

Hazit Ha'am, Revisionist journal, 195; attacks on Berl, 189

Hebrew language, 31, 98, 108, 133, 135; Berl brought up on, 3, 4, 7, 10; Berl's attitude to, 16–17, 38, 51, 63, 72, 81, 85–6; dispute over choice of, as national language, 85–7, 89, 132; knowledge of, in pioneering training groups, 210, 213; language of Second Aliyah pioneers, 28, 55

Hebrew literature: Berl's belief in importance of, in Jewish national movement, 144, 304, 305, 310; Berl's early exposure to, 3, 4, 7; published by Berl at Am Oved, 311–12, 314

Herzen, Alexander, Berl influenced by works of, 8, 106, 199, 313

Herzl, Theodore, Herzlian Zionism, 7, 12, 13, 20, 71, 102, 291; Berl and, 73, 258

387

Index

Index

390

Index

Index

legislative council scheme for Palestine, 201; Berl's opposition to, 173, 180–2
Lehi, 341; and Berl, 317
Lenin, 343
Leshchinsky, Yaakov, 312
Levin, Shmaryahu, 25, 101
Levite, Liova, 232, 295
Levkovitch (Lavi), Shlomo, 57, 60, 64, 110, 129, 130, 186, 243, 313
Levtov, Petahia, 93
Liebknecht, Karl, 79
Liessin, Abraham, 120, 124
Lilienblum, Moshe Leib, 7
Lima, Nehemia de, Berl visits, 270
Lipson, Mordechai, 141
Lithuania, 11, 306; Berl visits, 186–7; Tzeirei Zion in, 133, 135
Livenstein, Eliezer, 231, 245
Locker, Berl, 132, 133, 187; Berl and, 134, 135, 273
Lodz, Poland, 319; Berl visits, 211
London: Berl attends St James's Palace talks (1939), 275–6; Berl attends Zionist Actions Committee session (1919), 101, 102; Berl attends Zionist Conference (1920), 101–4; Berl meets British Labor Party members, 176–7, 261; Berl meets Jewish Agency offices team, 256–7, 258; Berl meets Zionist leaders (1930), 172–5; Berl receives medical treatment in, 261, 264, 272; Berl speaks at Conference of British Zionist Federation (1930), 175; Berl's links with Jewish high society in, 175–6, 258; Berl's talks with Jabotinsky in (1939), 282–4
London School of Economics, 142
Lourie, Arthur, Berl praises, 256
Lubianiker (Labon), Pinhas, 205n, 229, 241, 242, 248, 336
Lucerne, Berl attends 19th Zionist Congress in (1935), 222–3
Lufban, Yitzhak, hostility between Berl and, 138–40
Luzinsky, Kadish, 8
Lvov, Poland, Berl visits, 210–11

MacDonald, Malcolm, Colonial Secretary, 273, 274, 276
MacDonald, Ramsay, 177; 'MacDonald letter', 179, 180, 183, 187, 265

Magnes, Dr J. L., 119–20, 126, 171; Berl meets, 119
ha-Mahanot ha-Olim youth movement, 222, 248; Berl and, 233, 234–5, 238, 247, 299
malaria: Berl falls ill with, 34; Jewish settlers afflicted by, 35, 43, 57, 58, 59
Maletz, David, 231, 243
Mandate, 264, 266, 332; Berl and, 181, 262, 265, 267, 272
Manhattan Opera House, Berl attends fund-raising concert, 120–1
manual labor: Berl's failure at, in Russia, 18–19, 20; Berl perseveres at, in Palestine, 30–1, 33, 35, 37, 42, 47–8; Berl's view of, 46, 48, 72, 302
Maoz Hayim, 248
Mapai, 154, 161–2, 178, 183, 216, 223, 270, 341, 342; Berl addresses Rehovot Conference (1938), 235–9; Berl attends Central Committee meeting at Ayanot (1940), 298–9; Berl attends Council meeting in Jerusalem (1944), 330–1; Berl attends Council meeting in Tel Aviv (1931), 180–2; Berl attends his last session of Central Committee (July 1944), 339; Berl fears split in, 204, 242; Berl's concern over pro-Soviet orientation of, 294–6, 303, 325; Berl's explanation for causes of split in, 337; Berl's gradual alienation from, 162, 197–8, 199–200, 201, 202, 206–7, 299, 309, 323, 325; Berl's plans for reorganization of, 307–9; Berl's position in, 192, 193, 197, 207, 248, 328; debate between activists and moderates over British policy, 286–9; disunity of, 239–40, 242–3, 250, 277, 286, 296–300, 302, 325; Kfar Vitkin conference (1942), 324, 327–8, 331; and Revisionists, 183, 187, 189–207 passim; split in, 324–37 passim; stand on use of terror, 281–2; wins overwhelming majority in elections to Histadrut Conference (1944), 339; see also Faction B
Marks, Simon, 266; Berl meets, 175
Marxism, 10, 344–5; Berl and, 73, 84, 345; of Poalei Zion, 38; of ha-Shomer ha-Tzair, 162
Masaryk, Jan, Berl meets, 273

Index

Index

ha-Poel ha-Tzair (party weekly), 33, 51, 137, 138–9, 141, 142
pogroms, 78, 105, 322; see also Kishinev; Kristallnacht
Poland, 108, 193, 344; anti-Semitism in, 183; Berl refuses Ussishkin's invitation to visit, 223; Berl visits pioneering training farms in, 209–14, 216; Berl's condemnation of Zionist labor movement in wartime, 295–6; Nazi treatment of Polish Jewry, 275, 279, 284, 289; no Palestinian assistance to Jews in wartime, 290; return of he-Halutz emissaries from Russian-occupied, 294–5; Revisionists in, 187, 188, 195
Poriya settlement, 57
Prague, Berl attends 18th Zionist Congress in (1933), 195–6, 197
Prohorovski, Leib (Berl's uncle), 3, 8
Proudhon, Pierre Joseph, work published by Berl, 313
Pushkin, Alexander, 3

Rabinovitch, Ya'akov, 142
Rabinovitz, A. S., see Azar
Ramat Gan, Berl's home in, 317
Ramle Platform, 38
Rehovot, 7; Berl addresses Fourth Mapai Conference in (1938), 235–9, 243, 298; Berl's speech at Judean Workers' Union conference in (1918), 72–5; Berl's study month in, 304–5
Religious Workers party, 339
Remez, David, 50, 89, 124, 126, 132, 157, 158, 191, 206, 295; and Berl's anthology The Kibbutz and the Kvutza, 250, 251; disagrees with Berl over non-cooperation policy, 286; in Histadrut Secretariat, 130, 250, 297; proposes Berl as sole editor of Am Oved, 300, 302; spends vacation with Berl in Lucerne (1935), 223
Repetur, Berl, 145, 152, 326; breaks news of Beilinson's death to Berl, 261; opposes Berl's proposals on Betarists, 191; supported by Berl in illegal immigration activities, 274, 288
Reuters news agency, Cairo, 143
Revisionists, Revisionism, 145, 146, 149, 172, 187, 188–9, 281, 335; attempts at

reconciliation between Histadrut and, 201–6; attitude to Berl, 189; Berl demands commission of inquiry into terrorist groups within, 195, 196; Berl seeks dialog with, 282–3; Berl's attitude to, 180, 183, 188, 191, 193, 197, 201–6, 264; and murder of Arlosoroff, 194–6; see also Betar
Revusky, Abraham, 120, 127
Riga Betarists, Berl meets, 186–7
Rishon le-Zion, Berl addresses Fourth Conference of Judean Workers' Union in (1913), 53
roadbuilding project in northern Palestine, 111, 112, 113
Rommel, Erwin, North African offensive of, 308, 309, 323
Rosenberg, Arthur, Berl publishes work of, 312
Rosenblatt, Yossele, 120
Rosenblatt, Zvi, 194, 196, 197
Rotberg, Meir, 42, 51, 53, 60; and ha-Mashbir project, 63, 64, 128
Rotenstreich, Nathan, Berl's attitude towards, 315
Rothschild, Baron Edmond de, 29
Rousseau, Jean-Jacques, Berl publishes works of, 313
Rubashov (Shazar), Zalman, 156, 290, 313; Berl's admiration for, 91; on Davar's editorial staff, 141, 142, 149, 192, 200; lectures at Berl's study month, 304; speaks at Fourth Ahdut ha-Avoda conference (1924), 133, 135; view of Berl, 49, 310, 345
Rumania, Nazi take-over of, 289
Ruppin, Arthur, 25, 101, 178; describes Berl, 345; negotiates with Berl at Kinneret, 43, 44, 45, 46; proposes establishment of workers' bank, 104
Russia, Tsarist, 24, 35, 43; Berl influenced by revolutionary literature of, 8–9, 10, 199; Berl's childhood and youth in, 1–22, 144; influence of 1905 Revolution on Berl, 10, 15, 17, 18, 84, 100, 345, 346, 350; Jewish avoidance of military duty in, 21, 26; relations between Jews and non-Jews in, 2, 13, 14–15; Social Democratic Party, 8; see also Pale of Settlement; Social Revolutionary Party

395

Index

relations with, 115, 145, 228, 229, 304, 342; relations with ha-Kibbutz ha-Meuhad, 215, 216; Socialist League of, 324, 325, 339

Sick Fund, Berl's involvement with, 50, 53, 262

Sieff, Israel, Sieff family, Berl's links with, 175, 258, 266

Sifriyat ha-Poalim publishing house, 301

Silberfarb, M., reports on Berl's propaganda work in southern Russia, 16

Silone, Ignazio, *School for Dictators*, published by Berl, 312

Silver, Dr Abba Hillel, Berl's attack on, 278

Simon, Ernst, 149, 170

Slutzkin, A. M., 126

Slutzkin, Bluma, *see* Miron, Bluma

Smiella, Berl witnesses pogrom in, 15

Social Revolutionary Party, Russia, 8, 9, 10, 15, 117, 174

socialism: of Ahdut ha-Avoda, 88–9, 103; of American Jewry, 86; Berl organizes discussions on, at Kinneret, 64–5; Berl's conception of, 73–4, 88, 106–7, 147–8, 149, 188, 233; Berl's early exposure to debates on, 8–10, 13–16; decline of European, 296; lectures on, at Berl's study month, 304; primacy of Zionism over, 86; works of socialist writers published by Berl, 312–13; *see also* socialist Zionism

Socialist International, Palestinian labor movement's participation in, 87, 88, 89, 161n

socialist Zionism, 147–8; attitude of American Jewry to, 86; of Ben Gurion, 86, 344; Berl publishes works of founders of, 269, 313; Berl's conception of, 73–4, 148, 345; of Second Aliyah, 61, 152; struggle between communism and, 107, 109; of Third Aliyah, 112, 152

Society for the Dissemination of Knowledge, Russia, 17, 21

Sokolow, Nahum, 25, 53, 187

Solel Boneh, 124, 156–7, 158; Berl's explanation for failure of, 157

Soviet Union, 233, 357; Berl's attitude towards, 148, 232, 294, 295, 296, 325, 337; Berl's wartime broadcast to Jews in, 309–10; emigration of Labor Brigade

members to, 156, 225; German invasion of, 309; Jews in, 87, 101, 105, 109; non-aggression pact with Nazi Germany, 279, 293, 294; persecution of Zionism in, 148, 152, 232, 289, 294, 295; returned he-Halutz emissaries' favorable view of, 294–6; *see also* Bolshevik Revolution

Spanish Civil War, 296; Berl attends debate on, at British Labor Party conference, 259–60

Spinoza, Baruch, Berl visits house of, 269

Sprinzak, Yosef, 25, 173, 178, 290, 293, 330, 336; attitude to British, 286, 289; and Revisionists, 191, 193; and unification of kibbutz movement, 233, 243, 299

S.R.P., *see* Social Revolutionary Party

S.S.R.P., *see* Zionist Socialist Labor Party

Stalin, Josef, Berl's view of, 148, 224, 294

Stavsky, Avraham, trial of, Berl's attitude to, 194–5, 196–7, 200–1

Stendhal, *The Charterhouse of Parma*, Berl publishes, 314

Stock (Sadan), Dov, 144, 194; Berl's relations with, 170, 315

Stockholm, Berl attends Poalei Zion conference in (1919), 101, 107–9

Storrs, Sir Ronald, Berl's negotiations with, 69

Strashun, Shmuel, 2

Strashun, Zelda Rachel, *see* Katznelson, Zelda

study month, organized by Berl (1941), 300, 302–5, 307; Berl tells story of his life at, 305

Sudetenland, negotiations between Hitler and Chamberlain over, 273

Sursuk family, 110

Syria, 98, 99, 186

Syrkin, Nachman, 13; Berl and, 134, 269, 313

Szold, Henrietta, 282

Tabenkin, Eva, 57, 59

Tabenkin, Moshe, 247

Tabenkin, Yitzhak, 25, 63, 112, 126, 127, 223, 269, 303, 320, 343, 356; in Agricultural union, 50, 53; and Ahdut ha-Avoda, 89, 92, 102, 114, 152, 155, 160; and Berl's Youth Center project, 219,

Index

THE LIBRARY / JEWISH THEOLOGICAL SEMINARY
NEW YORK, NY 10027

3 1407 00137401 6

LIBRARY